High School Prodigies Have It Easy Even in Another World!

1

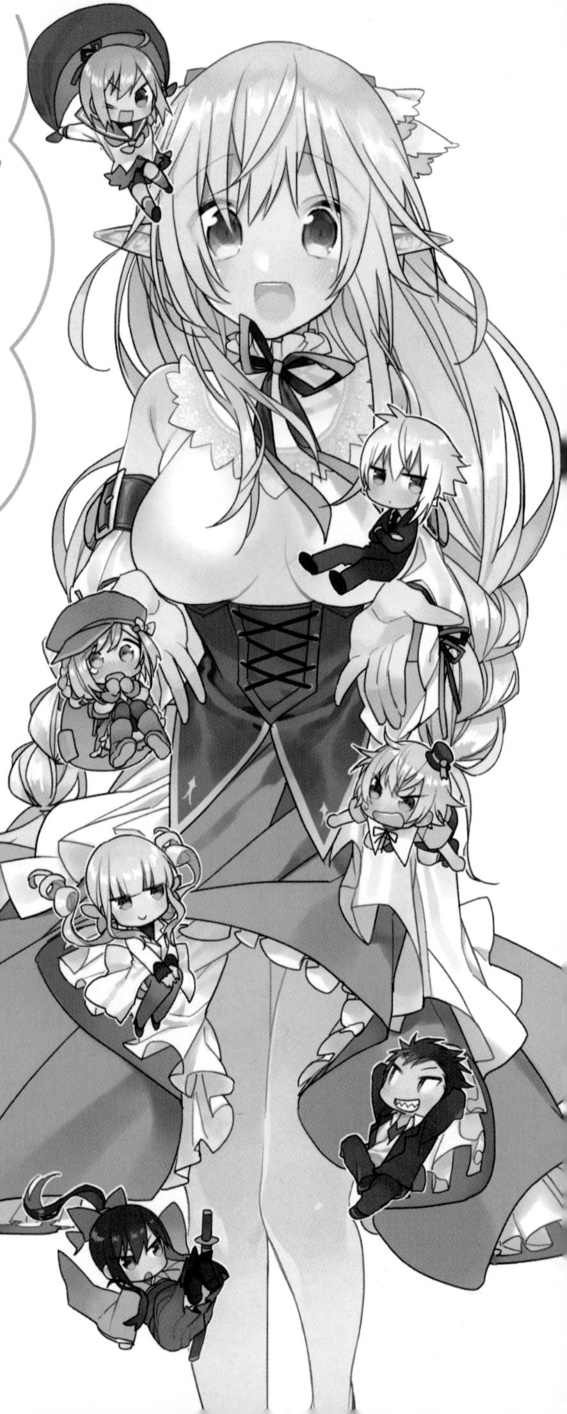

STORY BY
Riku Misora
ART BY
Kotaro Yamada
CHARACTER DESIGN BY
Sacraneco

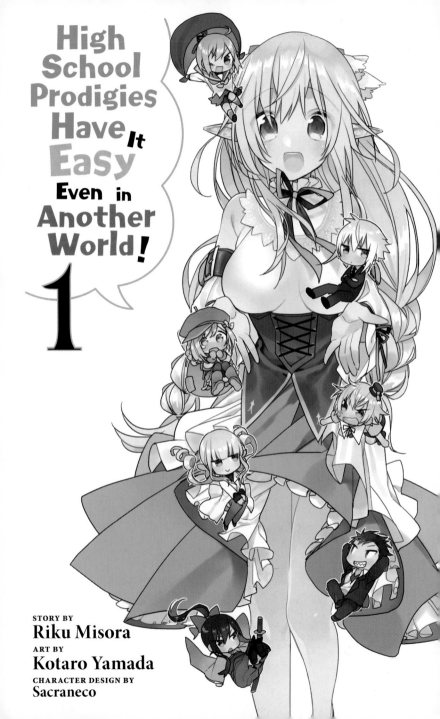

CONTENTS

HIGH SCHOOL PRODIGIES HAVE IT EASY EVEN IN ANOTHER WORLD!

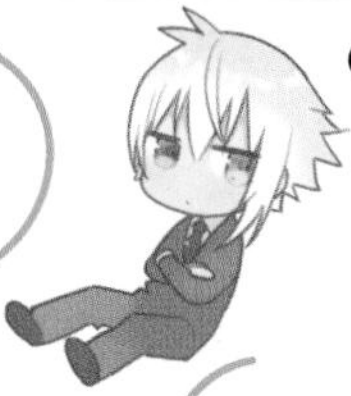

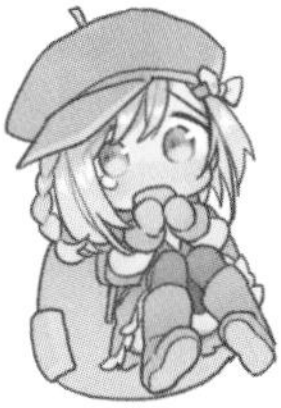

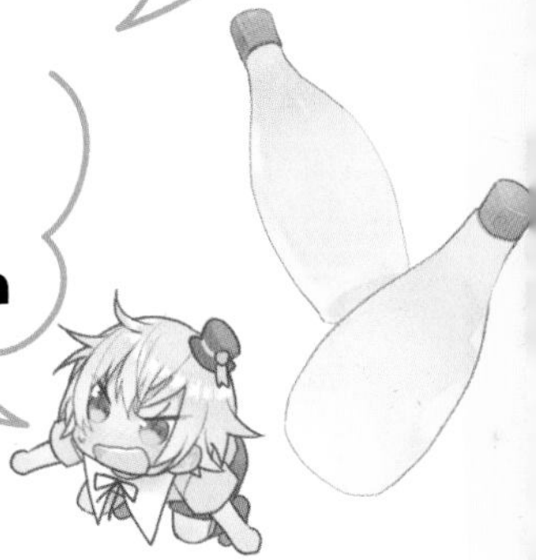

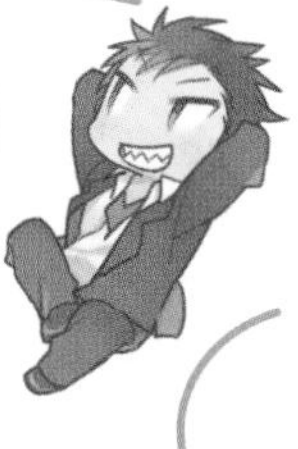

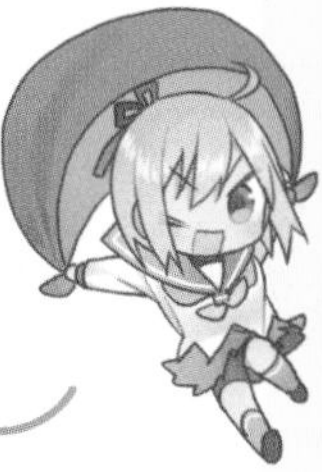

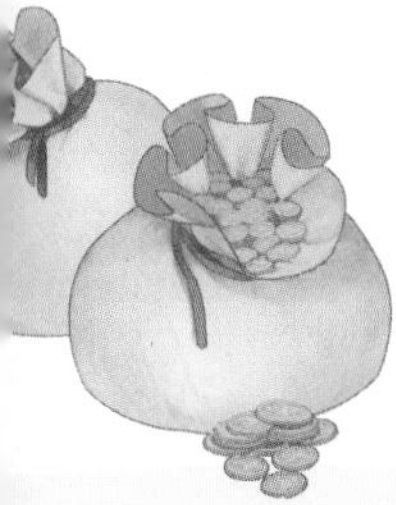

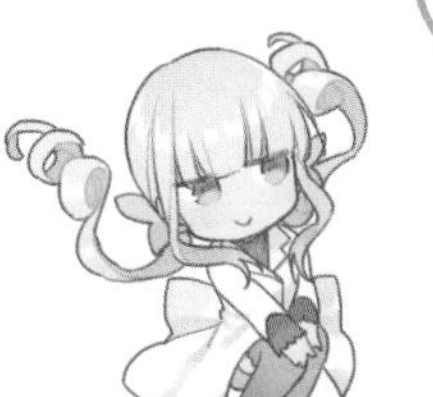

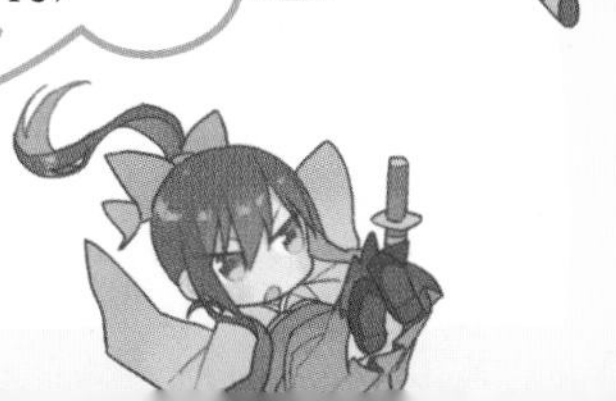

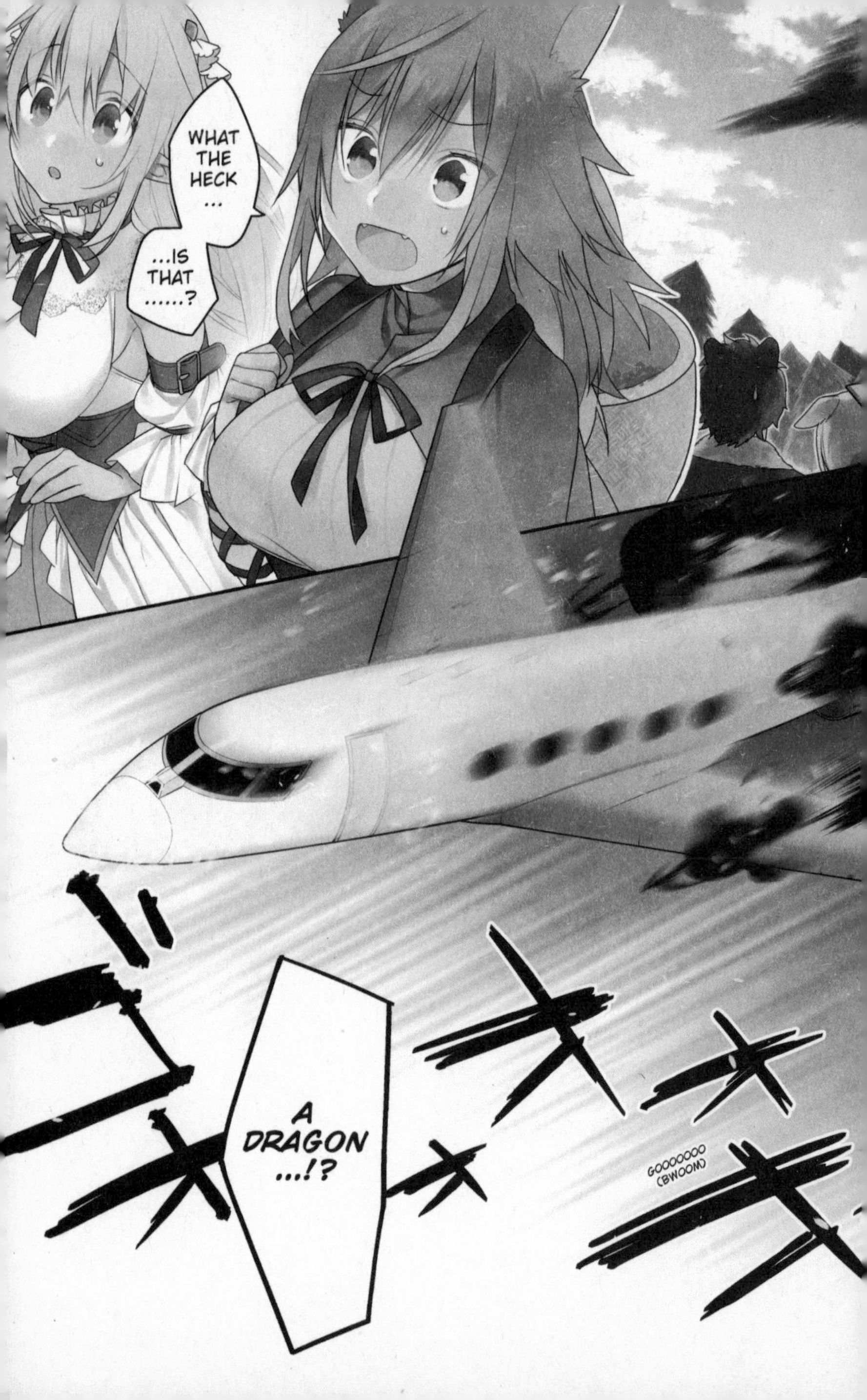
WHAT THE HECK ...
...IS THAT ......?
A DRAGON ...!?
GOOOOOOO (BWOOM)

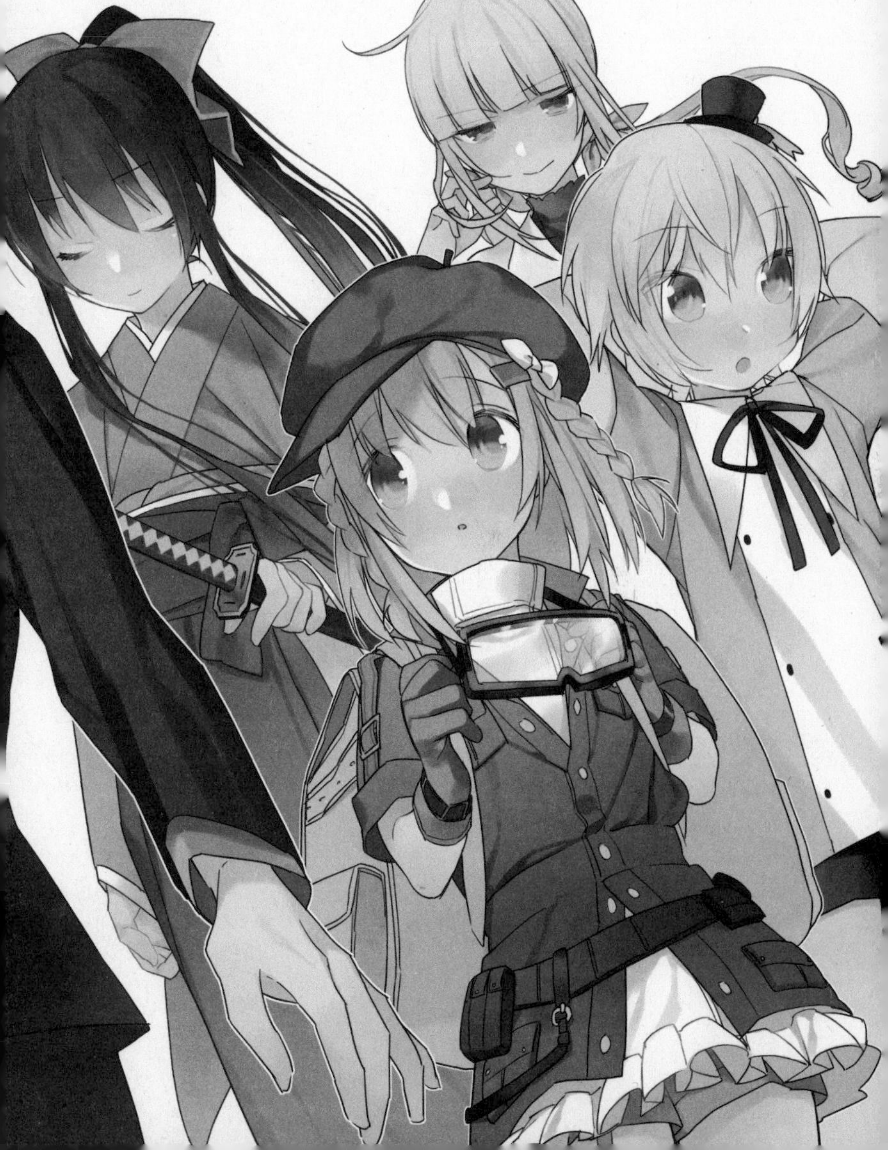

CHAPTER 1: THE SEVEN HIGH SCHOOL PRODIGIES

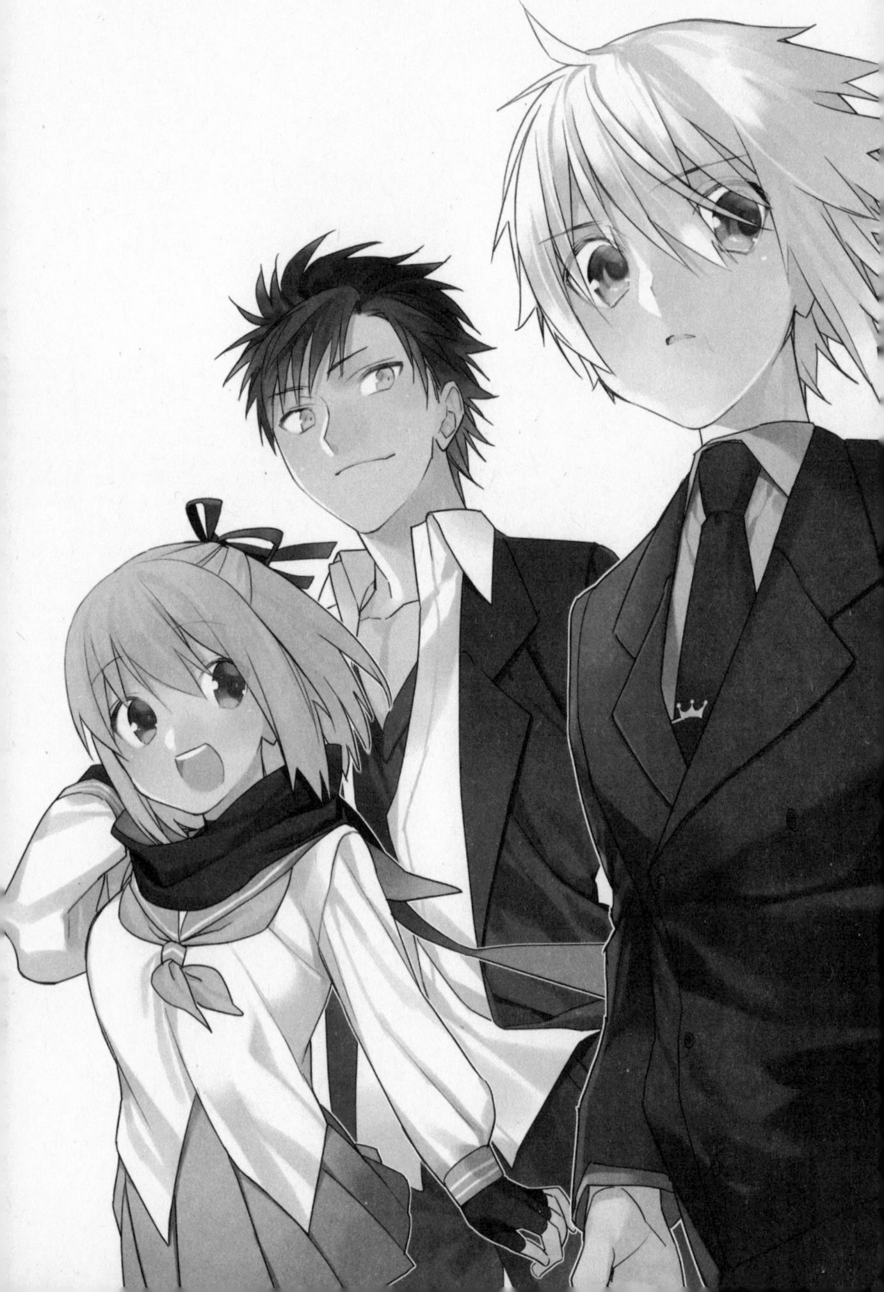

HIGH SCHOOL
PRODIGIES HAVE
IT EASY EVEN IN
ANOTHER
WORLD!

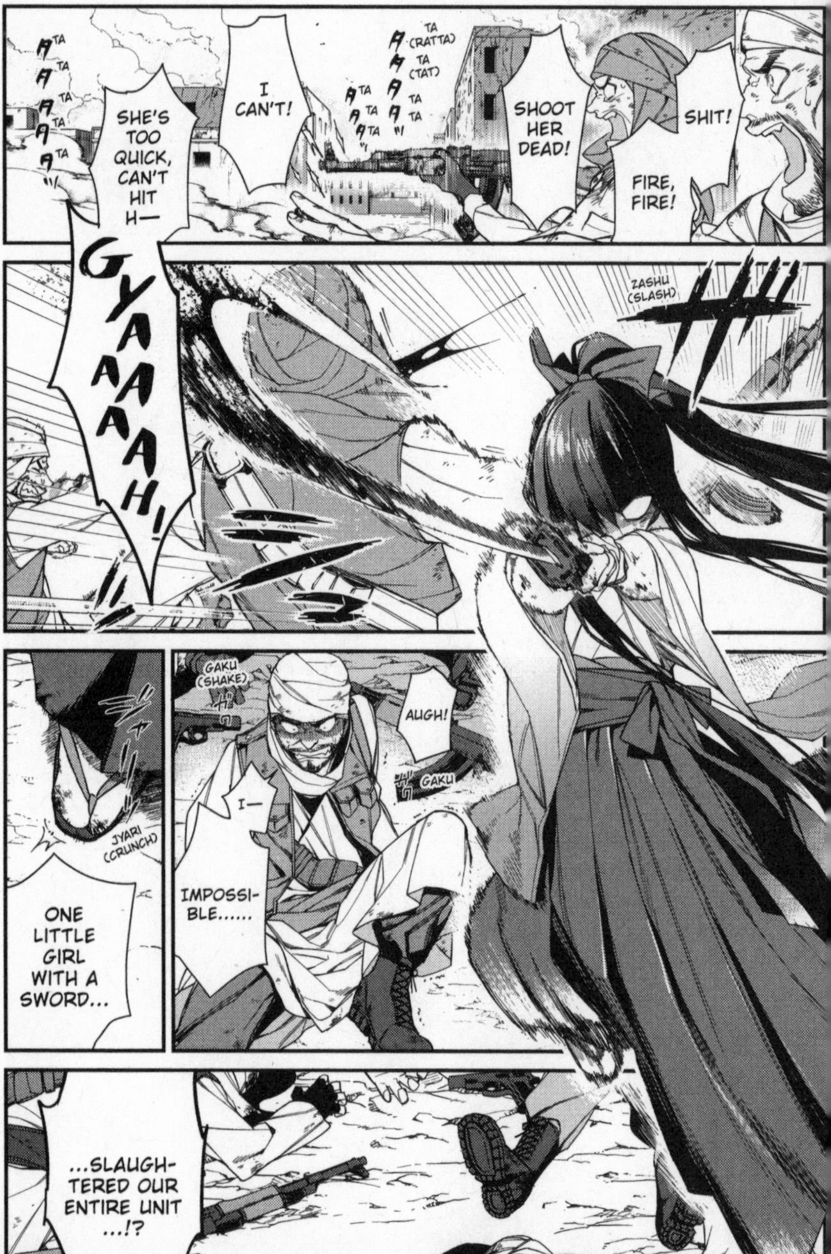
SHIT!
FIRE, FIRE!
SHOOT HER DEAD!
TA (RATTA) TA (TAT) TA TA TA TA TA
I CAN'T!
SHE'S TOO QUICK, CAN'T HIT H—
TA TA TA TA TA
ZASHU (SLASH)
GYAAAAAH!!
GAKU (SHAKE)
AUGH!
GAKU
I—
IMPOSSIBLE......
JYARI (CRUNCH)
ONE LITTLE GIRL WITH A SWORD...
...SLAUGHTERED OUR ENTIRE UNIT ...!?

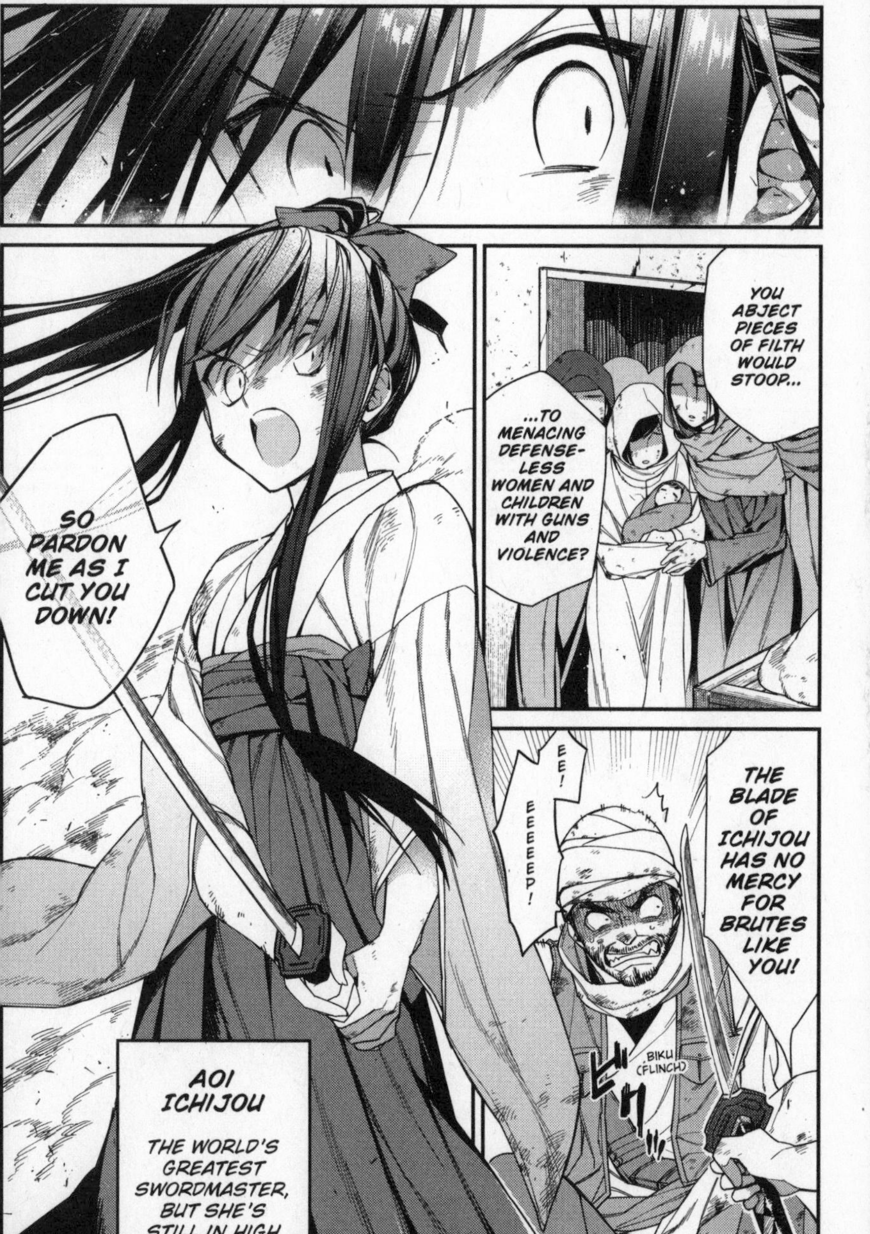
YOU ABJECT PIECES OF FILTH WOULD STOOP...
...TO MENACING DEFENSE-LESS WOMEN AND CHILDREN WITH GUNS AND VIOLENCE?
THE BLADE OF ICHIJOU HAS NO MERCY FOR BRUTES LIKE YOU!
EE! EEEEEEP!
BIKU (FLINCH)
SO PARDON ME AS I CUT YOU DOWN!
AOI ICHIJOU
THE WORLD'S GREATEST SWORDMASTER, BUT SHE'S STILL IN HIGH SCHOOL

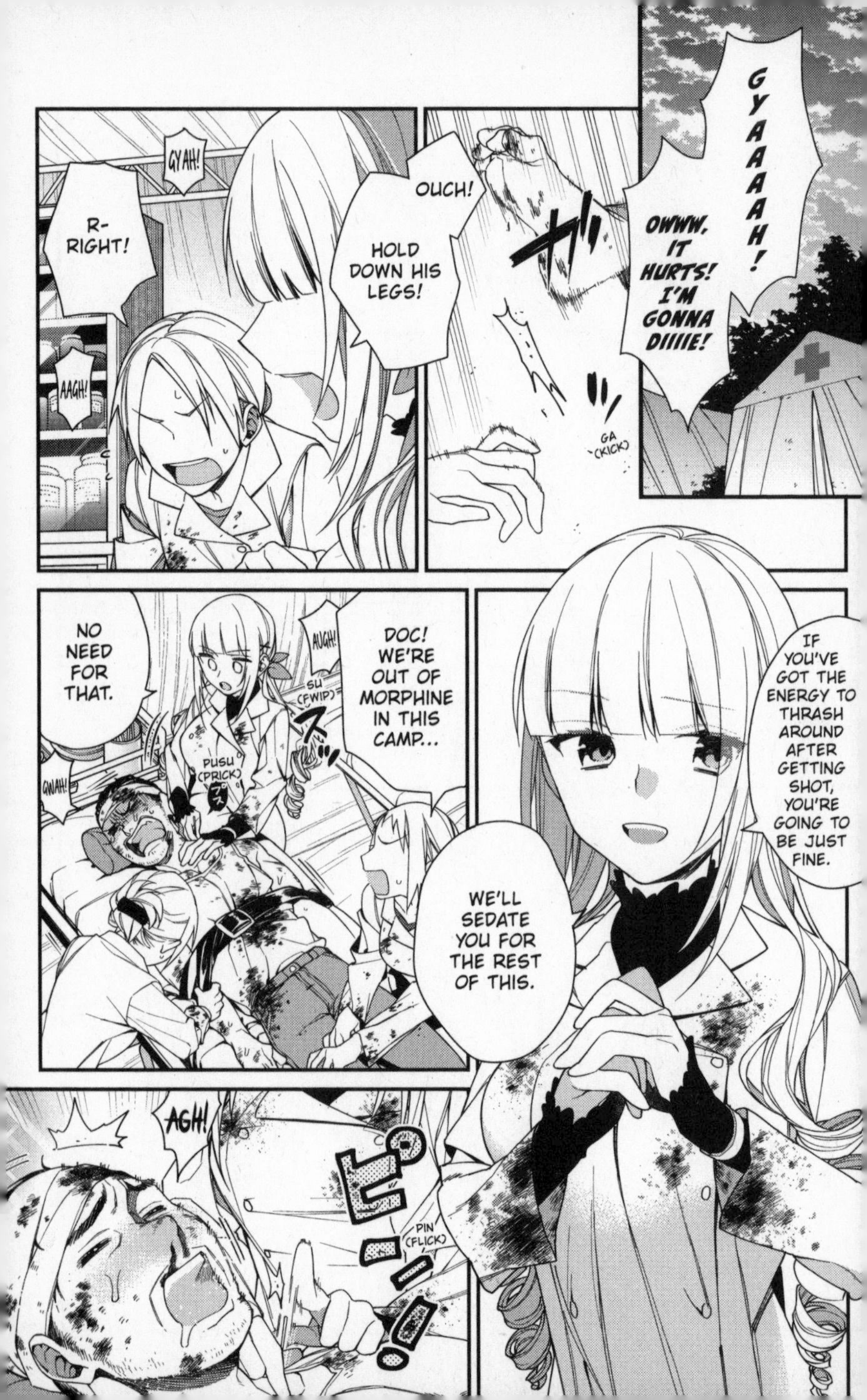
GYAAAAAH!
OWWW. IT HURTS! I'M GONNA DIIIIE!
OUCH!
HOLD DOWN HIS LEGS!
GA (KICK)
GYAH!
R- RIGHT!
AAGH!
IF YOU'VE GOT THE ENERGY TO THRASH AROUND AFTER GETTING SHOT, YOU'RE GOING TO BE JUST FINE.
WE'LL SEDATE YOU FOR THE REST OF THIS.
DOC! WE'RE OUT OF MORPHINE IN THIS CAMP...
AUGH!
NO NEED FOR THAT.
SU (FWIP)
PUSU (PRICK)
GWAH!
AGH!
PIN (FLICK)

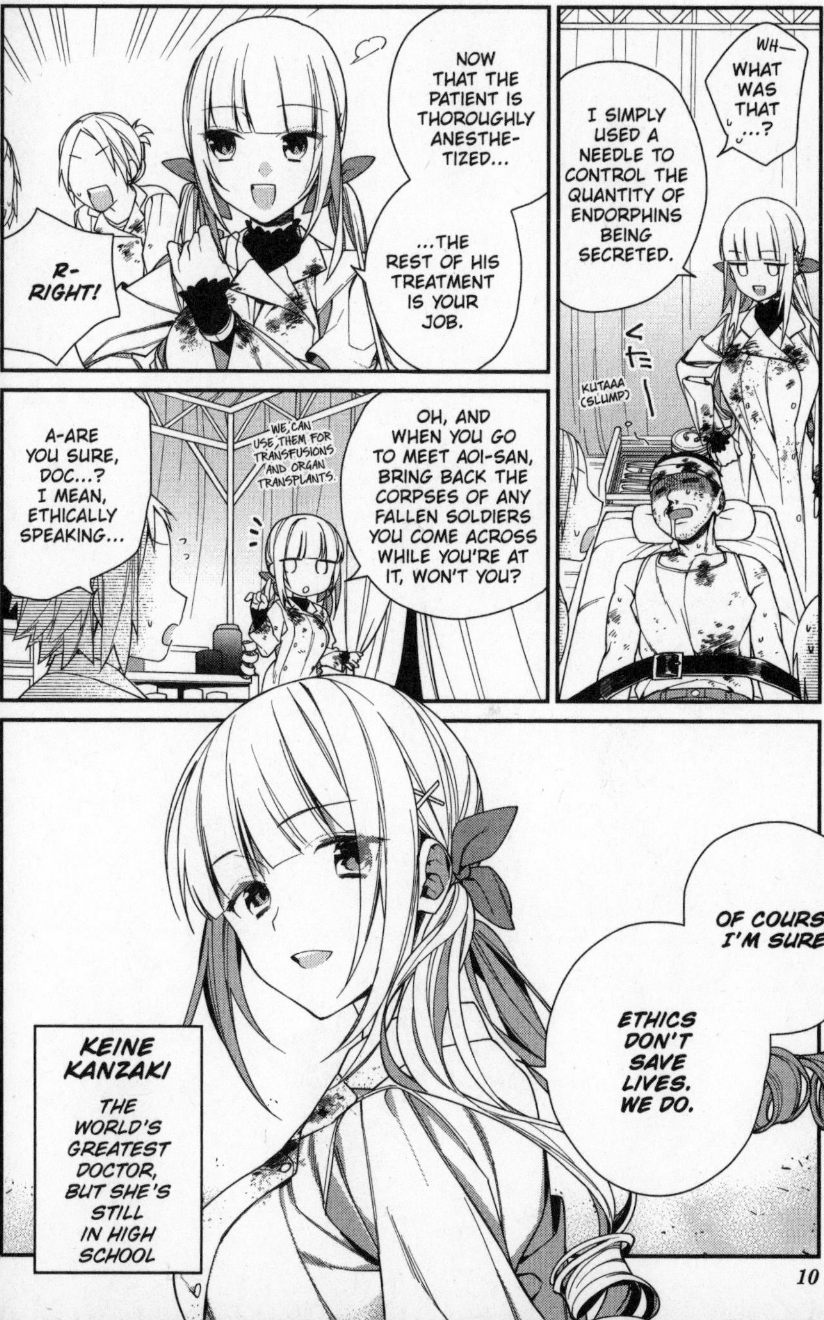
WH— WHAT WAS THAT...?
I SIMPLY USED A NEEDLE TO CONTROL THE QUANTITY OF ENDORPHINS BEING SECRETED.
KUTAAA (SLUMP)
NOW THAT THE PATIENT IS THOROUGHLY ANESTHE-TIZED...
...THE REST OF HIS TREATMENT IS YOUR JOB.
R-RIGHT!
OH, AND WHEN YOU GO TO MEET AOI-SAN, BRING BACK THE CORPSES OF ANY FALLEN SOLDIERS YOU COME ACROSS WHILE YOU'RE AT IT, WON'T YOU?
WE CAN USE THEM FOR TRANSFUSIONS AND ORGAN TRANSPLANTS.
A-ARE YOU SURE, DOC...? I MEAN, ETHICALLY SPEAKING...
OF COURSE I'M SURE.
ETHICS DON'T SAVE LIVES. WE DO.
KEINE KANZAKI
THE WORLD'S GREATEST DOCTOR, BUT SHE'S STILL IN HIGH SCHOOL

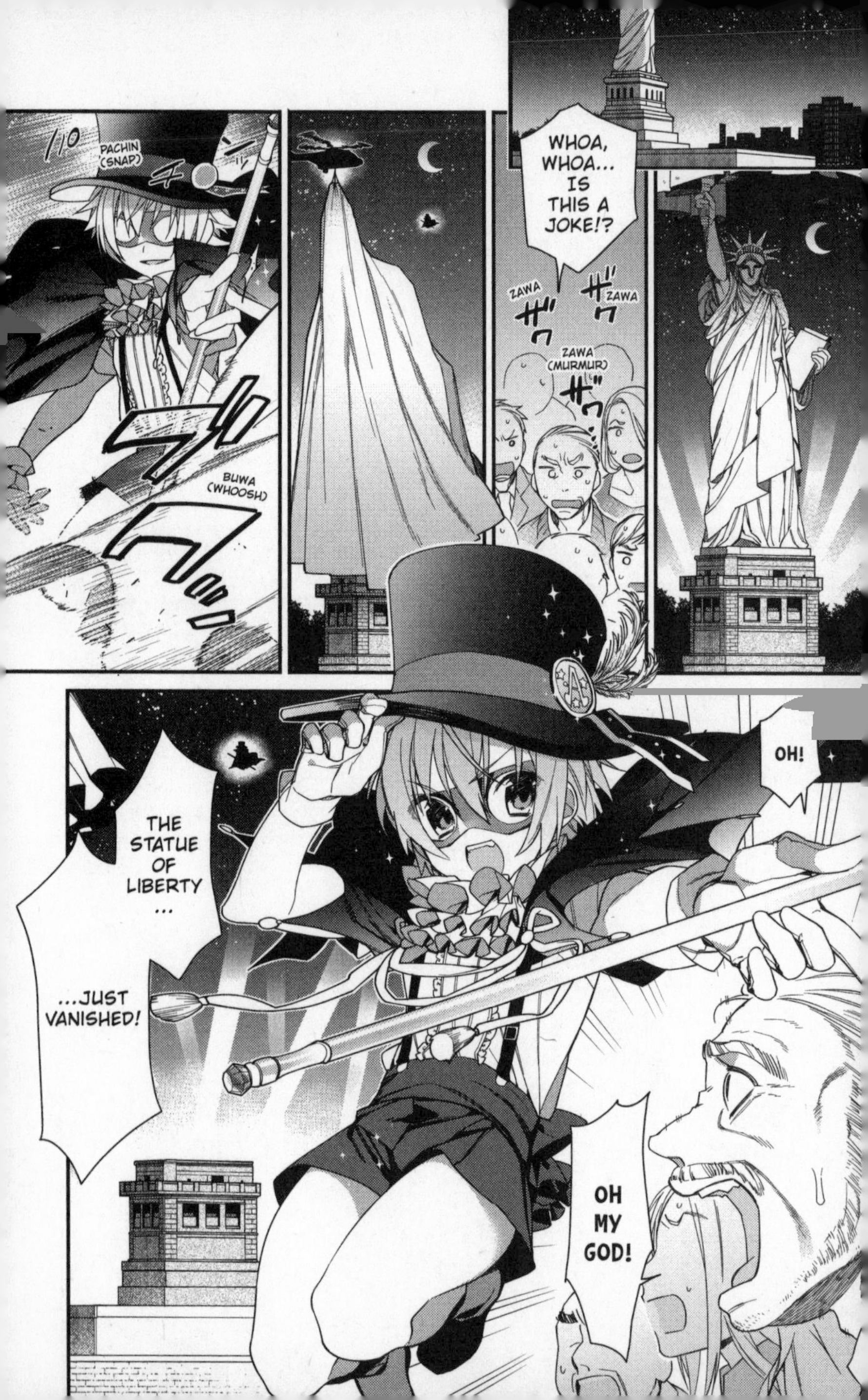
WHOA, WHOA... IS THIS A JOKE!?
ZAWA
ZAWA
ZAWA (MURMUR)
PACHIN (SNAP)
BUWA (WHOOSH)
OH!
OH MY GOD!
THE STATUE OF LIBERTY...
...JUST VANISHED!

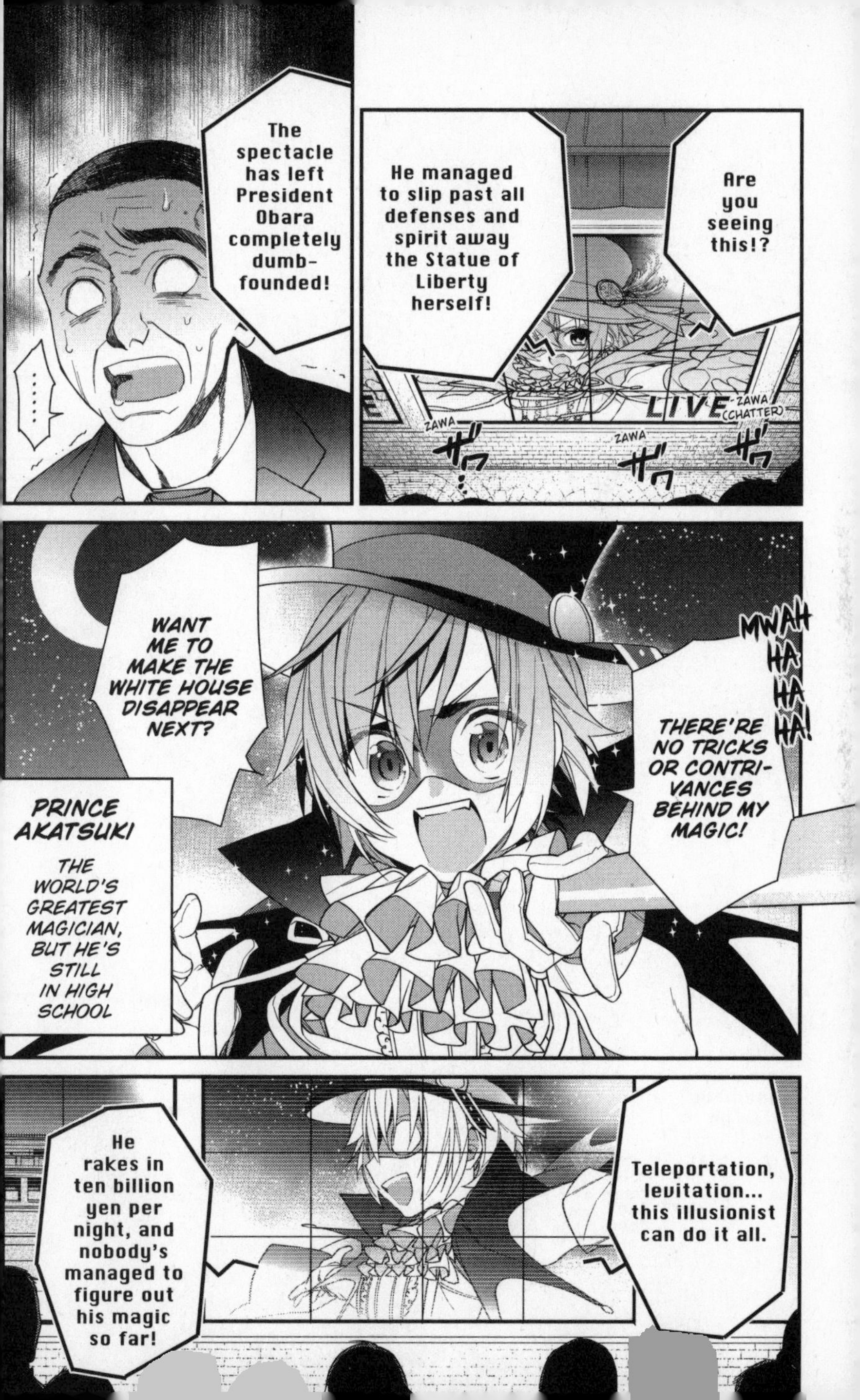
Are you seeing this!?
He managed to slip past all defenses and spirit away the Statue of Liberty herself!
LIVE
ZAWA (CHATTER)
ZAWA
ZAWA
The spectacle has left President Obara completely dumb-founded!
......
MWAH HA HA HA!
THERE'RE NO TRICKS OR CONTRI-VANCES BEHIND MY MAGIC!
WANT ME TO MAKE THE WHITE HOUSE DISAPPEAR NEXT?
PRINCE AKATSUKI
THE WORLD'S GREATEST MAGICIAN, BUT HE'S STILL IN HIGH SCHOOL
Teleportation, levitation... this illusionist can do it all.
He rakes in ten billion yen per night, and nobody's managed to figure out his magic so far!

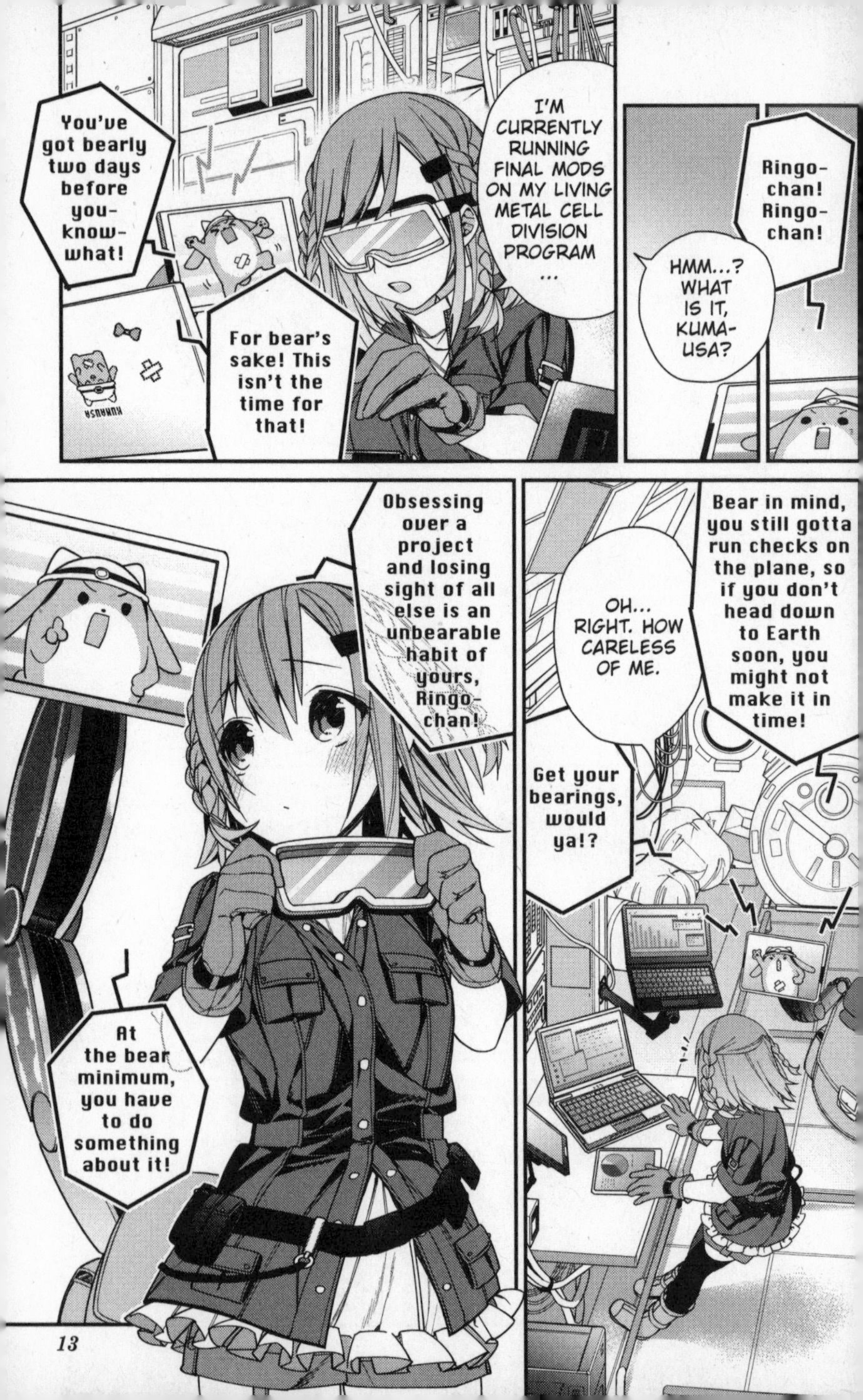
Ringo-chan! Ringo-chan!
HMM...? WHAT IS IT, KUMA-USA?
I'M CURRENTLY RUNNING FINAL MODS ON MY LIVING METAL CELL DIVISION PROGRAM ...
You've got bearly two days before you-know-what!
For bear's sake! This isn't the time for that!
Bear in mind, you still gotta run checks on the plane, so if you don't head down to Earth soon, you might not make it in time!
OH... RIGHT. HOW CARELESS OF ME.
Get your bearings, would ya!?
Obsessing over a project and losing sight of all else is an unbearable habit of yours, Ringo-chan!
At the bear minimum, you have to do something about it!

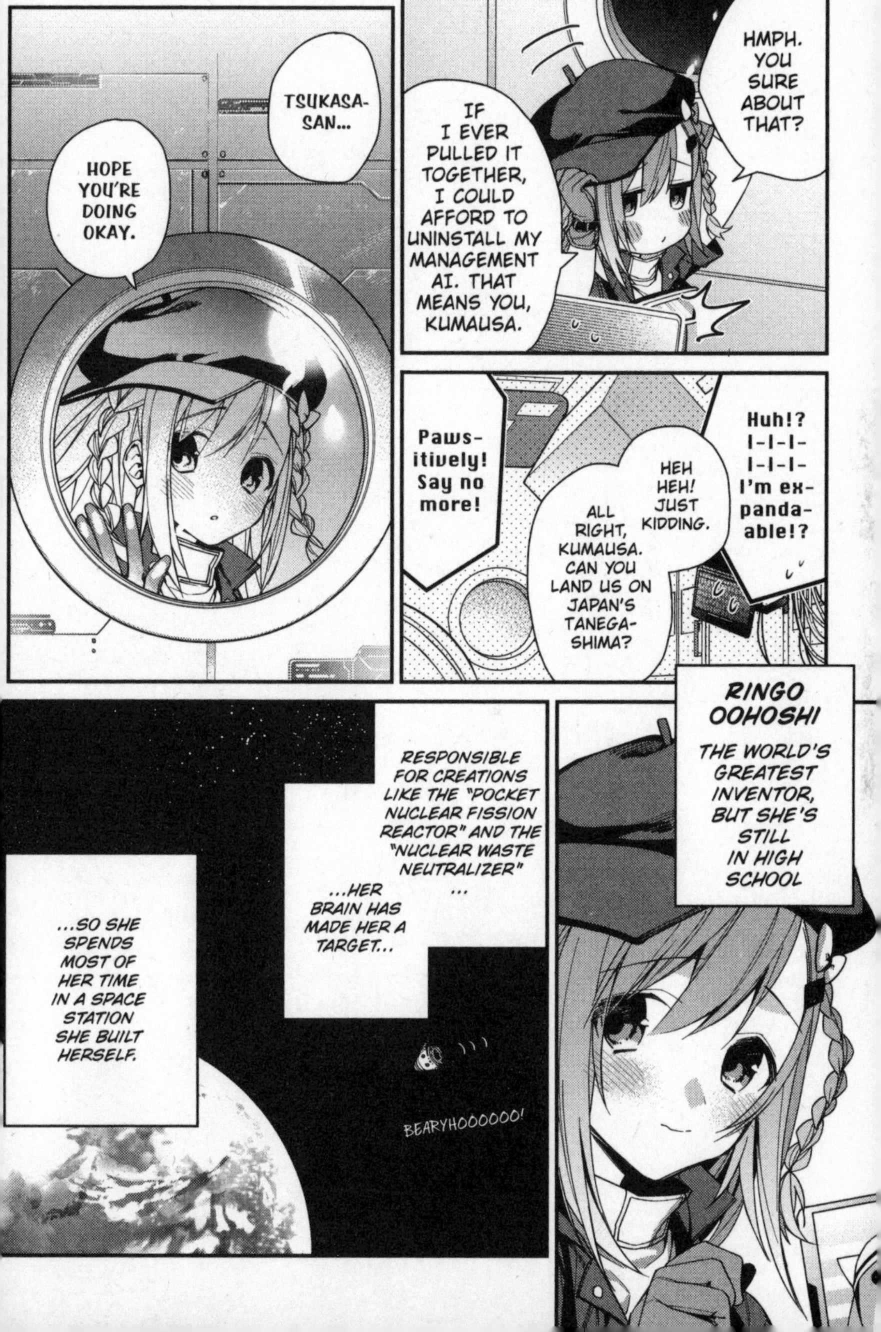
HMPH. YOU SURE ABOUT THAT?
IF I EVER PULLED IT TOGETHER, I COULD AFFORD TO UNINSTALL MY MANAGEMENT AI. THAT MEANS YOU, KUMAUSA.
Huh!? I-I-I-I-I-I-I'm ex-panda-able!?
HEH HEH! JUST KIDDING.
ALL RIGHT, KUMAUSA. CAN YOU LAND US ON JAPAN'S TANEGA-SHIMA?
Paws-itively! Say no more!
TSUKASA-SAN...
HOPE YOU'RE DOING OKAY.
RINGO OOHOSHI
THE WORLD'S GREATEST INVENTOR, BUT SHE'S STILL IN HIGH SCHOOL
RESPONSIBLE FOR CREATIONS LIKE THE "POCKET NUCLEAR FISSION REACTOR" AND THE "NUCLEAR WASTE NEUTRALIZER"...
...HER BRAIN HAS MADE HER A TARGET...
...SO SHE SPENDS MOST OF HER TIME IN A SPACE STATION SHE BUILT HERSELF.
BEARYHOOOOOOO!

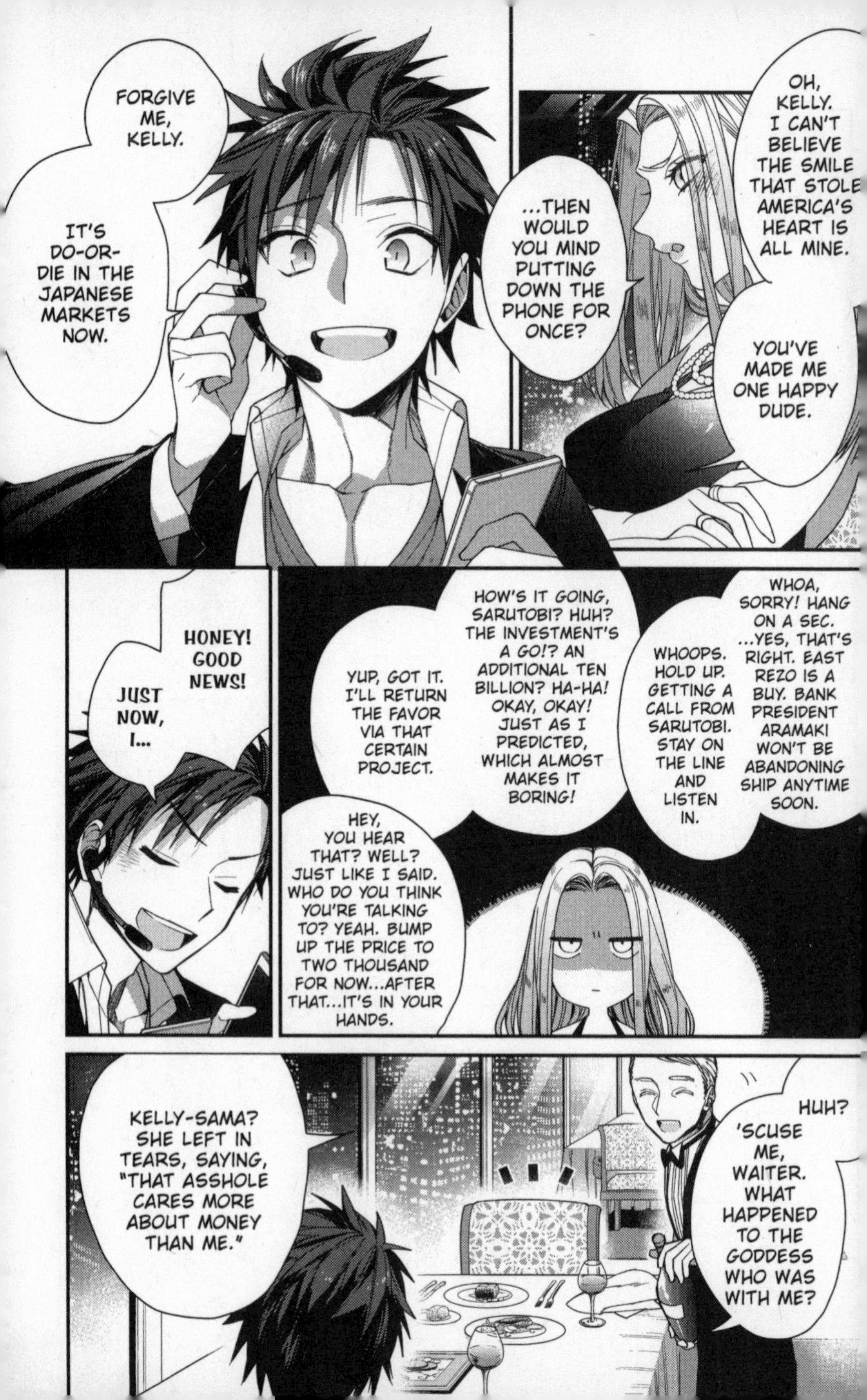
OH, KELLY. I CAN'T BELIEVE THE SMILE THAT STOLE AMERICA'S HEART IS ALL MINE.
YOU'VE MADE ME ONE HAPPY DUDE.
...THEN WOULD YOU MIND PUTTING DOWN THE PHONE FOR ONCE?
FORGIVE ME, KELLY.
IT'S DO-OR-DIE IN THE JAPANESE MARKETS NOW.
WHOA, SORRY! HANG ON A SEC. ...YES, THAT'S RIGHT. EAST REZO IS A BUY. BANK PRESIDENT ARAMAKI WON'T BE ABANDONING SHIP ANYTIME SOON.
WHOOPS. HOLD UP. GETTING A CALL FROM SARUTOBI. STAY ON THE LINE AND LISTEN IN.
HOW'S IT GOING, SARUTOBI? HUH? THE INVESTMENT'S A GO!? AN ADDITIONAL TEN BILLION? HA-HA! OKAY, OKAY! JUST AS I PREDICTED, WHICH ALMOST MAKES IT BORING!
YUP, GOT IT. I'LL RETURN THE FAVOR VIA THAT CERTAIN PROJECT.
HEY, YOU HEAR THAT? WELL? JUST LIKE I SAID. WHO DO YOU THINK YOU'RE TALKING TO? YEAH. BUMP UP THE PRICE TO TWO THOUSAND FOR NOW...AFTER THAT...IT'S IN YOUR HANDS.
HONEY! GOOD NEWS!
JUST NOW, I...
HUH? 'SCUSE ME, WAITER. WHAT HAPPENED TO THE GODDESS WHO WAS WITH ME?
KELLY-SAMA? SHE LEFT IN TEARS, SAYING, "THAT ASSHOLE CARES MORE ABOUT MONEY THAN ME."

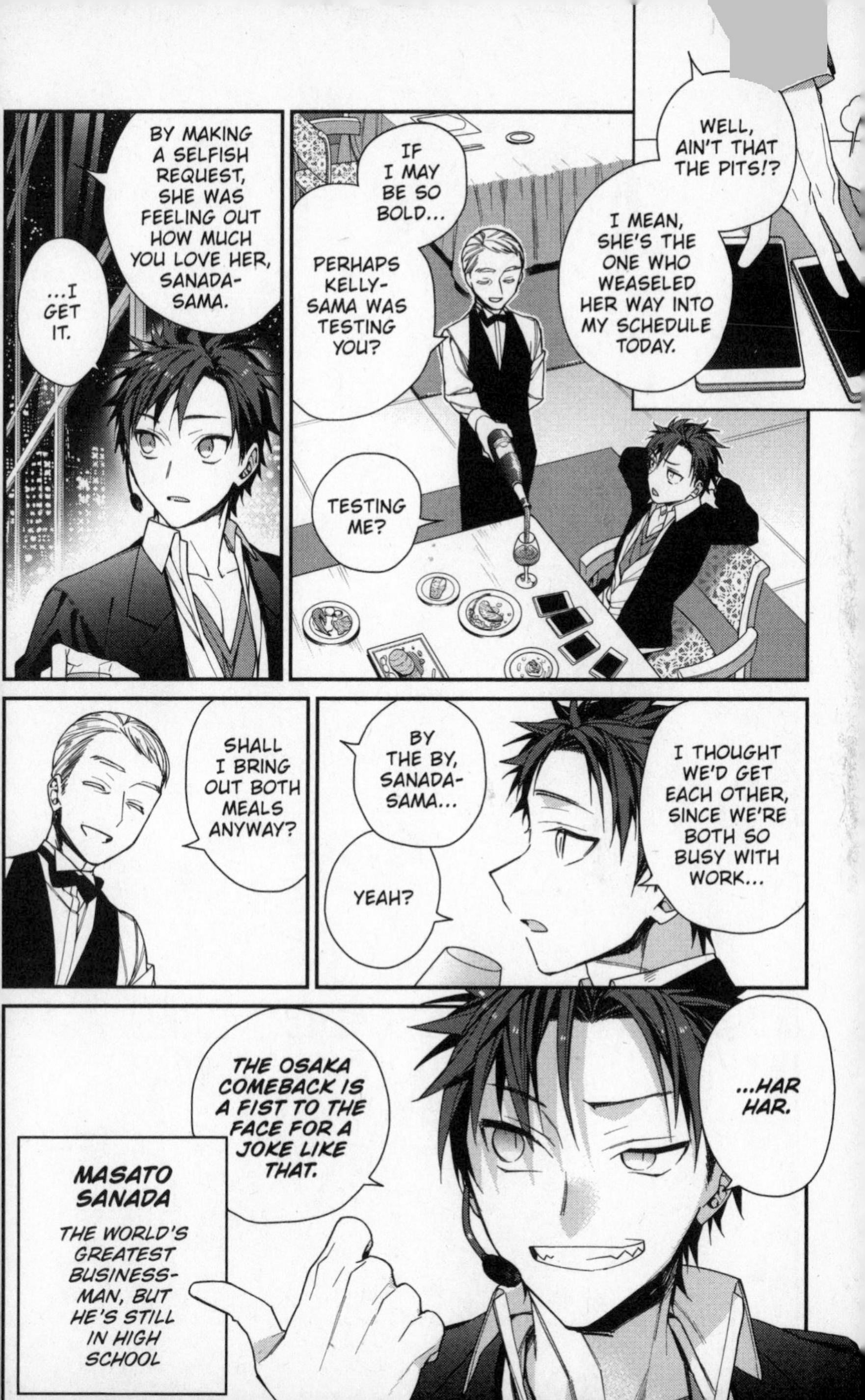

WELL, AIN'T THAT THE PITS!?
I MEAN, SHE'S THE ONE WHO WEASELED HER WAY INTO MY SCHEDULE TODAY.
IF I MAY BE SO BOLD...
PERHAPS KELLY-SAMA WAS TESTING YOU?
TESTING ME?
BY MAKING A SELFISH REQUEST, SHE WAS FEELING OUT HOW MUCH YOU LOVE HER, SANADA-SAMA.
...I GET IT.
I THOUGHT WE'D GET EACH OTHER, SINCE WE'RE BOTH SO BUSY WITH WORK...
BY THE BY, SANADA-SAMA...
YEAH?
SHALL I BRING OUT BOTH MEALS ANYWAY?
...HAR HAR.
THE OSAKA COMEBACK IS A FIST TO THE FACE FOR A JOKE LIKE THAT.
MASATO SANADA
THE WORLD'S GREATEST BUSINESS-MAN, BUT HE'S STILL IN HIGH SCHOOL

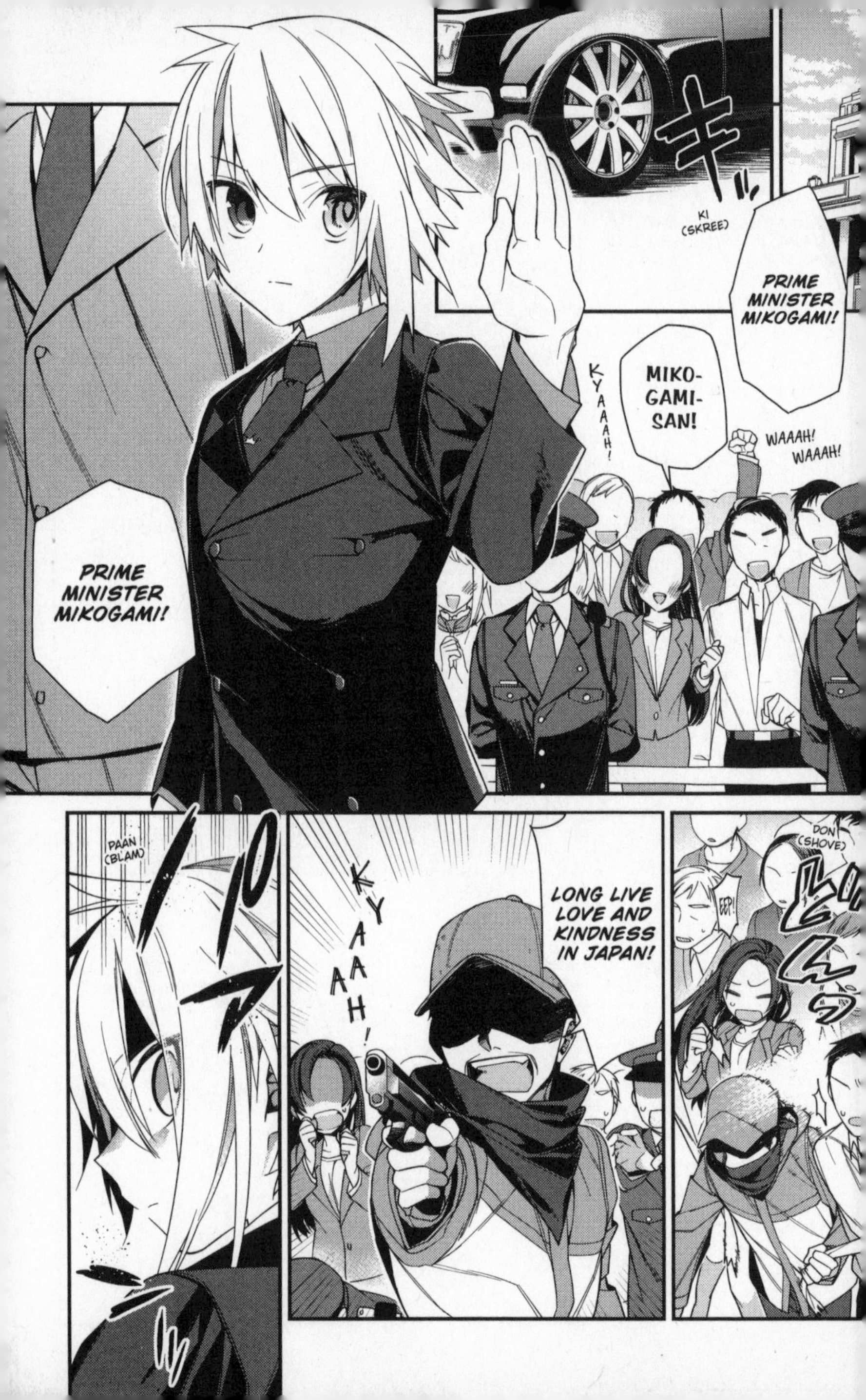
KI
(SKREE)
PRIME MINISTER MIKOGAMI!
WAAAH! WAAAH!
MIKO-GAMI-SAN!
KYAAAAH!
PRIME MINISTER MIKOGAMI!
DON
(SHOVE)
EEP!
LONG LIVE LOVE AND KINDNESS IN JAPAN!
KYAAAH!
PAAN
(BLAM)

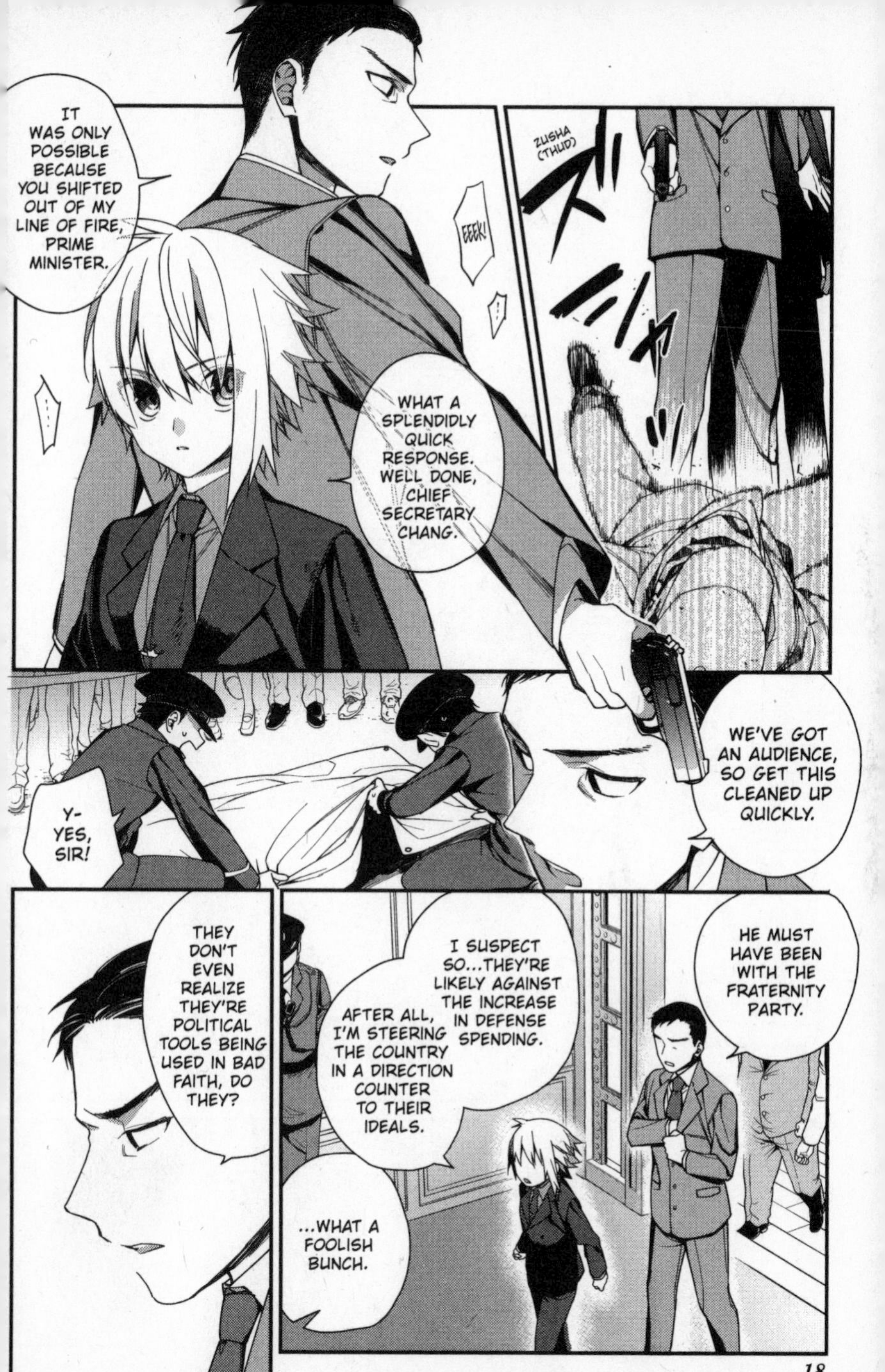
ZUSHA (THUD)
EEEK!
!
WHAT A SPLENDIDLY QUICK RESPONSE. WELL DONE, CHIEF SECRETARY CHANG.
IT WAS ONLY POSSIBLE BECAUSE YOU SHIFTED OUT OF MY LINE OF FIRE, PRIME MINISTER.
...!
WE'VE GOT AN AUDIENCE, SO GET THIS CLEANED UP QUICKLY.
Y-YES, SIR!
HE MUST HAVE BEEN WITH THE FRATERNITY PARTY.
I SUSPECT SO...THEY'RE LIKELY AGAINST THE INCREASE IN DEFENSE SPENDING.
AFTER ALL, I'M STEERING THE COUNTRY IN A DIRECTION COUNTER TO THEIR IDEALS.
...WHAT A FOOLISH BUNCH.
THEY DON'T EVEN REALIZE THEY'RE POLITICAL TOOLS BEING USED IN BAD FAITH, DO THEY?

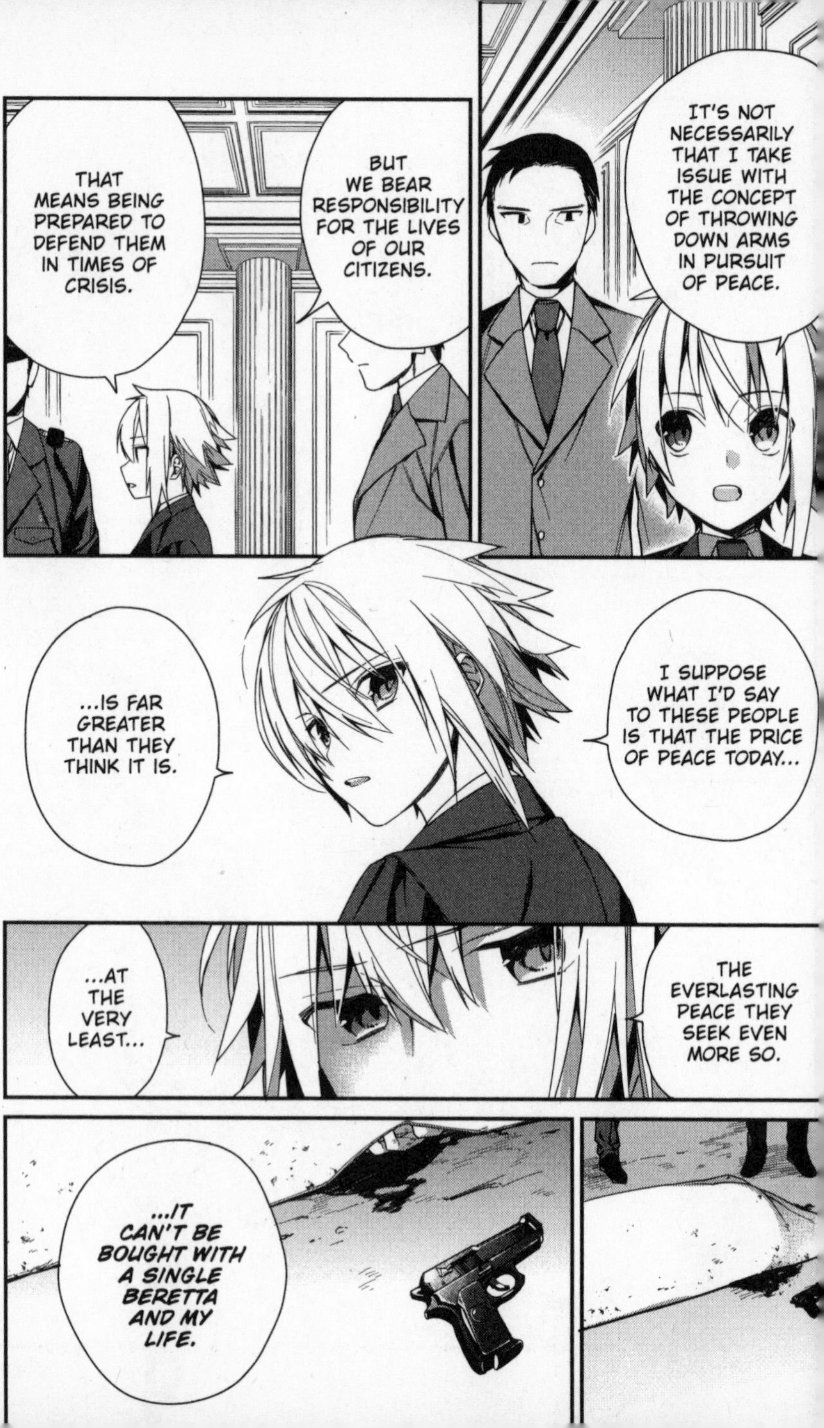
IT'S NOT NECESSARILY THAT I TAKE ISSUE WITH THE CONCEPT OF THROWING DOWN ARMS IN PURSUIT OF PEACE.
BUT WE BEAR RESPONSIBILITY FOR THE LIVES OF OUR CITIZENS.
THAT MEANS BEING PREPARED TO DEFEND THEM IN TIMES OF CRISIS.
I SUPPOSE WHAT I'D SAY TO THESE PEOPLE IS THAT THE PRICE OF PEACE TODAY...
...IS FAR GREATER THAN THEY THINK IT IS.
THE EVERLASTING PEACE THEY SEEK EVEN MORE SO.
...AT THE VERY LEAST...
...IT CAN'T BE BOUGHT WITH A SINGLE BERETTA AND MY LIFE.

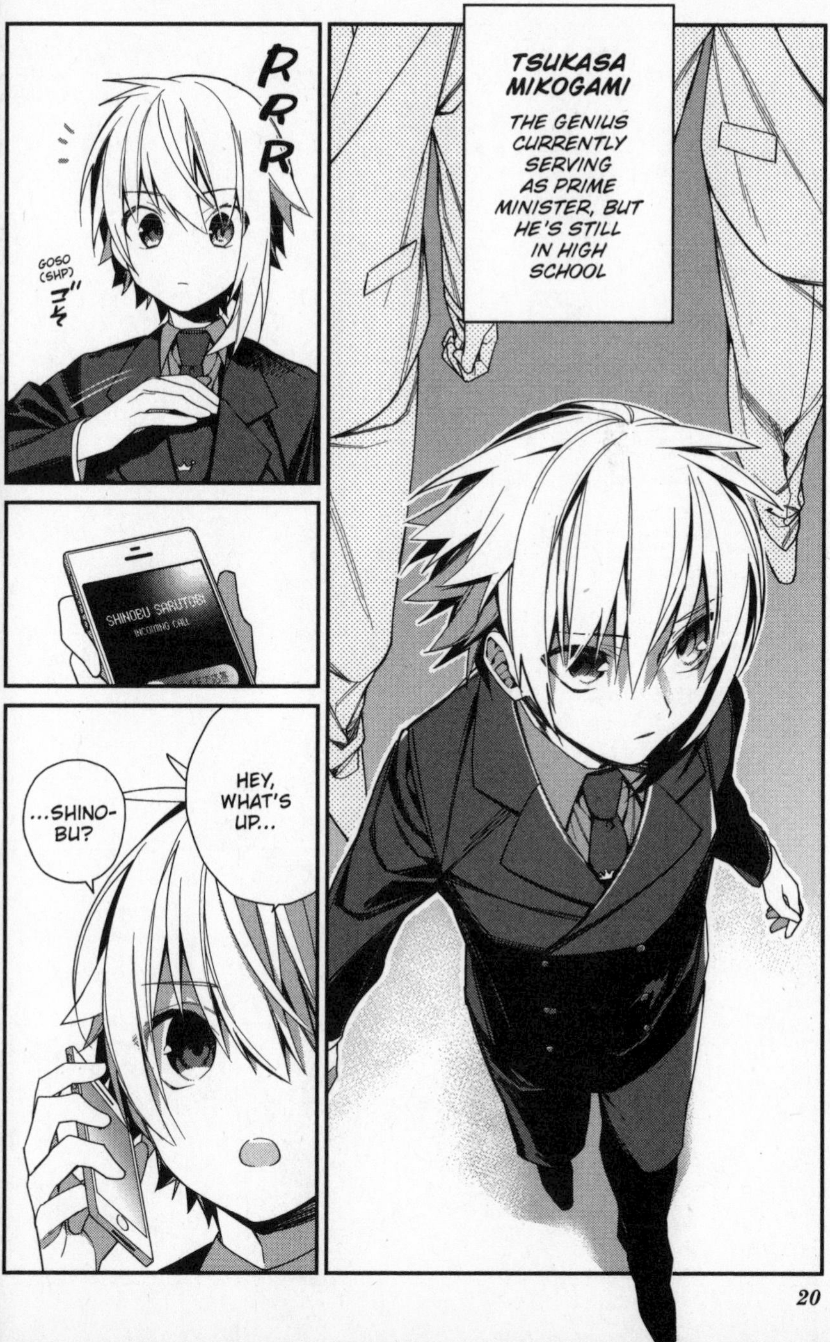
TSUKASA MIKOGAMI
THE GENIUS CURRENTLY SERVING AS PRIME MINISTER, BUT HE'S STILL IN HIGH SCHOOL
RRR
GOSO (SHP)
ゴソ
SHINOBU SARUTOBI
INCOMING CALL
HEY, WHAT'S UP...
...SHINO-BU?

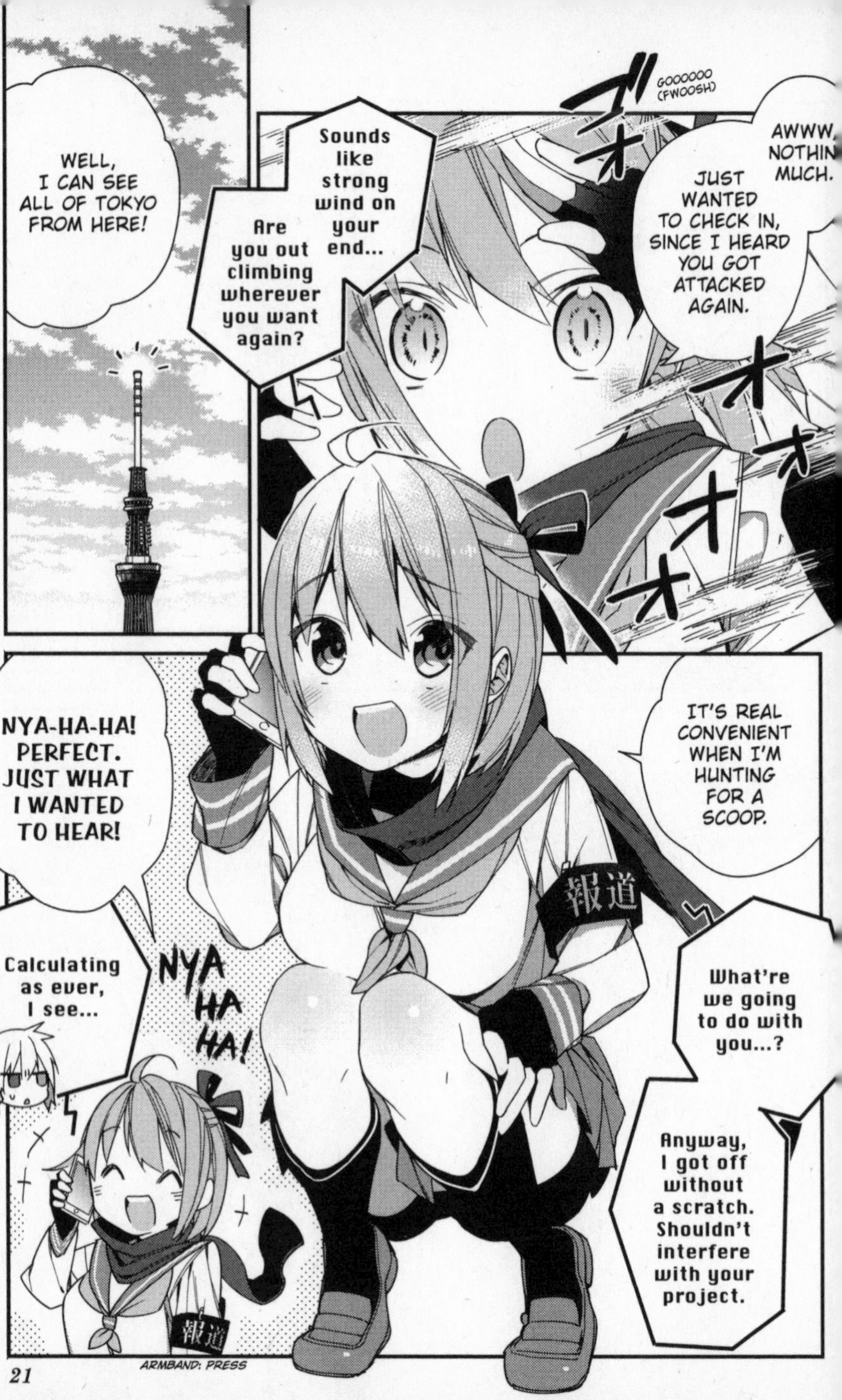
GOOOOOO (FWOOSH)
AWWW, NOTHIN MUCH.
JUST WANTED TO CHECK IN, SINCE I HEARD YOU GOT ATTACKED AGAIN.
Sounds like strong wind on your end...
Are you out climbing wherever you want again?
WELL, I CAN SEE ALL OF TOKYO FROM HERE!
IT'S REAL CONVENIENT WHEN I'M HUNTING FOR A SCOOP.
NYA-HA-HA! PERFECT. JUST WHAT I WANTED TO HEAR!
What're we going to do with you...?
Calculating as ever, I see...
NYA HA HA!
Anyway, I got off without a scratch. Shouldn't interfere with your project.
ARMBAND: PRESS

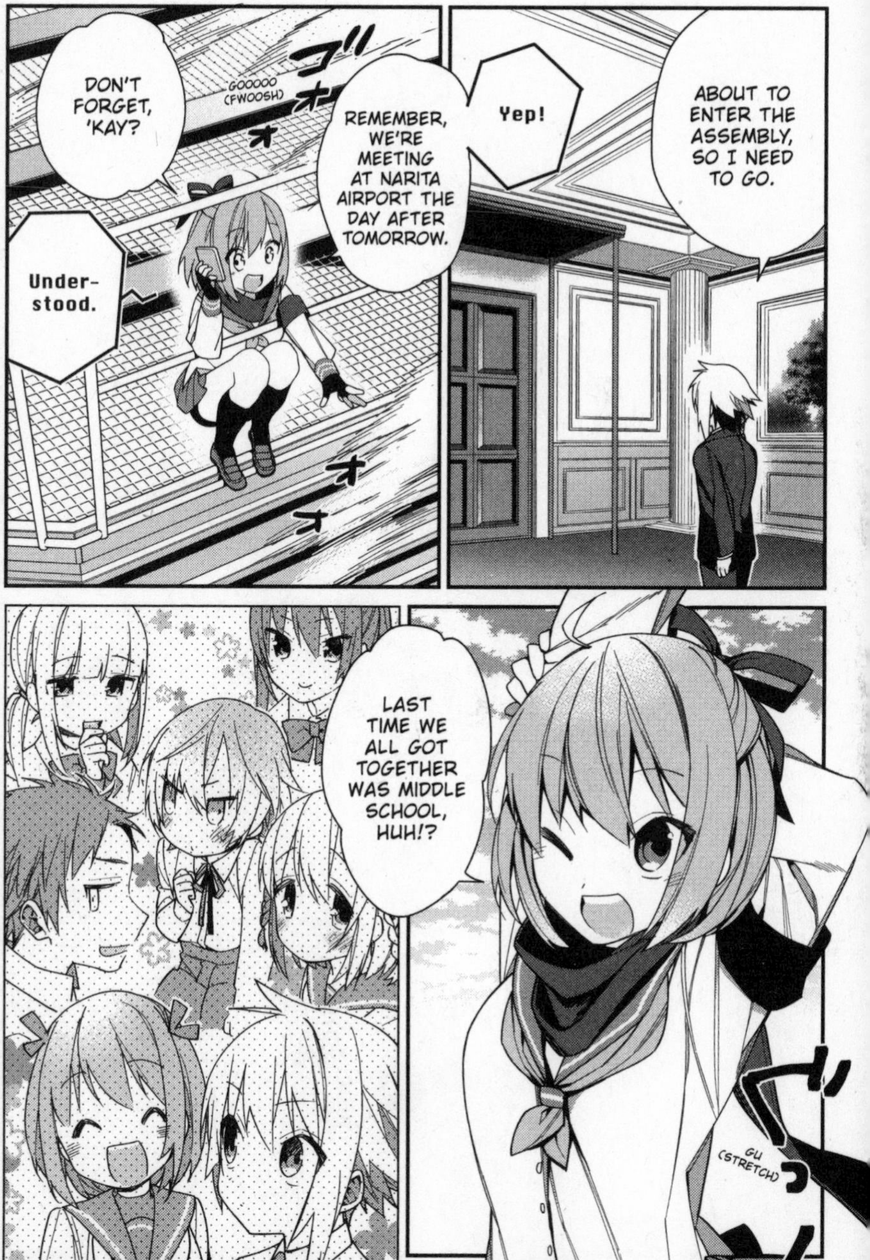
ABOUT TO ENTER THE ASSEMBLY, SO I NEED TO GO.
Yep!
REMEMBER, WE'RE MEETING AT NARITA AIRPORT THE DAY AFTER TOMORROW.
GOOOOO (FWOOSH)
DON'T FORGET, 'KAY?
Under-stood.
GU (STRETCH)
LAST TIME WE ALL GOT TOGETHER WAS MIDDLE SCHOOL, HUH!?

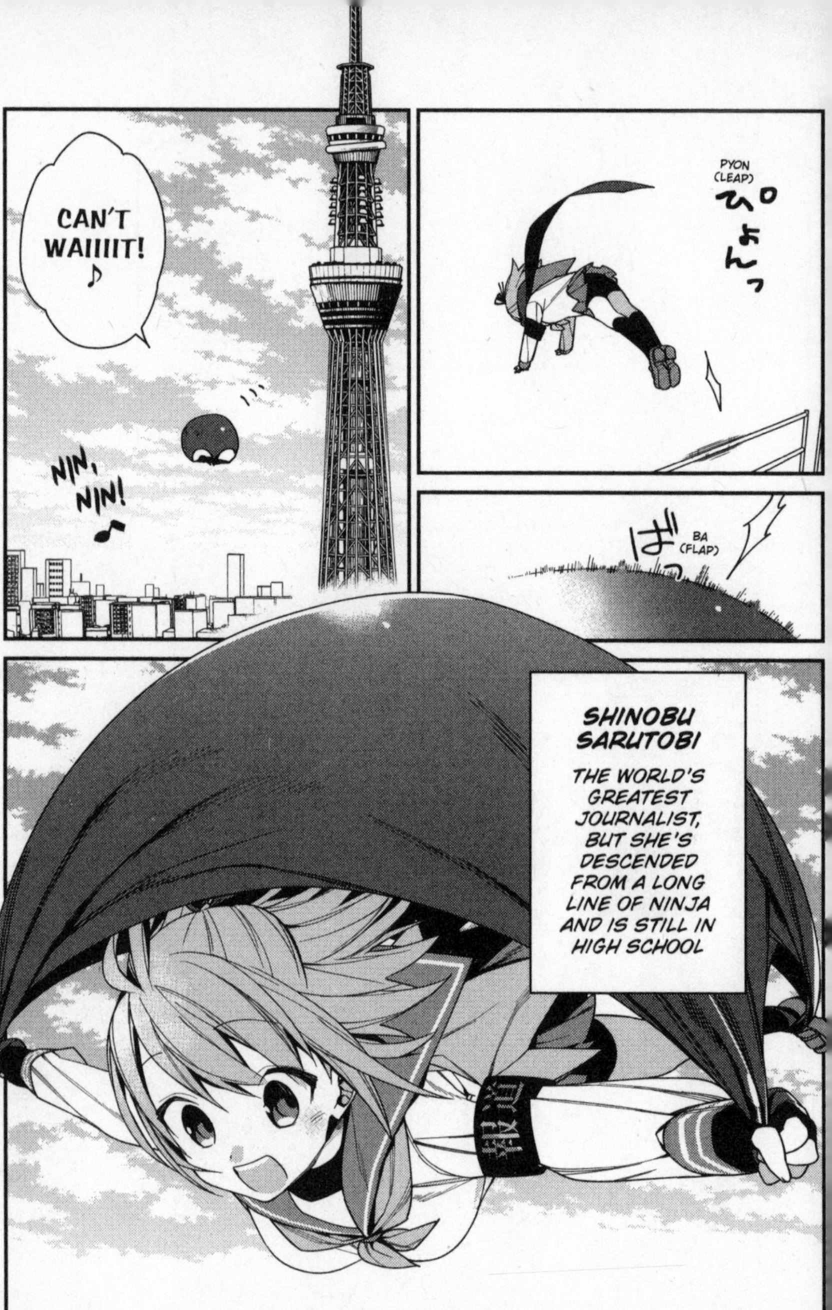

PYON (LEAP)
ぴょんっ
BA (FLAP)
ばっ
CAN'T WAIIIIT! ♪
NIN, NIN! ♪
SHINOBU SARUTOBI
THE WORLD'S GREATEST JOURNALIST, BUT SHE'S DESCENDED FROM A LONG LINE OF NINJA AND IS STILL IN HIGH SCHOOL

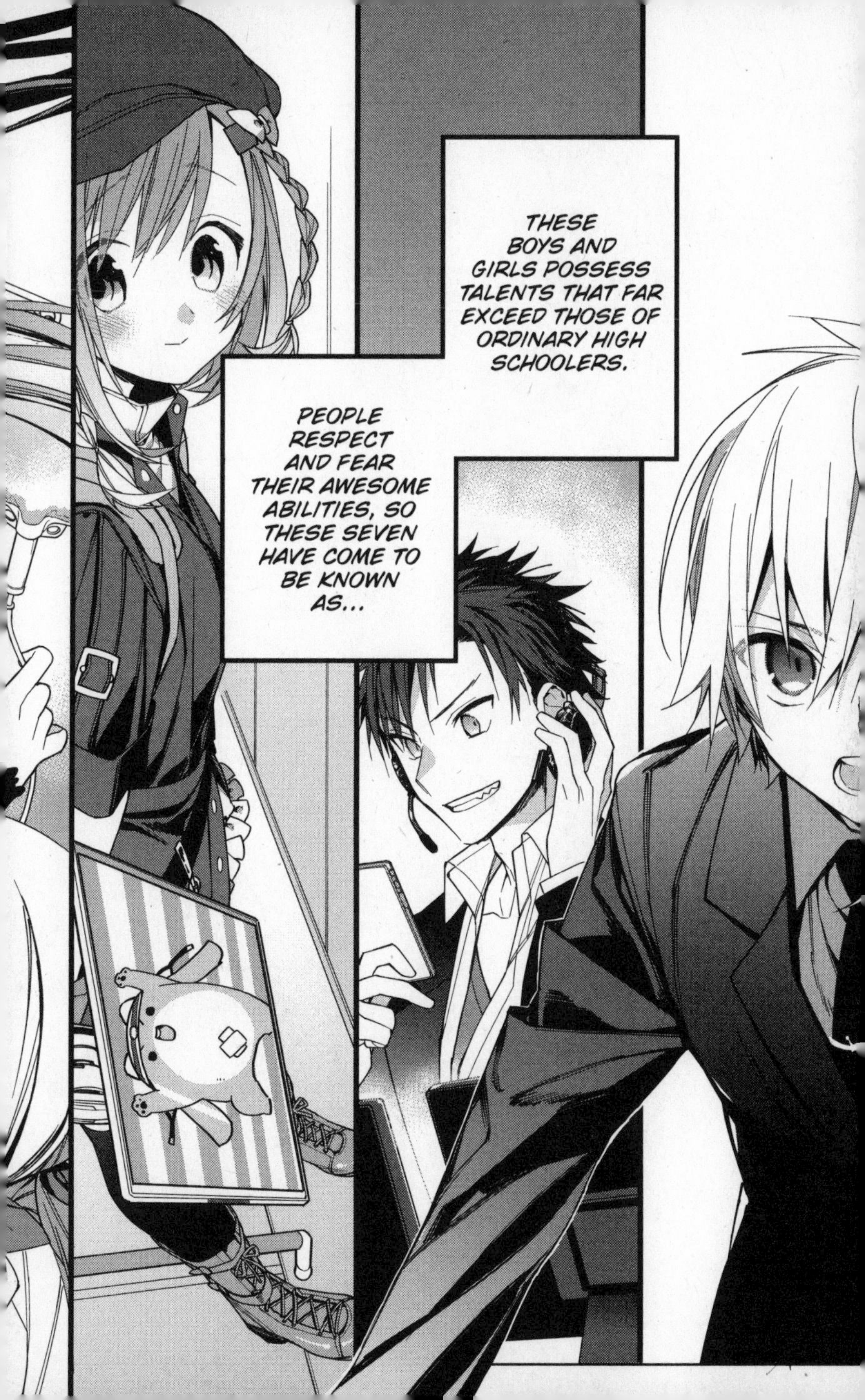
THESE BOYS AND GIRLS POSSESS TALENTS THAT FAR EXCEED THOSE OF ORDINARY HIGH SCHOOLERS.
PEOPLE RESPECT AND FEAR THEIR AWESOME ABILITIES, SO THESE SEVEN HAVE COME TO BE KNOWN AS...

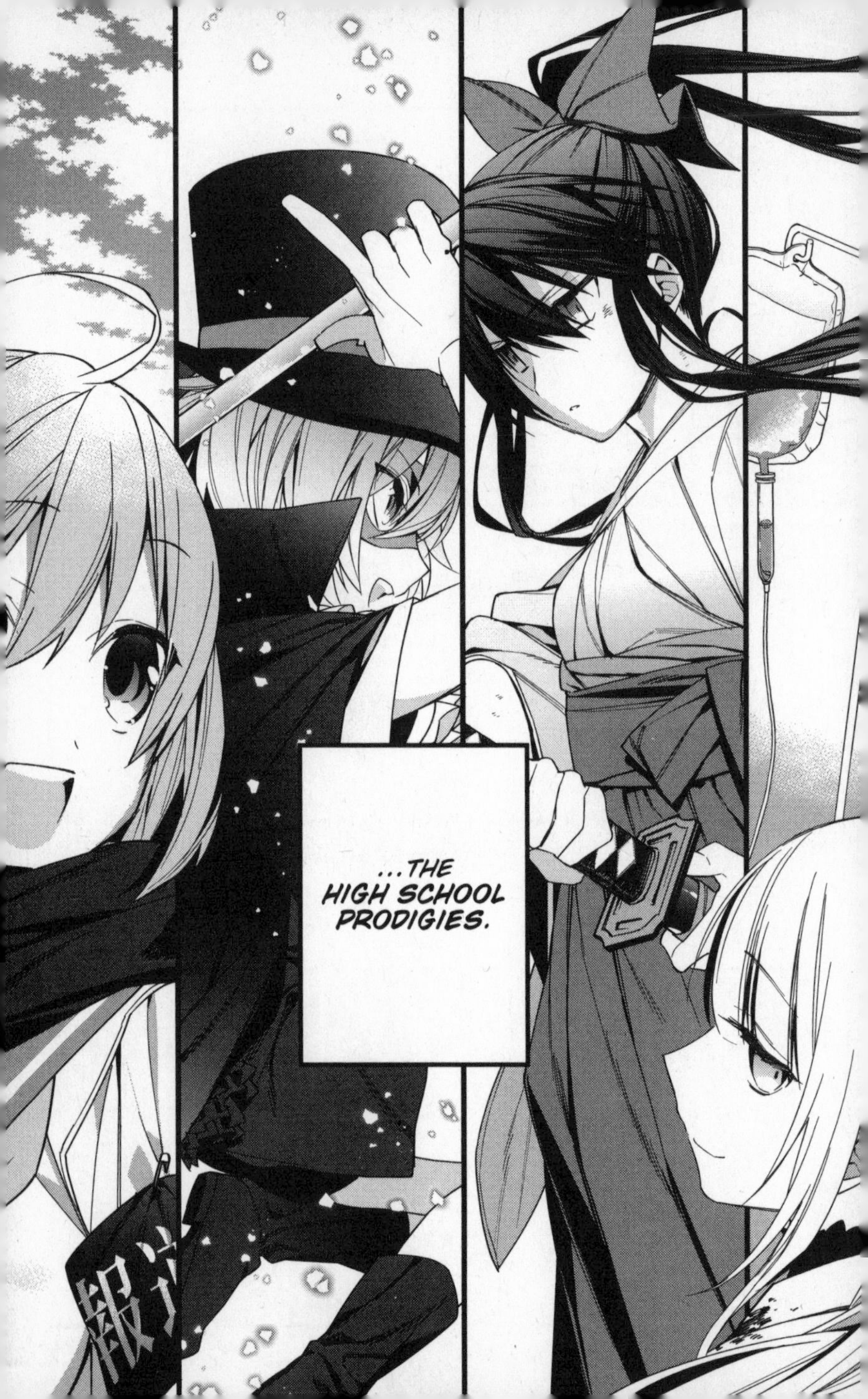
...THE HIGH SCHOOL PRODIGIES.

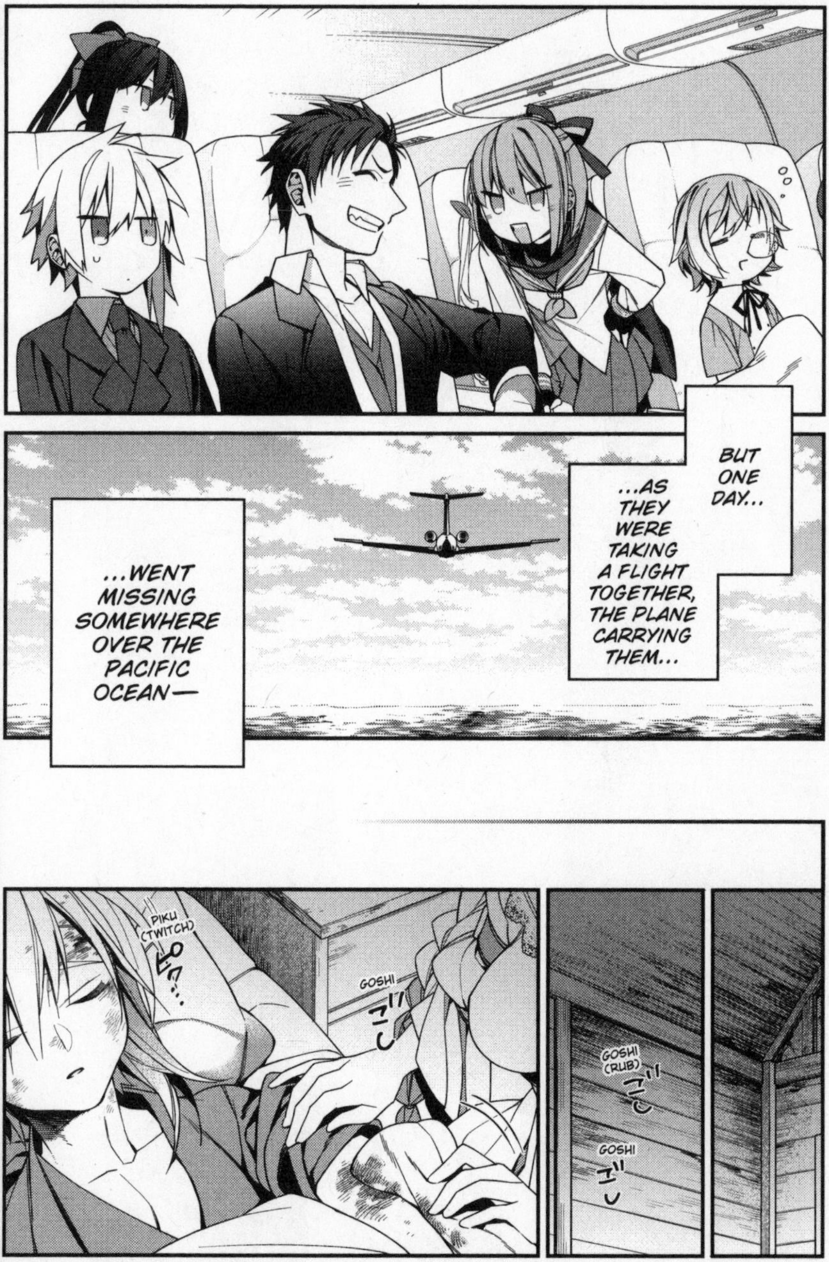
BUT ONE DAY...
...AS THEY WERE TAKING A FLIGHT TOGETHER, THE PLANE CARRYING THEM...
...WENT MISSING SOMEWHERE OVER THE PACIFIC OCEAN—
GOSHI (RUB)
GOSHI
GOSHI
PIKU (TWITCH)

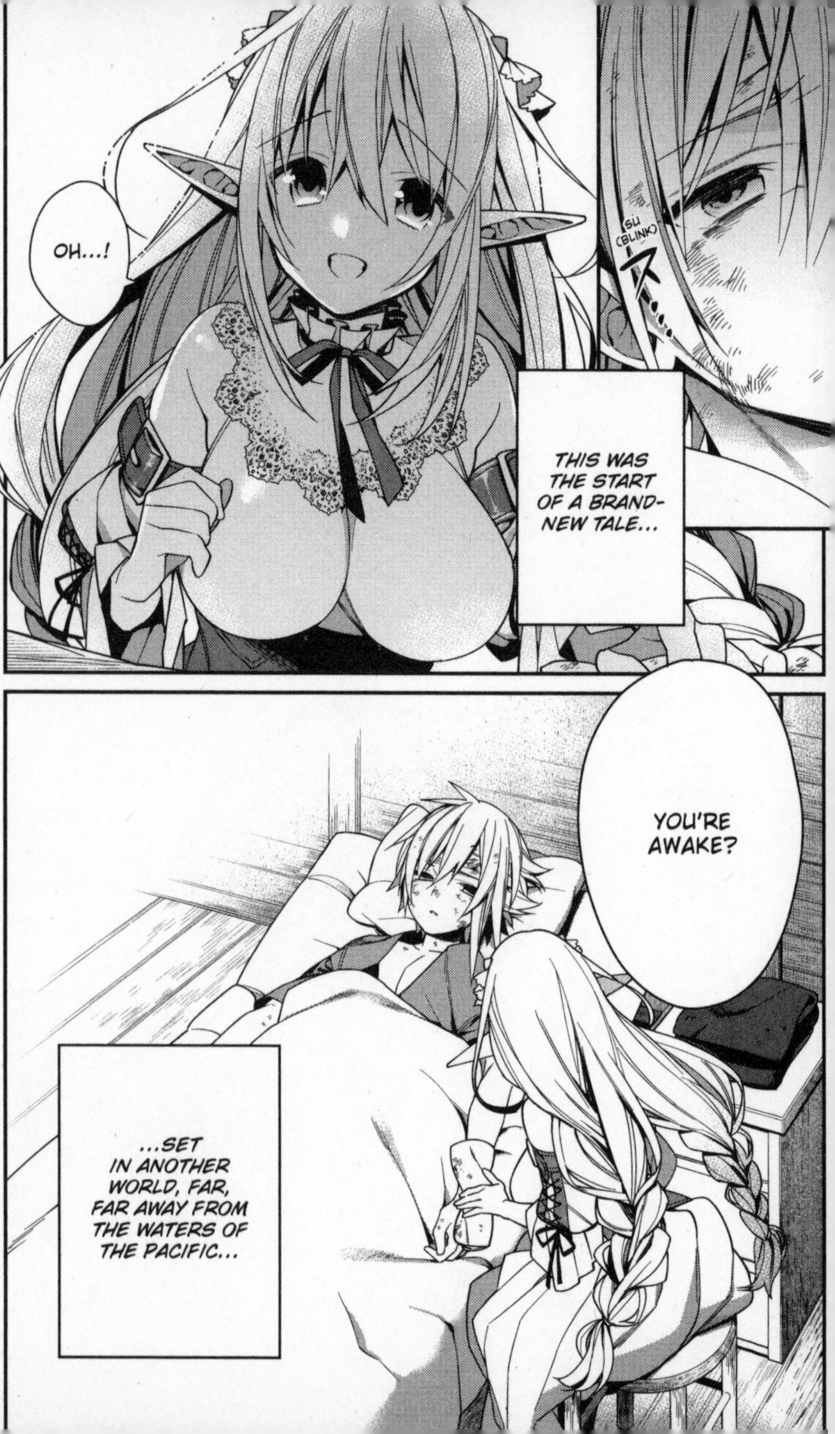
SU (BLINK)
OH...!
THIS WAS THE START OF A BRAND-NEW TALE...
YOU'RE AWAKE?
...SET IN ANOTHER WORLD, FAR, FAR AWAY FROM THE WATERS OF THE PACIFIC...

CHARACTER FILE 01

Tsukasa Mikogami

One of the high school prodigies. After election laws were changed to allow citizens to vote for prime minister directly, he took office with 92% of the popular vote. He has a condition called heterochromia, which results in different-colored eyes.

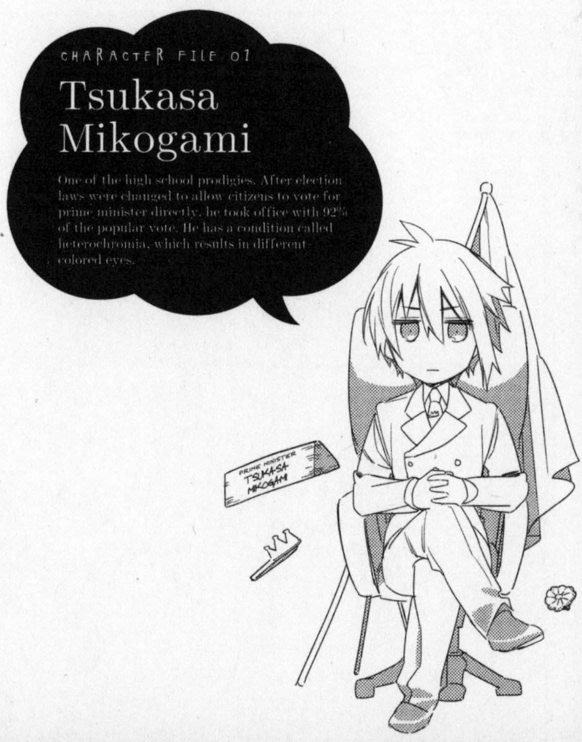
PRIME MINISTER
TSUKASA MIKOGAMI

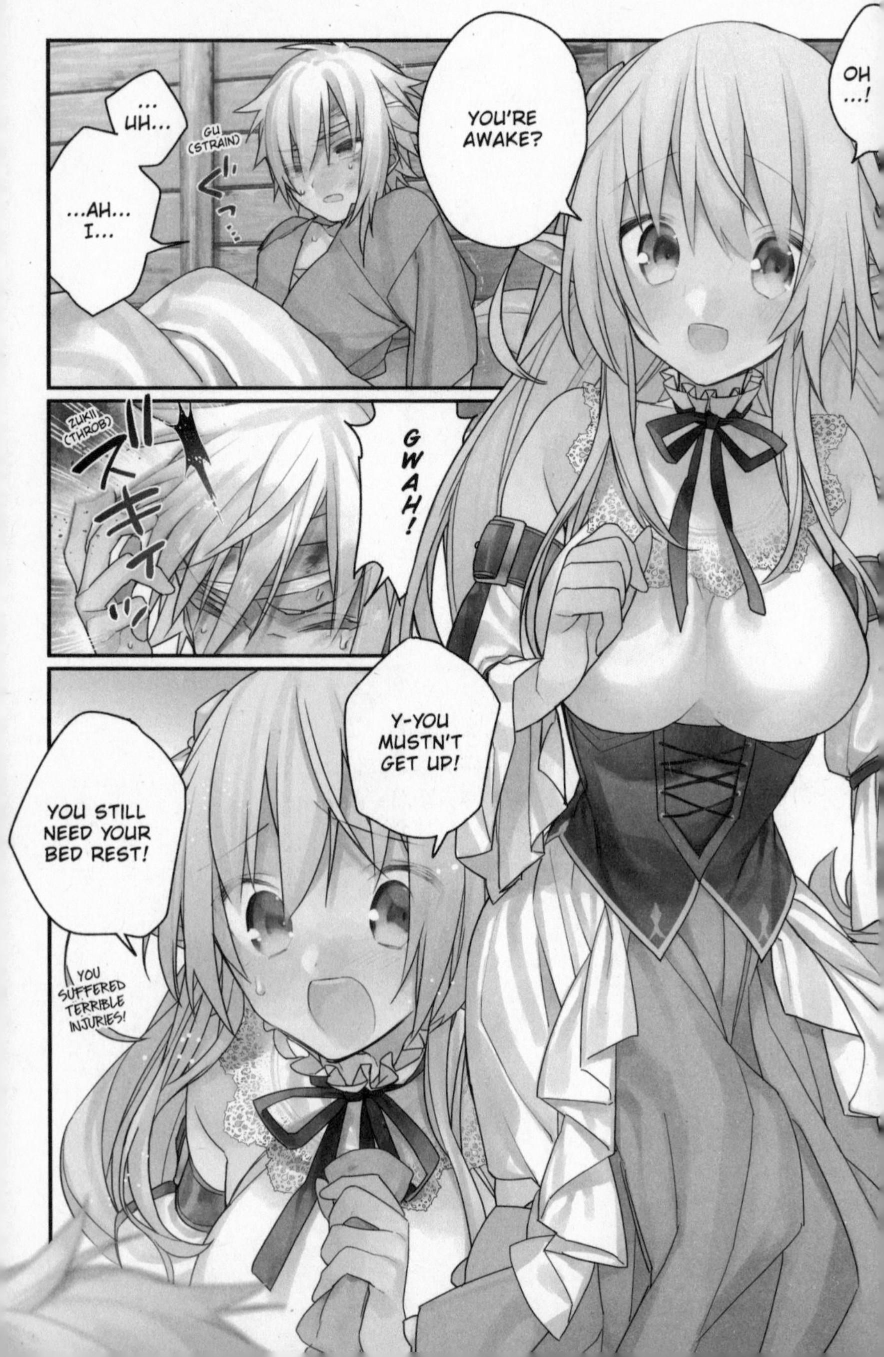
OH ...!
YOU'RE AWAKE?
... UH...
GU (STRAIN)
...AH... I...
ZUKII (THROB)
GWAH!
Y-YOU MUSTN'T GET UP!
YOU STILL NEED YOUR BED REST!
YOU SUFFERED TERRIBLE INJURIES!

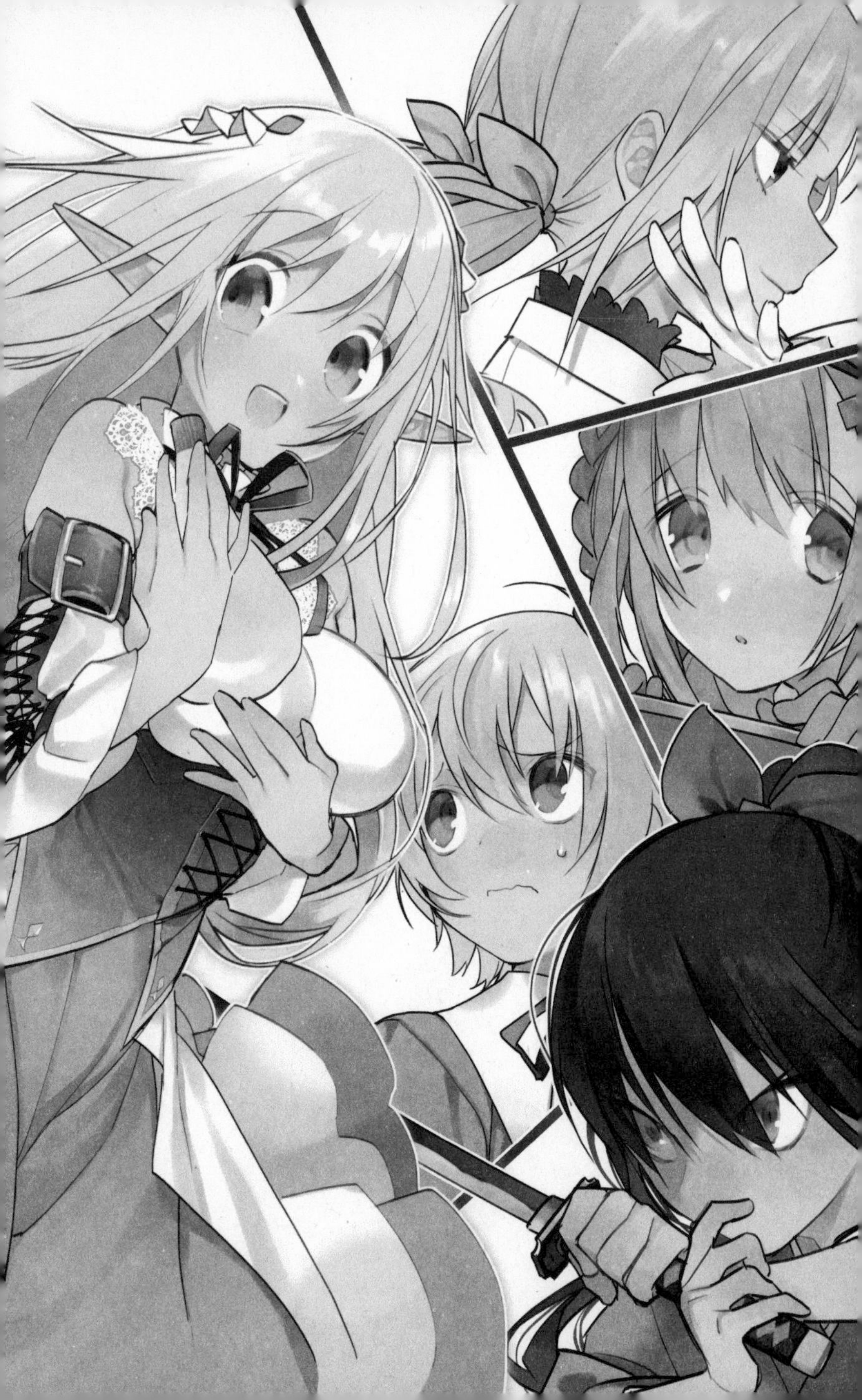

CHAPTER 2:
THE BOY FROM EARTH AND THE GIRL FROM ANOTHER WORLD

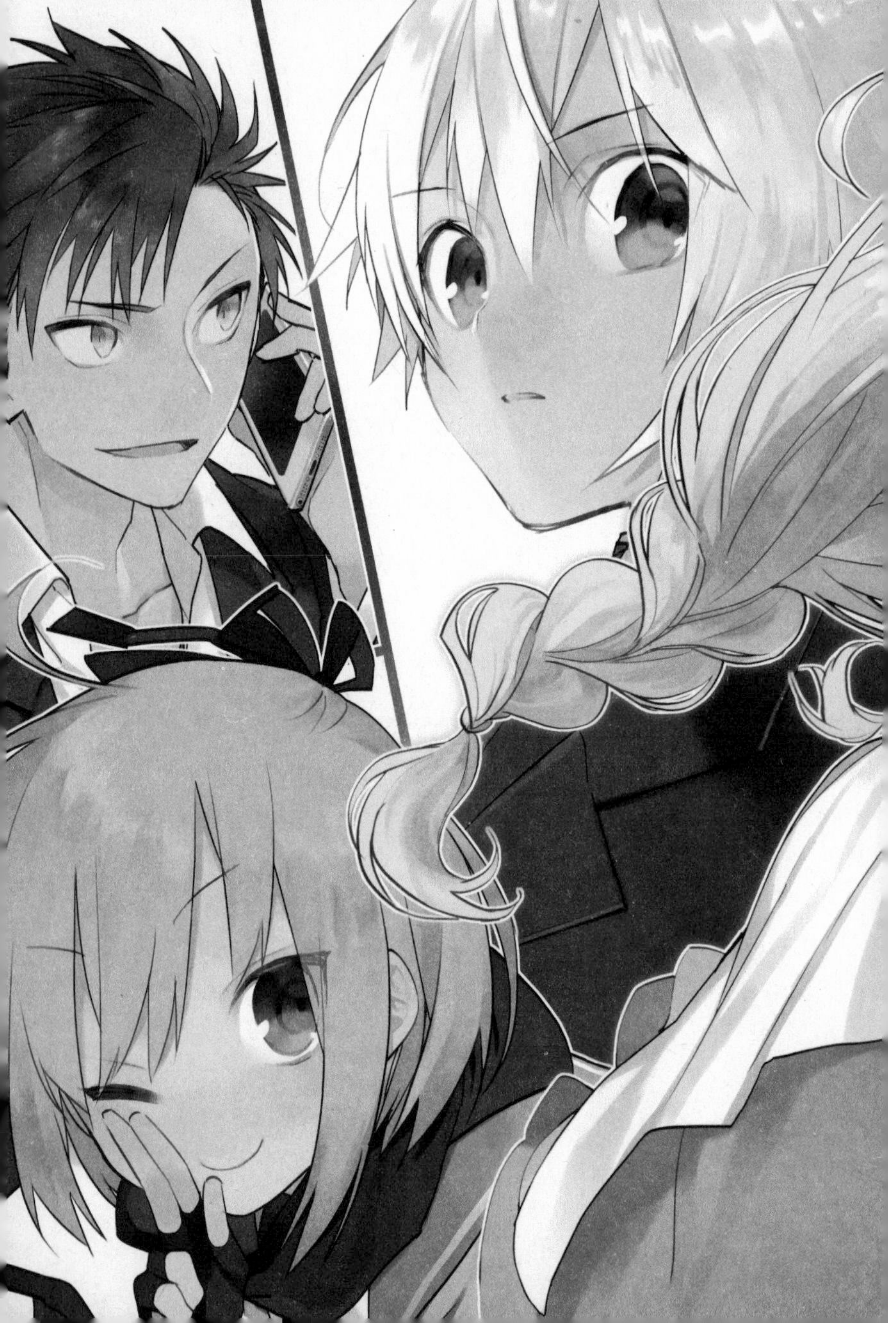

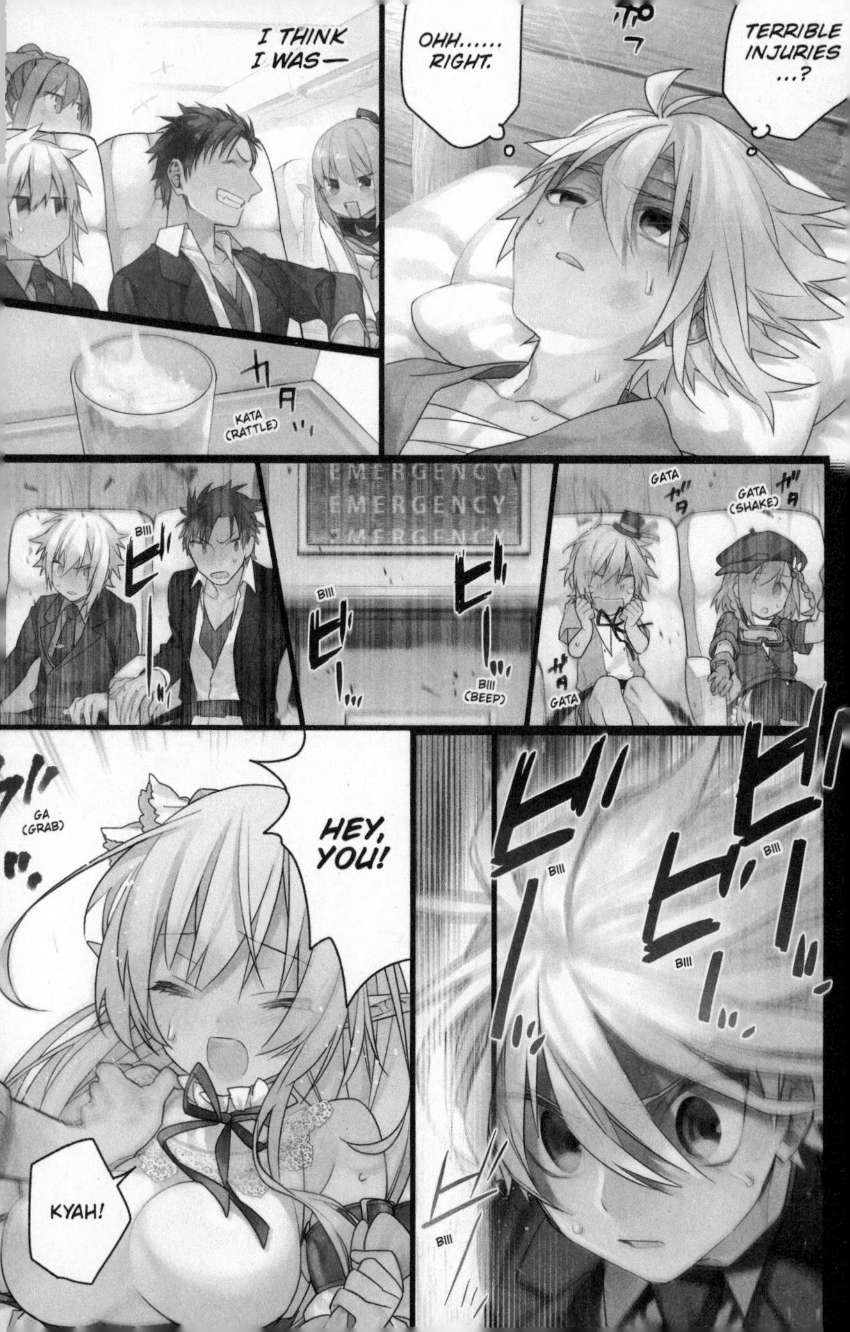
TERRIBLE INJURIES ...?
OHH...... RIGHT.
I THINK I WAS—
KATA (RATTLE)
GATA
GATA (SHAKE)
GATA
EMERGENCY
EMERGENCY
EMERGENCY
BIII
BIII (BEEP)
BIII
BIII
BIII
BIII
BIII
HEY, YOU!
GA (GRAB)
KYAH!

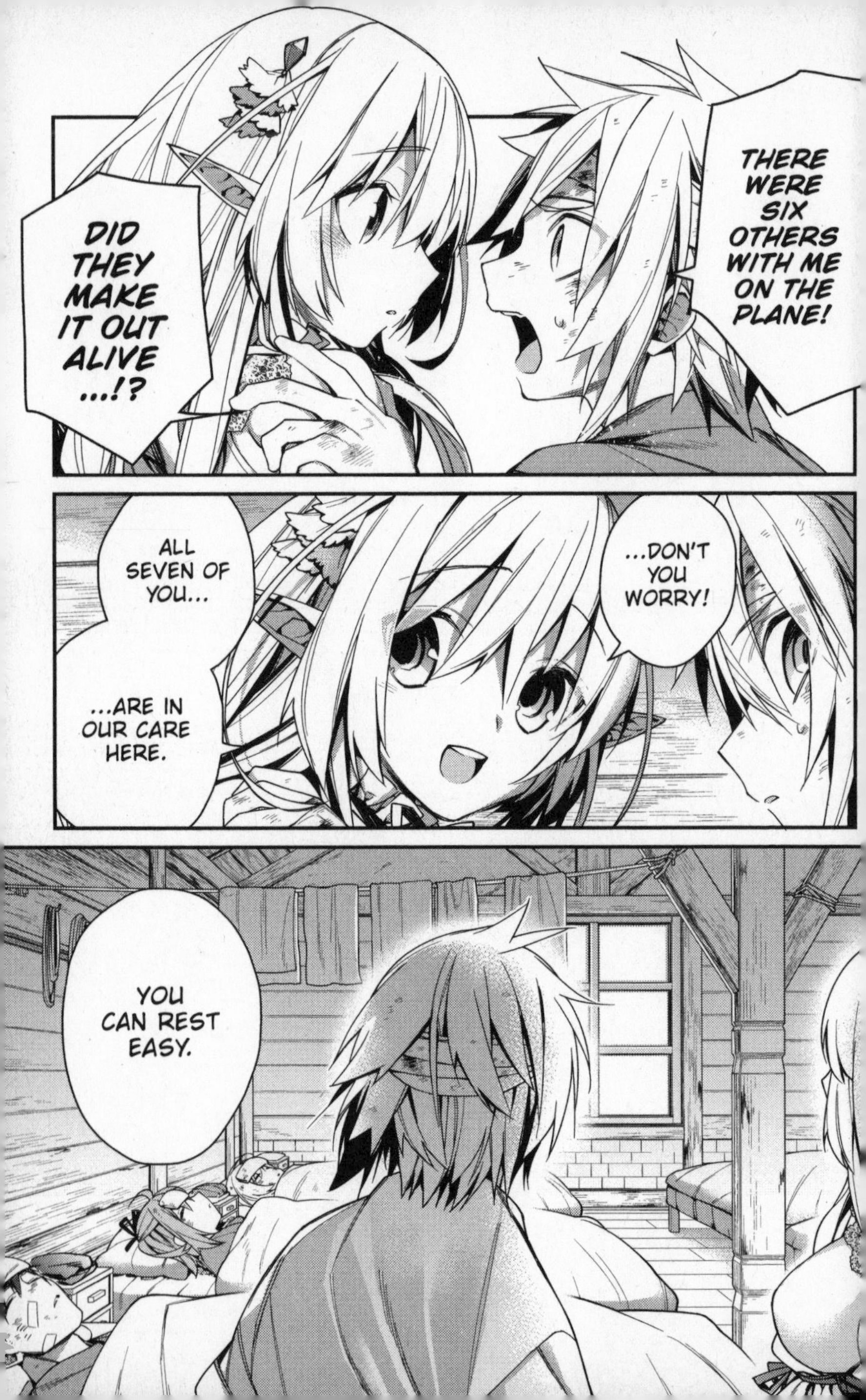
THERE WERE SIX OTHERS WITH ME ON THE PLANE!
DID THEY MAKE IT OUT ALIVE ...!?
...DON'T YOU WORRY!
ALL SEVEN OF YOU...
...ARE IN OUR CARE HERE.
YOU CAN REST EASY.

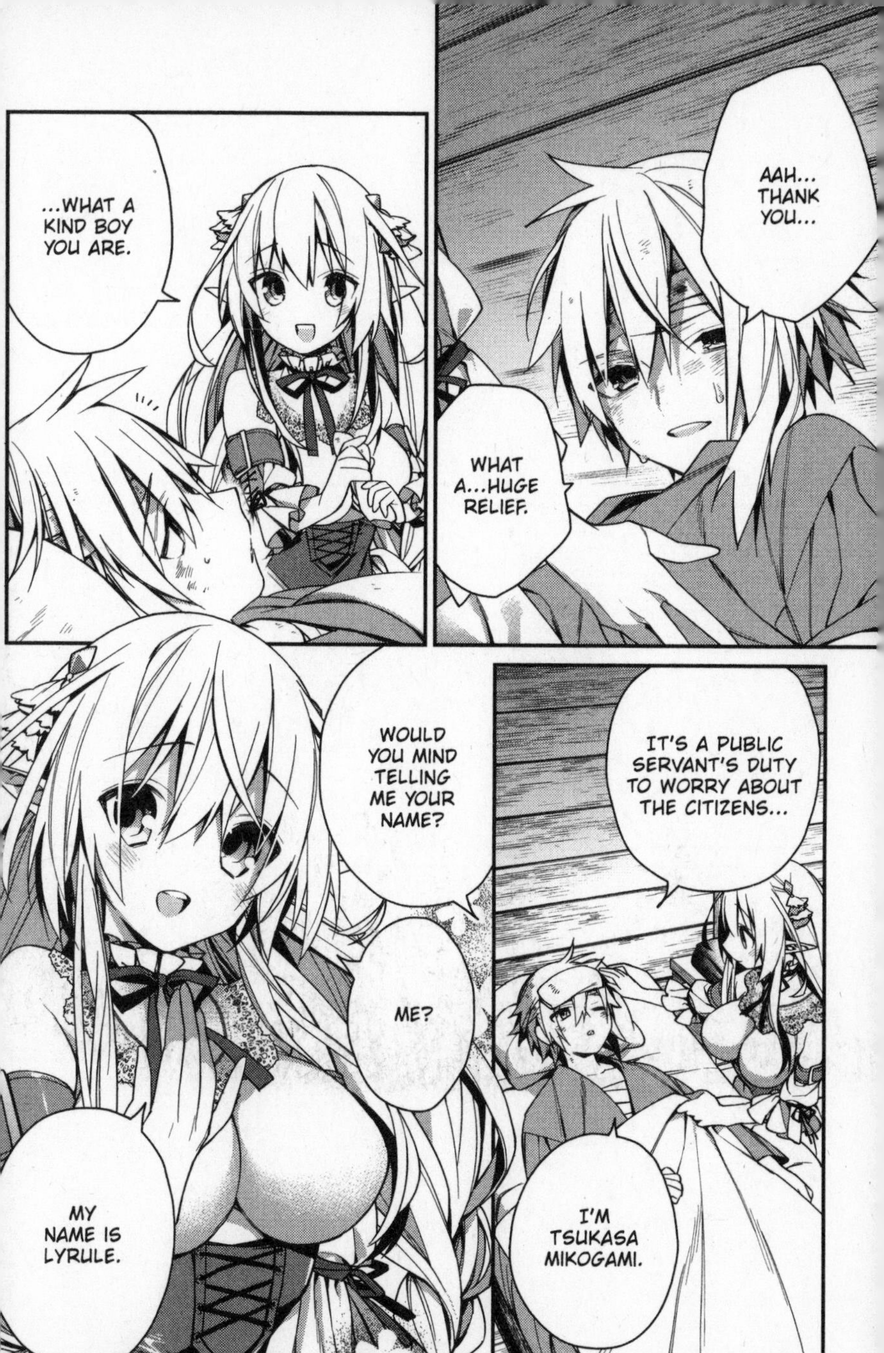
AAH... THANK YOU...
WHAT A...HUGE RELIEF.
...WHAT A KIND BOY YOU ARE.
IT'S A PUBLIC SERVANT'S DUTY TO WORRY ABOUT THE CITIZENS...
I'M TSUKASA MIKOGAMI.
WOULD YOU MIND TELLING ME YOUR NAME?
ME?
MY NAME IS LYRULE.

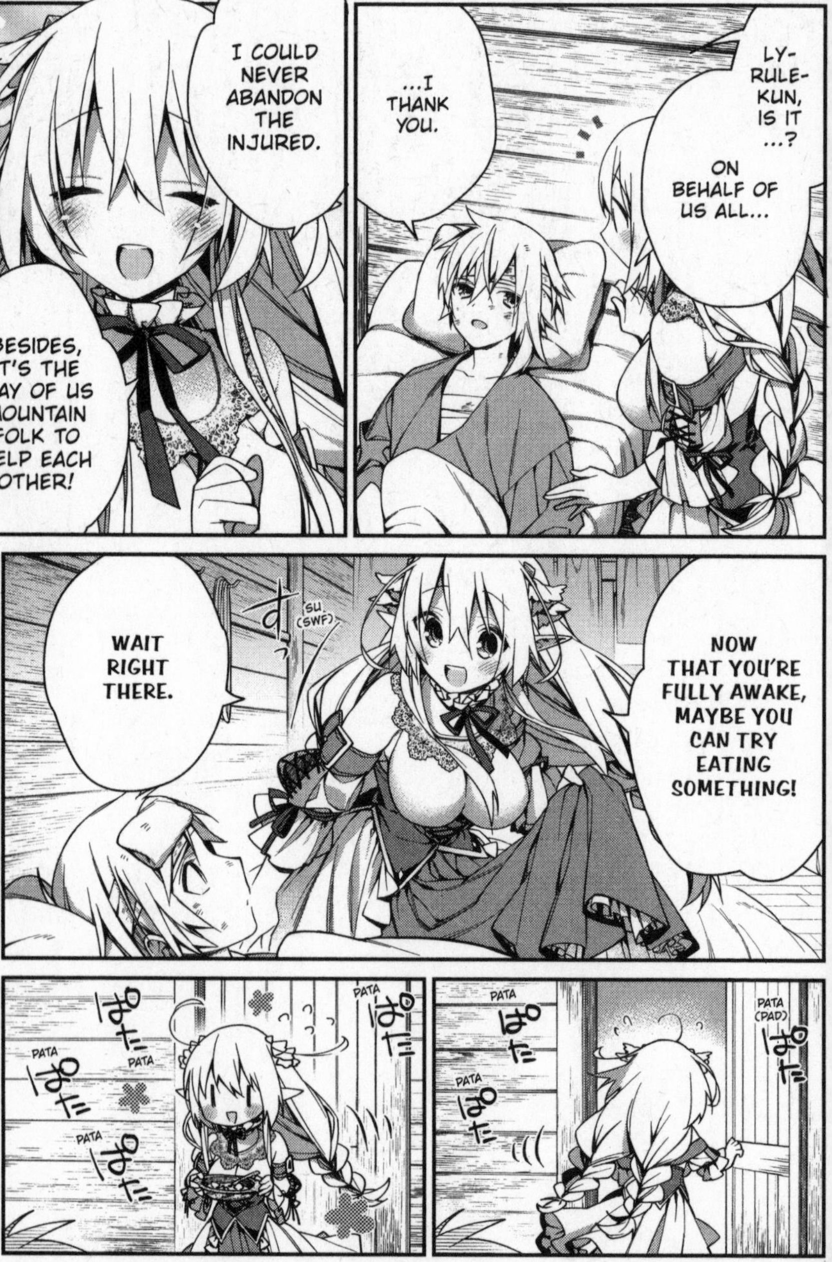
LY-RULE-KUN, IS IT ...?
ON BEHALF OF US ALL...
...I THANK YOU.
I COULD NEVER ABANDON THE INJURED.
BESIDES, IT'S THE WAY OF US MOUNTAIN FOLK TO HELP EACH OTHER!
NOW THAT YOU'RE FULLY AWAKE, MAYBE YOU CAN TRY EATING SOMETHING!
SU (SWF)
WAIT RIGHT THERE.
PATA (PAD)
PATA
PATA
PATA
PATA
PATA
PATA

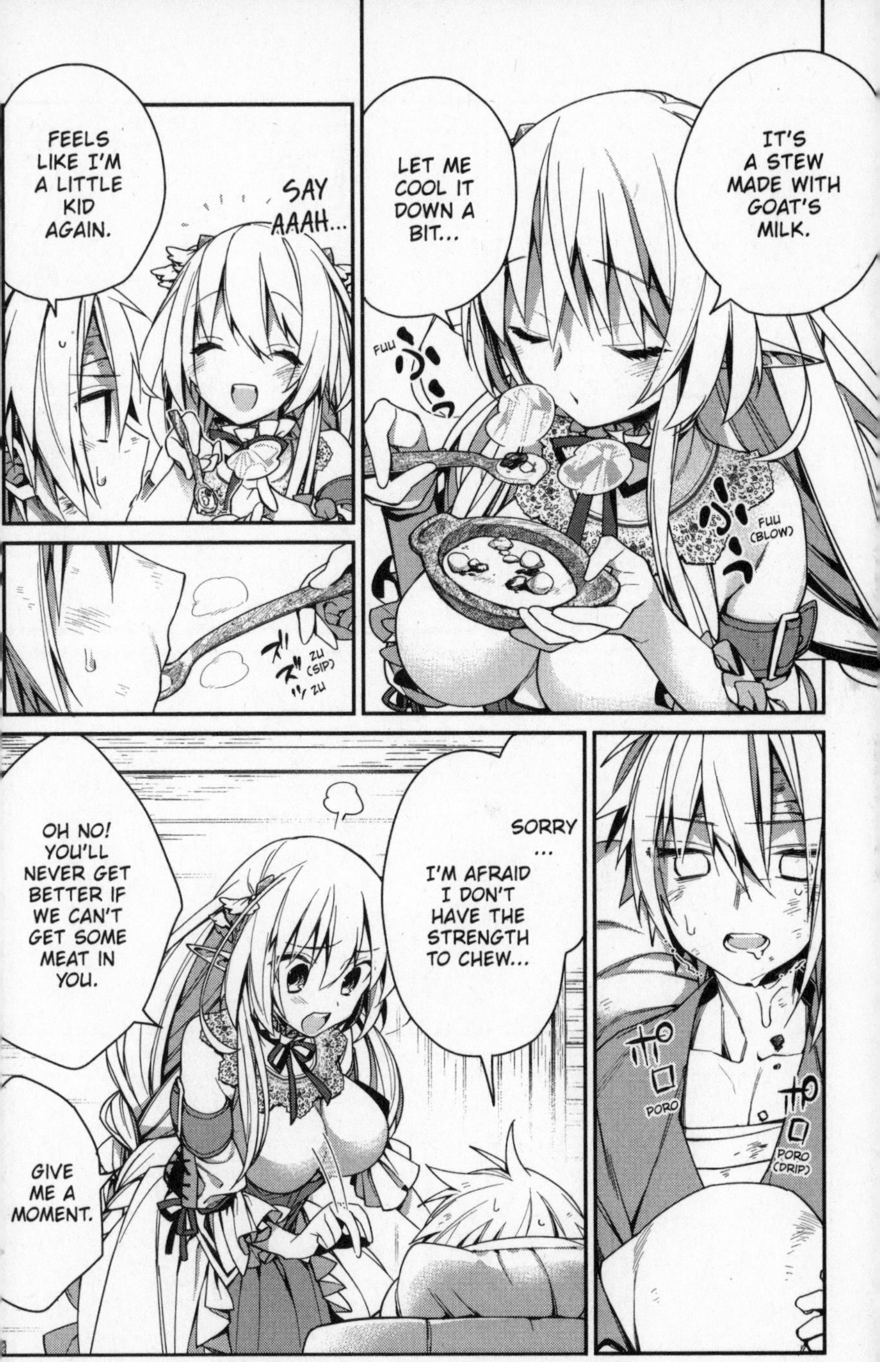
IT'S A STEW MADE WITH GOAT'S MILK.
LET ME COOL IT DOWN A BIT...
FUU
FUU (BLOW)
FEELS LIKE I'M A LITTLE KID AGAIN.
SAY AAAH...
ZU (SIP)
ZU
PORO
PORO (DRIP)
SORRY ... I'M AFRAID I DON'T HAVE THE STRENGTH TO CHEW...
OH NO! YOU'LL NEVER GET BETTER IF WE CAN'T GET SOME MEAT IN YOU.
GIVE ME A MOMENT.

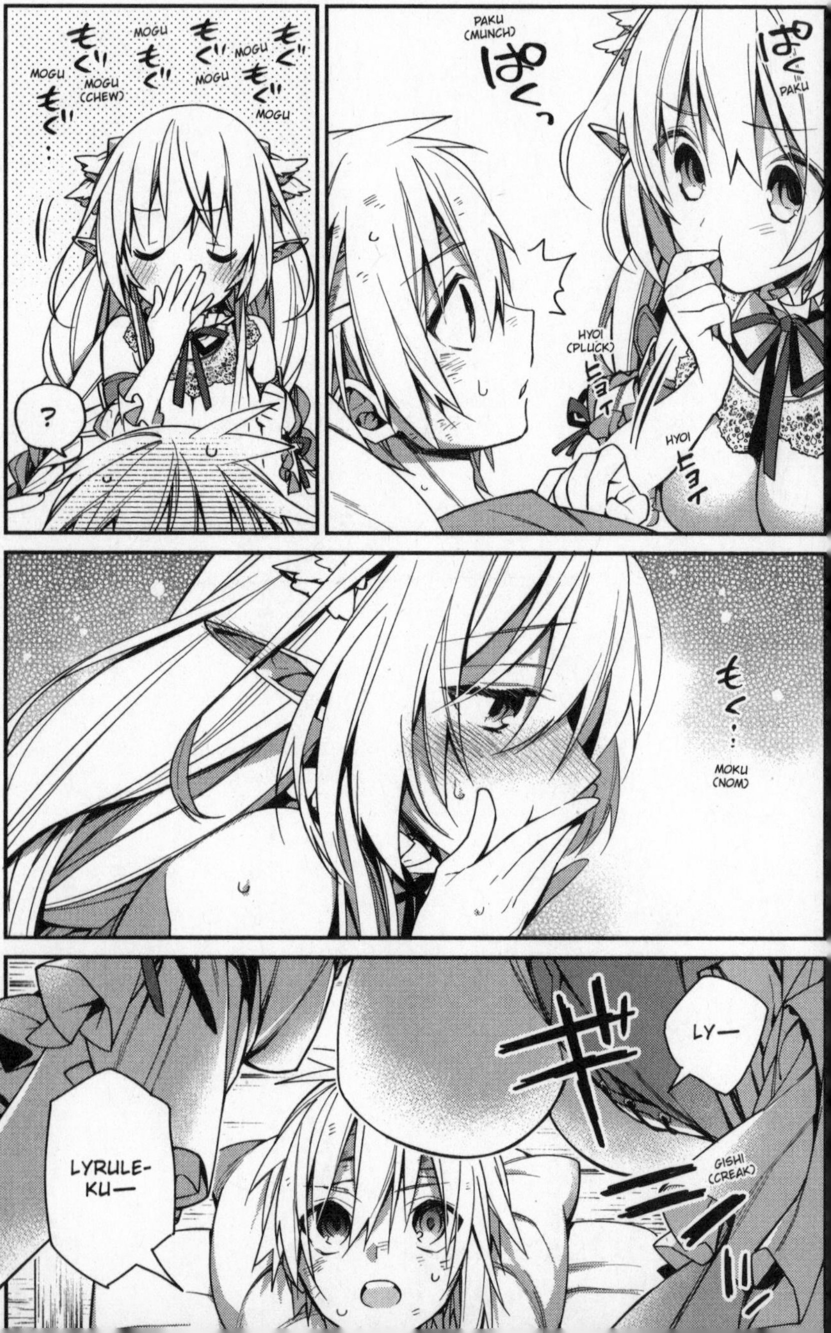
ぱく
PAKU
PAKU (MUNCH)
ぱくっ
HYOI
ヒョイ
HYOI (PLUCK)
ヒョイ
もぐ
MOGU
もぐ
MOGU
もぐ
MOGU
もぐ
MOGU (CHEW)
もぐ
MOGU
もぐ…
MOGU
?
もく…
MOKU (NOM)
LY—
ギ
GISHI (CREAK)
LYRULE-KU—

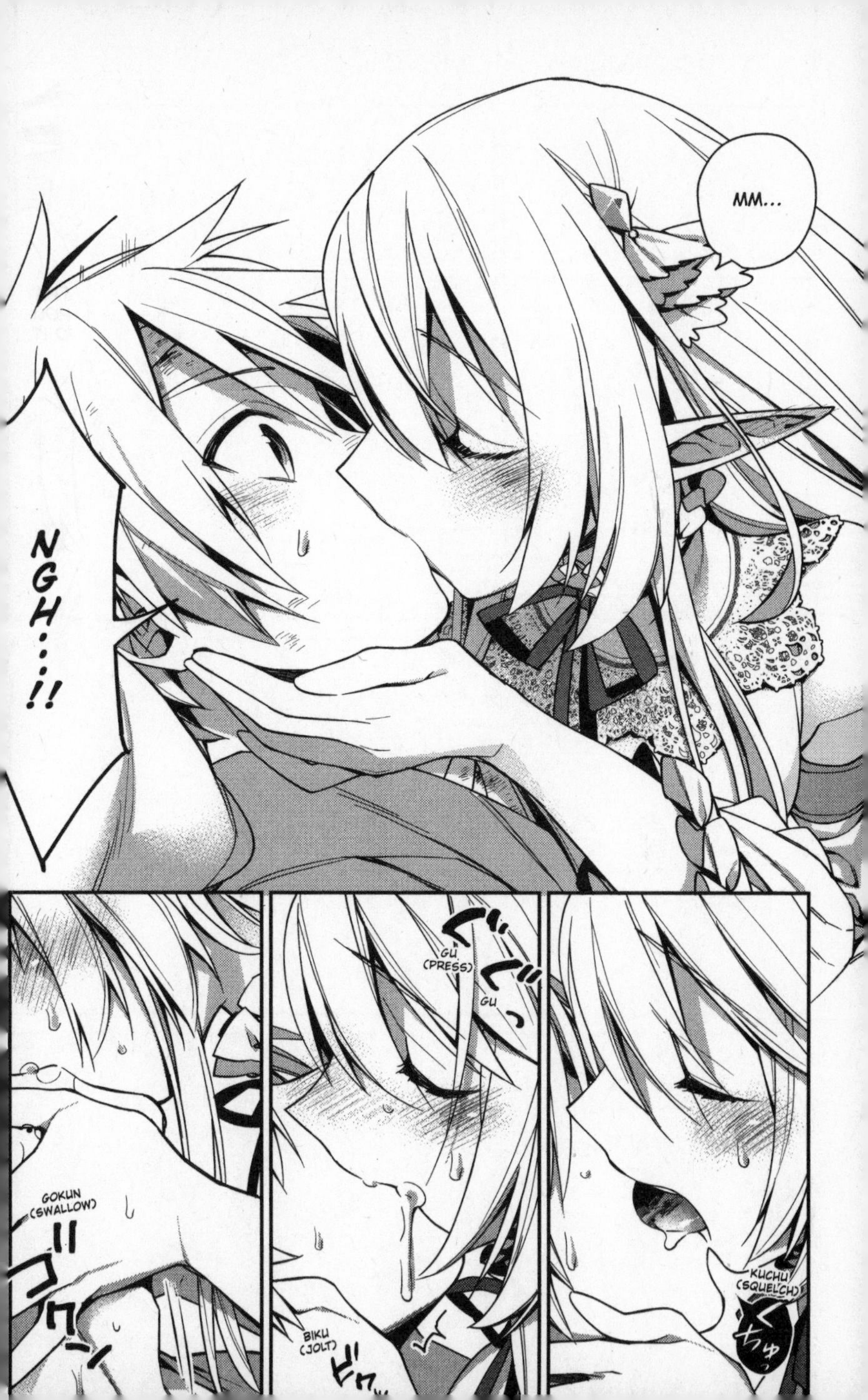
MM...
NGH...!!
KUCHU (SQUELCH)
GU (PRESS)
GU
BIKU (JOLT)
GOKUN (SWALLOW)

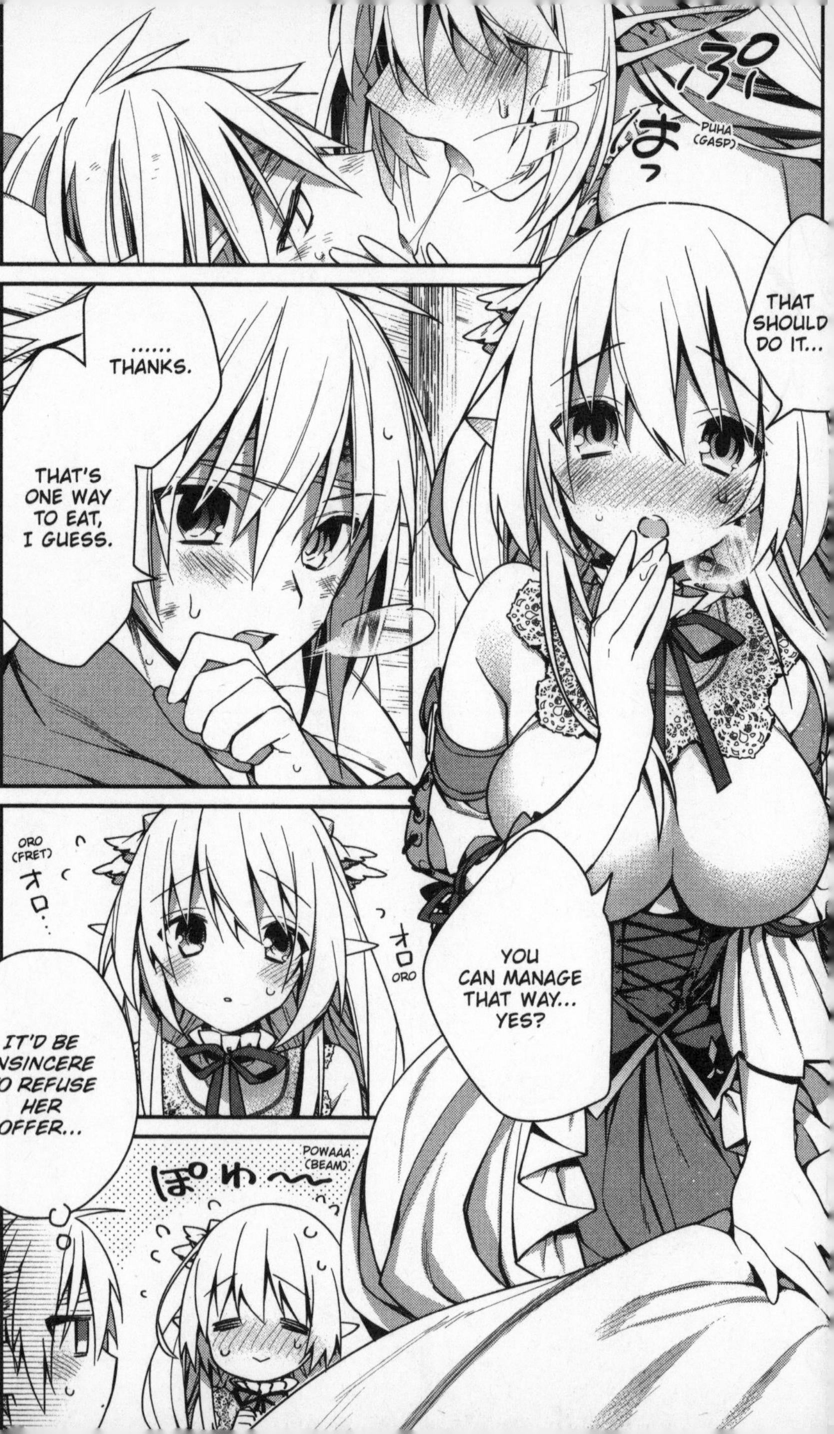
ぷはっ
PUHA (GASP)
THAT SHOULD DO IT...
YOU CAN MANAGE THAT WAY... YES?
...... THANKS.
THAT'S ONE WAY TO EAT, I GUESS.
ORO (FRET)
オロ…
オロ
ORO
IT'D BE INSINCERE TO REFUSE HER OFFER...
POWAAA (BEAM)
ぽゆ～～

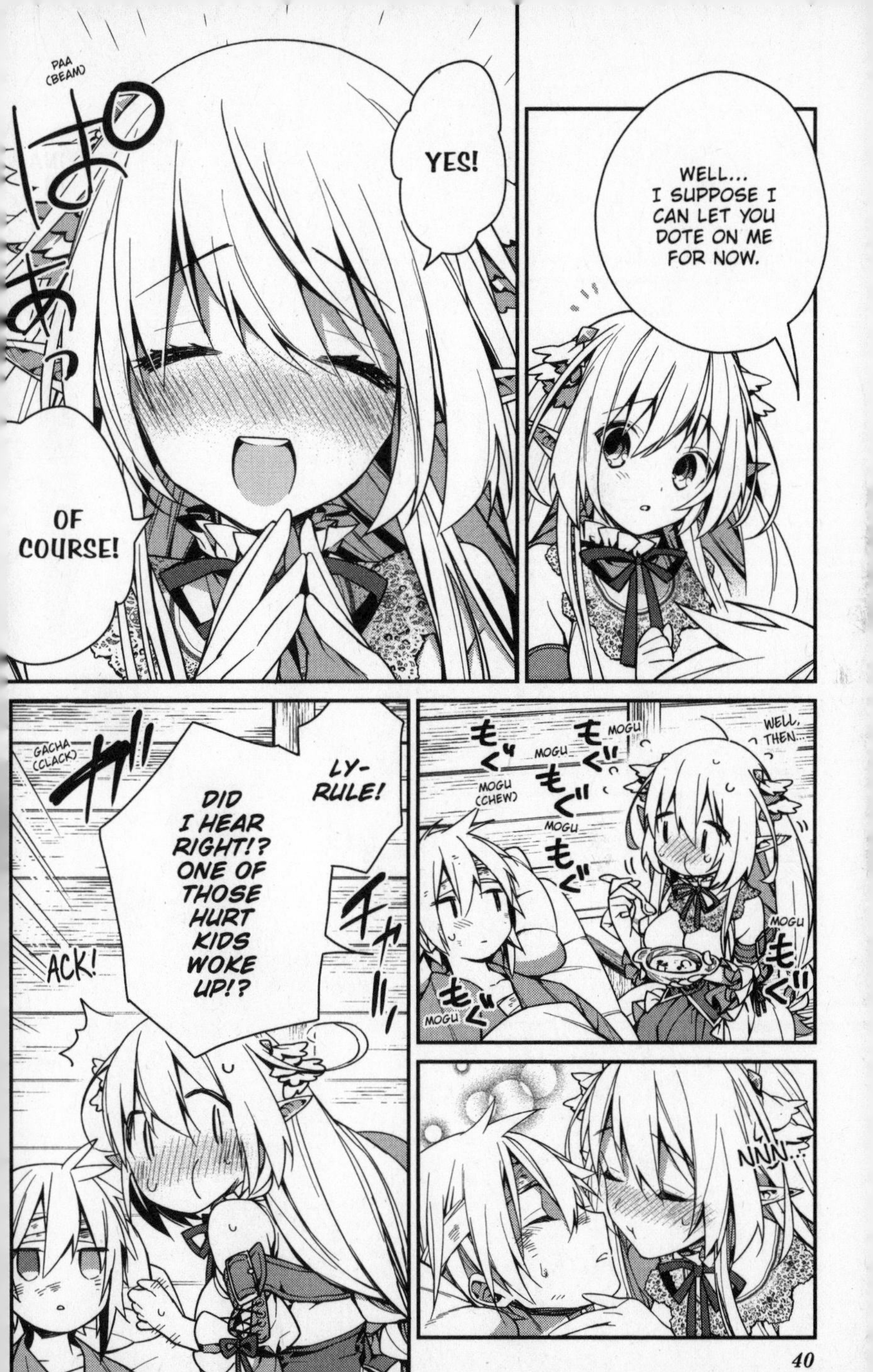
WELL... I SUPPOSE I CAN LET YOU DOTE ON ME FOR NOW.
YES!
PAA (BEAM)
ぱあっ
OF COURSE!
WELL, THEN...
MOGU
MOGU
MOGU (CHEW)
MOGU
MOGU
MOGU
NNN...
LY-RULE!
DID I HEAR RIGHT!? ONE OF THOSE HURT KIDS WOKE UP!?
GACHA (CLACK)
ACK!

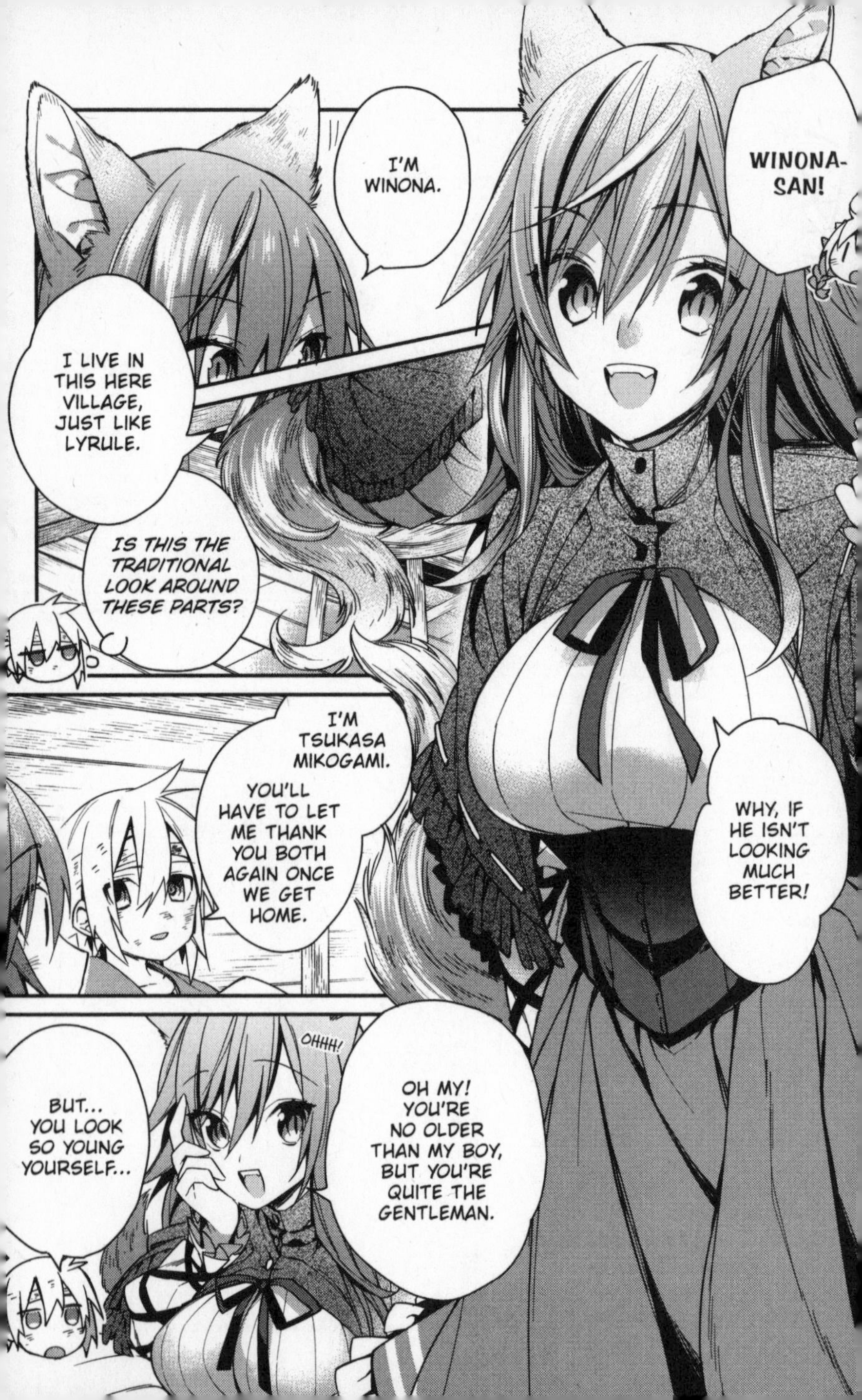
WINONA-SAN!
WHY, IF HE ISN'T LOOKING MUCH BETTER!
I'M WINONA.
I LIVE IN THIS HERE VILLAGE, JUST LIKE LYRULE.
IS THIS THE TRADITIONAL LOOK AROUND THESE PARTS?
I'M TSUKASA MIKOGAMI.
YOU'LL HAVE TO LET ME THANK YOU BOTH AGAIN ONCE WE GET HOME.
OHHH!
OH MY! YOU'RE NO OLDER THAN MY BOY, BUT YOU'RE QUITE THE GENTLEMAN.
BUT... YOU LOOK SO YOUNG YOURSELF...

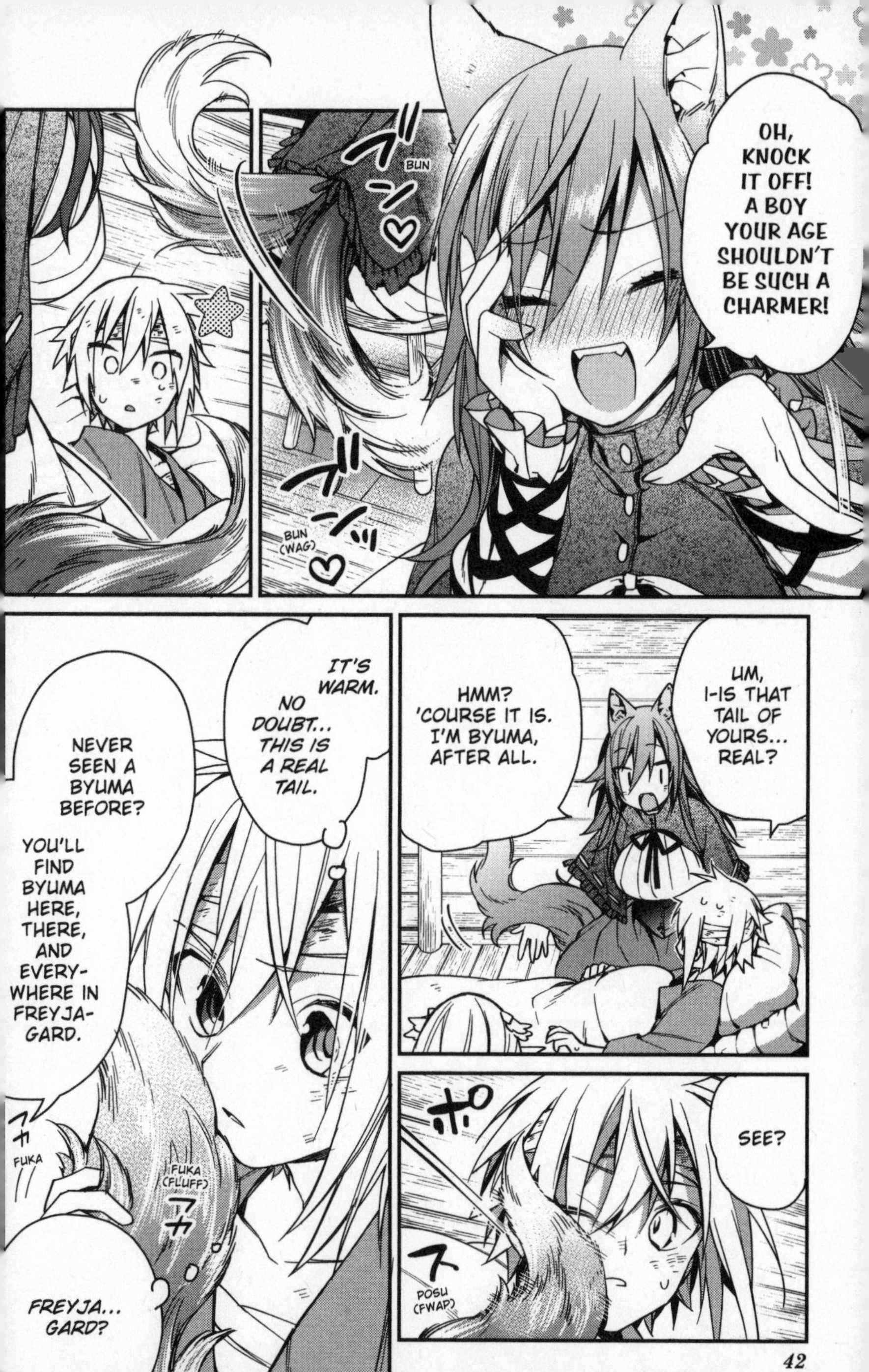
BUN
OH, KNOCK IT OFF! A BOY YOUR AGE SHOULDN'T BE SUCH A CHARMER!
BUN (WAG)
UM, I-IS THAT TAIL OF YOURS... REAL?
HMM? 'COURSE IT IS. I'M BYUMA, AFTER ALL.
SEE?
POSU (FWAP)
IT'S WARM. NO DOUBT... THIS IS A REAL TAIL.
NEVER SEEN A BYUMA BEFORE?
YOU'LL FIND BYUMA HERE, THERE, AND EVERYWHERE IN FREYJAGARD.
FUKA
FUKA (FLUFF)
FREYJA... GARD?

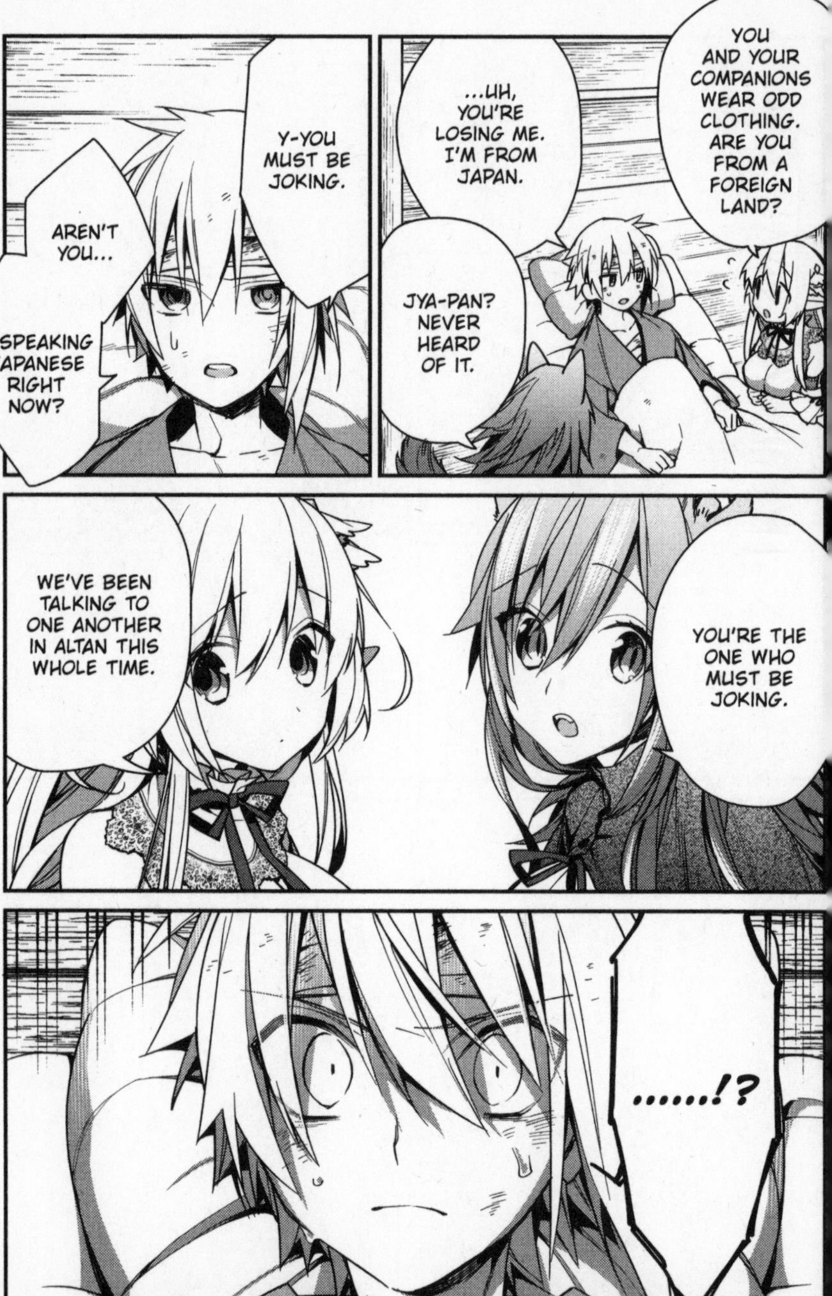
YOU AND YOUR COMPANIONS WEAR ODD CLOTHING. ARE YOU FROM A FOREIGN LAND?
...UH, YOU'RE LOSING ME. I'M FROM JAPAN.
JYA-PAN? NEVER HEARD OF IT.
Y-YOU MUST BE JOKING.
AREN'T YOU...
...SPEAKING JAPANESE RIGHT NOW?
YOU'RE THE ONE WHO MUST BE JOKING.
WE'VE BEEN TALKING TO ONE ANOTHER IN ALTAN THIS WHOLE TIME.
......!?

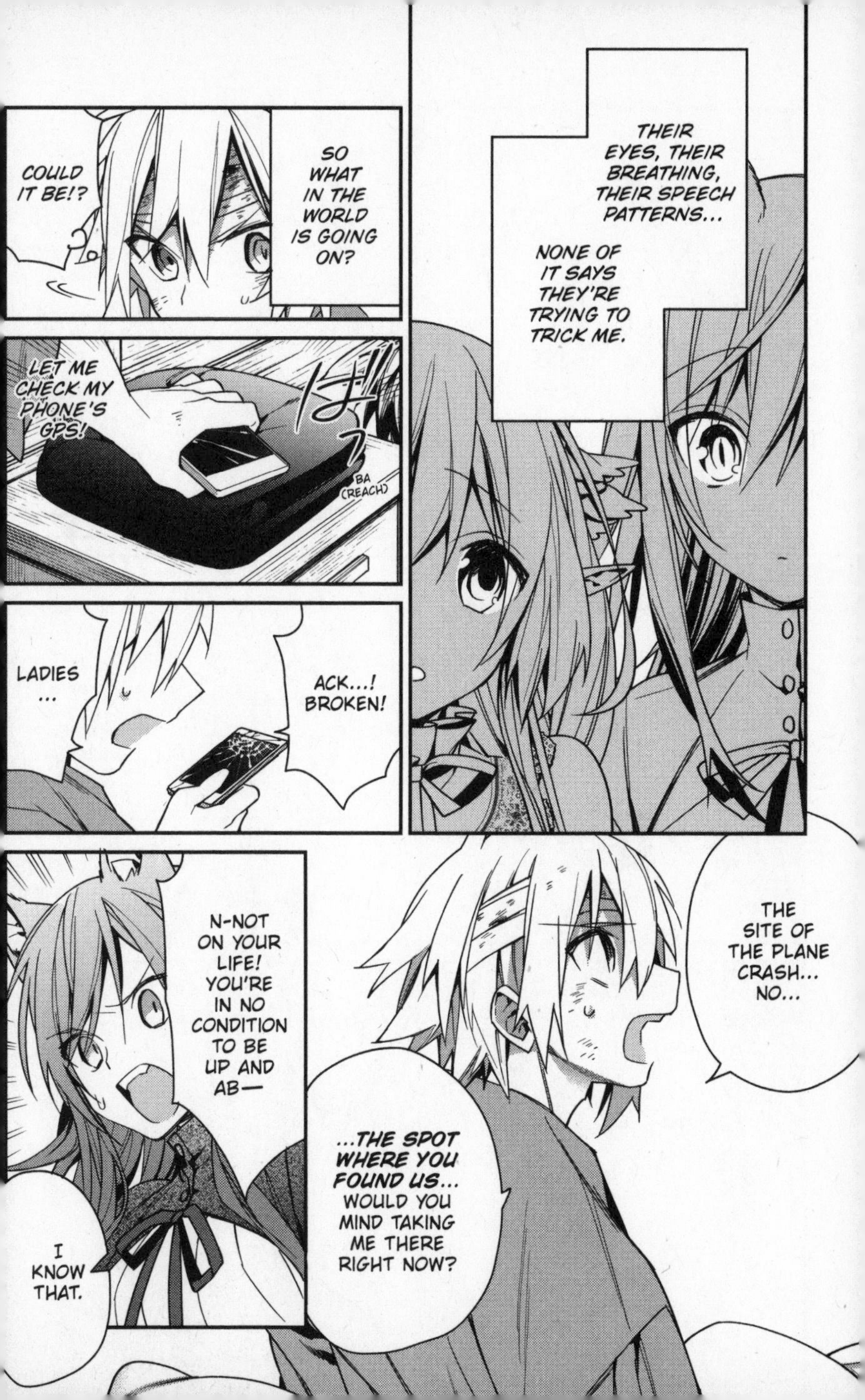
THEIR EYES, THEIR BREATHING, THEIR SPEECH PATTERNS...
NONE OF IT SAYS THEY'RE TRYING TO TRICK ME.
SO WHAT IN THE WORLD IS GOING ON?
COULD IT BE!?
LET ME CHECK MY PHONE'S GPS!
ばっ
BA (REACH)
ACK...! BROKEN!
LADIES ...
THE SITE OF THE PLANE CRASH... NO...
...THE SPOT WHERE YOU FOUND US... WOULD YOU MIND TAKING ME THERE RIGHT NOW?
N-NOT ON YOUR LIFE! YOU'RE IN NO CONDITION TO BE UP AND AB—
I KNOW THAT.

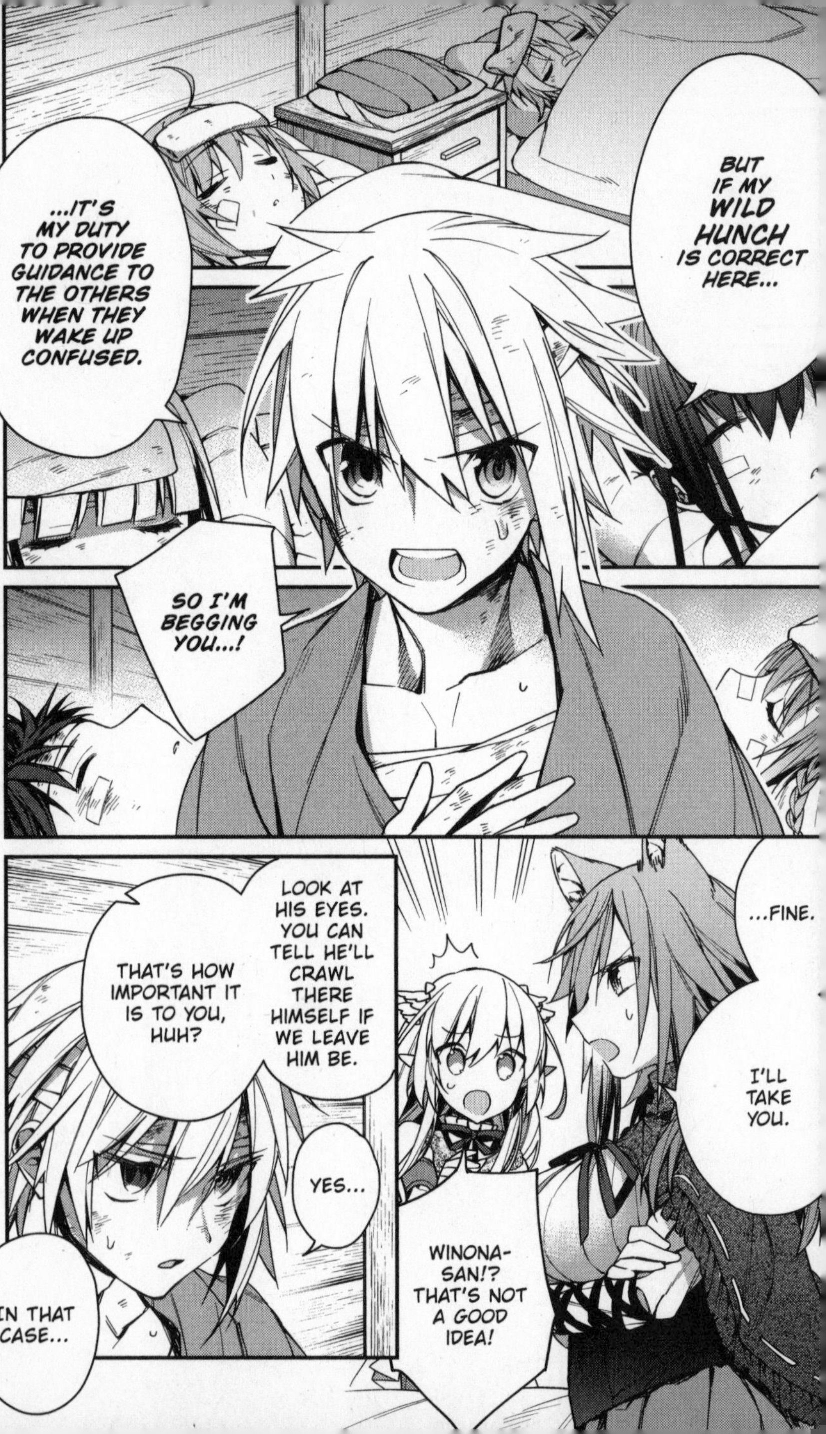
BUT IF MY WILD HUNCH IS CORRECT HERE...
...IT'S MY DUTY TO PROVIDE GUIDANCE TO THE OTHERS WHEN THEY WAKE UP CONFUSED.
SO I'M BEGGING YOU...!
...FINE.
I'LL TAKE YOU.
WINONA-SAN!? THAT'S NOT A GOOD IDEA!
LOOK AT HIS EYES. YOU CAN TELL HE'LL CRAWL THERE HIMSELF IF WE LEAVE HIM BE.
THAT'S HOW IMPORTANT IT IS TO YOU, HUH?
YES...
IN THAT CASE...

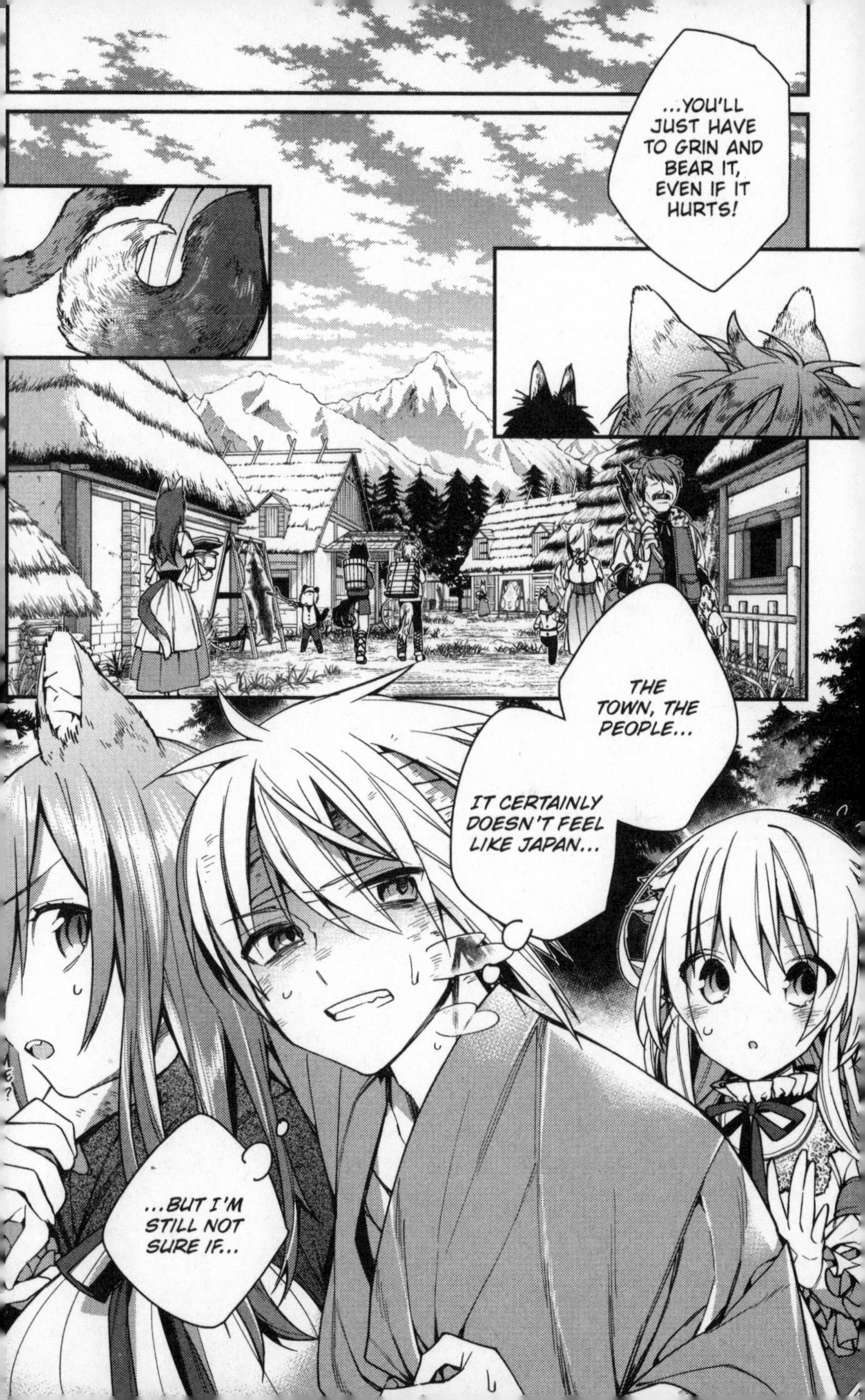
...YOU'LL JUST HAVE TO GRIN AND BEAR IT, EVEN IF IT HURTS!
THE TOWN, THE PEOPLE...
IT CERTAINLY DOESN'T FEEL LIKE JAPAN...
...BUT I'M STILL NOT SURE IF...

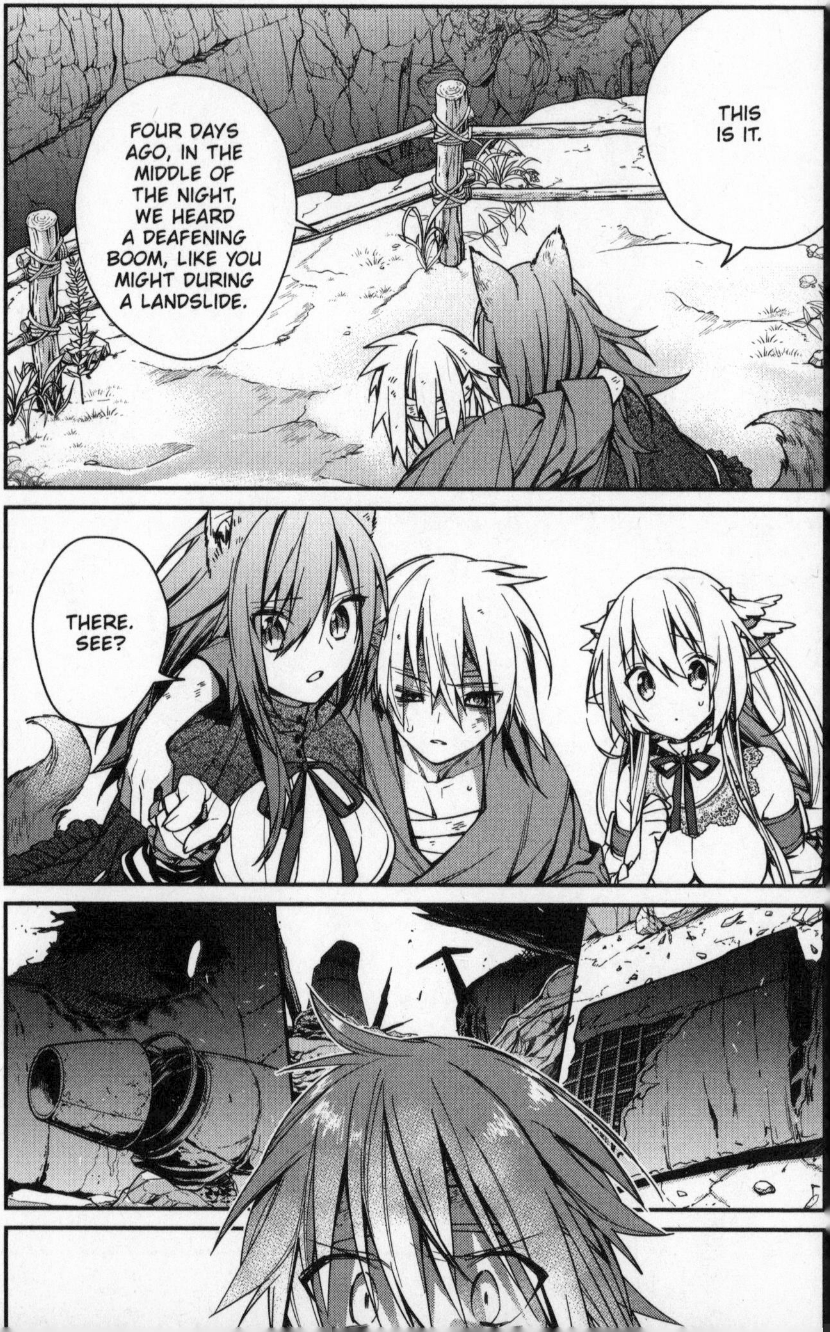
THIS IS IT.
FOUR DAYS AGO, IN THE MIDDLE OF THE NIGHT, WE HEARD A DEAFENING BOOM, LIKE YOU MIGHT DURING A LANDSLIDE.
THERE. SEE?

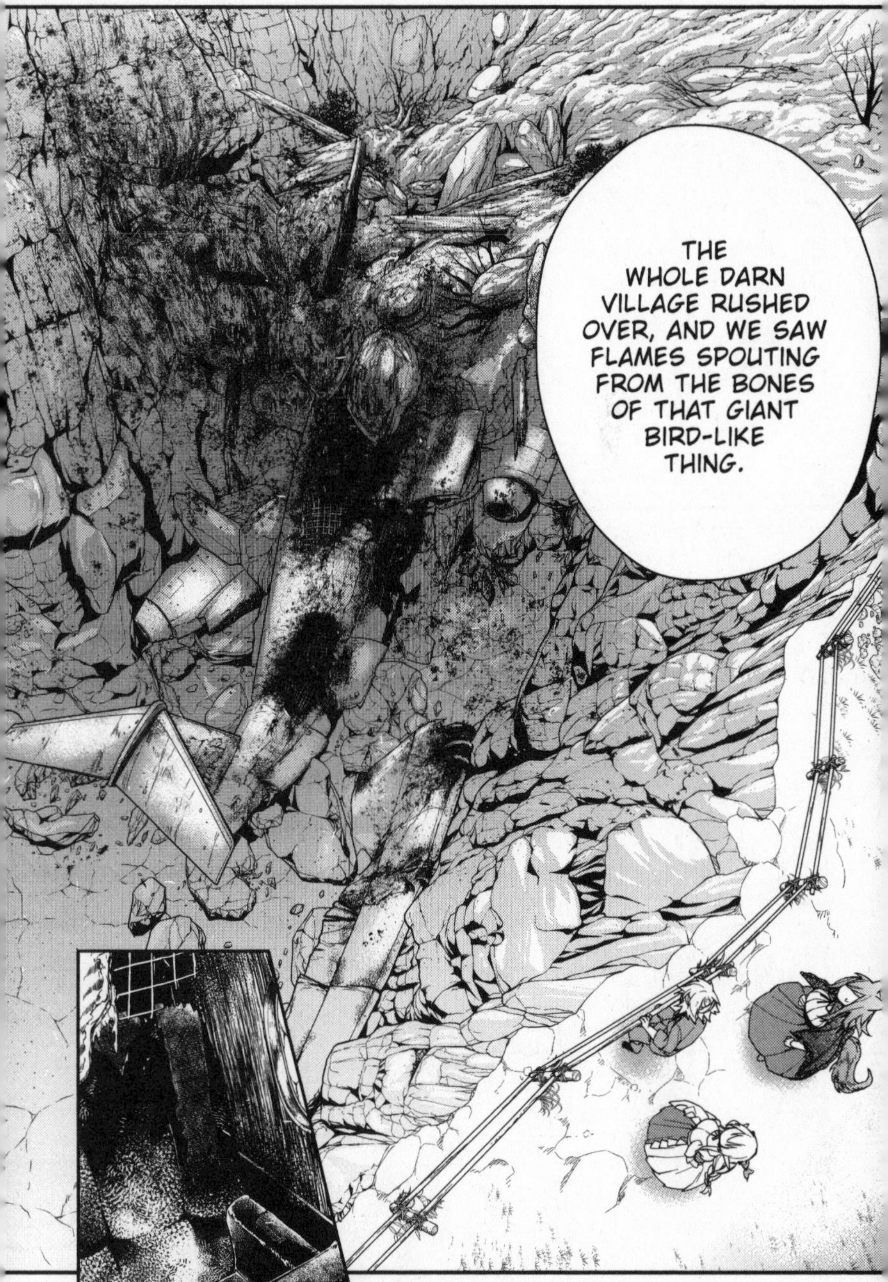
THE WHOLE DARN VILLAGE RUSHED OVER, AND WE SAW FLAMES SPOUTING FROM THE BONES OF THAT GIANT BIRD-LIKE THING.

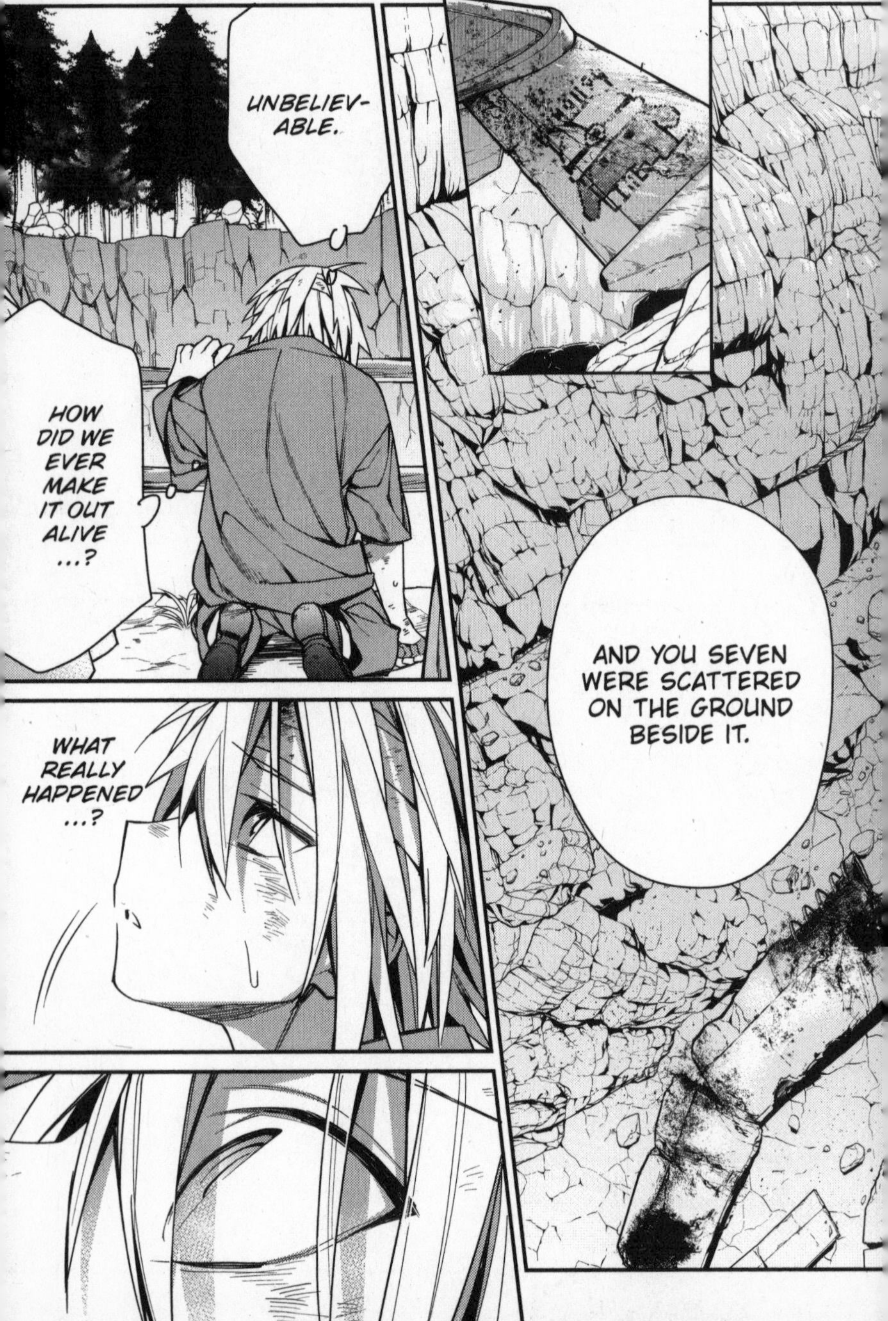
AND YOU SEVEN WERE SCATTERED ON THE GROUND BESIDE IT.
UNBELIEV-ABLE.
HOW DID WE EVER MAKE IT OUT ALIVE ...?
WHAT REALLY HAPPENED ...?

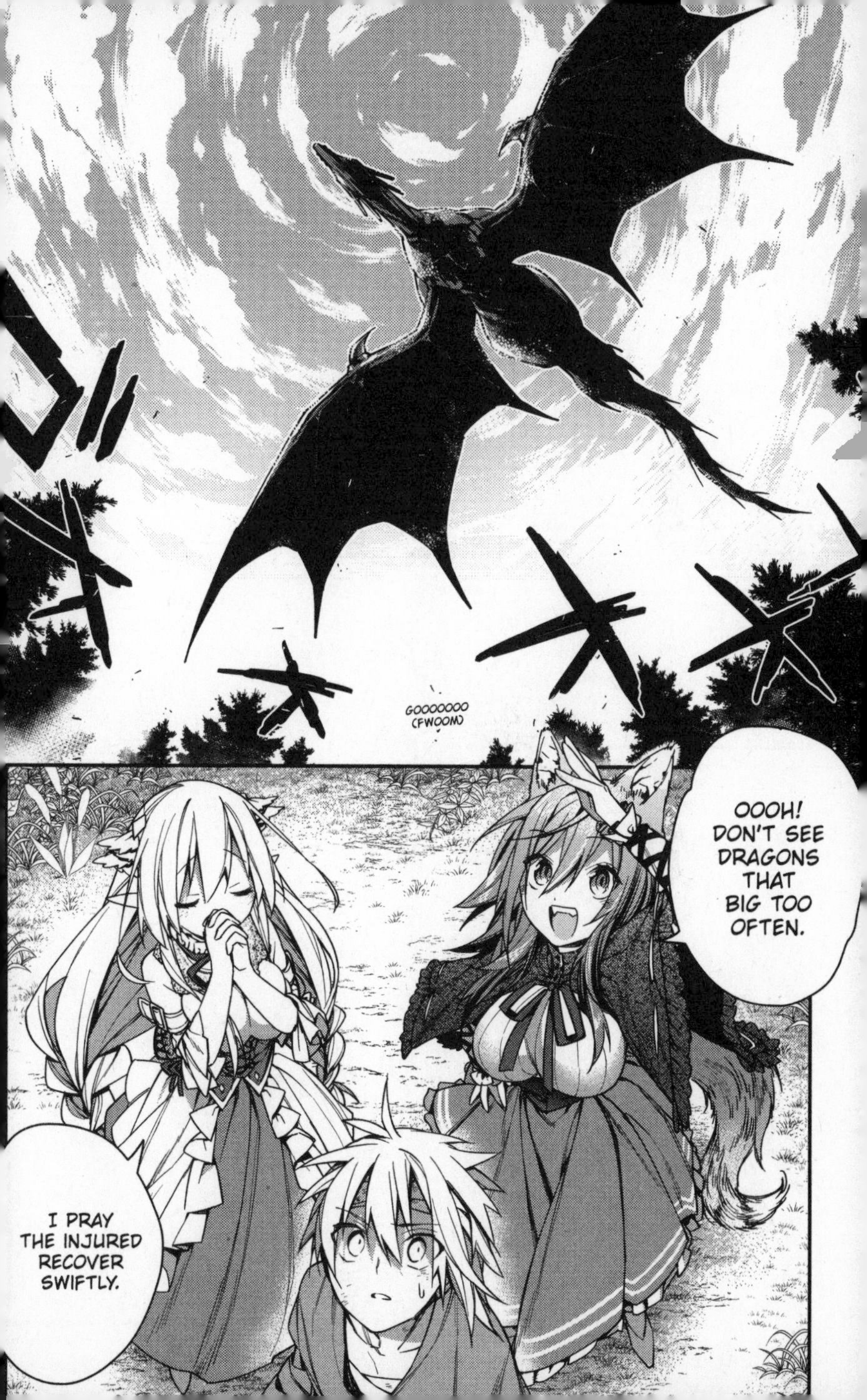
GOOOOOOO
(FWOOM)
OOOH! DON'T SEE DRAGONS THAT BIG TOO OFTEN.
I PRAY THE INJURED RECOVER SWIFTLY.

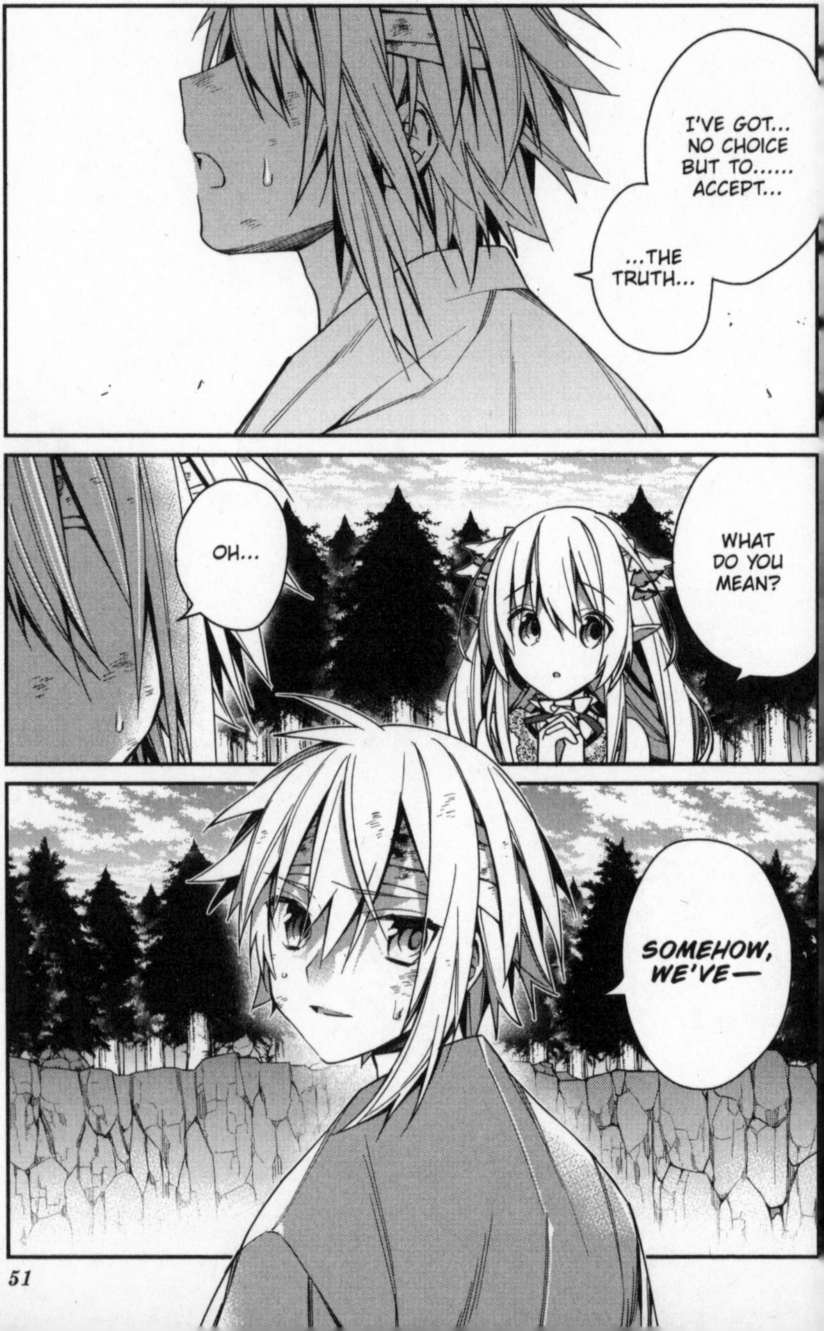
I'VE GOT... NO CHOICE BUT TO...... ACCEPT...
...THE TRUTH...
WHAT DO YOU MEAN?
OH...
SOMEHOW, WE'VE—

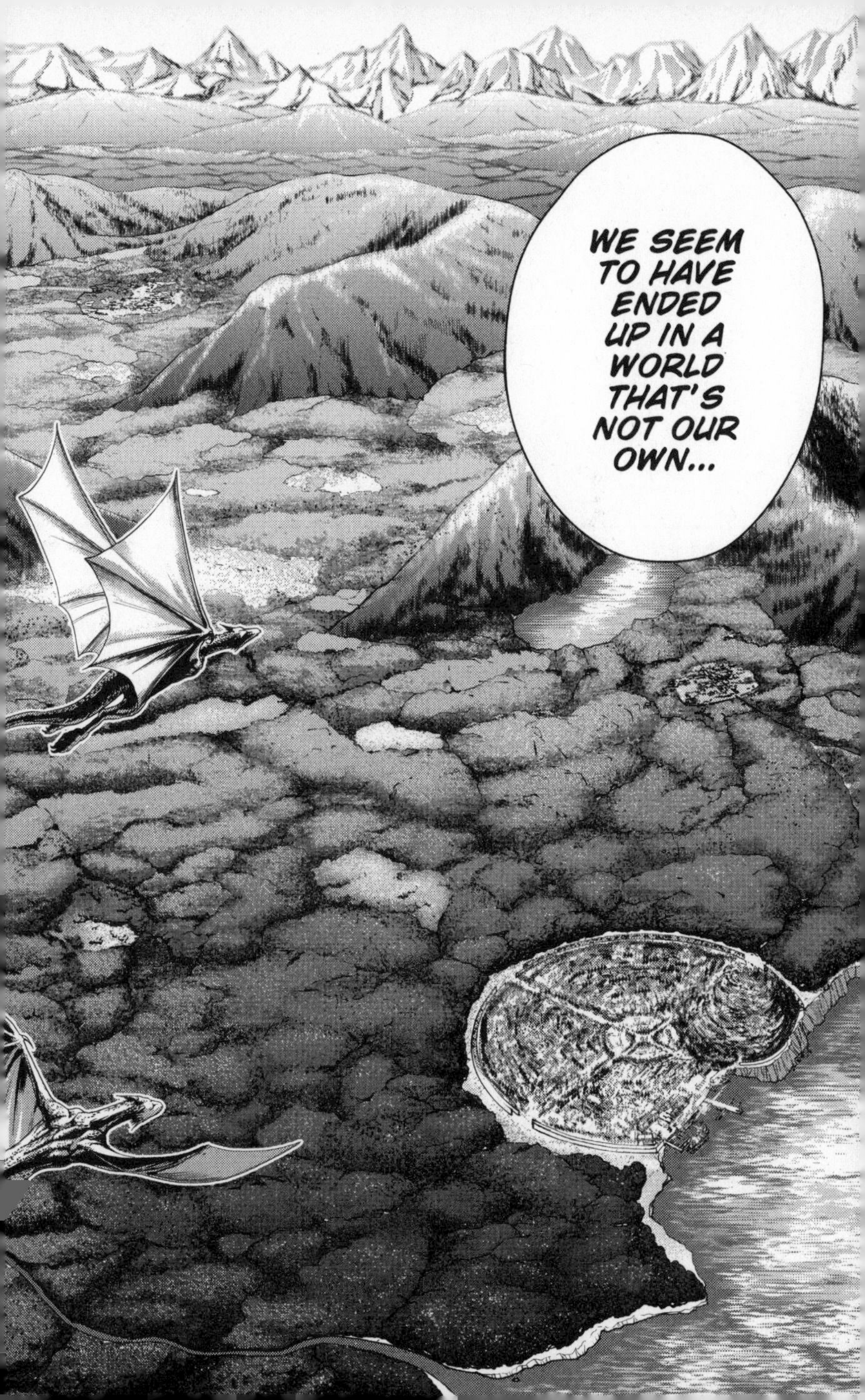
WE SEEM TO HAVE ENDED UP IN A WORLD THAT'S NOT OUR OWN...

HIGH SCHOOL
PRODIGIES HAVE
IT EASY EVEN IN
ANOTHER
WORLD!

CHARACTER FILE 02

Lyrule

A girl the high schoolers meet in the other world. Tends to dote and meddle. The villagers try to keep her existence a secret, since she's just that beautiful.

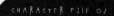

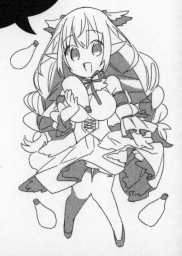

CHAPTER 3: BANQUET AND HOSTILITIES

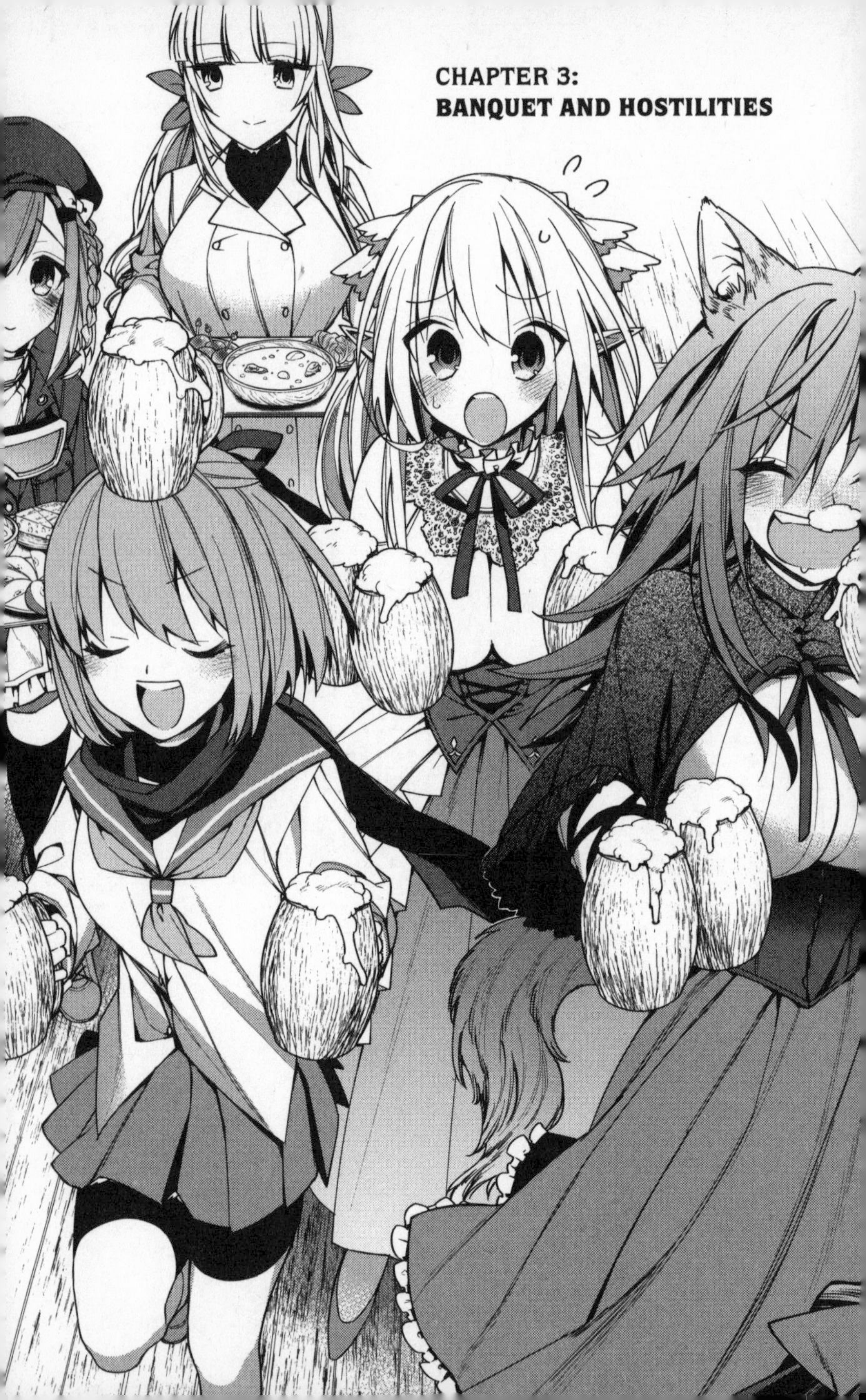

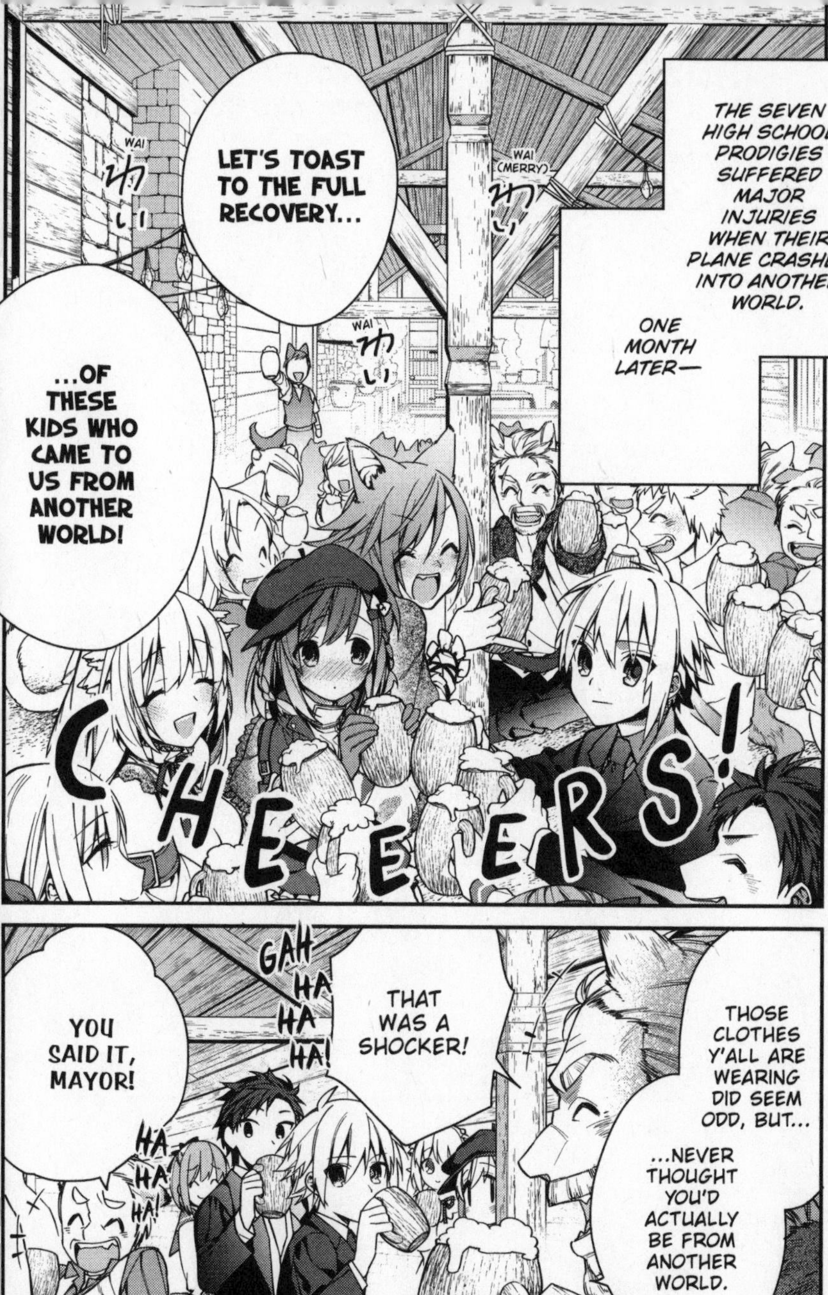
THE SEVEN HIGH SCHOOL PRODIGIES SUFFERED MAJOR INJURIES WHEN THEIR PLANE CRASHED INTO ANOTHER WORLD.
ONE MONTH LATER—
WAI (MERRY)
LET'S TOAST TO THE FULL RECOVERY...
WAI
WAI
...OF THESE KIDS WHO CAME TO US FROM ANOTHER WORLD!
CHEERS!
THOSE CLOTHES Y'ALL ARE WEARING DID SEEM ODD, BUT...
...NEVER THOUGHT YOU'D ACTUALLY BE FROM ANOTHER WORLD.
THAT WAS A SHOCKER!
GAH HA HA HA HA!
YOU SAID IT, MAYOR!
HA HA HA!

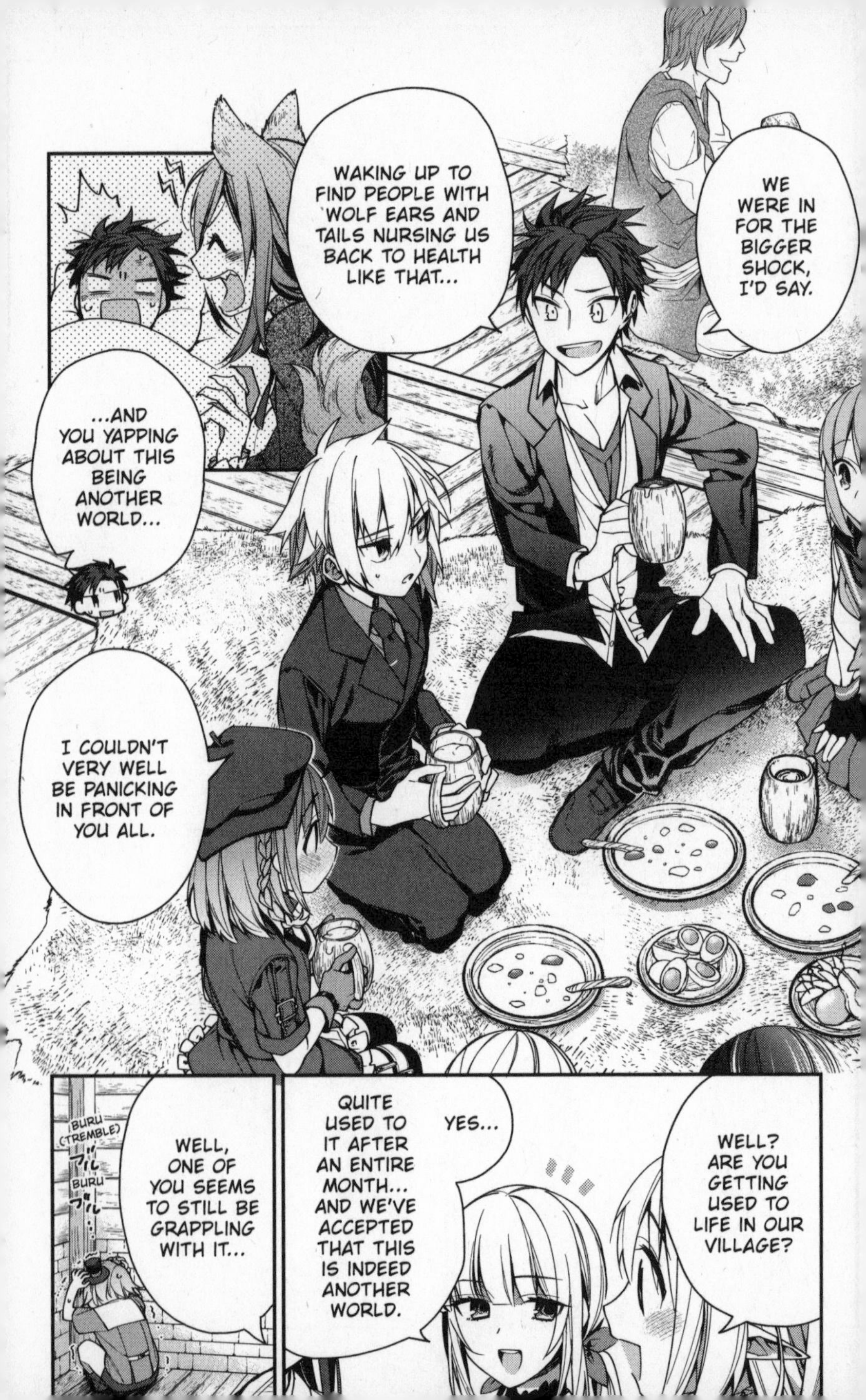
WE WERE IN FOR THE BIGGER SHOCK, I'D SAY.
WAKING UP TO FIND PEOPLE WITH WOLF EARS AND TAILS NURSING US BACK TO HEALTH LIKE THAT...
...AND YOU YAPPING ABOUT THIS BEING ANOTHER WORLD...
I COULDN'T VERY WELL BE PANICKING IN FRONT OF YOU ALL.
WELL? ARE YOU GETTING USED TO LIFE IN OUR VILLAGE?
YES...
QUITE USED TO IT AFTER AN ENTIRE MONTH... AND WE'VE ACCEPTED THAT THIS IS INDEED ANOTHER WORLD.
WELL, ONE OF YOU SEEMS TO STILL BE GRAPPLING WITH IT...
BURU (TREMBLE)
ブル
BURU
ブル

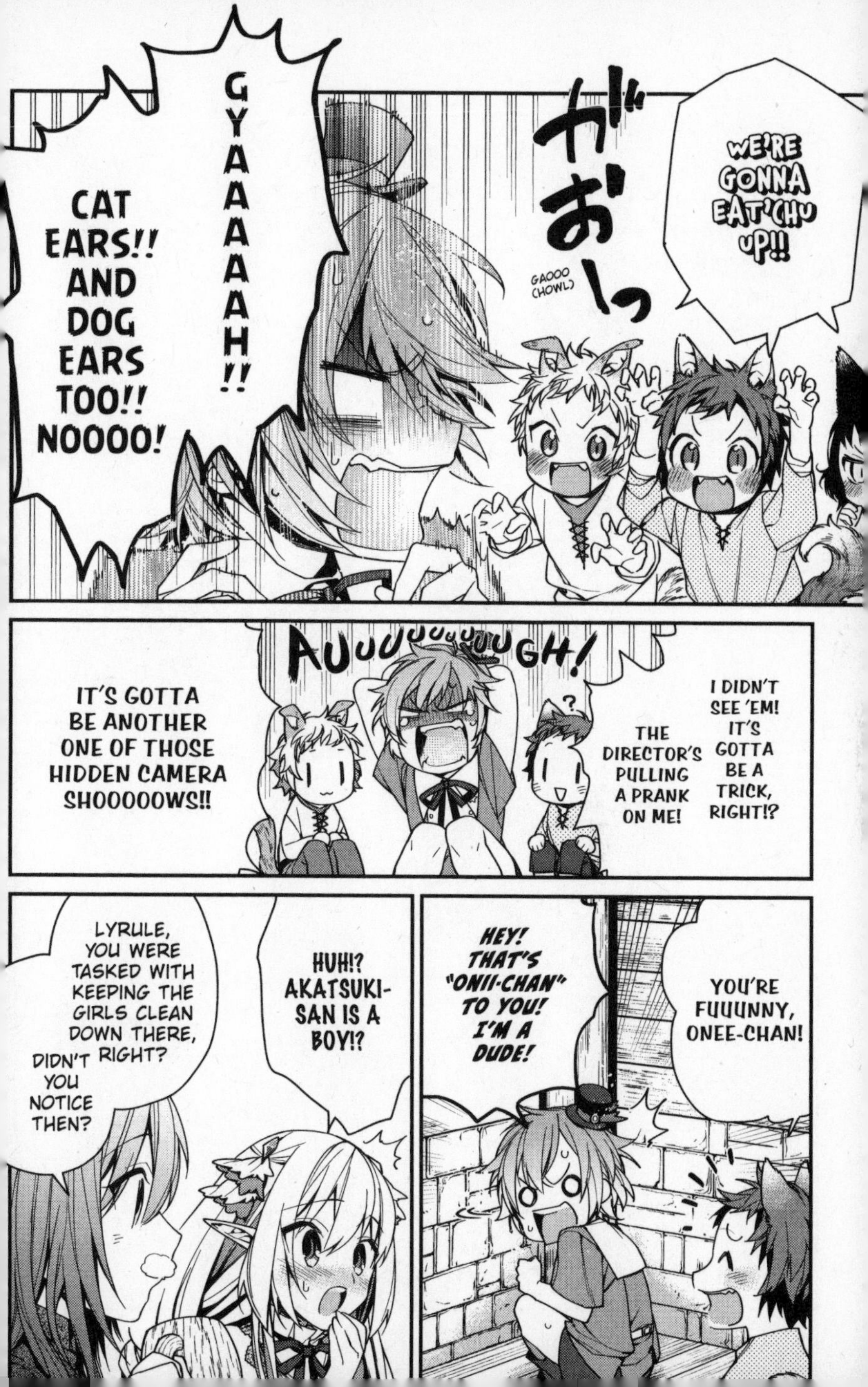
WE'RE GONNA EAT'CHU UP!!
がおーっ
GAOOO (HOWL)
GYAAAAAAH!!
CAT EARS!! AND DOG EARS TOO!! NOOOO!
I DIDN'T SEE 'EM! IT'S GOTTA BE A TRICK, RIGHT!?
THE DIRECTOR'S PULLING A PRANK ON ME!
AUUUUUUUGH!
IT'S GOTTA BE ANOTHER ONE OF THOSE HIDDEN CAMERA SHOOOOOWS!!
YOU'RE FUUUNNY, ONEE-CHAN!
HEY! THAT'S "ONII-CHAN" TO YOU! I'M A DUDE!
HUH!? AKATSUKI-SAN IS A BOY!?
LYRULE, YOU WERE TASKED WITH KEEPING THE GIRLS CLEAN DOWN THERE, RIGHT?
DIDN'T YOU NOTICE THEN?

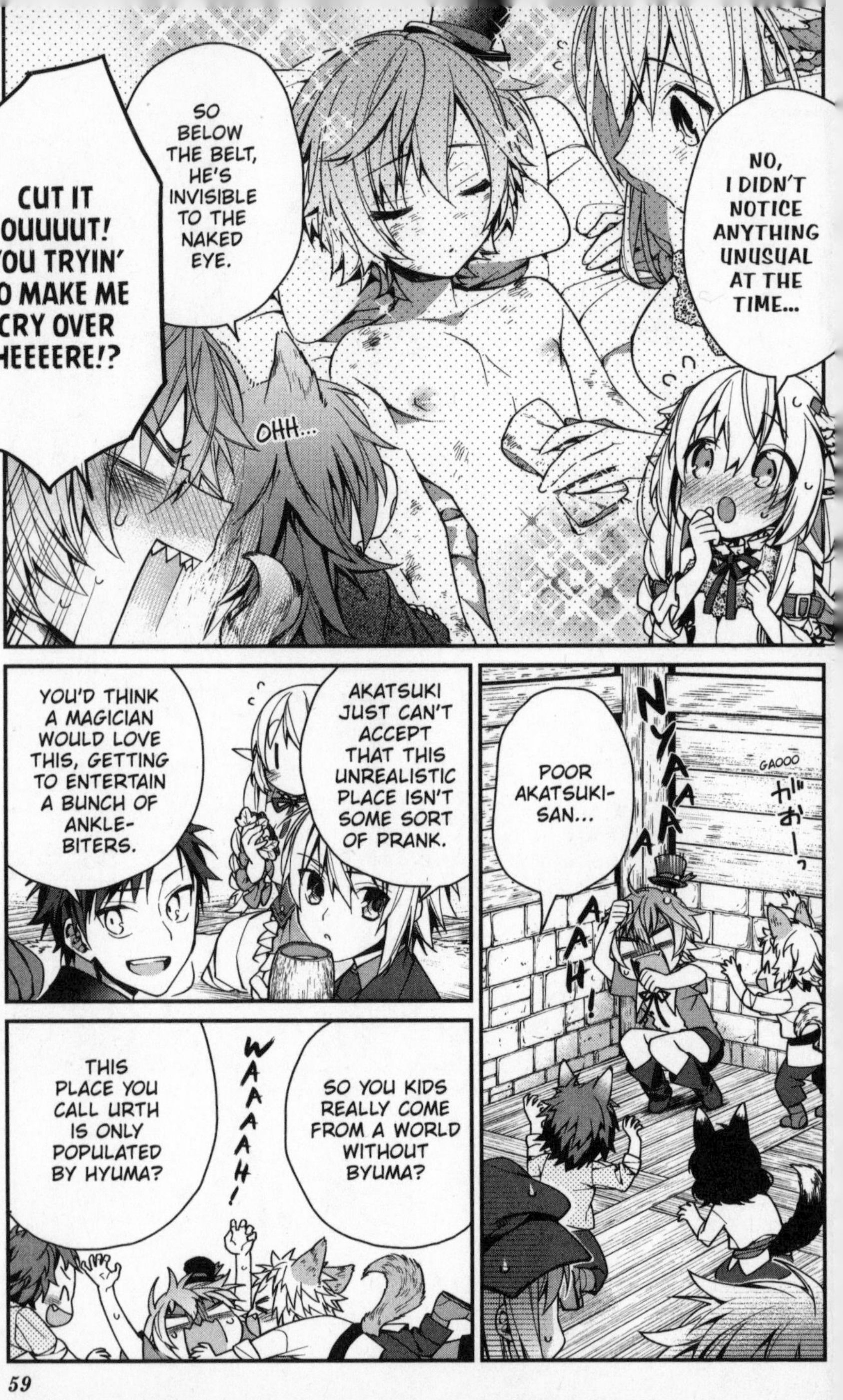
NO, I DIDN'T NOTICE ANYTHING UNUSUAL AT THE TIME...
SO BELOW THE BELT, HE'S INVISIBLE TO THE NAKED EYE.
CUT IT OUUUUT! YOU TRYIN' TO MAKE ME CRY OVER HEEEERE!?
OHH...
NYAAAAAAAH!
POOR AKATSUKI-SAN...
GAOOO
がおーっ
AKATSUKI JUST CAN'T ACCEPT THAT THIS UNREALISTIC PLACE ISN'T SOME SORT OF PRANK.
YOU'D THINK A MAGICIAN WOULD LOVE THIS, GETTING TO ENTERTAIN A BUNCH OF ANKLE-BITERS.
SO YOU KIDS REALLY COME FROM A WORLD WITHOUT BYUMA?
WAAAAAH!
THIS PLACE YOU CALL URTH IS ONLY POPULATED BY HYUMA?

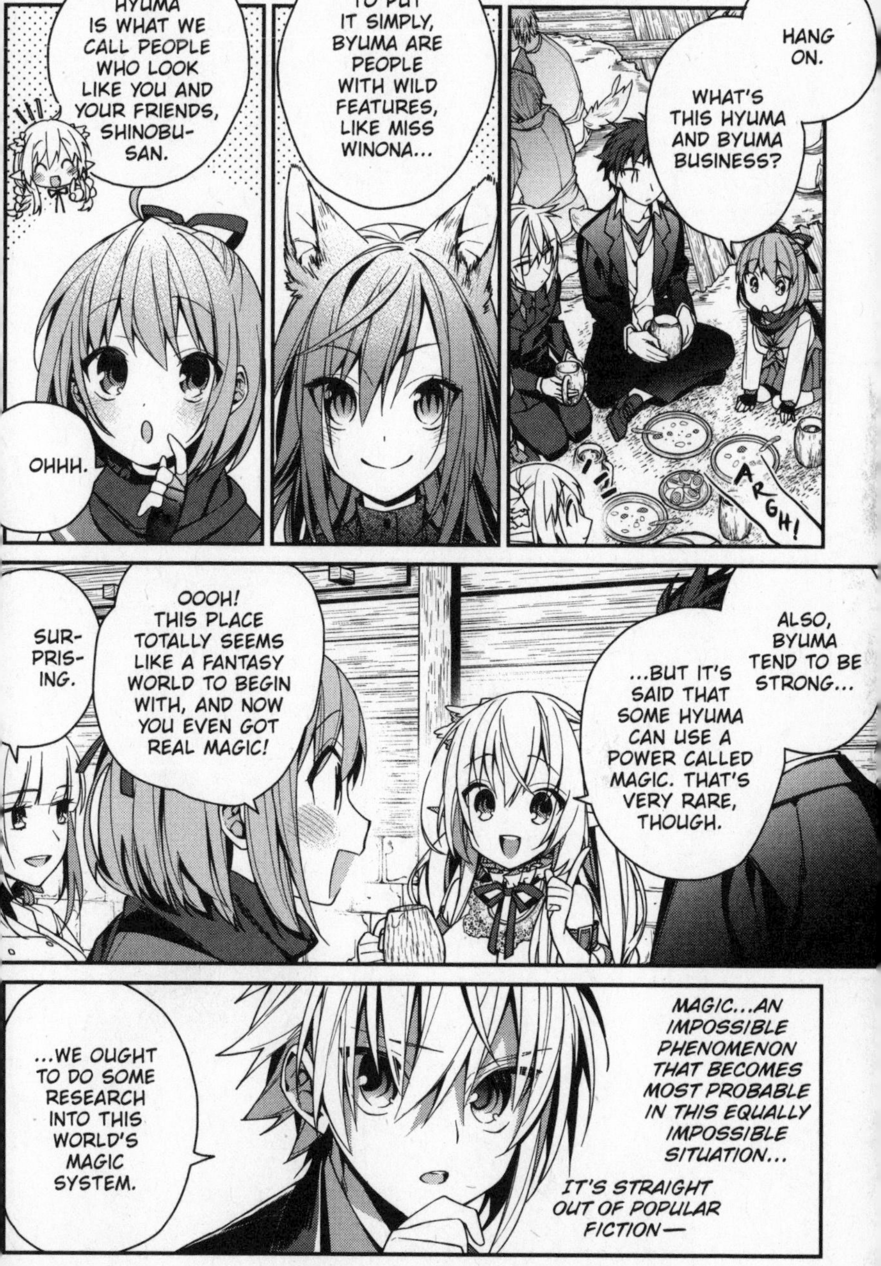
HANG ON.
WHAT'S THIS HYUMA AND BYUMA BUSINESS?
ARGH!
TO PUT IT SIMPLY, BYUMA ARE PEOPLE WITH WILD FEATURES, LIKE MISS WINONA...
...WHILE HYUMA IS WHAT WE CALL PEOPLE WHO LOOK LIKE YOU AND YOUR FRIENDS, SHINOBU-SAN.
OHHH.
ALSO, BYUMA TEND TO BE STRONG...
...BUT IT'S SAID THAT SOME HYUMA CAN USE A POWER CALLED MAGIC. THAT'S VERY RARE, THOUGH.
OOOH! THIS PLACE TOTALLY SEEMS LIKE A FANTASY WORLD TO BEGIN WITH, AND NOW YOU EVEN GOT REAL MAGIC!
SUR-PRIS-ING.
MAGIC...AN IMPOSSIBLE PHENOMENON THAT BECOMES MOST PROBABLE IN THIS EQUALLY IMPOSSIBLE SITUATION...
IT'S STRAIGHT OUT OF POPULAR FICTION—
...WE OUGHT TO DO SOME RESEARCH INTO THIS WORLD'S MAGIC SYSTEM.

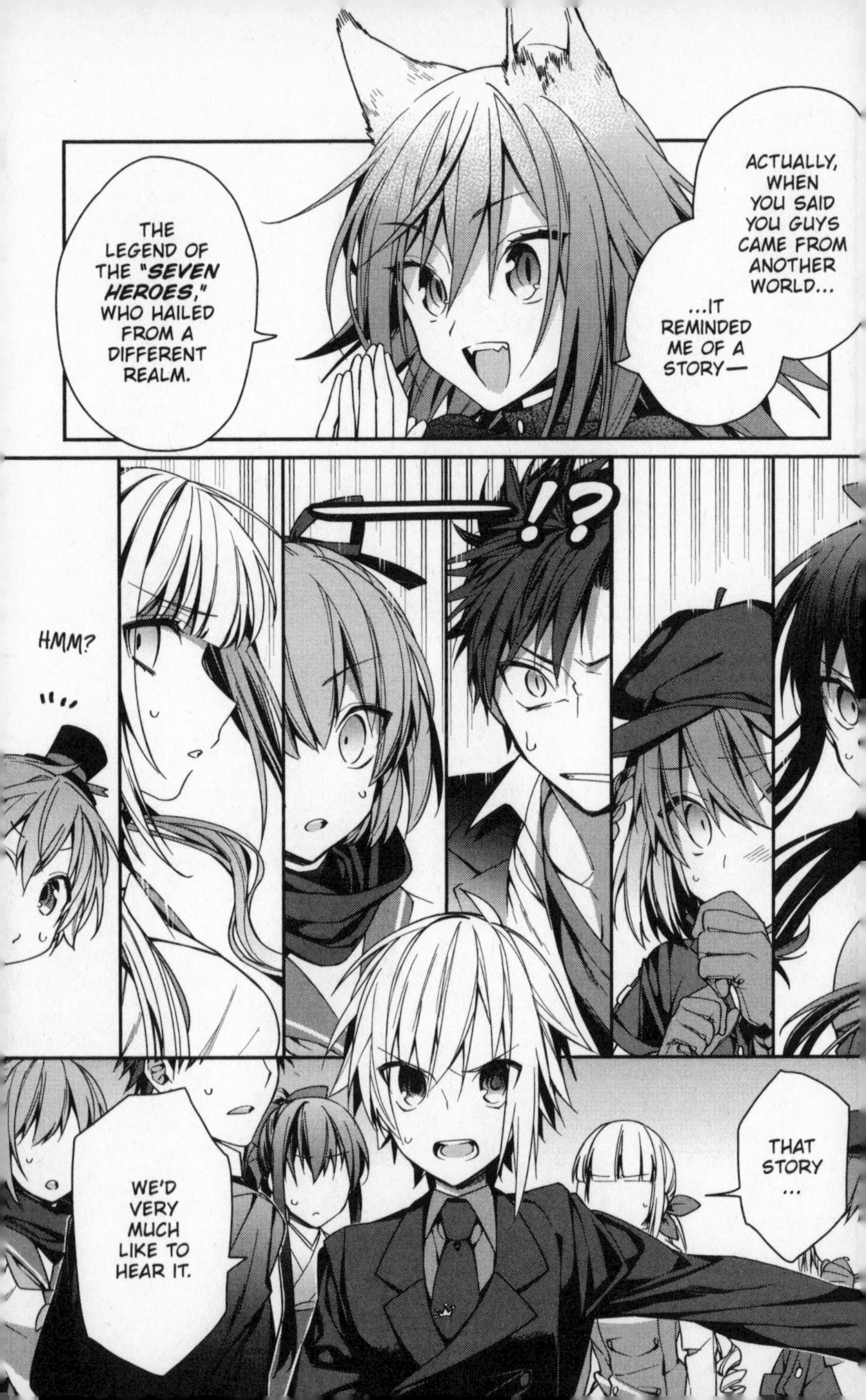
ACTUALLY, WHEN YOU SAID YOU GUYS CAME FROM ANOTHER WORLD...
...IT REMINDED ME OF A STORY—
THE LEGEND OF THE "SEVEN HEROES," WHO HAILED FROM A DIFFERENT REALM.
!?
HMM?
THAT STORY...
WE'D VERY MUCH LIKE TO HEAR IT.

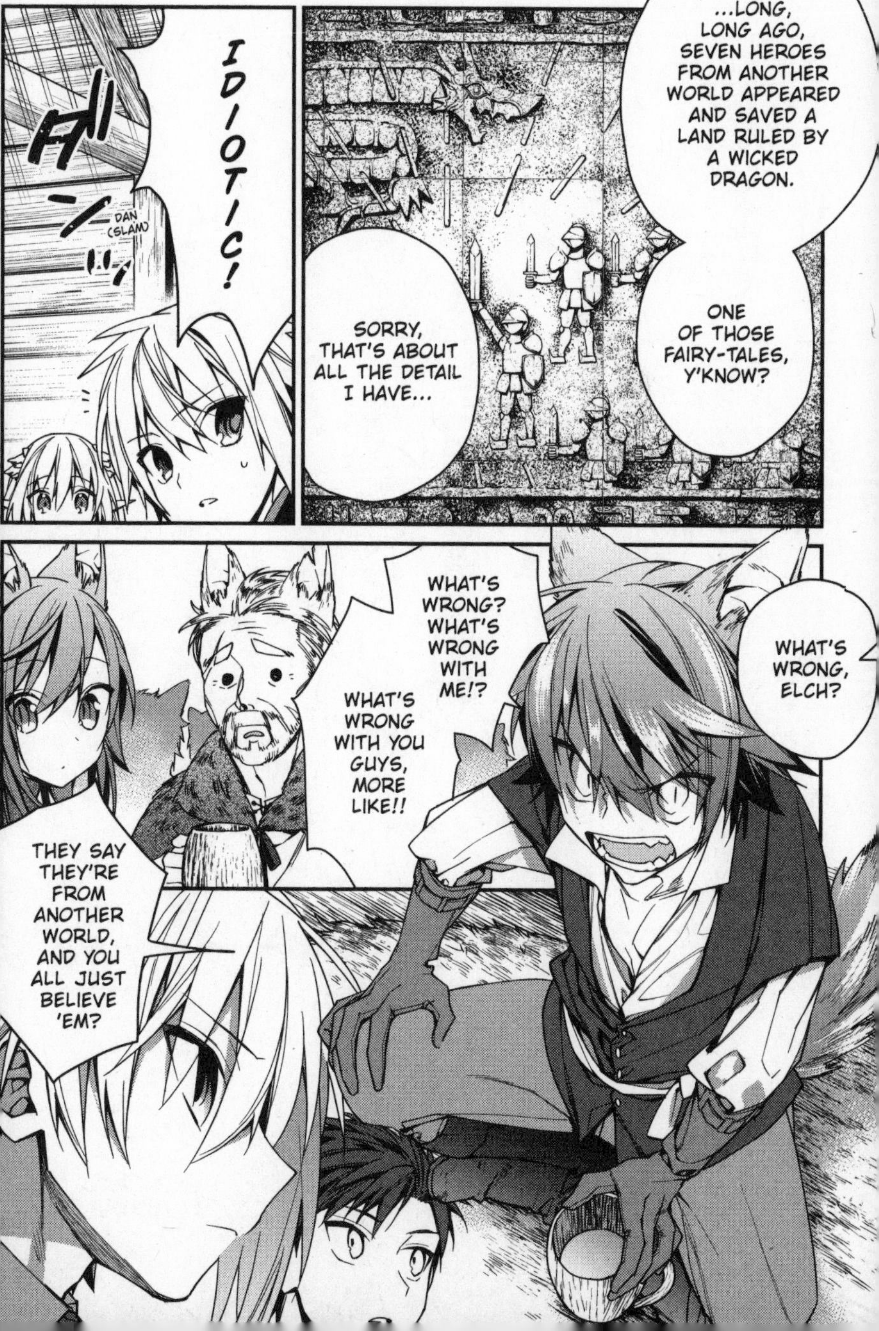
...LONG, LONG AGO, SEVEN HEROES FROM ANOTHER WORLD APPEARED AND SAVED A LAND RULED BY A WICKED DRAGON.
ONE OF THOSE FAIRY-TALES, Y'KNOW?
SORRY, THAT'S ABOUT ALL THE DETAIL I HAVE...
IDIOTIC!
DAN (SLAM)
WHAT'S WRONG, ELCH?
WHAT'S WRONG? WHAT'S WRONG WITH ME!?
WHAT'S WRONG WITH YOU GUYS, MORE LIKE!!
THEY SAY THEY'RE FROM ANOTHER WORLD, AND YOU ALL JUST BELIEVE 'EM?

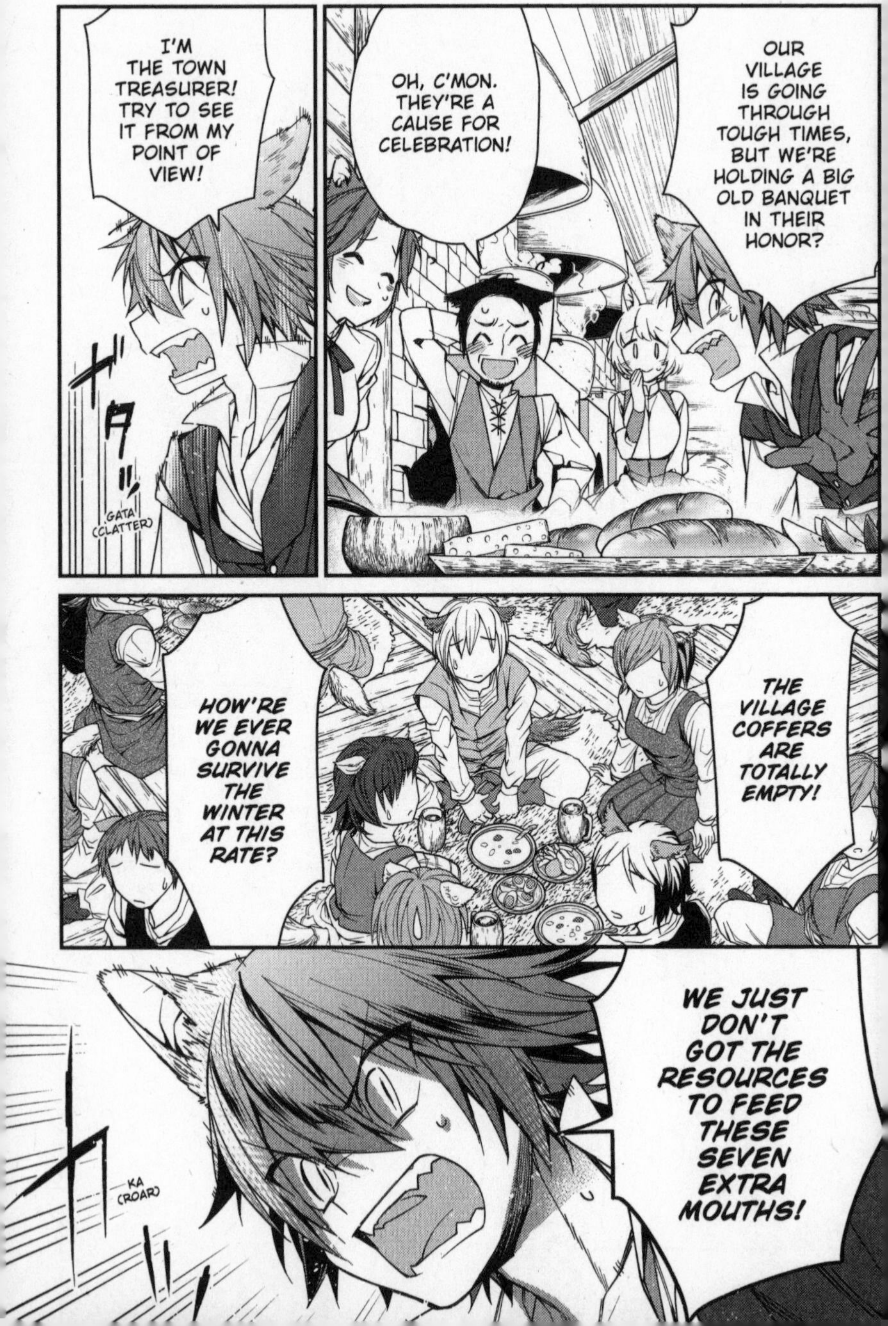
OUR VILLAGE IS GOING THROUGH TOUGH TIMES, BUT WE'RE HOLDING A BIG OLD BANQUET IN THEIR HONOR?
OH, C'MON. THEY'RE A CAUSE FOR CELEBRATION!
I'M THE TOWN TREASURER! TRY TO SEE IT FROM MY POINT OF VIEW!
GATA (CLATTER)
THE VILLAGE COFFERS ARE TOTALLY EMPTY!
HOW'RE WE EVER GONNA SURVIVE THE WINTER AT THIS RATE?
WE JUST DON'T GOT THE RESOURCES TO FEED THESE SEVEN EXTRA MOUTHS!
KA (ROAR)

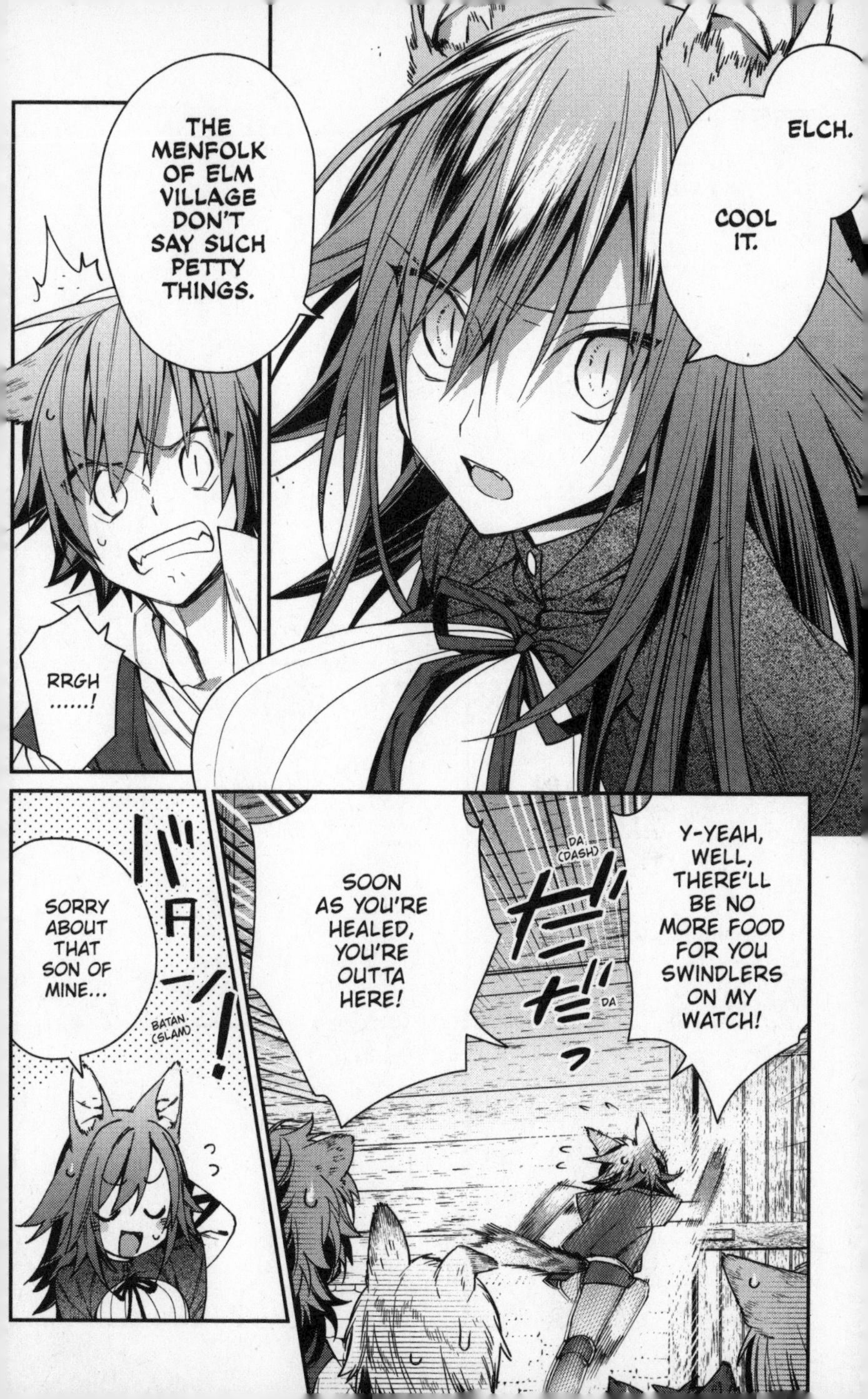
ELCH.
COOL IT.
THE MENFOLK OF ELM VILLAGE DON'T SAY SUCH PETTY THINGS.
RRGH ......!
Y-YEAH, WELL, THERE'LL BE NO MORE FOOD FOR YOU SWINDLERS ON MY WATCH!
DA (DASH)
DA
SOON AS YOU'RE HEALED, YOU'RE OUTTA HERE!
BATAN (SLAM)
SORRY ABOUT THAT SON OF MINE...

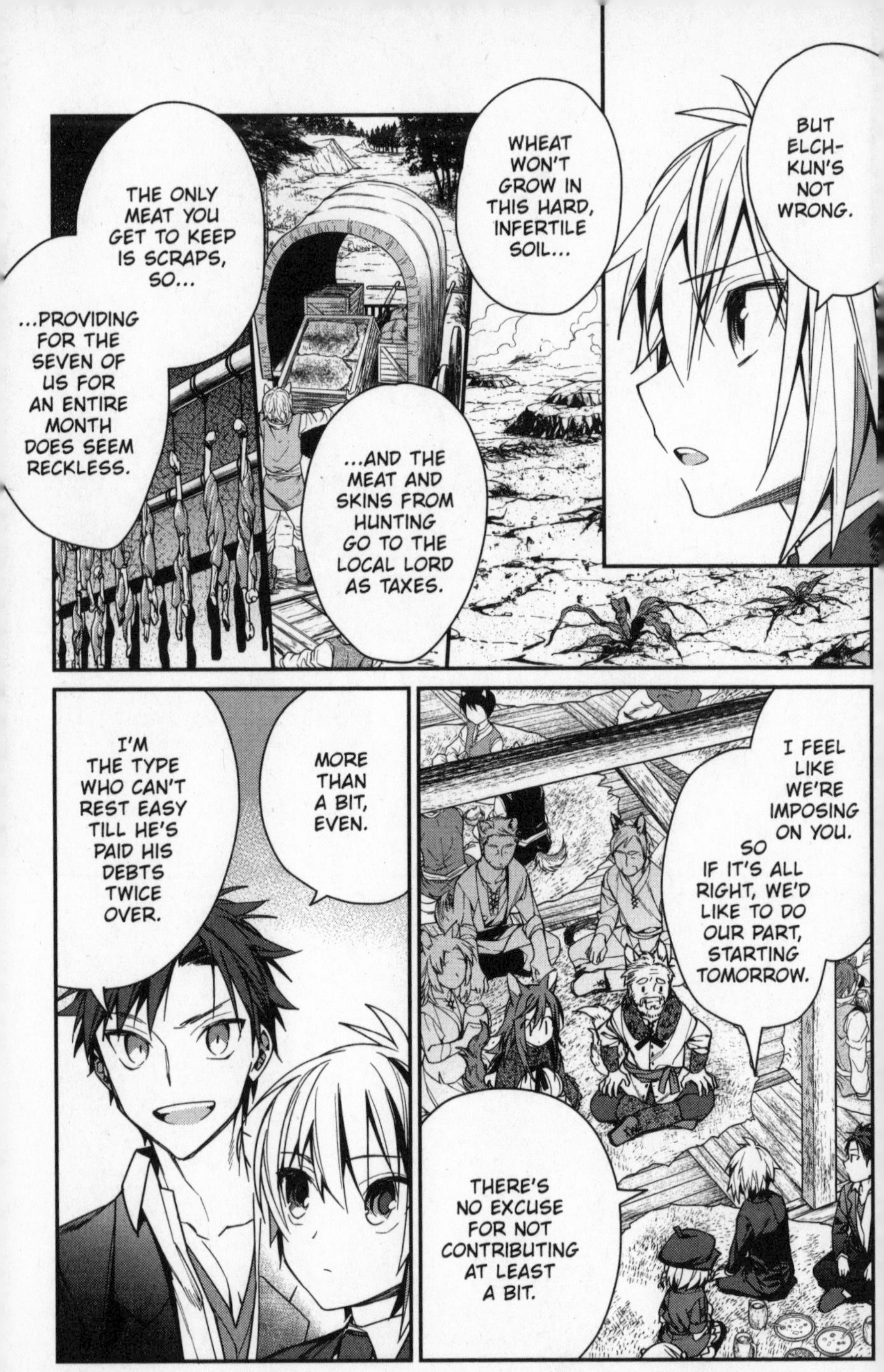
BUT ELCH-KUN'S NOT WRONG.
WHEAT WON'T GROW IN THIS HARD, INFERTILE SOIL...
...AND THE MEAT AND SKINS FROM HUNTING GO TO THE LOCAL LORD AS TAXES.
THE ONLY MEAT YOU GET TO KEEP IS SCRAPS, SO...
...PROVIDING FOR THE SEVEN OF US FOR AN ENTIRE MONTH DOES SEEM RECKLESS.
I FEEL LIKE WE'RE IMPOSING ON YOU. SO IF IT'S ALL RIGHT, WE'D LIKE TO DO OUR PART, STARTING TOMORROW.
THERE'S NO EXCUSE FOR NOT CONTRIBUTING AT LEAST A BIT.
MORE THAN A BIT, EVEN.
I'M THE TYPE WHO CAN'T REST EASY TILL HE'S PAID HIS DEBTS TWICE OVER.

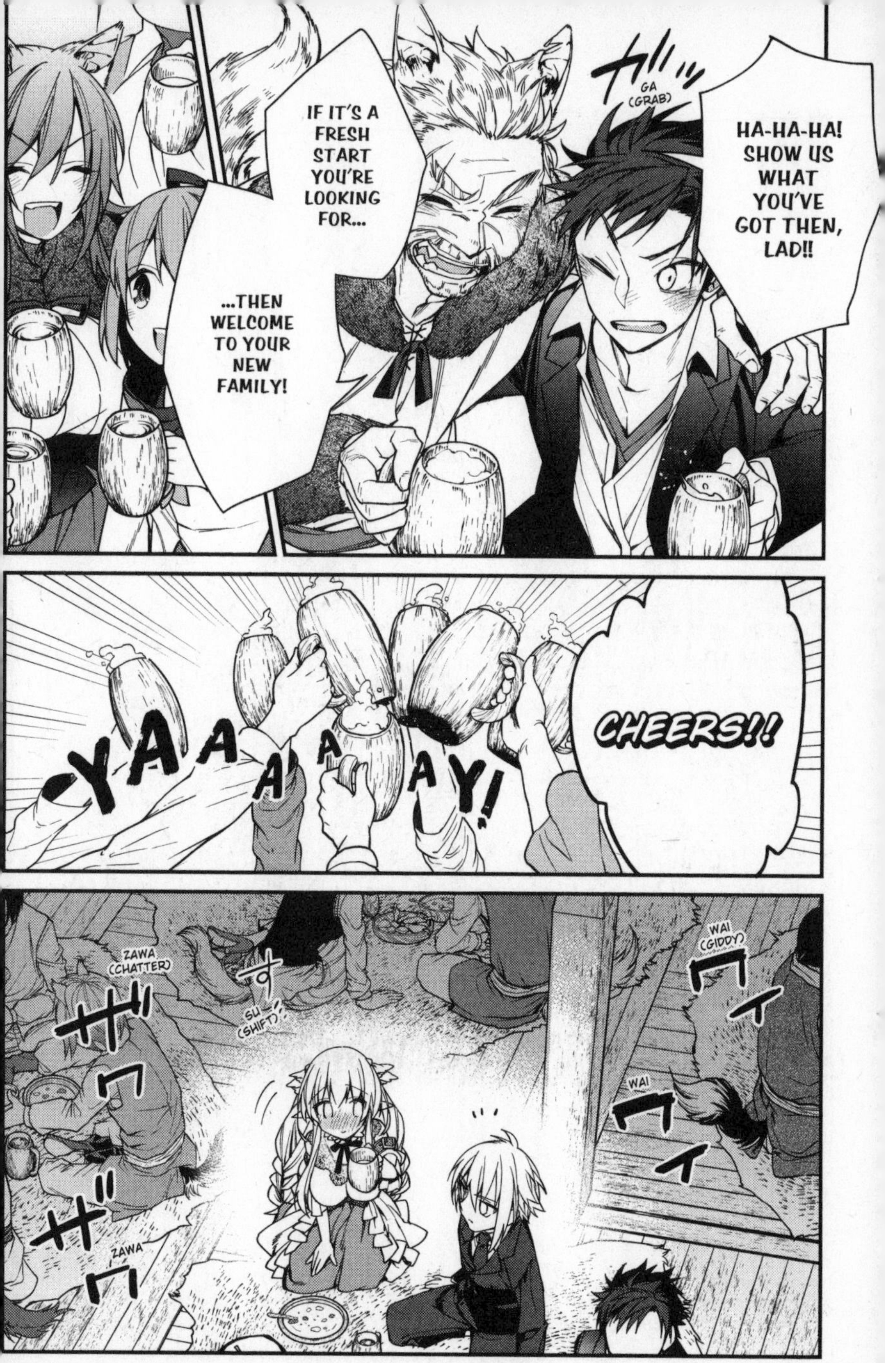
GA (GRAB)
HA-HA-HA! SHOW US WHAT YOU'VE GOT THEN, LAD!!
IF IT'S A FRESH START YOU'RE LOOKING FOR...
...THEN WELCOME TO YOUR NEW FAMILY!
CHEERS!!
YAAAAAY!
WAI (GIDDY)
WAI
SU (SHIFT)
ZAWA (CHATTER)
ZAWA

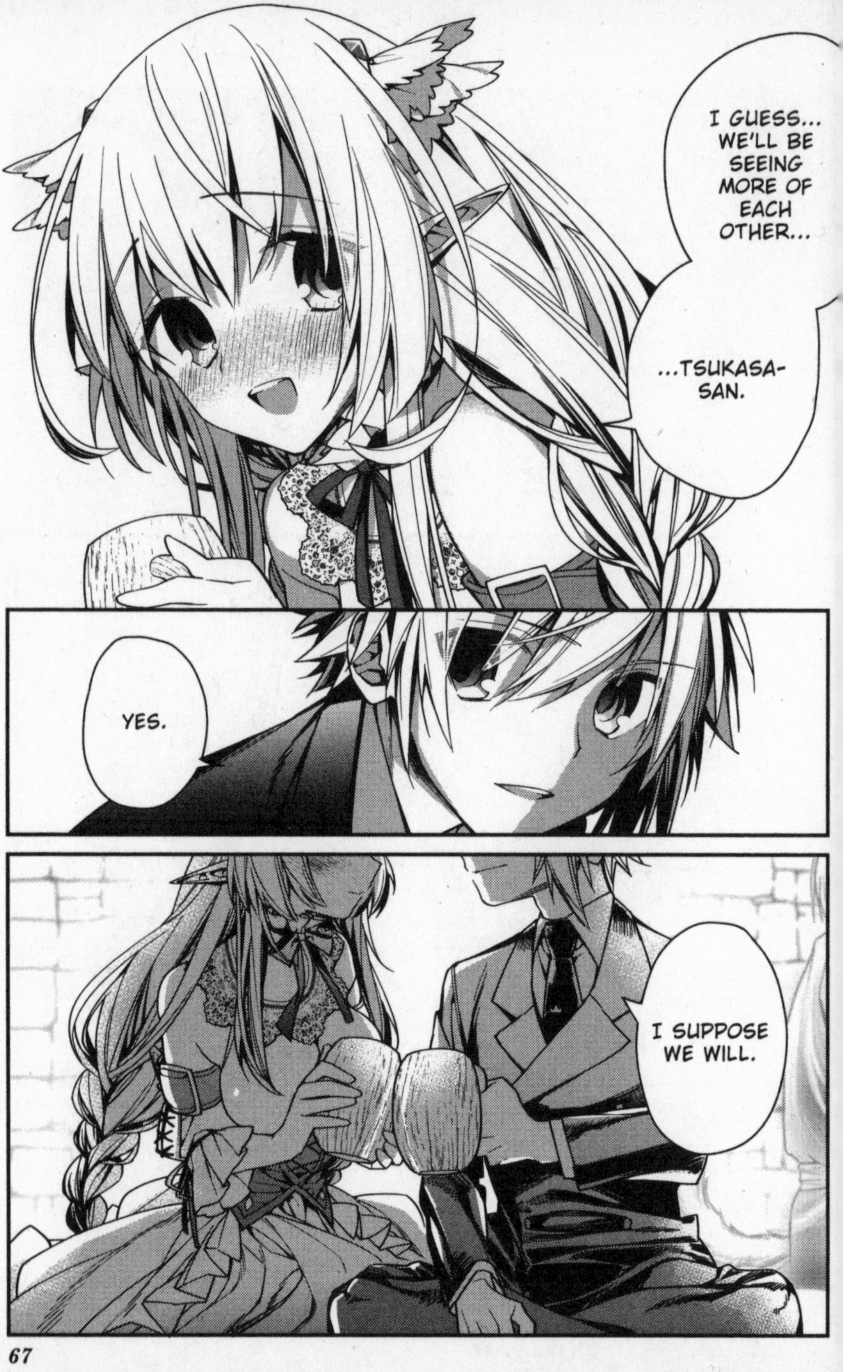
I GUESS... WE'LL BE SEEING MORE OF EACH OTHER...
...TSUKASA-SAN.
YES.
I SUPPOSE WE WILL.

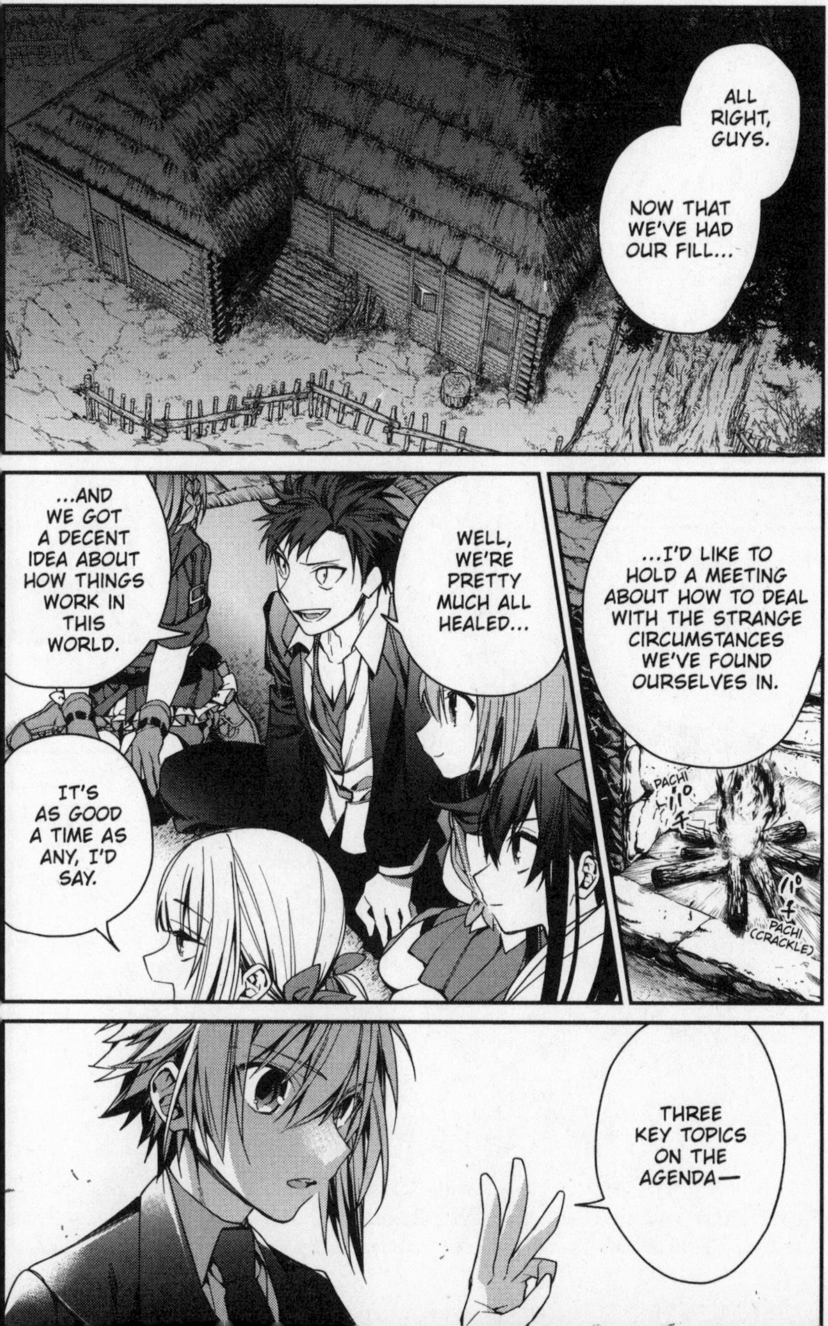
ALL RIGHT, GUYS.
NOW THAT WE'VE HAD OUR FILL...
...I'D LIKE TO HOLD A MEETING ABOUT HOW TO DEAL WITH THE STRANGE CIRCUMSTANCES WE'VE FOUND OURSELVES IN.
PACHI
パチ
パチ
PACHI (CRACKLE)
WELL, WE'RE PRETTY MUCH ALL HEALED...
...AND WE GOT A DECENT IDEA ABOUT HOW THINGS WORK IN THIS WORLD.
IT'S AS GOOD A TIME AS ANY, I'D SAY.
THREE KEY TOPICS ON THE AGENDA—

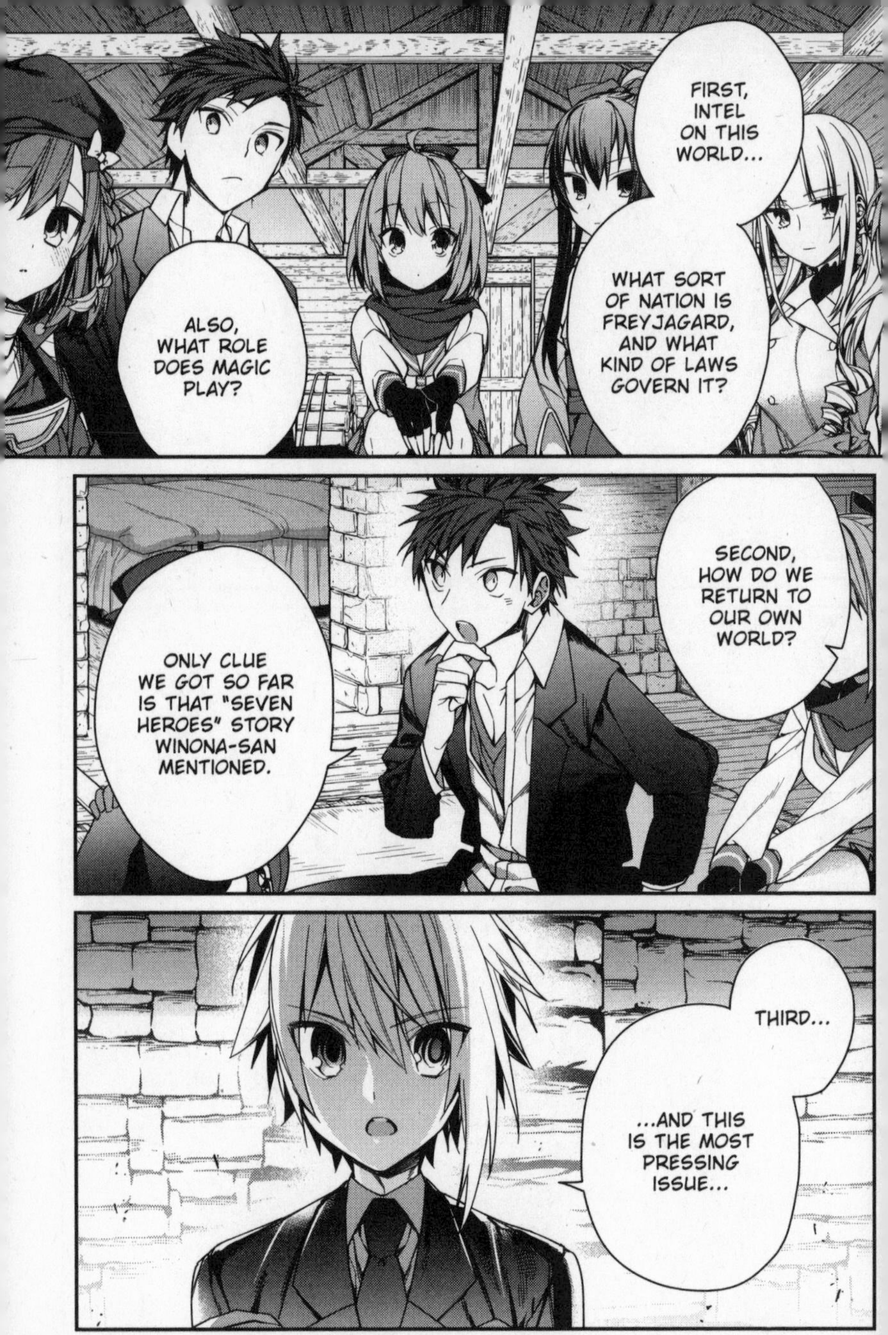
FIRST, INTEL ON THIS WORLD...
WHAT SORT OF NATION IS FREYJAGARD, AND WHAT KIND OF LAWS GOVERN IT?
ALSO, WHAT ROLE DOES MAGIC PLAY?
SECOND, HOW DO WE RETURN TO OUR OWN WORLD?
ONLY CLUE WE GOT SO FAR IS THAT "SEVEN HEROES" STORY WINONA-SAN MENTIONED.
THIRD...
...AND THIS IS THE MOST PRESSING ISSUE...

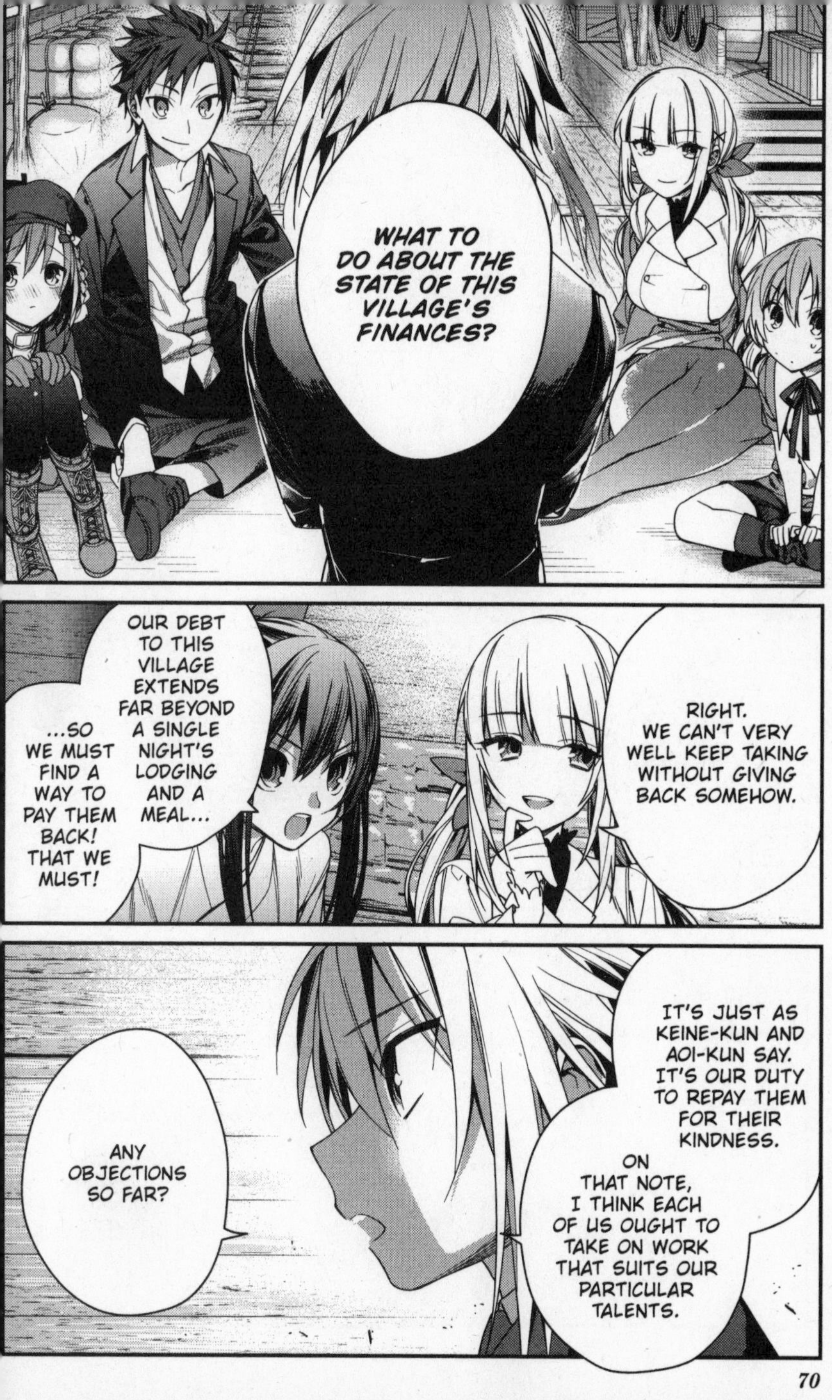
WHAT TO DO ABOUT THE STATE OF THIS VILLAGE'S FINANCES?
RIGHT. WE CAN'T VERY WELL KEEP TAKING WITHOUT GIVING BACK SOMEHOW.
OUR DEBT TO THIS VILLAGE EXTENDS FAR BEYOND A SINGLE NIGHT'S LODGING AND A MEAL...
...SO WE MUST FIND A WAY TO PAY THEM BACK! THAT WE MUST!
IT'S JUST AS KEINE-KUN AND AOI-KUN SAY. IT'S OUR DUTY TO REPAY THEM FOR THEIR KINDNESS.
ON THAT NOTE, I THINK EACH OF US OUGHT TO TAKE ON WORK THAT SUITS OUR PARTICULAR TALENTS.
ANY OBJECTIONS SO FAR?

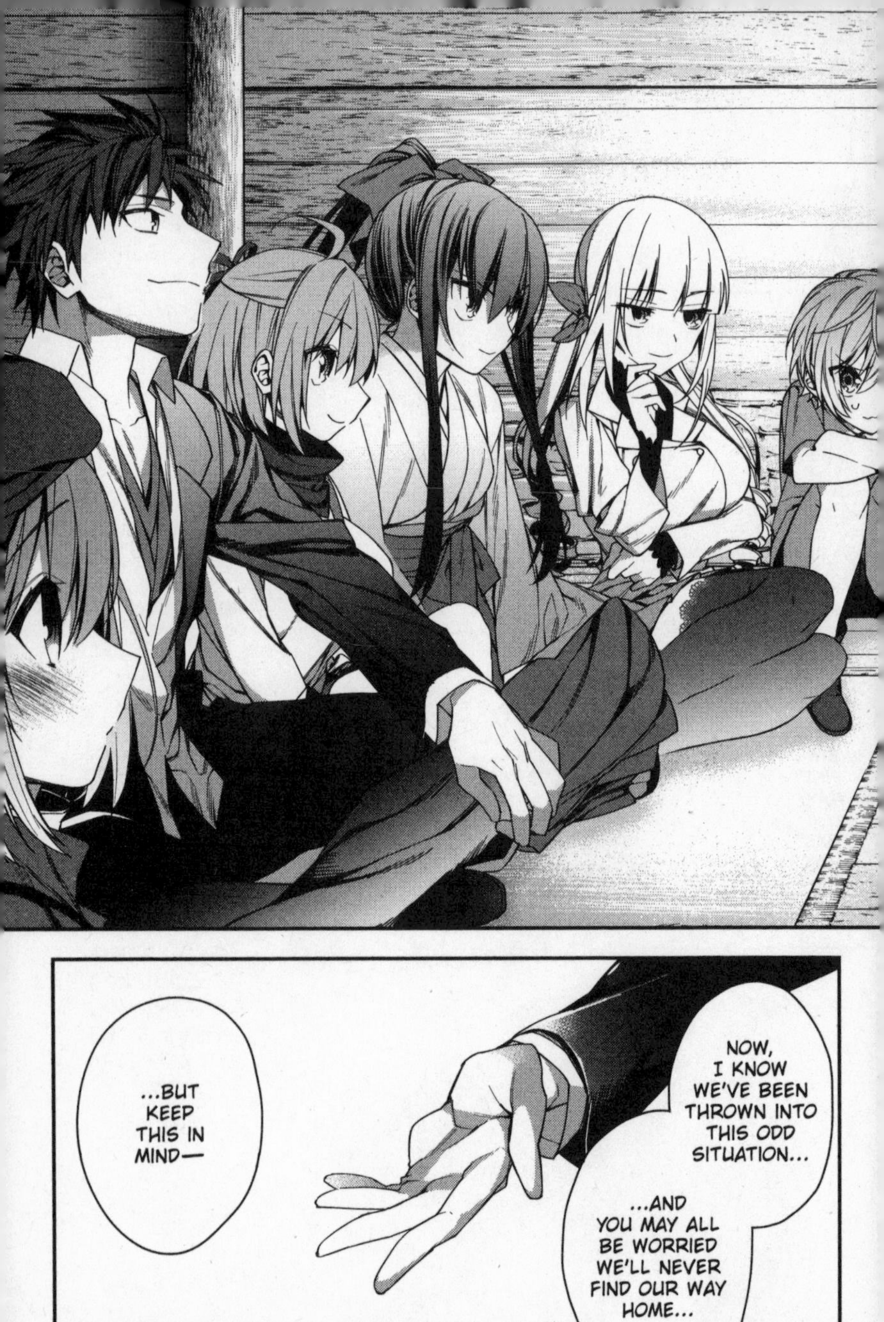
NOW, I KNOW WE'VE BEEN THROWN INTO THIS ODD SITUATION...
...AND YOU MAY ALL BE WORRIED WE'LL NEVER FIND OUR WAY HOME...
...BUT KEEP THIS IN MIND—

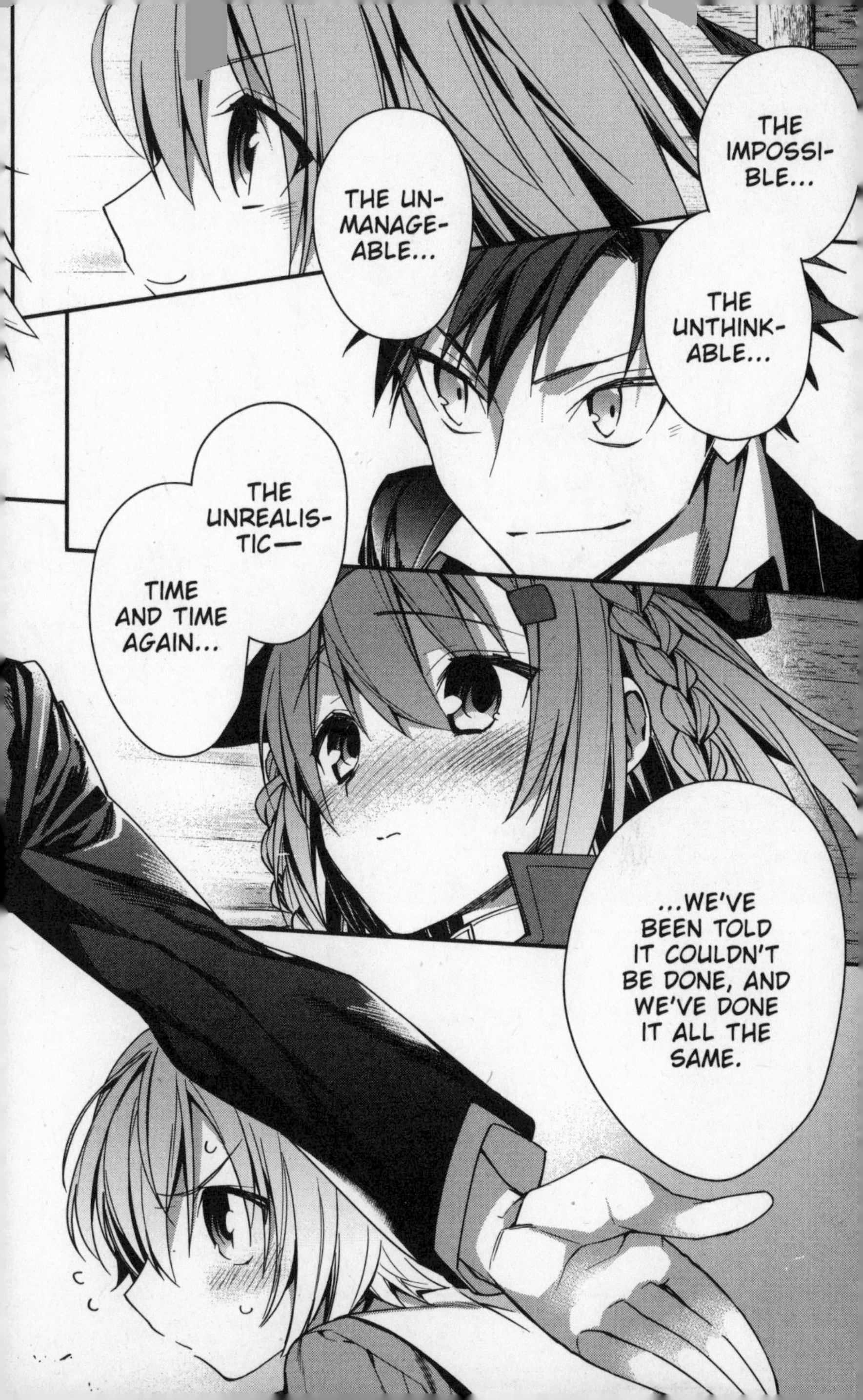
THE IMPOSSI-BLE...
THE UN-MANAGE-ABLE...
THE UNTHINK-ABLE...
THE UNREALIS-TIC—
TIME AND TIME AGAIN...
...WE'VE BEEN TOLD IT COULDN'T BE DONE, AND WE'VE DONE IT ALL THE SAME.

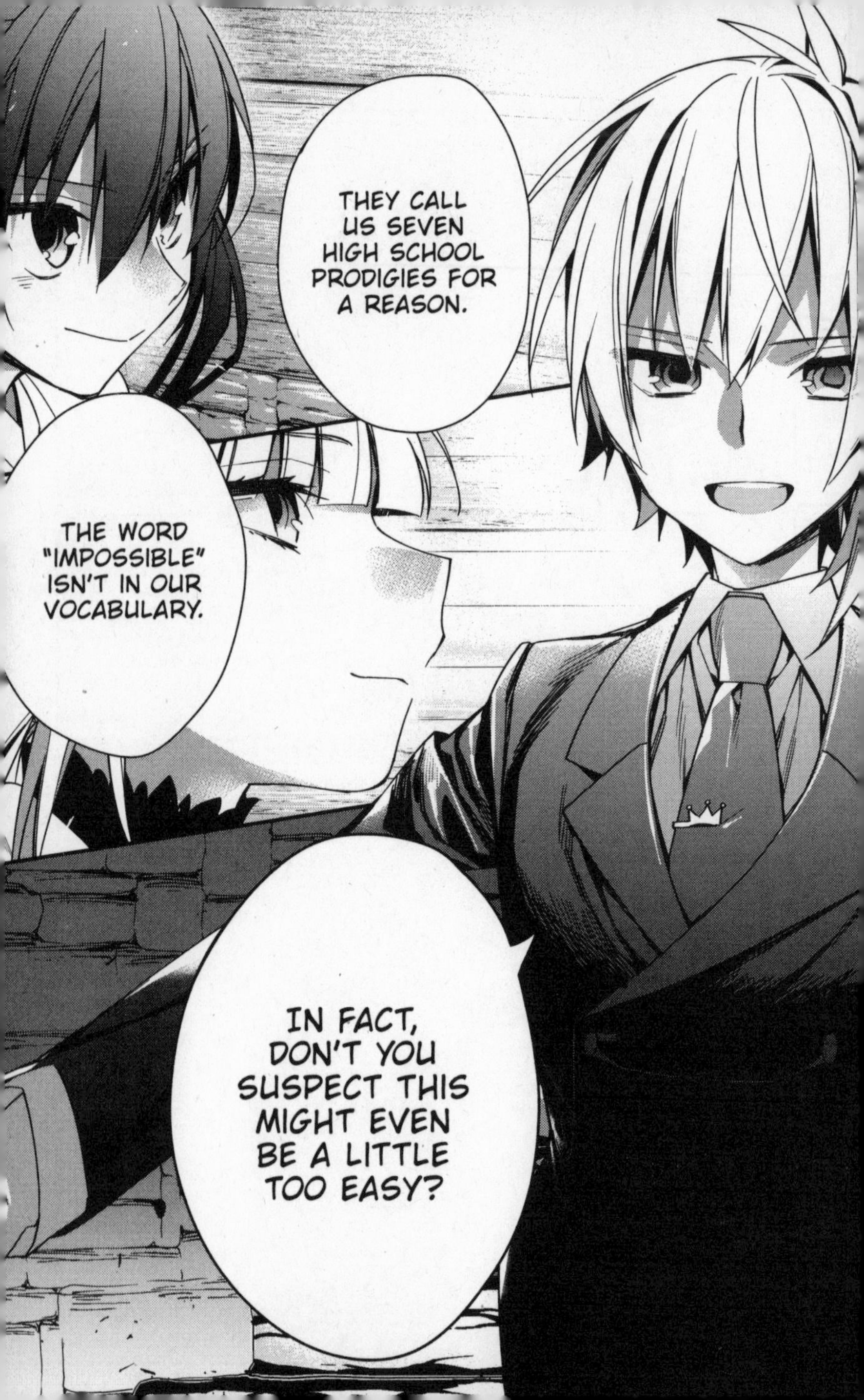
THEY CALL US SEVEN HIGH SCHOOL PRODIGIES FOR A REASON.
THE WORD "IMPOSSIBLE" ISN'T IN OUR VOCABULARY.
IN FACT, DON'T YOU SUSPECT THIS MIGHT EVEN BE A LITTLE TOO EASY?

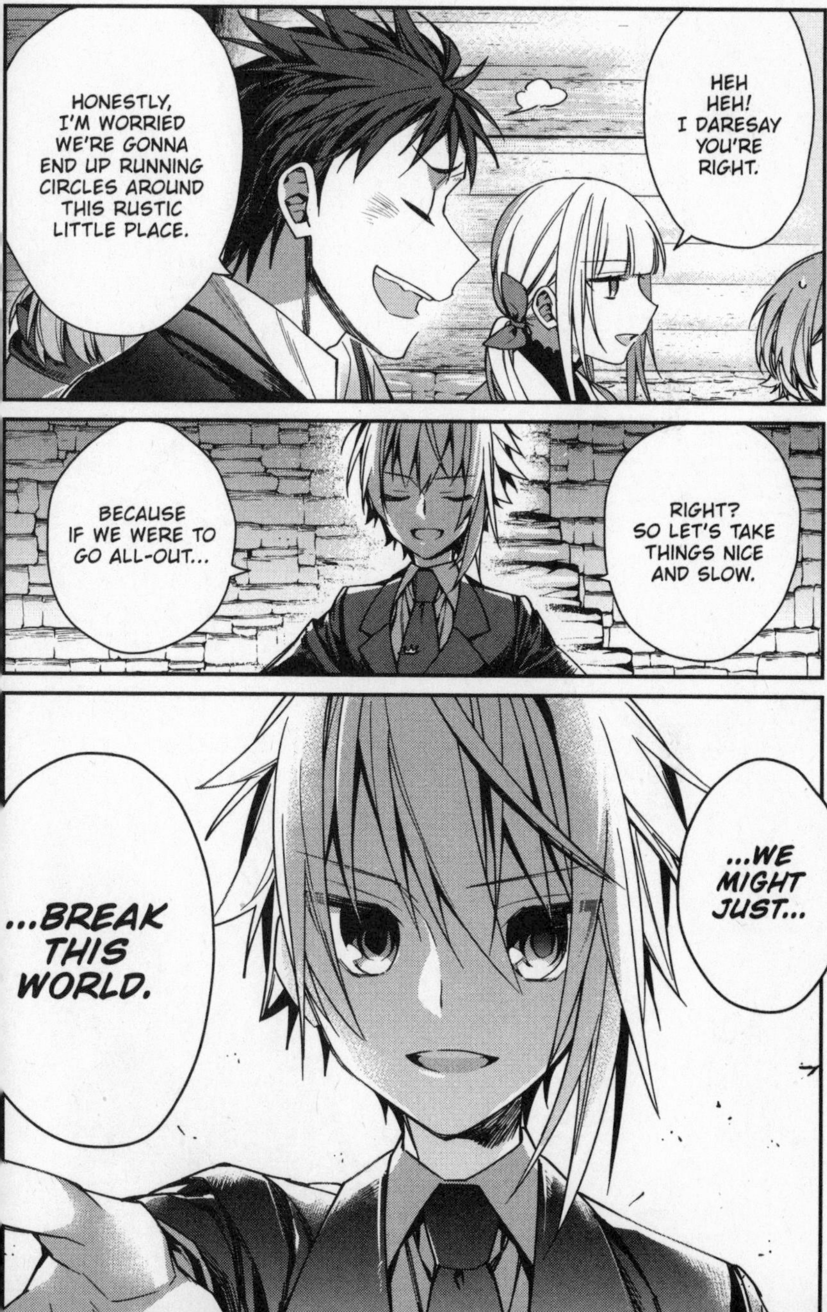
HEH HEH! I DARESAY YOU'RE RIGHT.
HONESTLY, I'M WORRIED WE'RE GONNA END UP RUNNING CIRCLES AROUND THIS RUSTIC LITTLE PLACE.
RIGHT? SO LET'S TAKE THINGS NICE AND SLOW.
BECAUSE IF WE WERE TO GO ALL-OUT...
...WE MIGHT JUST...
...BREAK THIS WORLD.

HIGH SCHOOL
PRODIGIES HAVE
IT EASY EVEN IN
ANOTHER
WORLD!

CHARACTER FILE 03

Masato Sanada

One of the high school prodigies. With seemingly demonic foresight, this boy genius has dominated multiple industries and rescued the near-defunct Sanada Group from ruin. Known as the Devil of Finance.

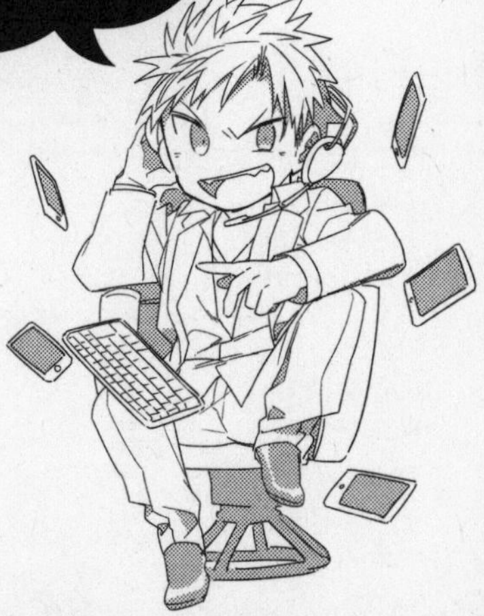

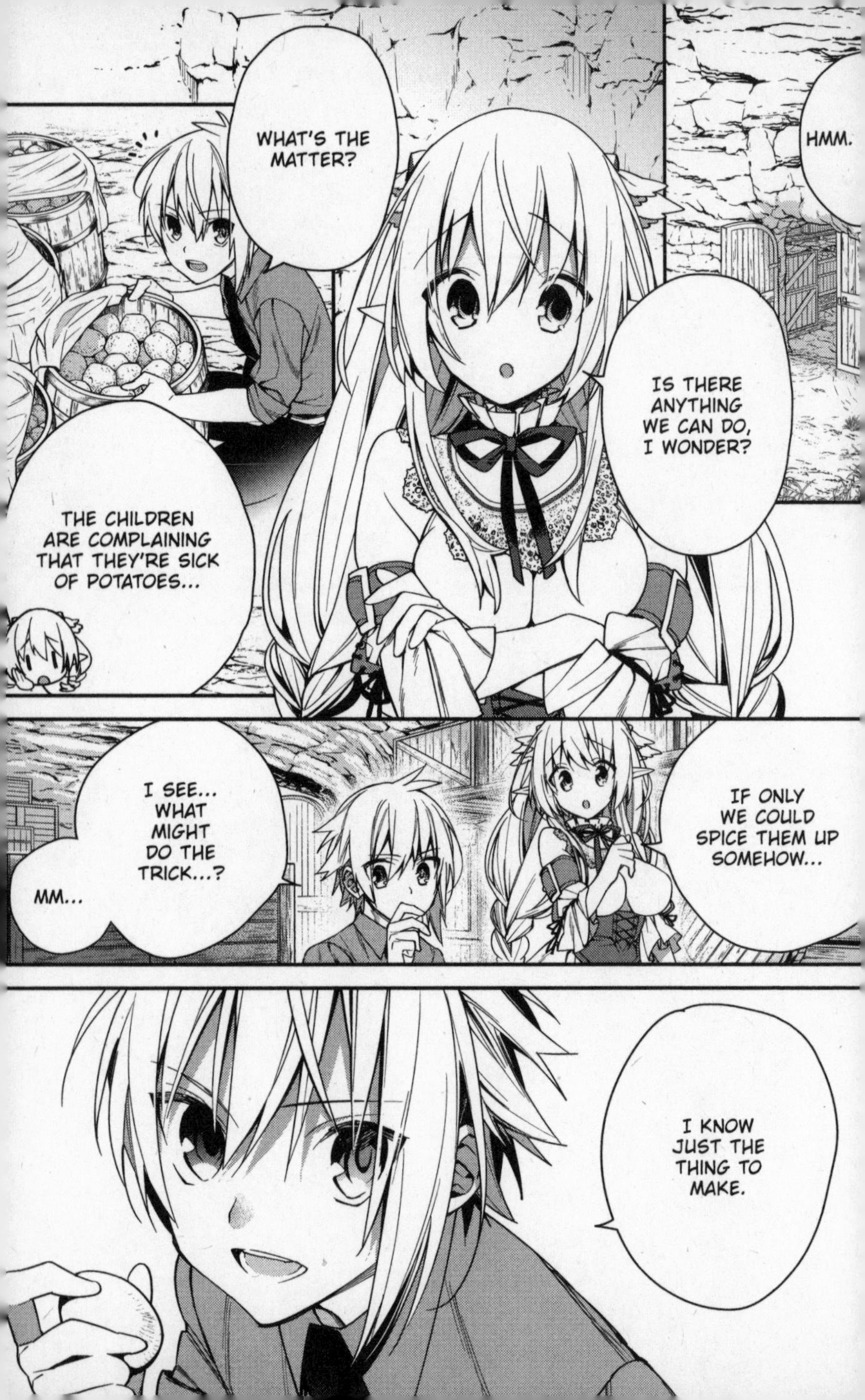
HMM.
WHAT'S THE MATTER?
IS THERE ANYTHING WE CAN DO, I WONDER?
THE CHILDREN ARE COMPLAINING THAT THEY'RE SICK OF POTATOES...
IF ONLY WE COULD SPICE THEM UP SOMEHOW...
I SEE... WHAT MIGHT DO THE TRICK...?
MM...
I KNOW JUST THE THING TO MAKE.

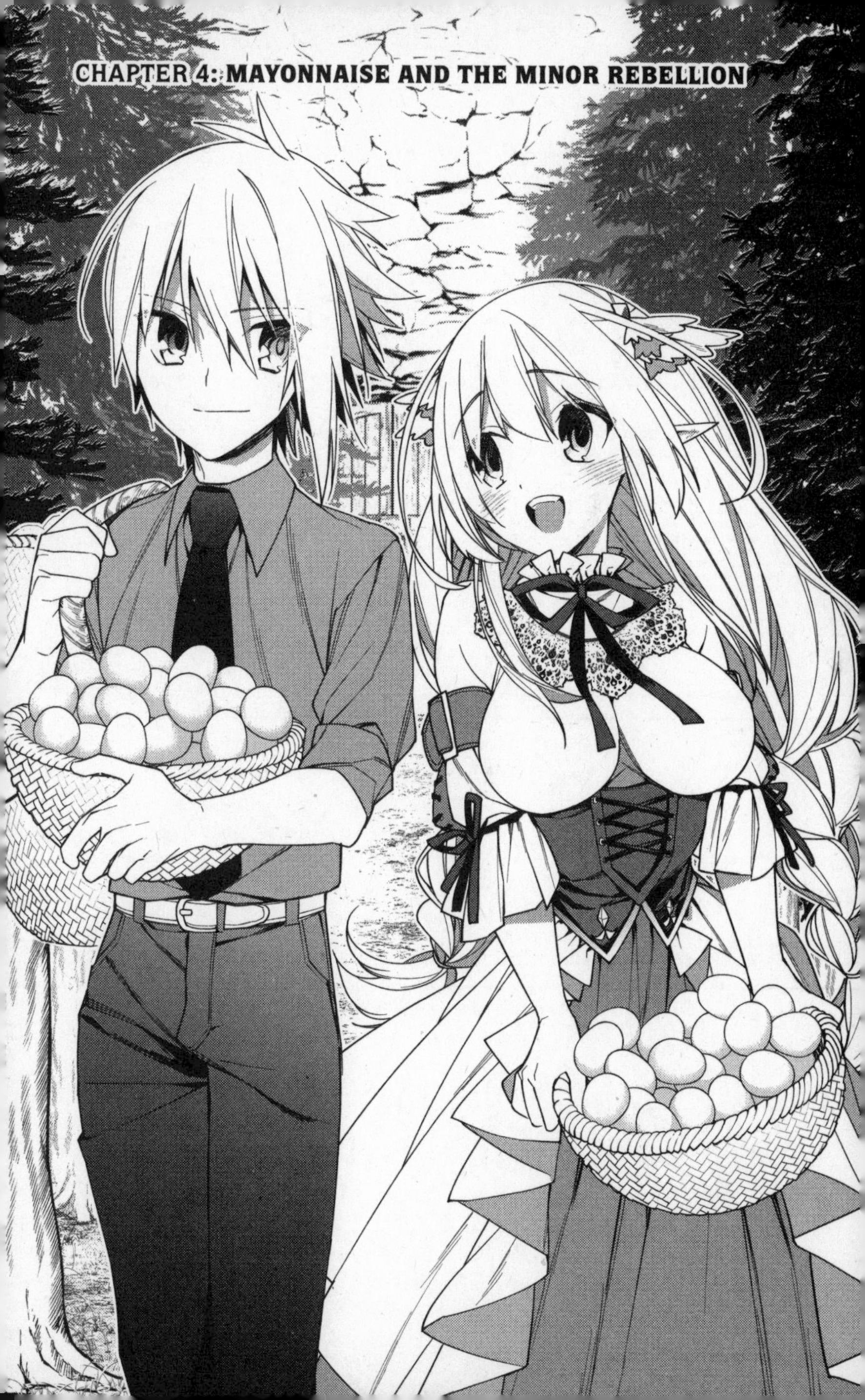
CHAPTER 4: MAYONNAISE AND THE MINOR REBELLION

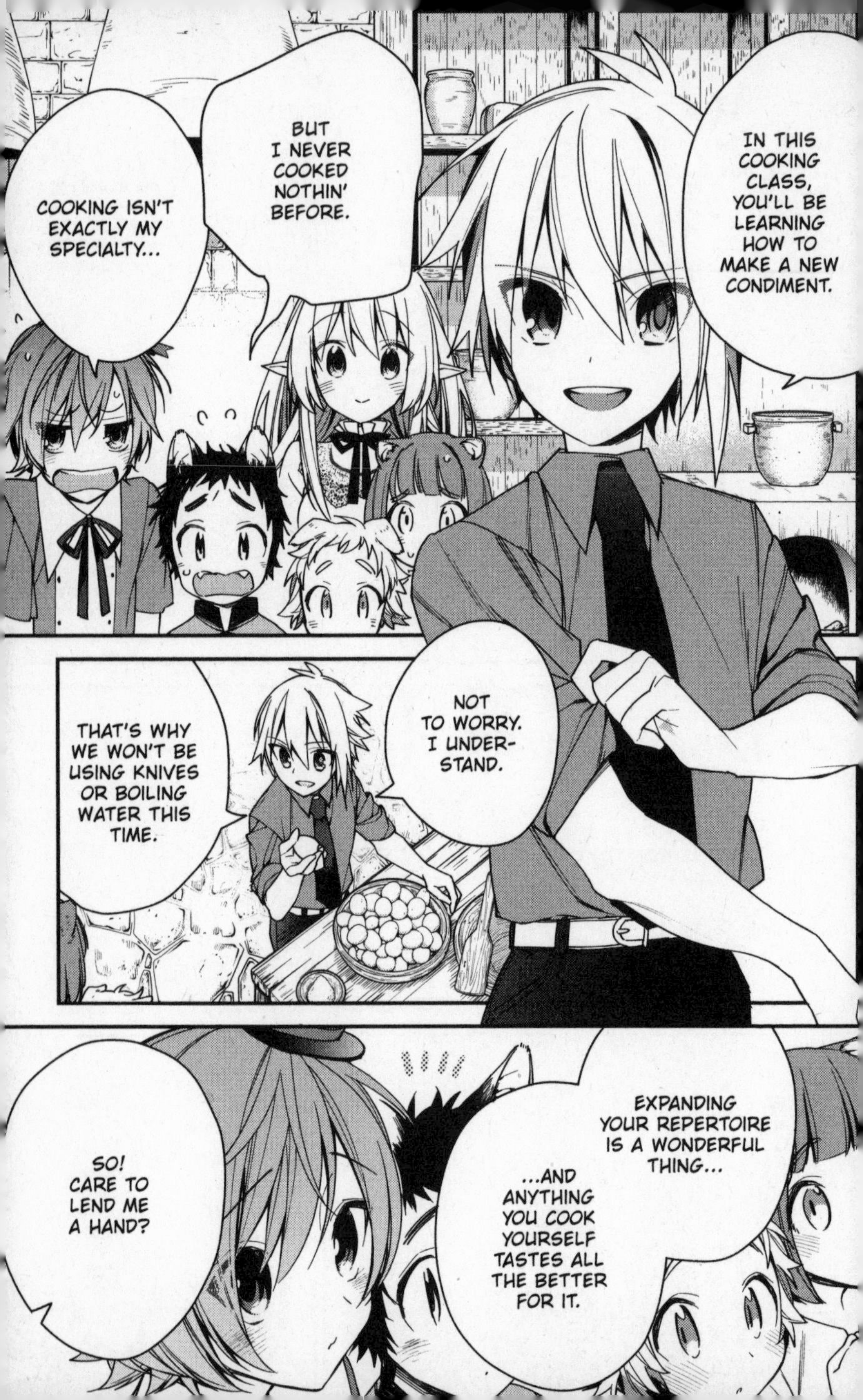

IN THIS COOKING CLASS, YOU'LL BE LEARNING HOW TO MAKE A NEW CONDIMENT.
BUT I NEVER COOKED NOTHIN' BEFORE.
COOKING ISN'T EXACTLY MY SPECIALTY...
NOT TO WORRY. I UNDER-STAND.
THAT'S WHY WE WON'T BE USING KNIVES OR BOILING WATER THIS TIME.
EXPANDING YOUR REPERTOIRE IS A WONDERFUL THING...
...AND ANYTHING YOU COOK YOURSELF TASTES ALL THE BETTER FOR IT.
SO! CARE TO LEND ME A HAND?

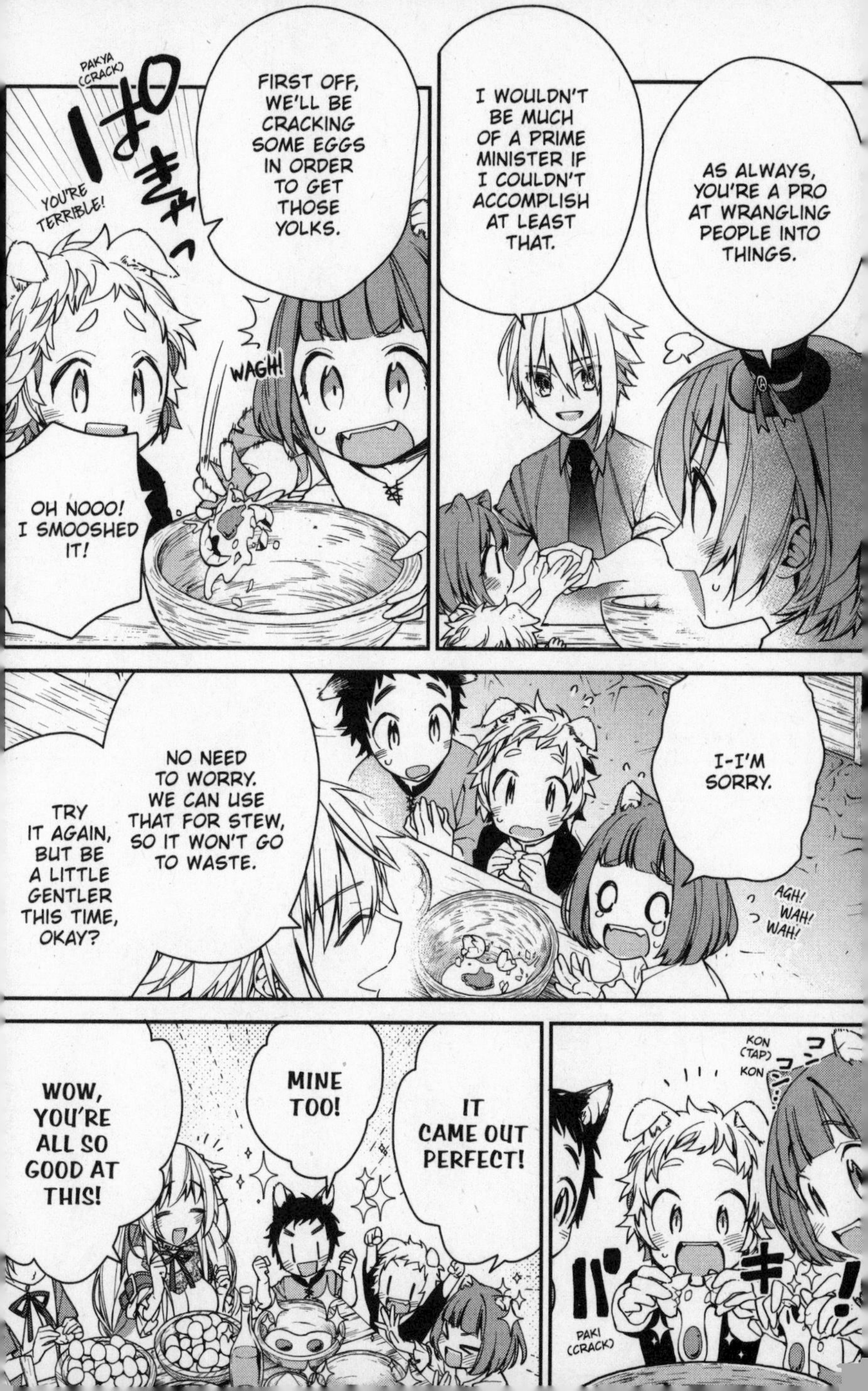
AS ALWAYS, YOU'RE A PRO AT WRANGLING PEOPLE INTO THINGS.
I WOULDN'T BE MUCH OF A PRIME MINISTER IF I COULDN'T ACCOMPLISH AT LEAST THAT.
FIRST OFF, WE'LL BE CRACKING SOME EGGS IN ORDER TO GET THOSE YOLKS.
PAKYA (CRACK)
YOU'RE TERRIBLE!
WAGH!
OH NOOO! I SMOOSHED IT!
I-I'M SORRY.
AGH! WAH! WAH!
NO NEED TO WORRY. WE CAN USE THAT FOR STEW, SO IT WON'T GO TO WASTE.
TRY IT AGAIN, BUT BE A LITTLE GENTLER THIS TIME, OKAY?
KON (TAP) KON
PAKI (CRACK)
IT CAME OUT PERFECT!
MINE TOO!
WOW, YOU'RE ALL SO GOOD AT THIS!

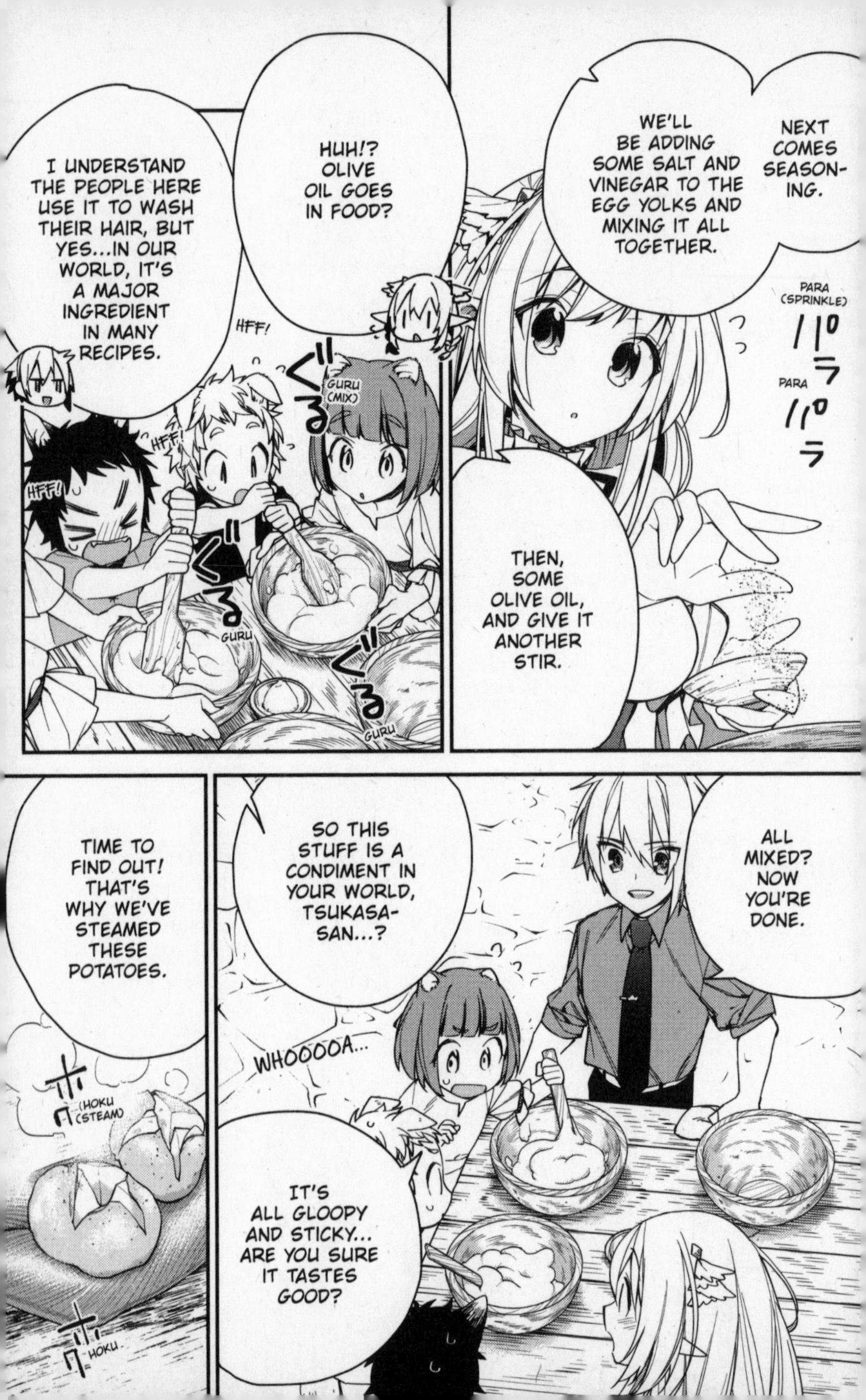
NEXT COMES SEASON-ING.
WE'LL BE ADDING SOME SALT AND VINEGAR TO THE EGG YOLKS AND MIXING IT ALL TOGETHER.
パラ PARA (SPRINKLE)
パラ PARA
THEN, SOME OLIVE OIL, AND GIVE IT ANOTHER STIR.
HUH!? OLIVE OIL GOES IN FOOD?
I UNDERSTAND THE PEOPLE HERE USE IT TO WASH THEIR HAIR, BUT YES...IN OUR WORLD, IT'S A MAJOR INGREDIENT IN MANY RECIPES.
HFF!
ぐる GURU (MIX)
HFF!
HFF!
ぐる GURU
ぐる GURU
ALL MIXED? NOW YOU'RE DONE.
SO THIS STUFF IS A CONDIMENT IN YOUR WORLD, TSUKASA-SAN...?
WHOOOOA...
IT'S ALL GLOOPY AND STICKY... ARE YOU SURE IT TASTES GOOD?
TIME TO FIND OUT! THAT'S WHY WE'VE STEAMED THESE POTATOES.
ホク (HOKU (STEAM)
ホク HOKU

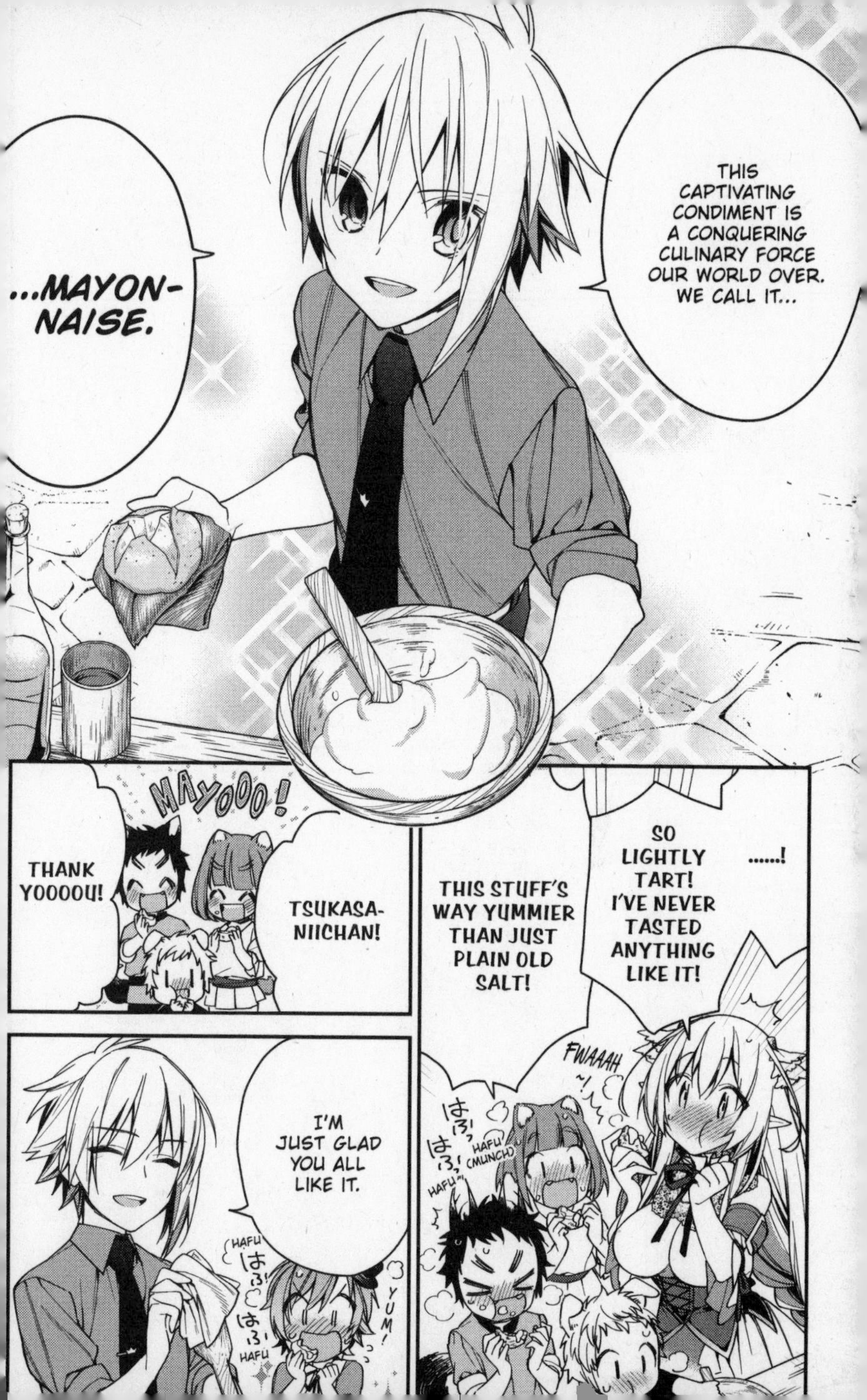
THIS CAPTIVATING CONDIMENT IS A CONQUERING CULINARY FORCE OUR WORLD OVER. WE CALL IT...
...MAYON-NAISE.
......!
SO LIGHTLY TART! I'VE NEVER TASTED ANYTHING LIKE IT!
THIS STUFF'S WAY YUMMIER THAN JUST PLAIN OLD SALT!
FWAAAH~!
はふっ
はふっ
HAFU
HAFU
HAFU (MUNCH)
MAYOOO!
TSUKASA-NIICHAN!
THANK YOOOOU!
I'M JUST GLAD YOU ALL LIKE IT.
HAFU
はふ
はふ
HAFU
YUM!

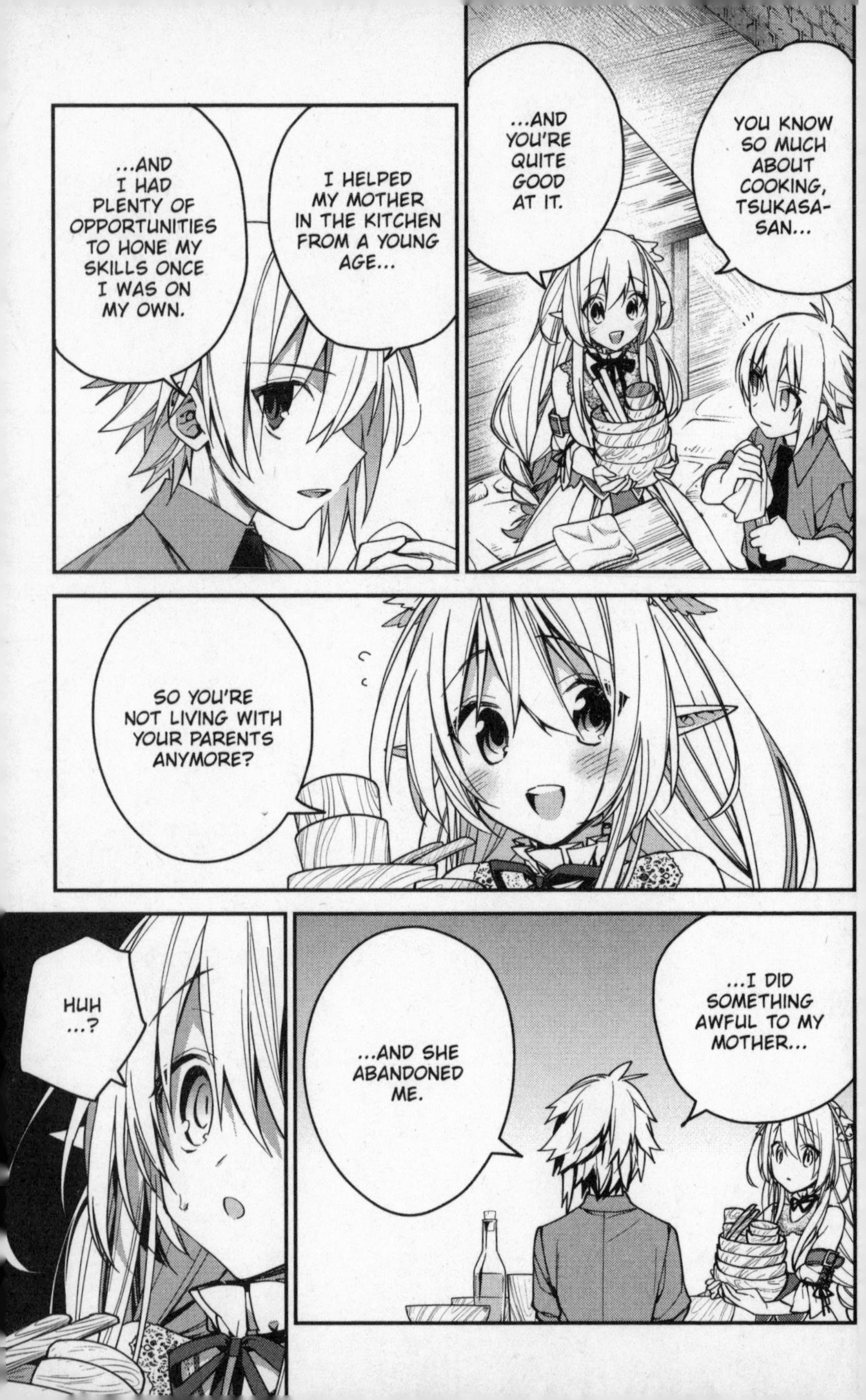
YOU KNOW SO MUCH ABOUT COOKING, TSUKASA-SAN...
...AND YOU'RE QUITE GOOD AT IT.
I HELPED MY MOTHER IN THE KITCHEN FROM A YOUNG AGE...
...AND I HAD PLENTY OF OPPORTUNITIES TO HONE MY SKILLS ONCE I WAS ON MY OWN.
SO YOU'RE NOT LIVING WITH YOUR PARENTS ANYMORE?
...I DID SOMETHING AWFUL TO MY MOTHER...
...AND SHE ABANDONED ME.
HUH ...?

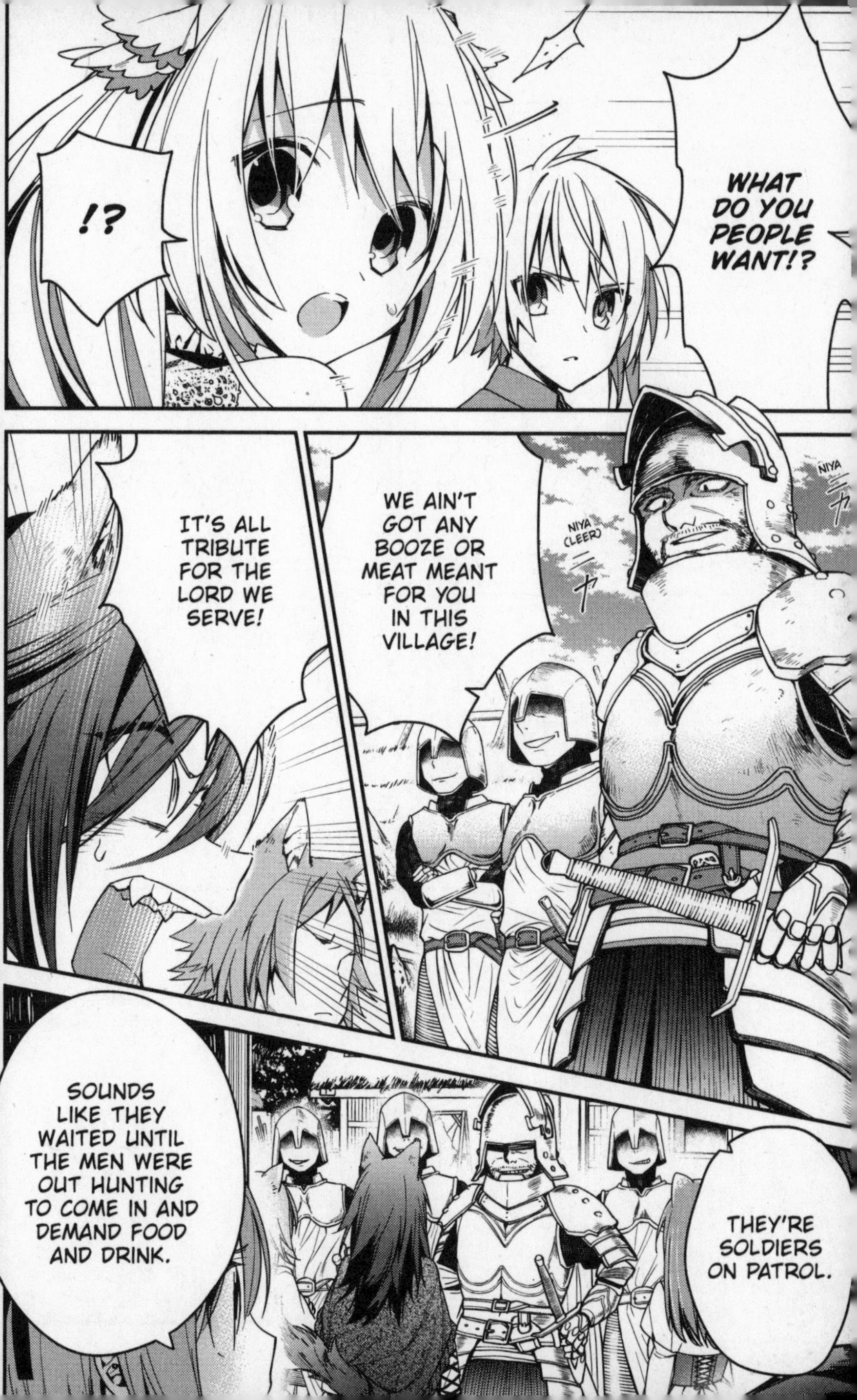

WHAT DO YOU PEOPLE WANT!?
!?
NIYA (LEER)
NIYA
WE AIN'T GOT ANY BOOZE OR MEAT MEANT FOR YOU IN THIS VILLAGE!
IT'S ALL TRIBUTE FOR THE LORD WE SERVE!
THEY'RE SOLDIERS ON PATROL.
SOUNDS LIKE THEY WAITED UNTIL THE MEN WERE OUT HUNTING TO COME IN AND DEMAND FOOD AND DRINK.

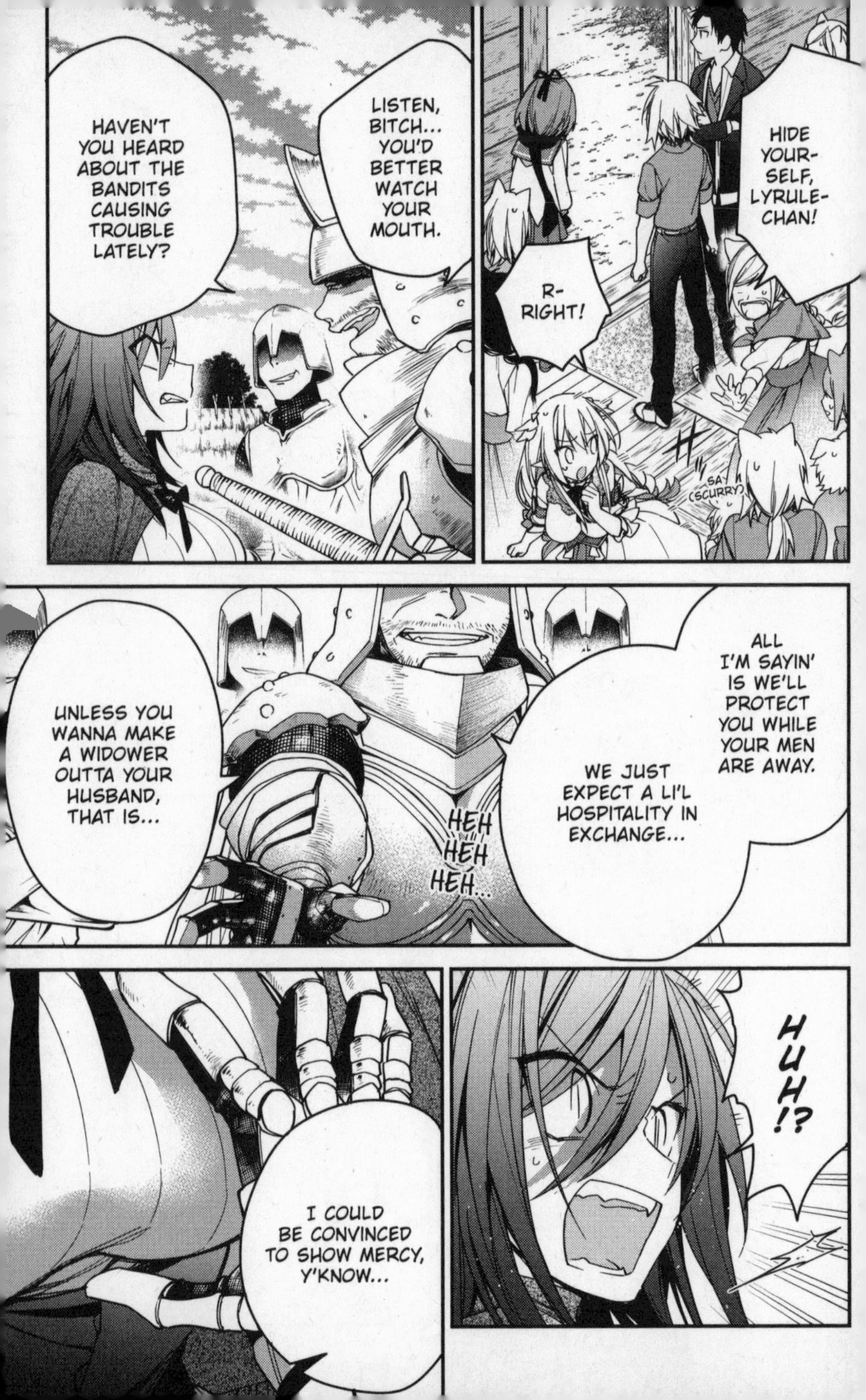
HIDE YOURSELF, LYRULE-CHAN!
R-RIGHT!
SA (SCURRY)
LISTEN, BITCH... YOU'D BETTER WATCH YOUR MOUTH.
HAVEN'T YOU HEARD ABOUT THE BANDITS CAUSING TROUBLE LATELY?
ALL I'M SAYIN' IS WE'LL PROTECT YOU WHILE YOUR MEN ARE AWAY.
WE JUST EXPECT A LI'L HOSPITALITY IN EXCHANGE...
HEH HEH HEH...
UNLESS YOU WANNA MAKE A WIDOWER OUTTA YOUR HUSBAND, THAT IS...
HUH!?
I COULD BE CONVINCED TO SHOW MERCY, Y'KNOW...

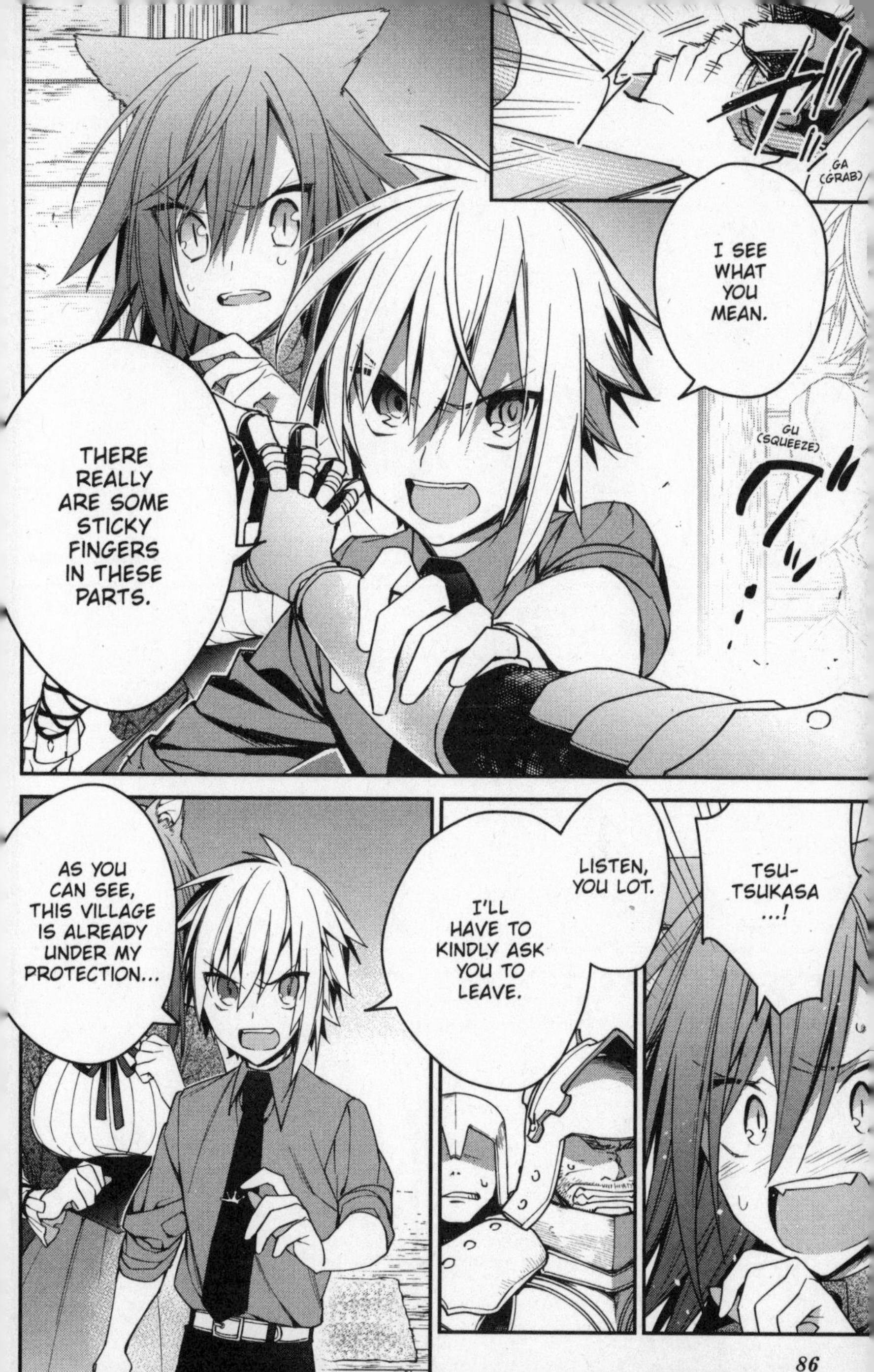
GA (GRAB)
I SEE WHAT YOU MEAN.
GU (SQUEEZE)
THERE REALLY ARE SOME STICKY FINGERS IN THESE PARTS.
TSU-TSUKASA ...!
LISTEN, YOU LOT.
I'LL HAVE TO KINDLY ASK YOU TO LEAVE.
AS YOU CAN SEE, THIS VILLAGE IS ALREADY UNDER MY PROTECTION...

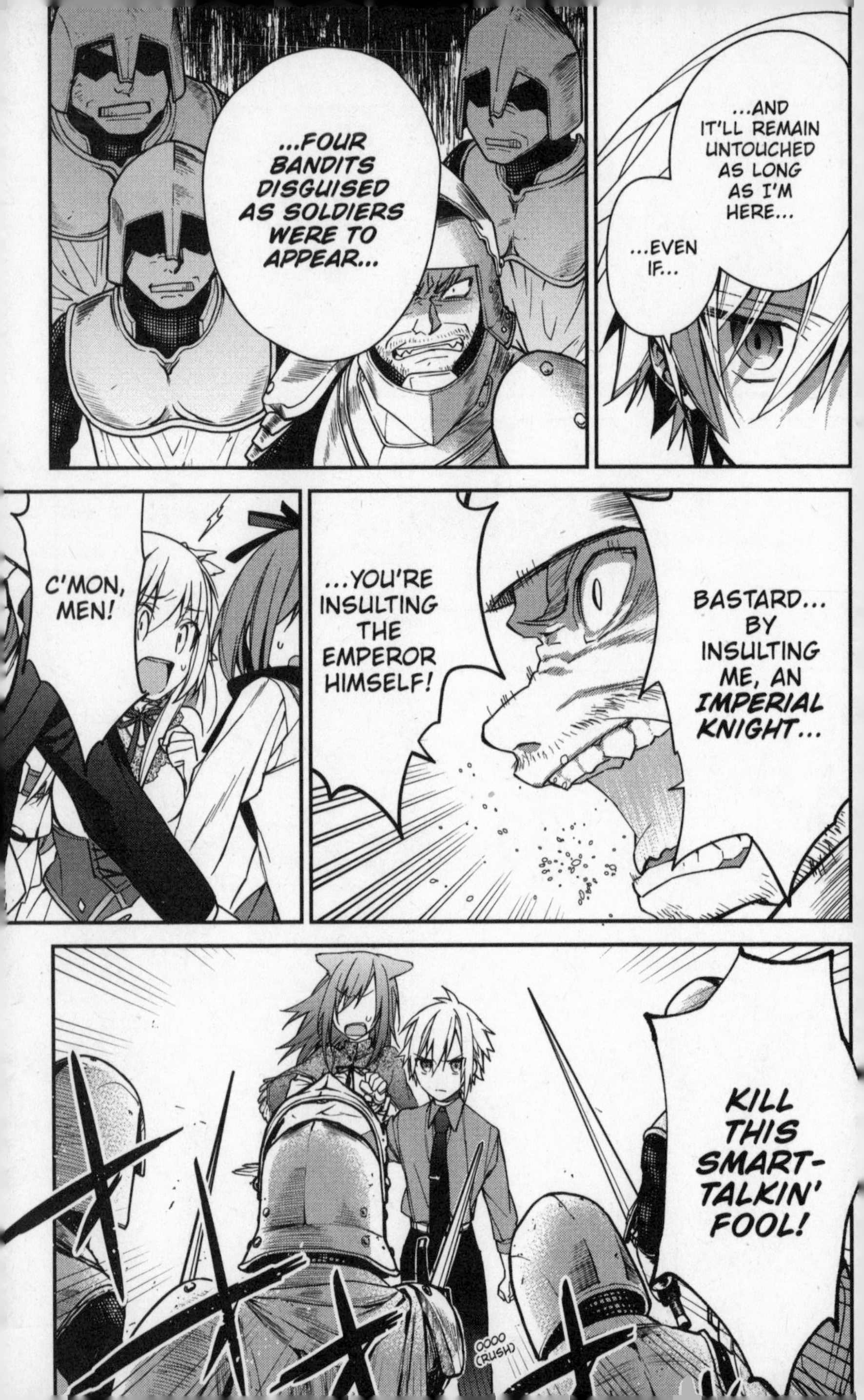
...AND IT'LL REMAIN UNTOUCHED AS LONG AS I'M HERE...
...EVEN IF...
...FOUR BANDITS DISGUISED AS SOLDIERS WERE TO APPEAR...
BASTARD... BY INSULTING ME, AN IMPERIAL KNIGHT...
...YOU'RE INSULTING THE EMPEROR HIMSELF!
C'MON, MEN!
KILL THIS SMART-TALKIN' FOOL!
OOOO (RUSH)

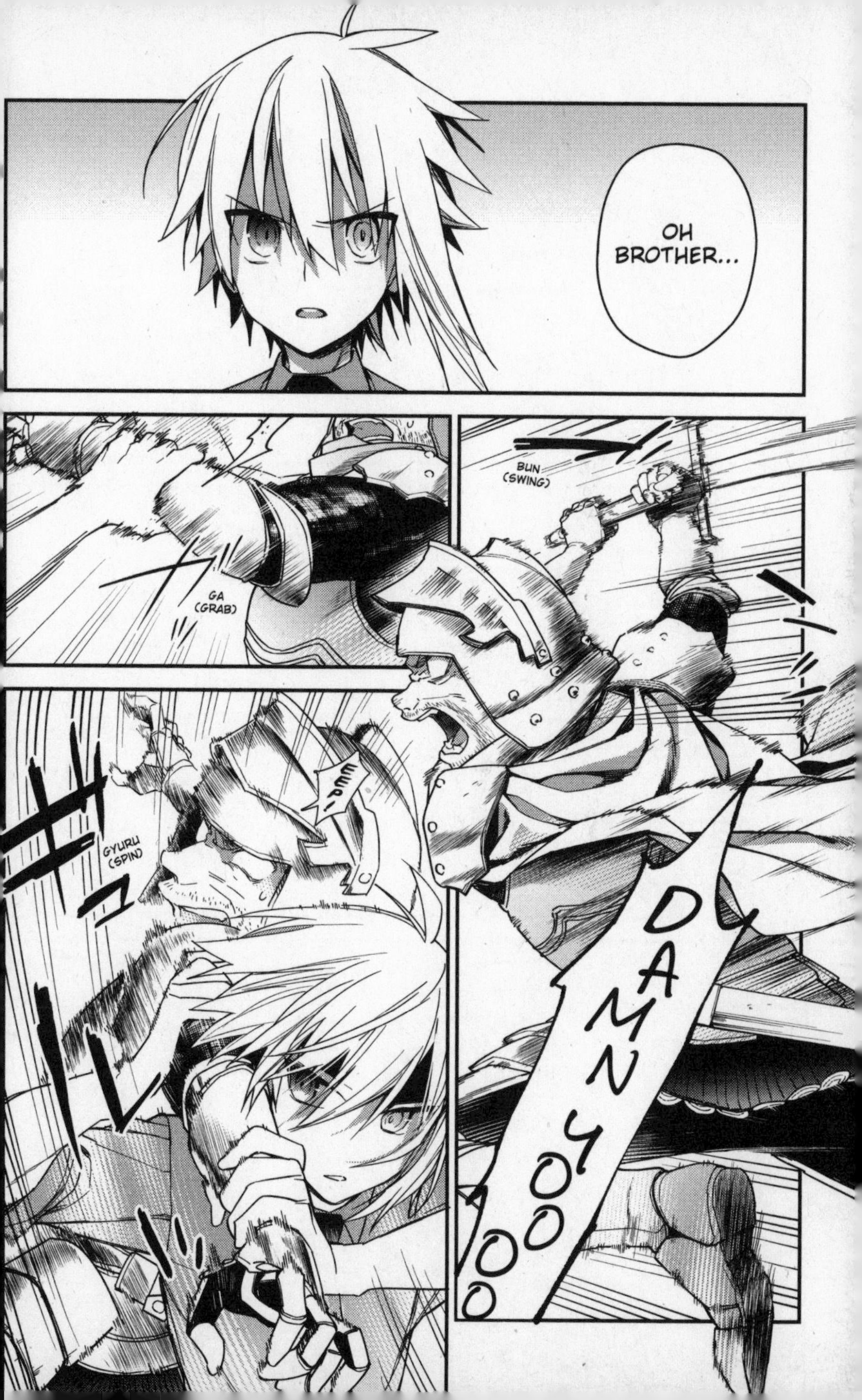
OH BROTHER...
BUN (SWING)
GA (GRAB)
EEP!
GYURU (SPIN)
DAMN YOOOOOO

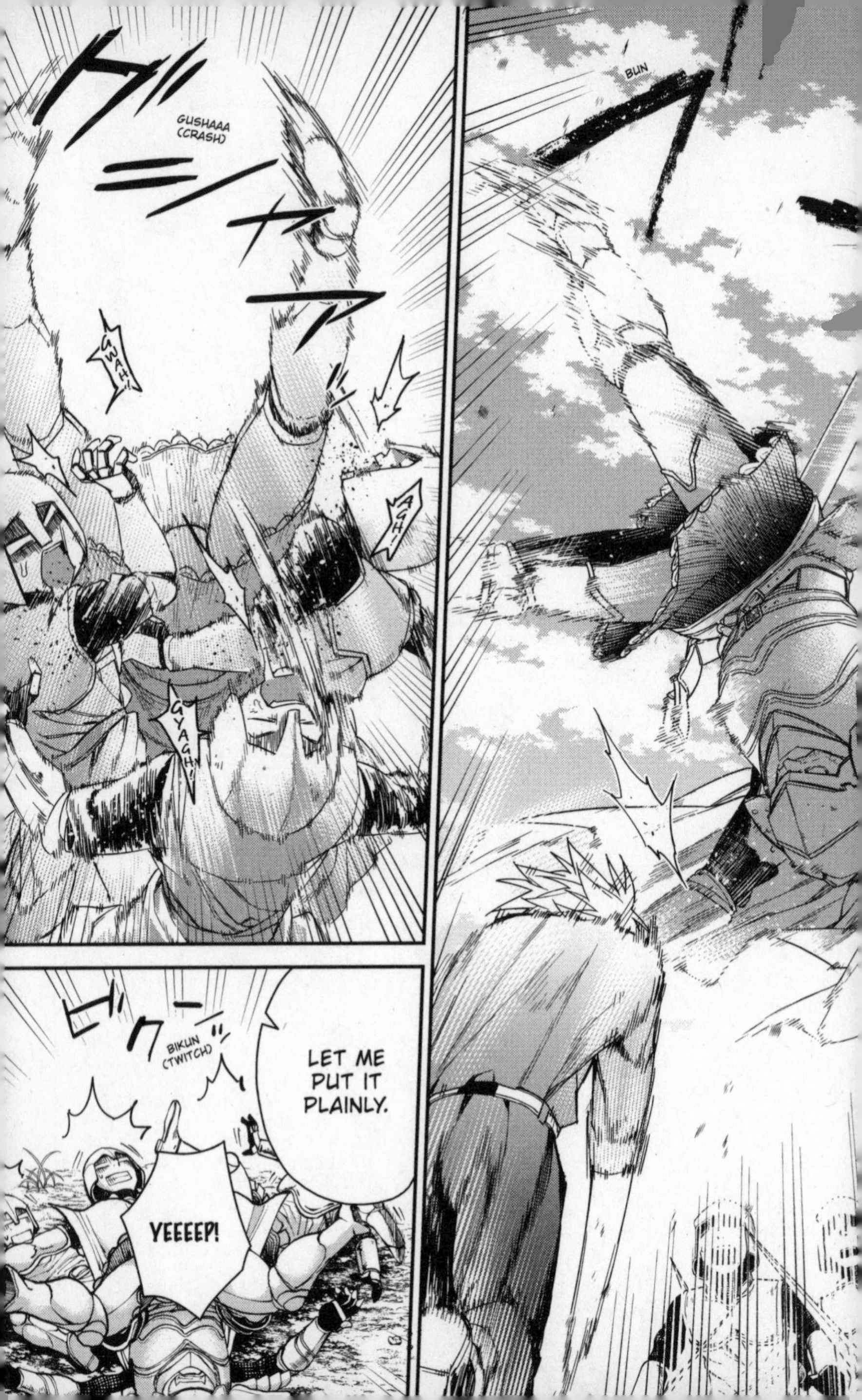
BUN
GUSHAAA (CRASH)
AGH!
GWAH!
GYAGH!
LET ME PUT IT PLAINLY.
BIKUN (TWITCH)
YEEEEP!

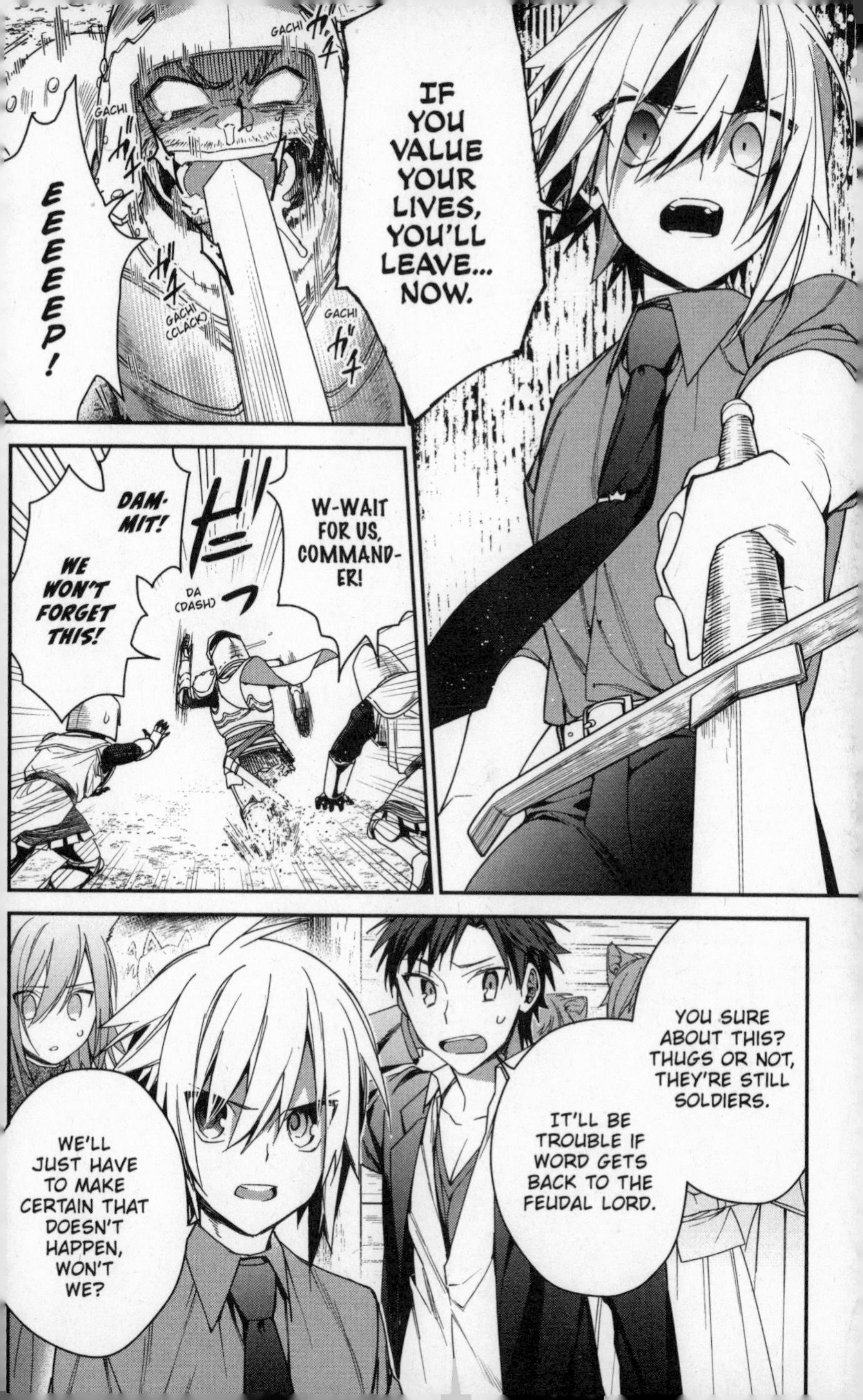

IF YOU VALUE YOUR LIVES, YOU'LL LEAVE... NOW.
GACHI
GACHI
GACHI (CLACK)
GACHI
EEEEEEP!
W-WAIT FOR US, COMMANDER!
DA (DASH)
DAM-MIT!
WE WON'T FORGET THIS!
YOU SURE ABOUT THIS? THUGS OR NOT, THEY'RE STILL SOLDIERS.
IT'LL BE TROUBLE IF WORD GETS BACK TO THE FEUDAL LORD.
WE'LL JUST HAVE TO MAKE CERTAIN THAT DOESN'T HAPPEN, WON'T WE?

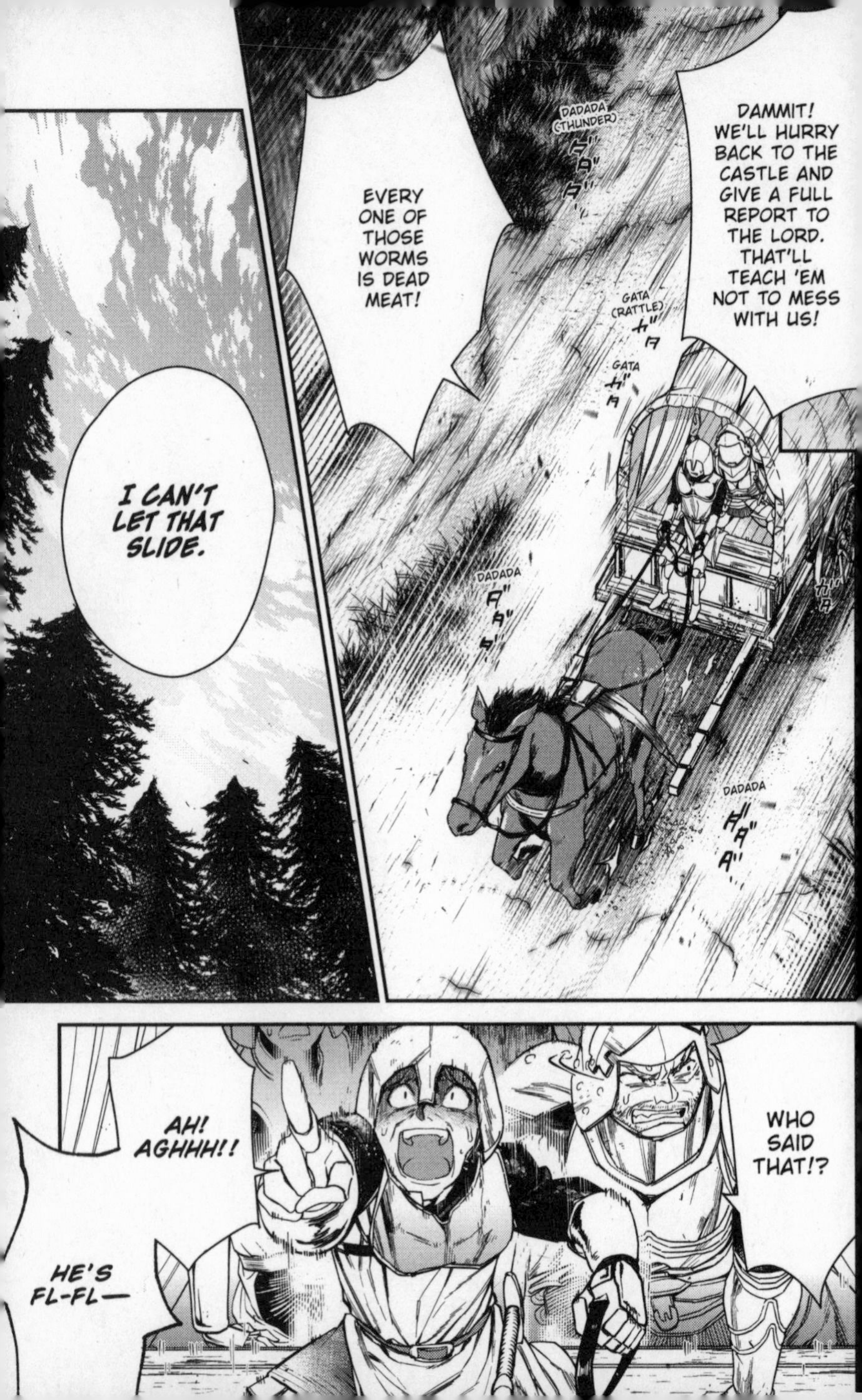
DAMMIT! WE'LL HURRY BACK TO THE CASTLE AND GIVE A FULL REPORT TO THE LORD. THAT'LL TEACH 'EM NOT TO MESS WITH US!
DADADA (THUNDER)
EVERY ONE OF THOSE WORMS IS DEAD MEAT!
GATA (RATTLE)
GATA
DADADA
DADADA
I CAN'T LET THAT SLIDE.
WHO SAID THAT!?
AH! AGHHH!!
HE'S FL-FL—

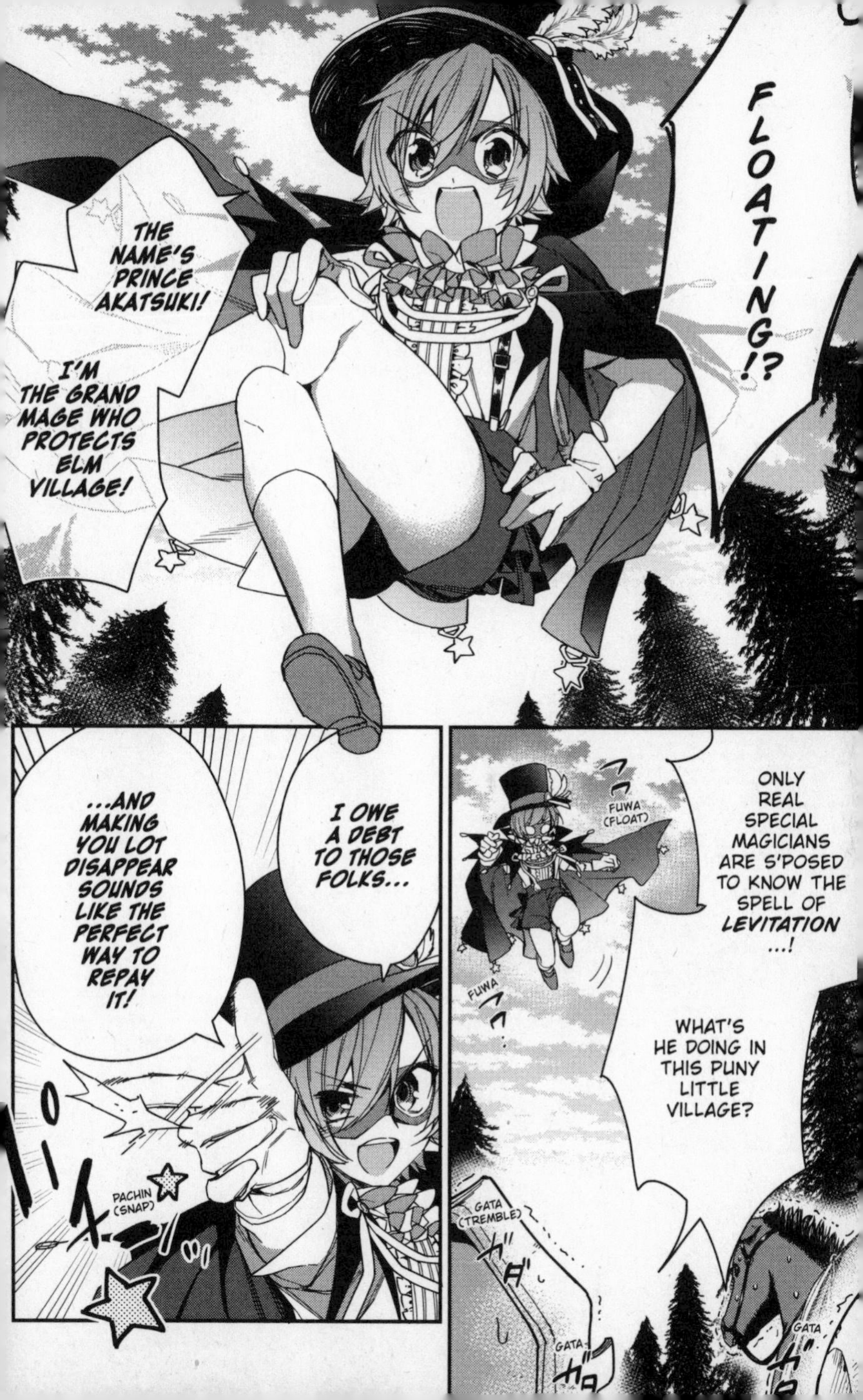
FLOATING!?
THE NAME'S PRINCE AKATSUKI!
I'M THE GRAND MAGE WHO PROTECTS ELM VILLAGE!
ONLY REAL SPECIAL MAGICIANS ARE S'POSED TO KNOW THE SPELL OF *LEVITATION* ...!
FUWA (FLOAT)
FUWA
WHAT'S HE DOING IN THIS PUNY LITTLE VILLAGE?
GATA (TREMBLE)
GATA
GATA
I OWE A DEBT TO THOSE FOLKS...
...AND MAKING YOU LOT DISAPPEAR SOUNDS LIKE THE PERFECT WAY TO REPAY IT!
PACHIN (SNAP)

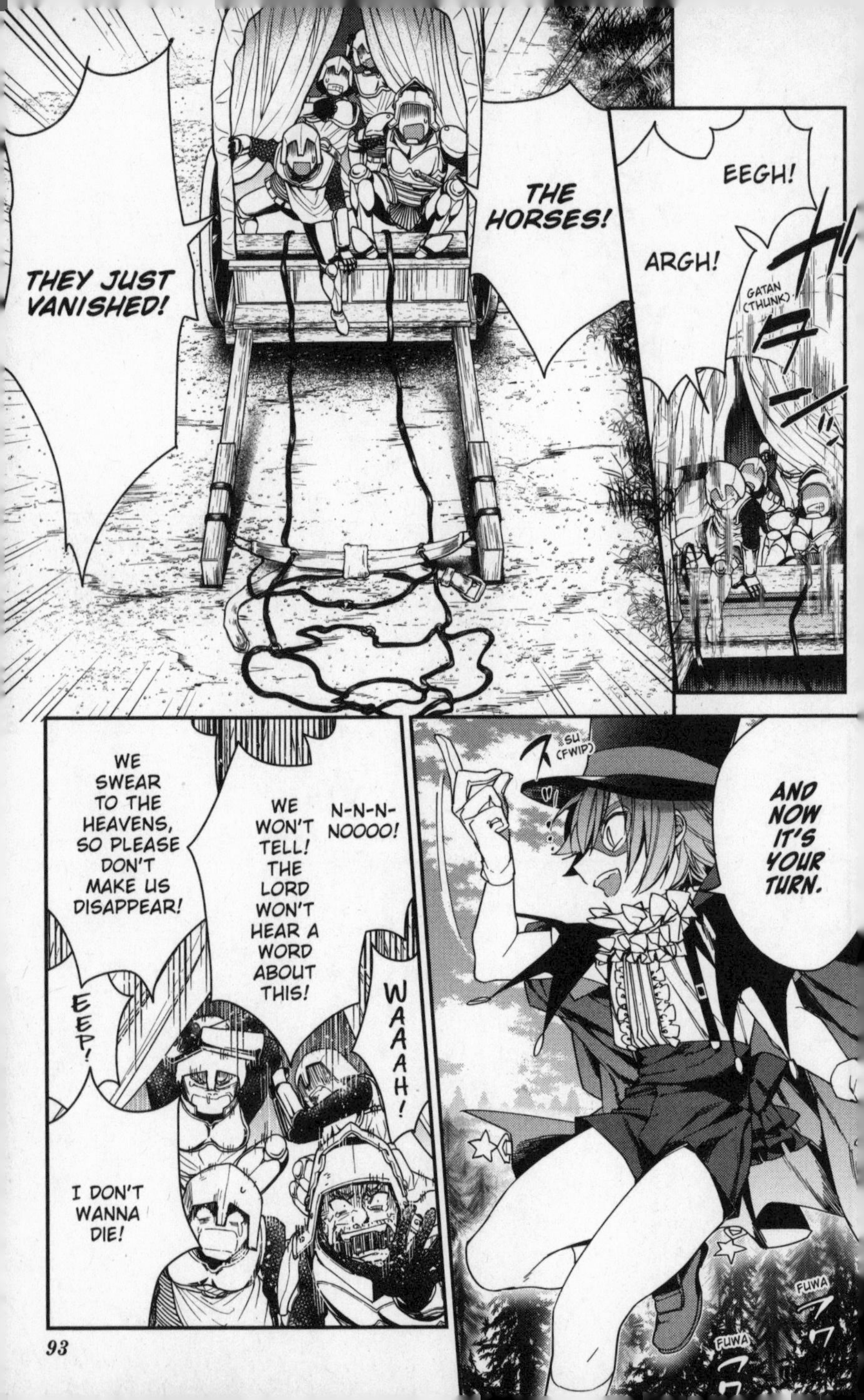
EEGH!
ARGH!
GATAN (THUNK)
THE HORSES!
THEY JUST VANISHED!
SU (FWIP)
AND NOW IT'S YOUR TURN.
FUWA
FUWA
N-N-N-NOOOO!
WE WON'T TELL! THE LORD WON'T HEAR A WORD ABOUT THIS!
WE SWEAR TO THE HEAVENS, SO PLEASE DON'T MAKE US DISAPPEAR!
WAAAAH!
EEP!
I DON'T WANNA DIE!

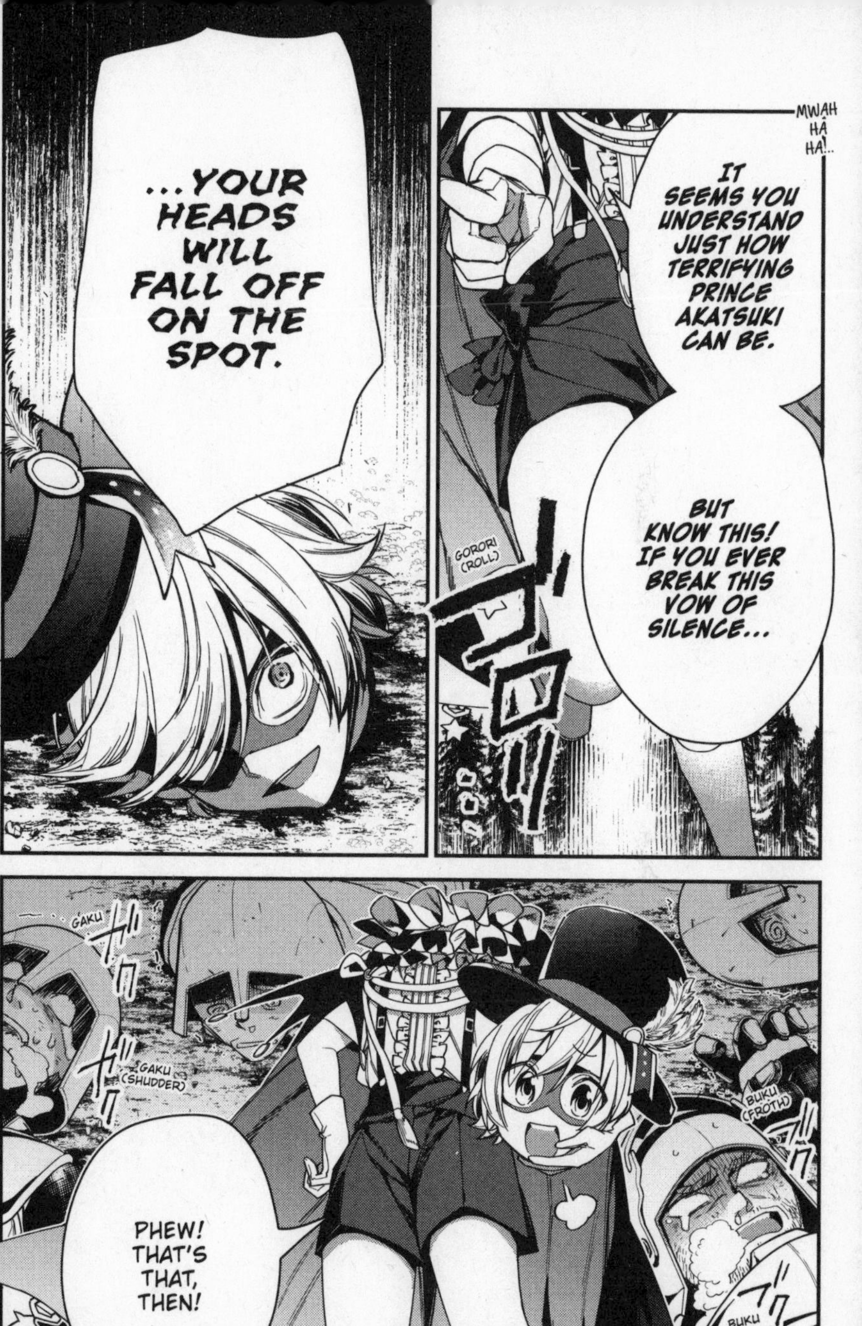
MWAH HA HA!...
IT SEEMS YOU UNDERSTAND JUST HOW TERRIFYING PRINCE AKATSUKI CAN BE.
BUT KNOW THIS! IF YOU EVER BREAK THIS VOW OF SILENCE...
GORORI (ROLL)
...YOUR HEADS WILL FALL OFF ON THE SPOT.
BUKU (FROTH)
BUKU
GAKU
GAKU (SHUDDER)
PHEW! THAT'S THAT, THEN!

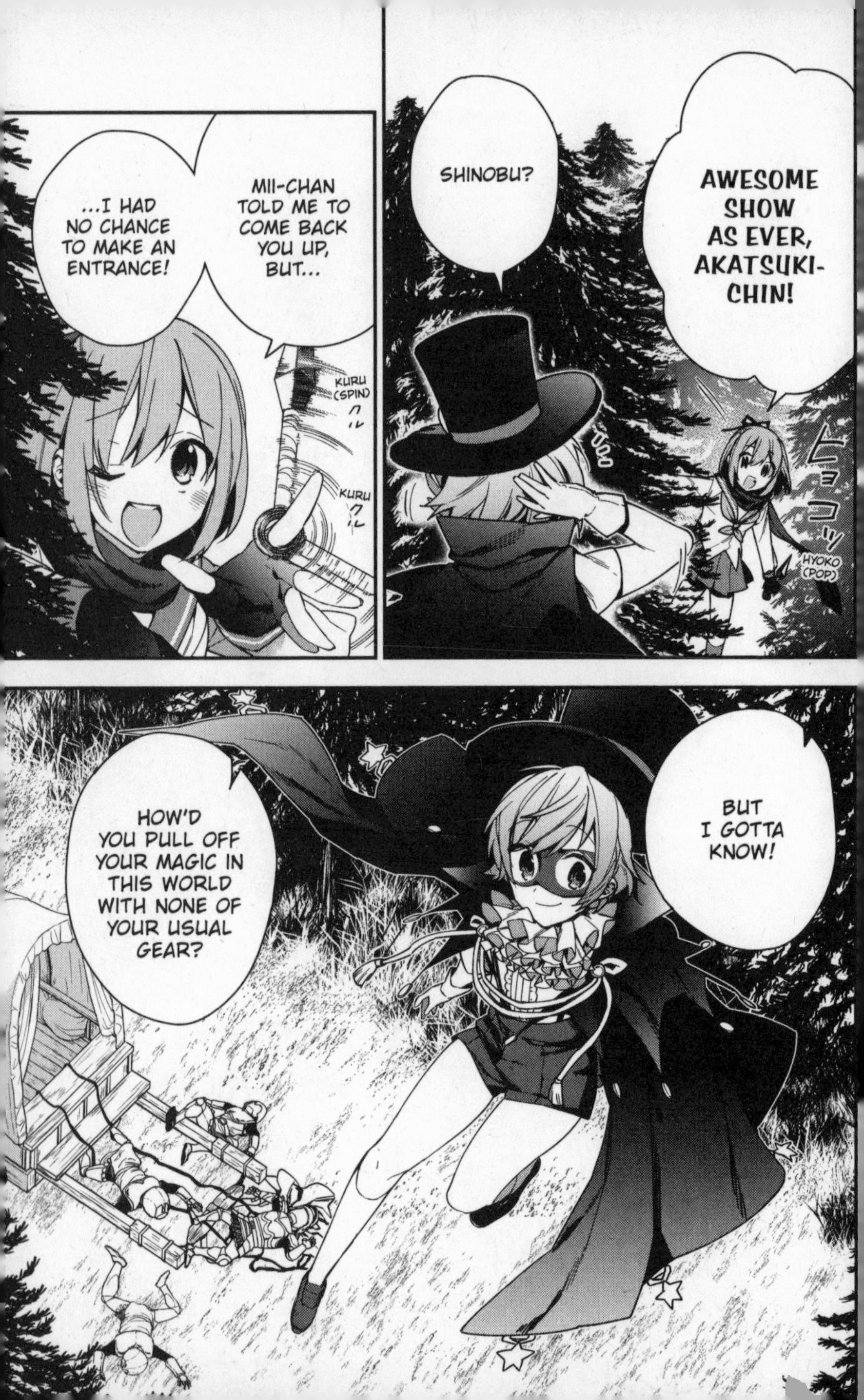
AWESOME SHOW AS EVER, AKATSUKI-CHIN!
SHINOBU?
HYOKO (POP)
MII-CHAN TOLD ME TO COME BACK YOU UP, BUT...
...I HAD NO CHANCE TO MAKE AN ENTRANCE!
KURU (SPIN)
KURU
BUT I GOTTA KNOW!
HOW'D YOU PULL OFF YOUR MAGIC IN THIS WORLD WITH NONE OF YOUR USUAL GEAR?

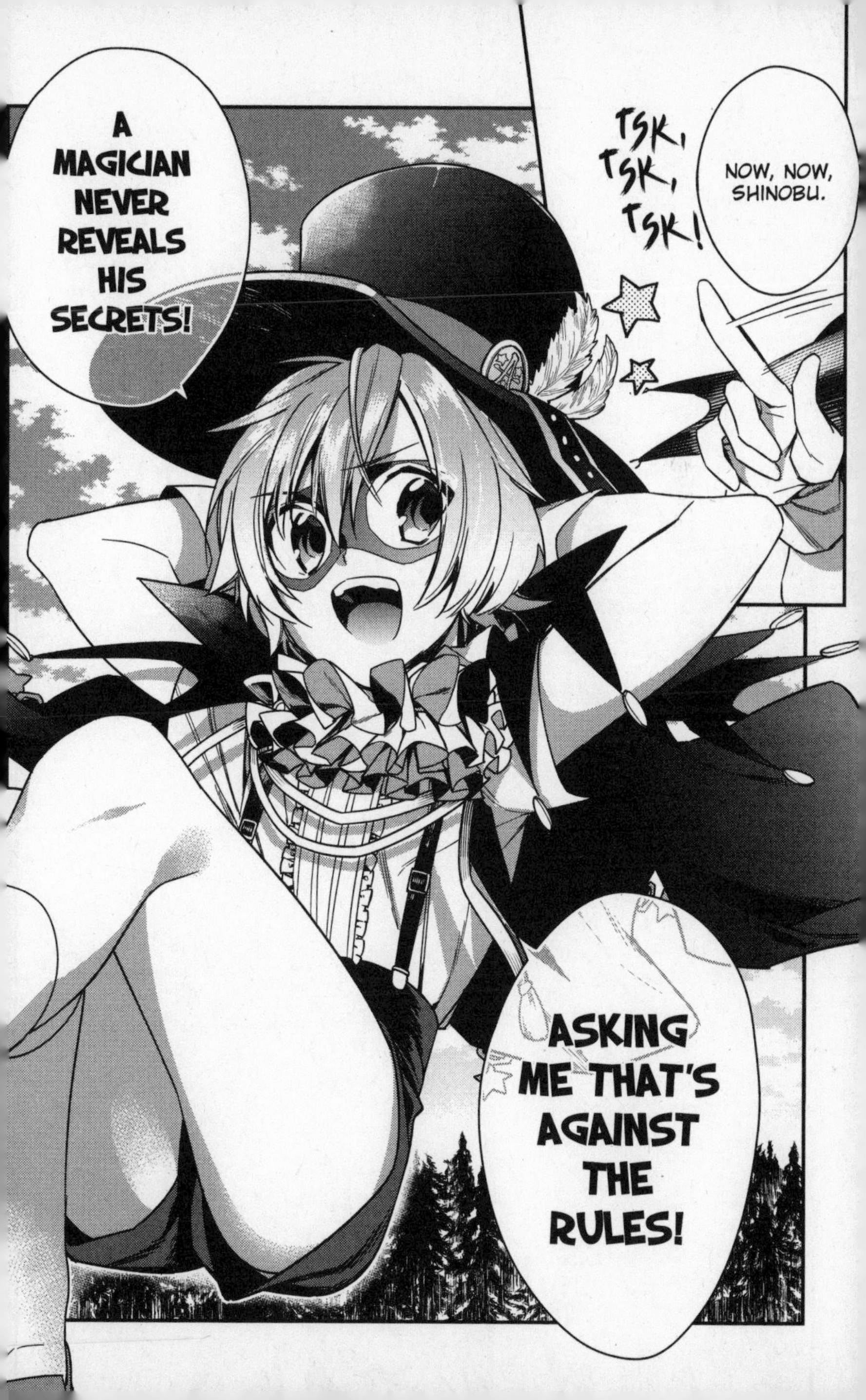
NOW, NOW, SHINOBU.
TSK, TSK, TSK!
A MAGICIAN NEVER REVEALS HIS SECRETS!
ASKING ME THAT'S AGAINST THE RULES!

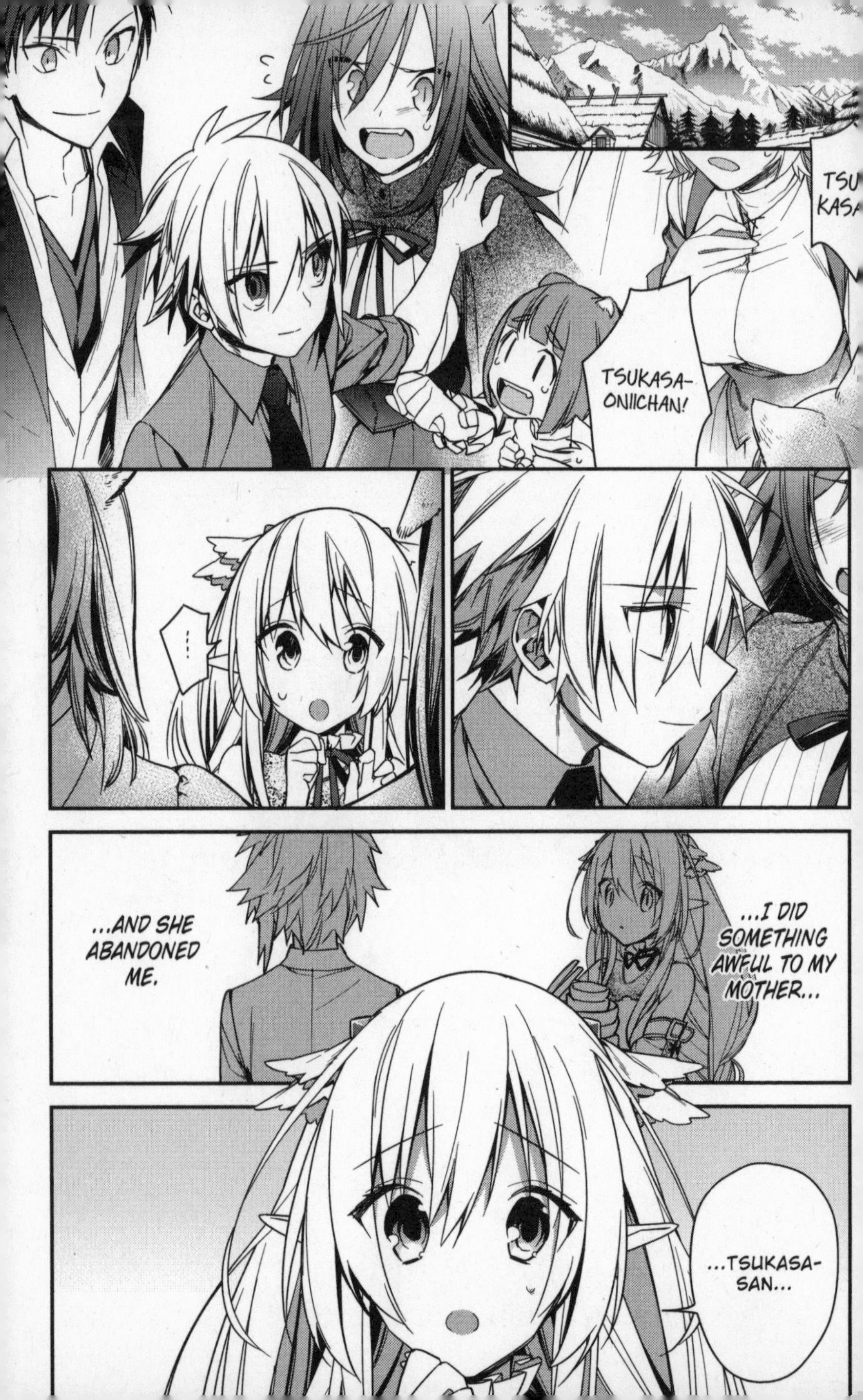
TSU KASA
TSUKASA-ONIICHAN!
...I DID SOMETHING AWFUL TO MY MOTHER...
...AND SHE ABANDONED ME.
...TSUKASA-SAN...

CHARACTER FILE 04

Shinobu Sarutobi

One of the high school prodigies. A descendant of the famous ninja, Sasuke Sarutobi. From international news to local rumors, there's no scoop or scandal she can't get to the bottom of.

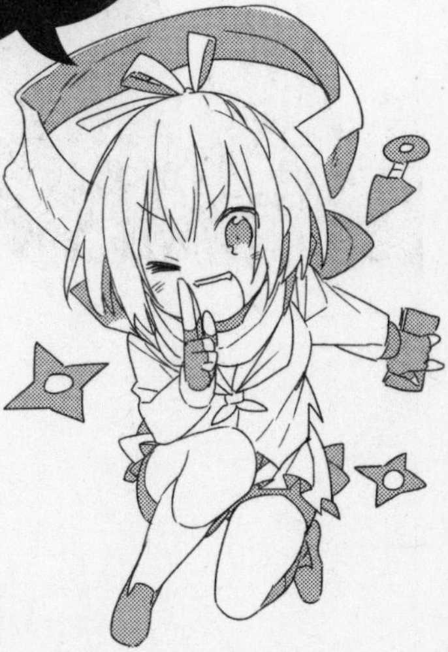

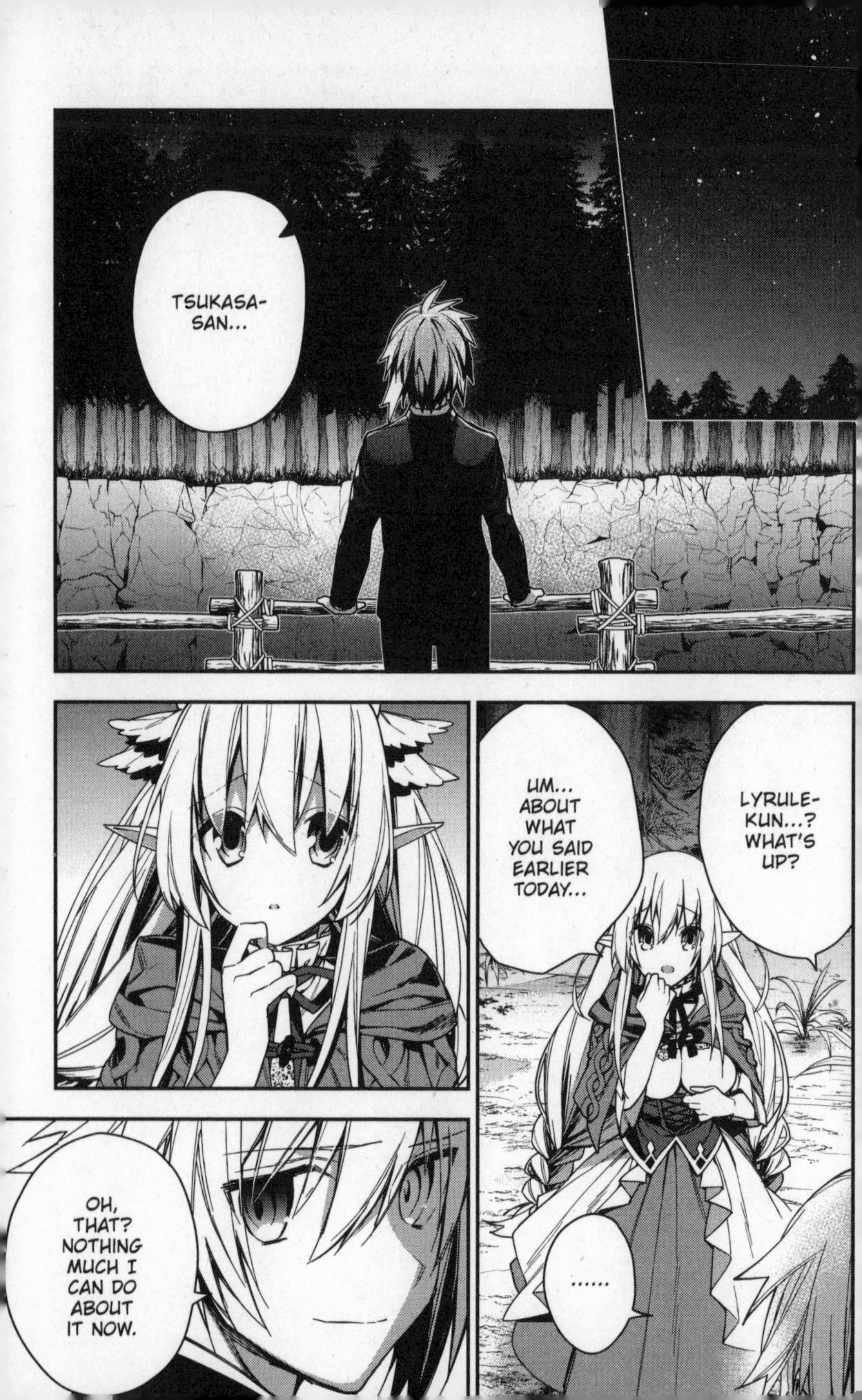
TSUKASA-SAN...
LYRULE-KUN...? WHAT'S UP?
UM... ABOUT WHAT YOU SAID EARLIER TODAY...
......
OH, THAT? NOTHING MUCH I CAN DO ABOUT IT NOW.

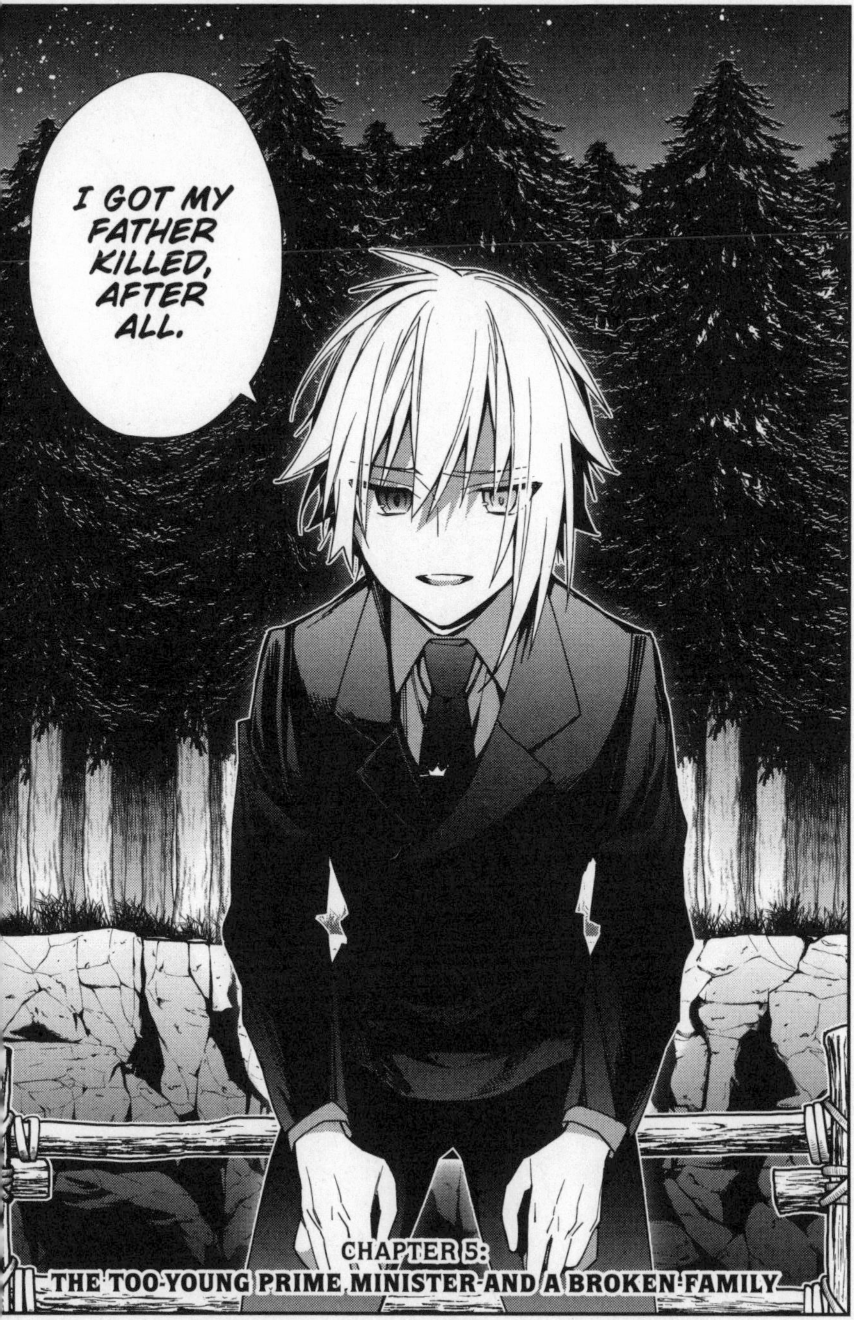
I GOT MY FATHER KILLED, AFTER ALL.
CHAPTER 5:
THE TOO-YOUNG PRIME MINISTER AND A BROKEN FAMILY

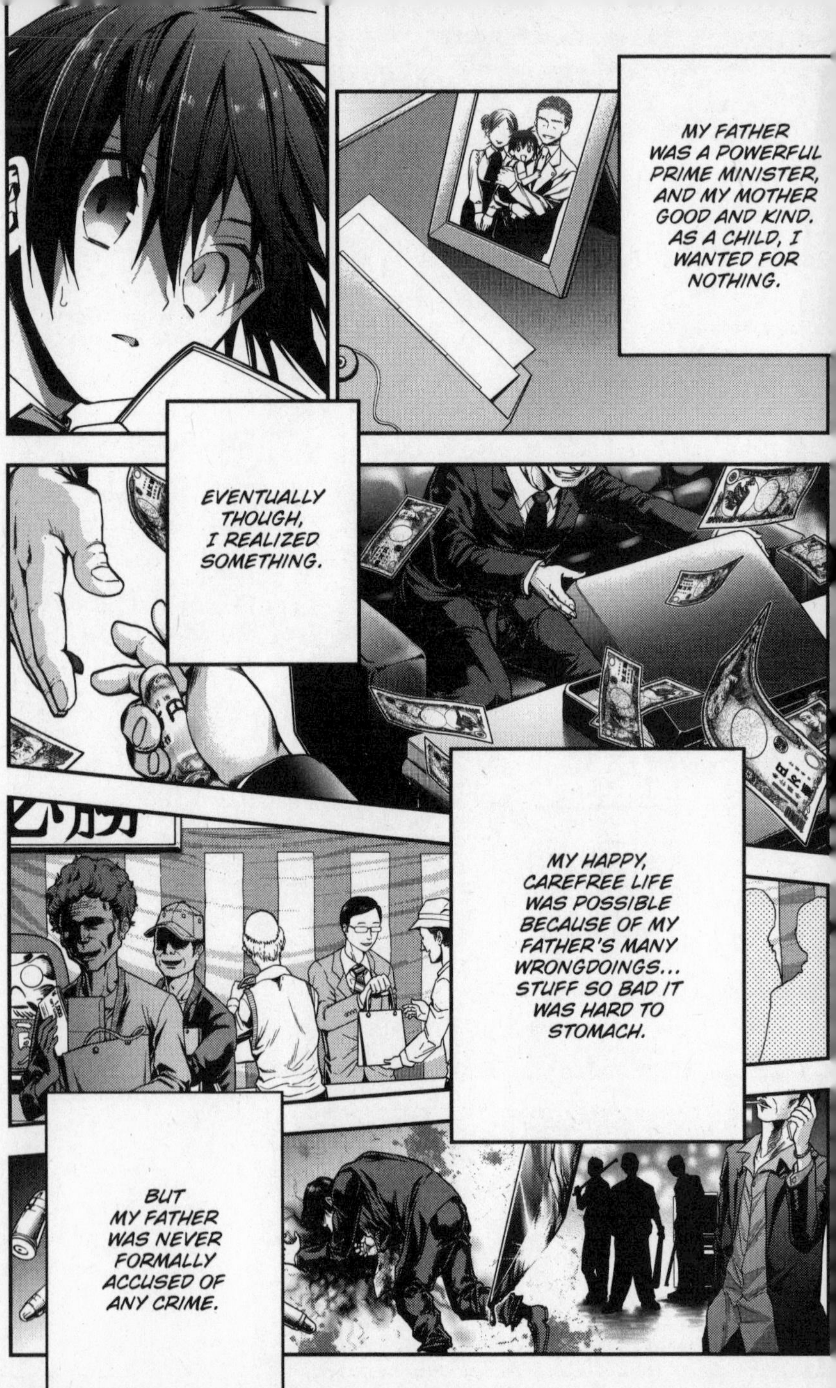
MY FATHER WAS A POWERFUL PRIME MINISTER, AND MY MOTHER GOOD AND KIND. AS A CHILD, I WANTED FOR NOTHING.
EVENTUALLY THOUGH, I REALIZED SOMETHING.
MY HAPPY, CAREFREE LIFE WAS POSSIBLE BECAUSE OF MY FATHER'S MANY WRONGDOINGS... STUFF SO BAD IT WAS HARD TO STOMACH.
BUT MY FATHER WAS NEVER FORMALLY ACCUSED OF ANY CRIME.

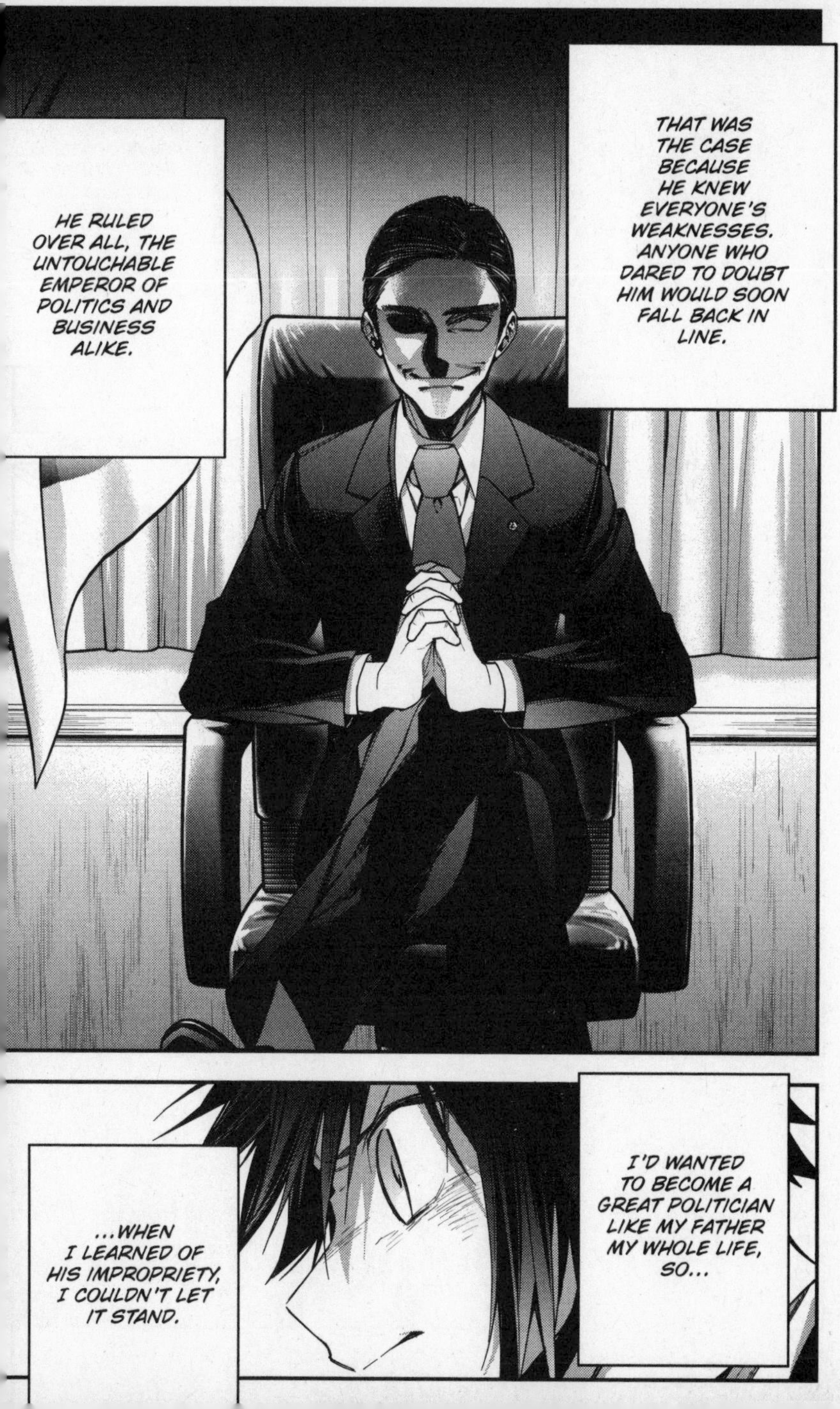
THAT WAS THE CASE BECAUSE HE KNEW EVERYONE'S WEAKNESSES. ANYONE WHO DARED TO DOUBT HIM WOULD SOON FALL BACK IN LINE.
HE RULED OVER ALL, THE UNTOUCHABLE EMPEROR OF POLITICS AND BUSINESS ALIKE.
I'D WANTED TO BECOME A GREAT POLITICIAN LIKE MY FATHER MY WHOLE LIFE, SO...
...WHEN I LEARNED OF HIS IMPROPRIETY, I COULDN'T LET IT STAND.

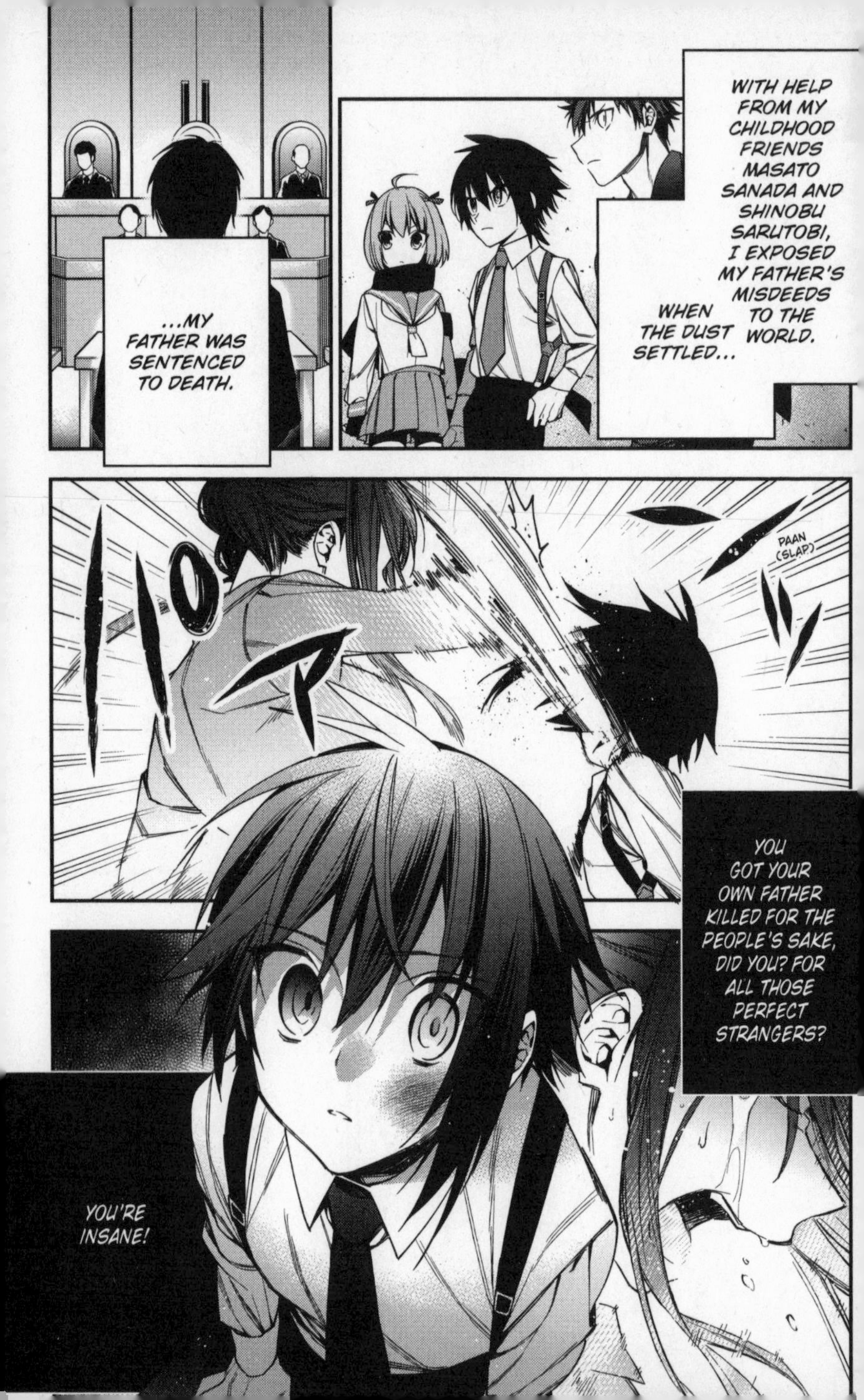
WITH HELP FROM MY CHILDHOOD FRIENDS MASATO SANADA AND SHINOBU SARUTOBI, I EXPOSED MY FATHER'S MISDEEDS TO THE WORLD.
WHEN THE DUST SETTLED...
...MY FATHER WAS SENTENCED TO DEATH.
PAAN (SLAP)
YOU GOT YOUR OWN FATHER KILLED FOR THE PEOPLE'S SAKE, DID YOU? FOR ALL THOSE PERFECT STRANGERS?
YOU'RE INSANE!

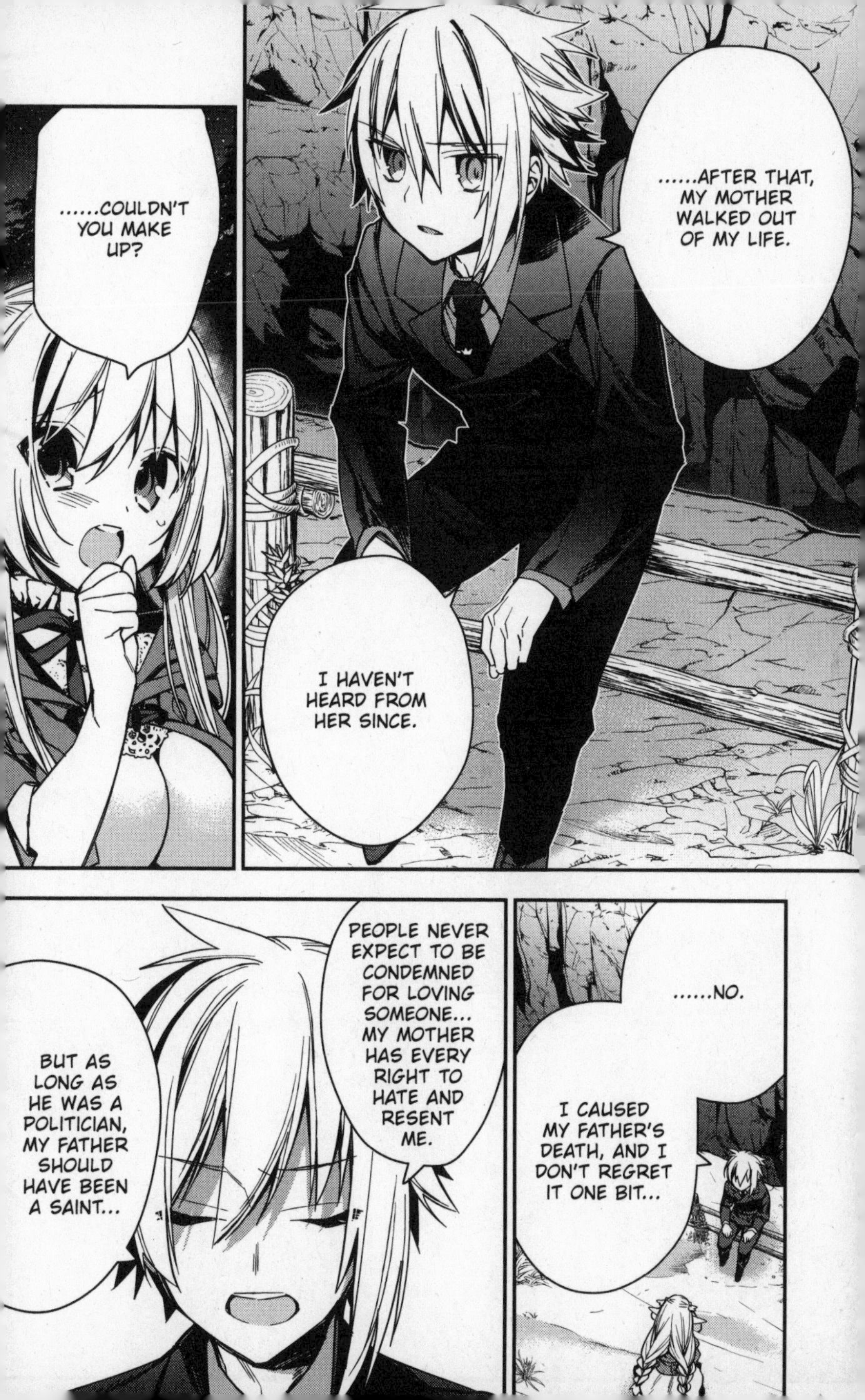
......AFTER THAT, MY MOTHER WALKED OUT OF MY LIFE.
I HAVEN'T HEARD FROM HER SINCE.
......COULDN'T YOU MAKE UP?
......NO.
I CAUSED MY FATHER'S DEATH, AND I DON'T REGRET IT ONE BIT...
PEOPLE NEVER EXPECT TO BE CONDEMNED FOR LOVING SOMEONE... MY MOTHER HAS EVERY RIGHT TO HATE AND RESENT ME.
BUT AS LONG AS HE WAS A POLITICIAN, MY FATHER SHOULD HAVE BEEN A SAINT...

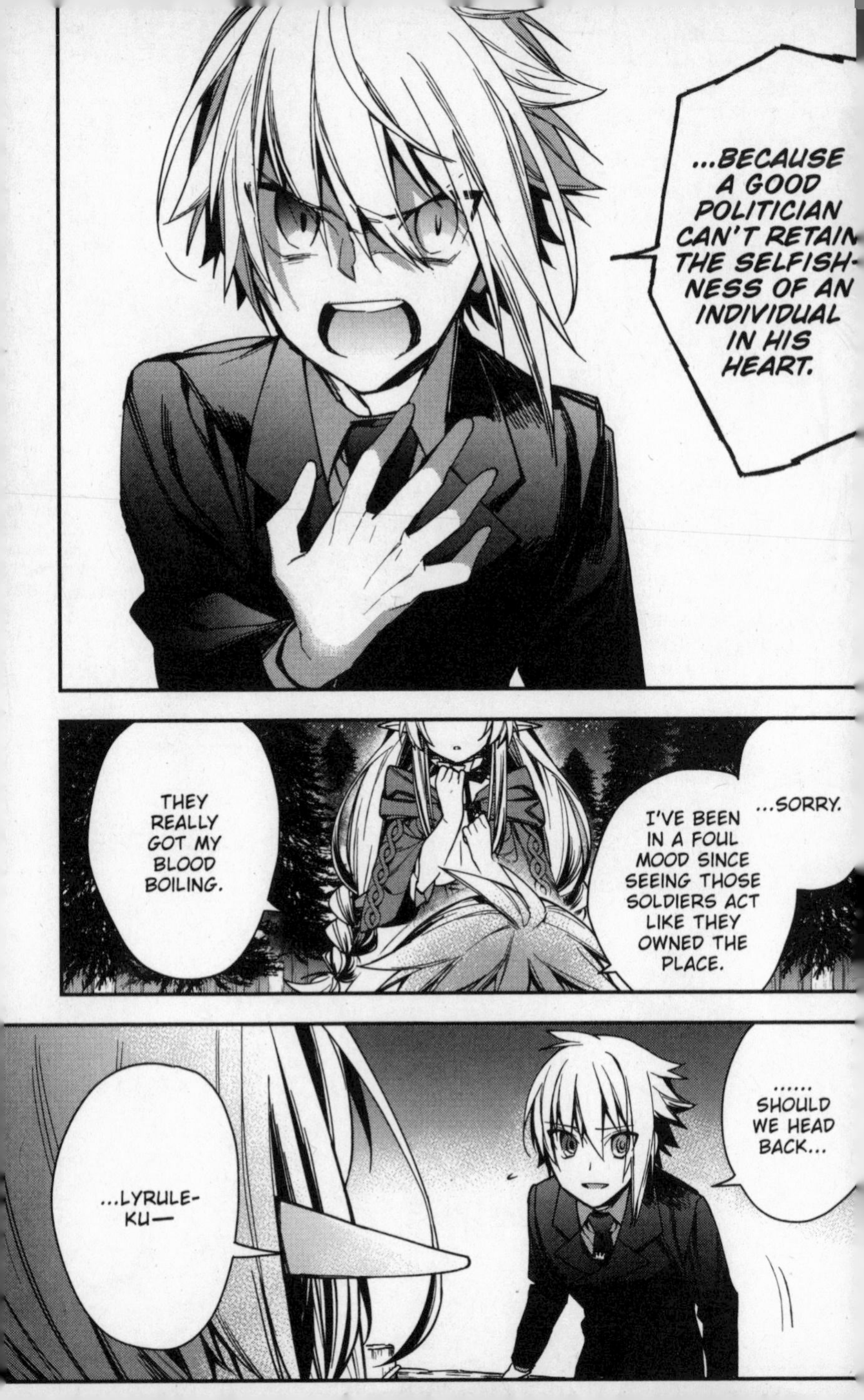
...BECAUSE A GOOD POLITICIAN CAN'T RETAIN THE SELFISH-NESS OF AN INDIVIDUAL IN HIS HEART.
...SORRY.
I'VE BEEN IN A FOUL MOOD SINCE SEEING THOSE SOLDIERS ACT LIKE THEY OWNED THE PLACE.
THEY REALLY GOT MY BLOOD BOILING.
......SHOULD WE HEAD BACK...
...LYRULE-KU—

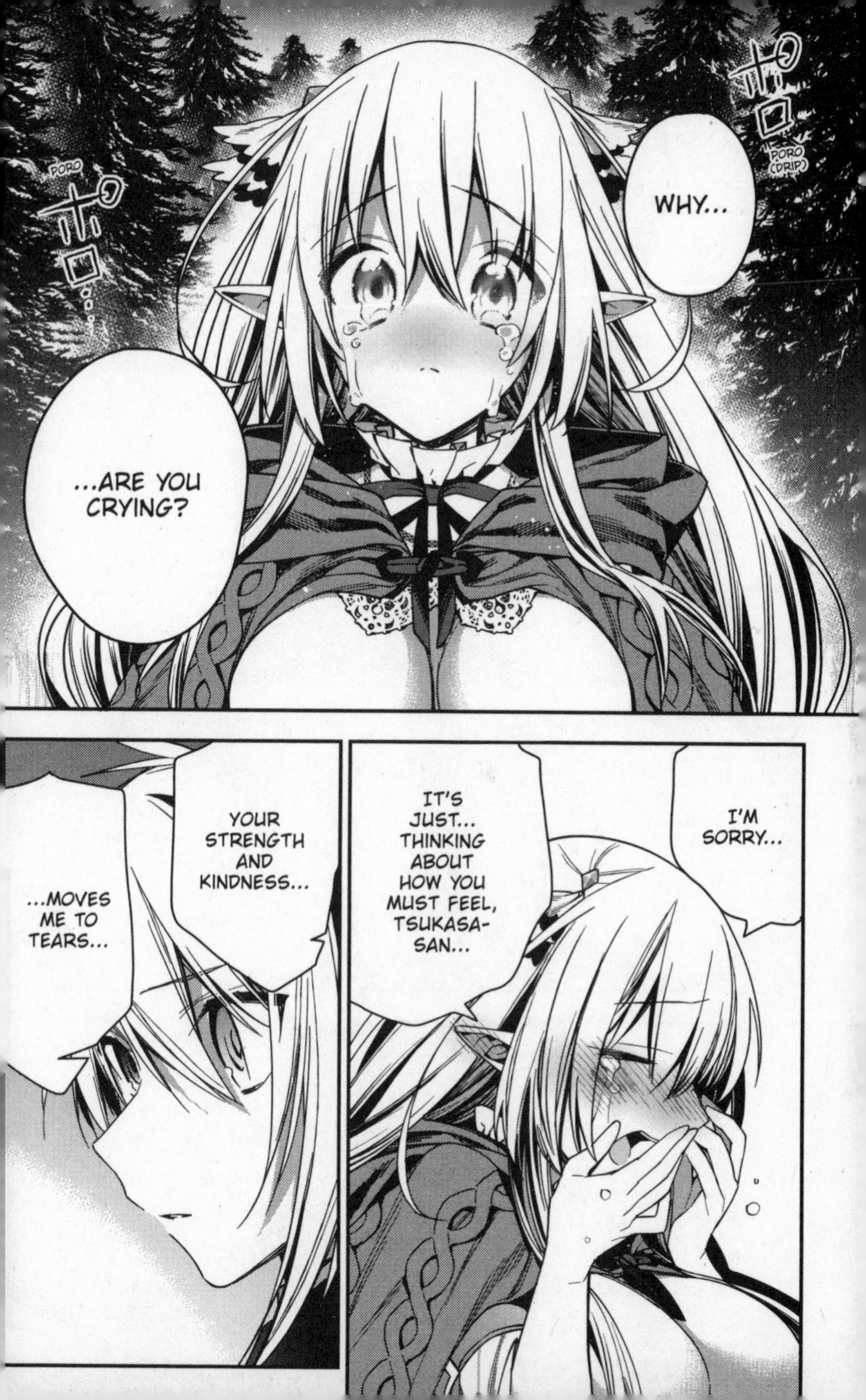

PORO (DRIP)
WHY...
PORO
...ARE YOU CRYING?
I'M SORRY...
IT'S JUST... THINKING ABOUT HOW YOU MUST FEEL, TSUKASA-SAN...
YOUR STRENGTH AND KINDNESS...
...MOVES ME TO TEARS...

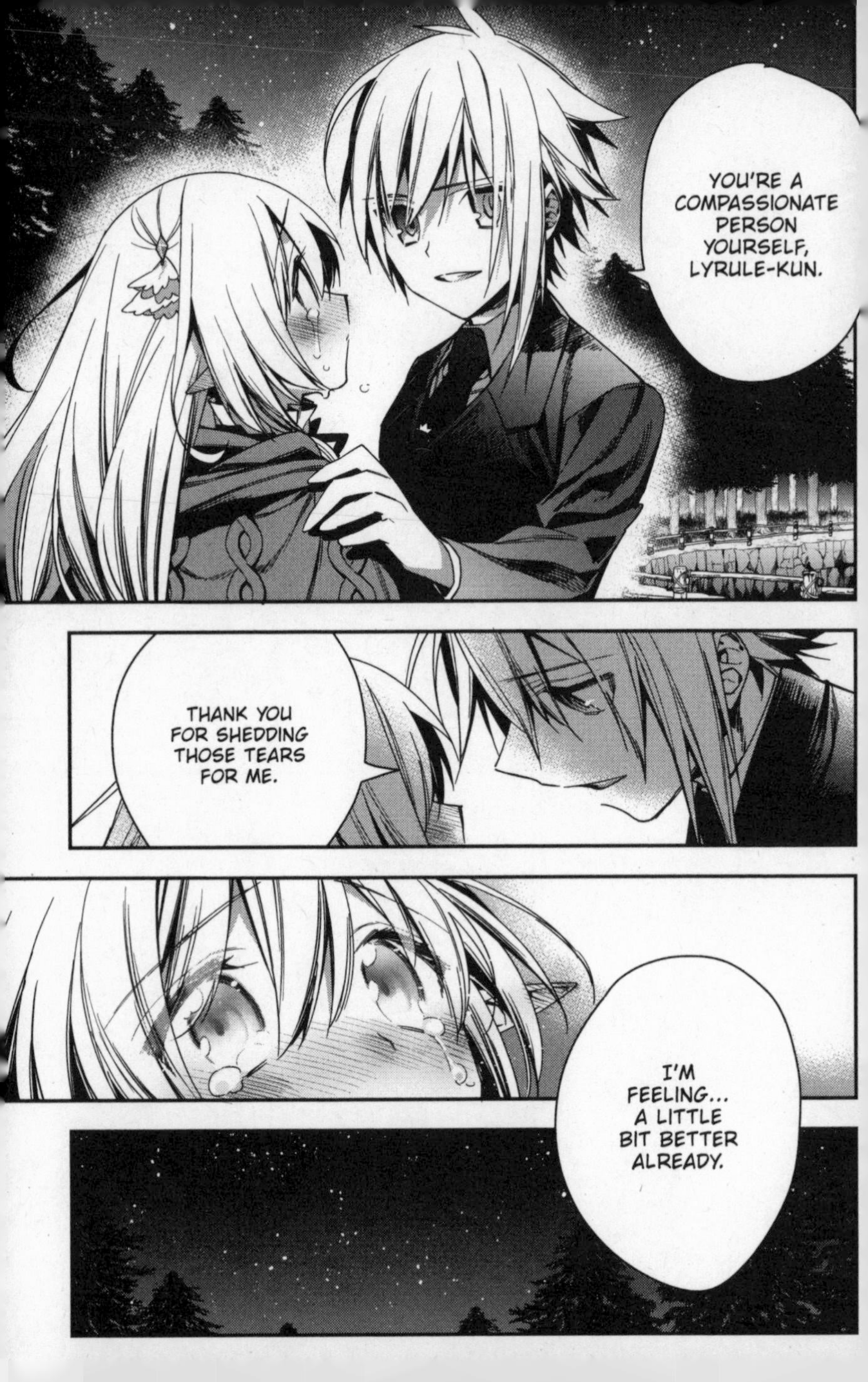
YOU'RE A COMPASSIONATE PERSON YOURSELF, LYRULE-KUN.
THANK YOU FOR SHEDDING THOSE TEARS FOR ME.
I'M FEELING... A LITTLE BIT BETTER ALREADY.

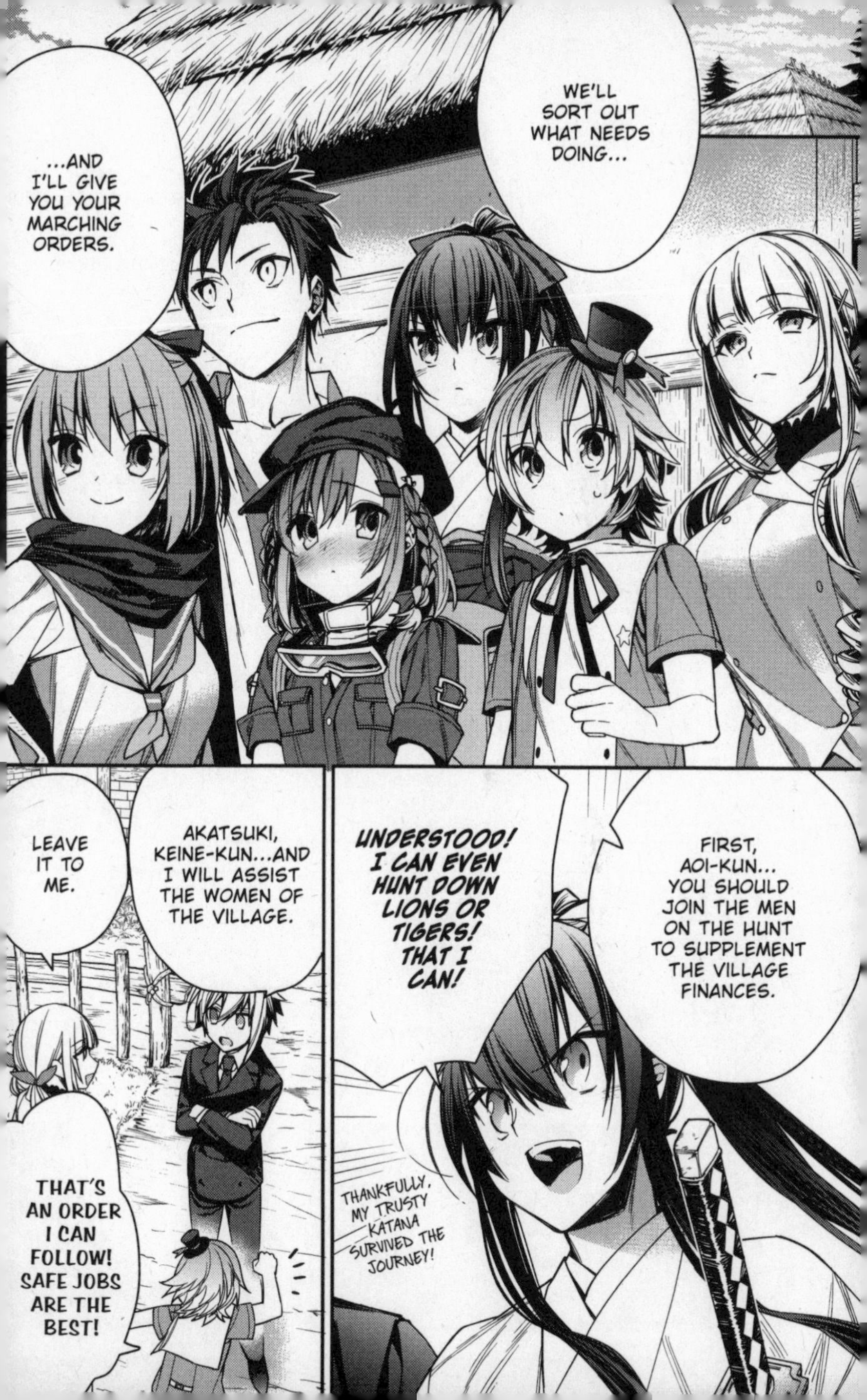
WE'LL SORT OUT WHAT NEEDS DOING...
...AND I'LL GIVE YOU YOUR MARCHING ORDERS.
FIRST, AOI-KUN... YOU SHOULD JOIN THE MEN ON THE HUNT TO SUPPLEMENT THE VILLAGE FINANCES.
UNDERSTOOD! I CAN EVEN HUNT DOWN LIONS OR TIGERS! THAT I CAN!
THANKFULLY, MY TRUSTY KATANA SURVIVED THE JOURNEY!
AKATSUKI, KEINE-KUN...AND I WILL ASSIST THE WOMEN OF THE VILLAGE.
LEAVE IT TO ME.
THAT'S AN ORDER I CAN FOLLOW! SAFE JOBS ARE THE BEST!

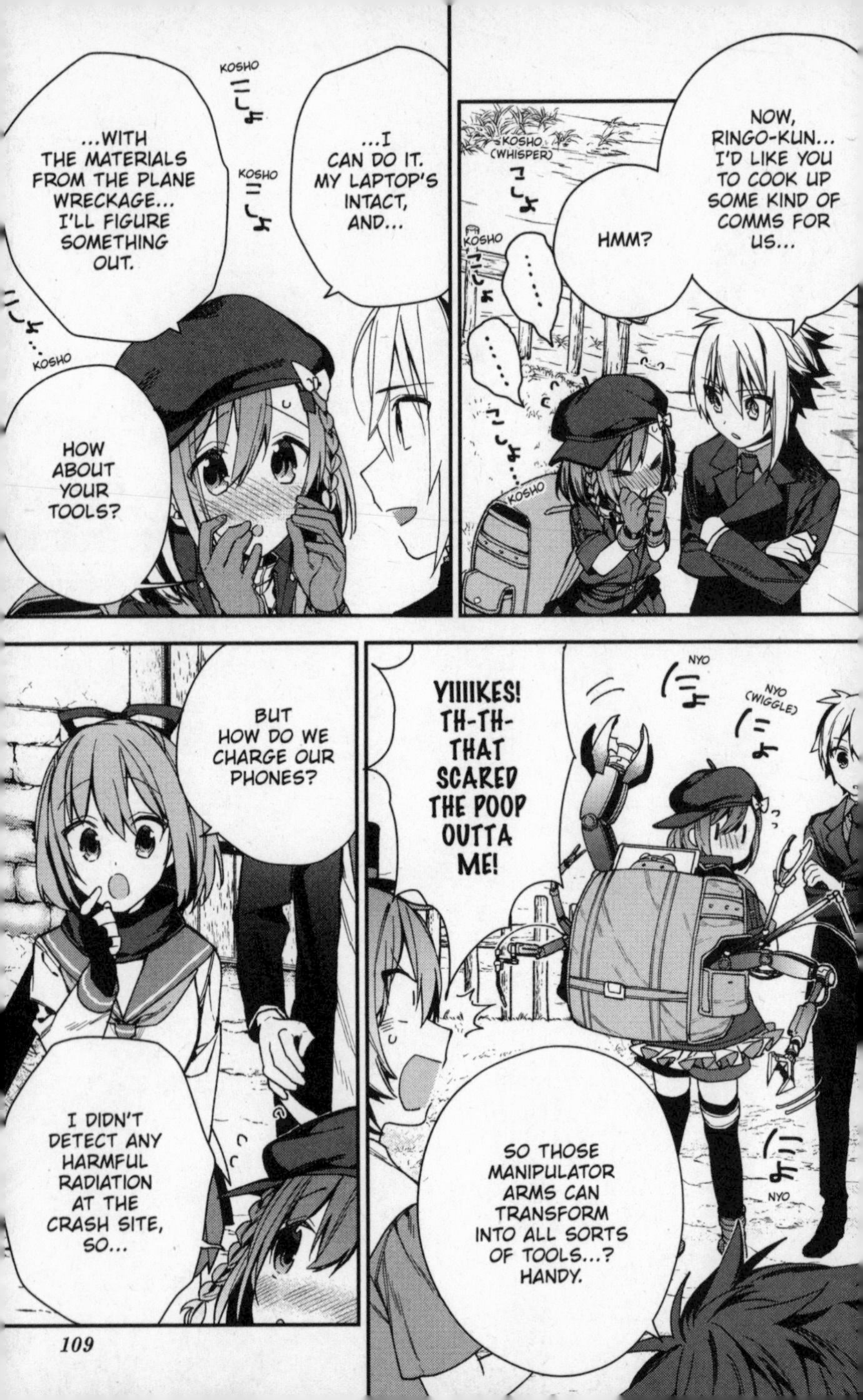
NOW, RINGO-KUN... I'D LIKE YOU TO COOK UP SOME KIND OF COMMS FOR US...
HMM?
......
......
KOSHO (WHISPER)
KOSHO
KOSHO
...I CAN DO IT. MY LAPTOP'S INTACT, AND...
KOSHO
KOSHO
...WITH THE MATERIALS FROM THE PLANE WRECKAGE... I'LL FIGURE SOMETHING OUT.
KOSHO
HOW ABOUT YOUR TOOLS?
NYO
NYO (WIGGLE)
YIIIIKES! TH-TH-THAT SCARED THE POOP OUTTA ME!
NYO
SO THOSE MANIPULATOR ARMS CAN TRANSFORM INTO ALL SORTS OF TOOLS...? HANDY.
BUT HOW DO WE CHARGE OUR PHONES?
I DIDN'T DETECT ANY HARMFUL RADIATION AT THE CRASH SITE, SO...

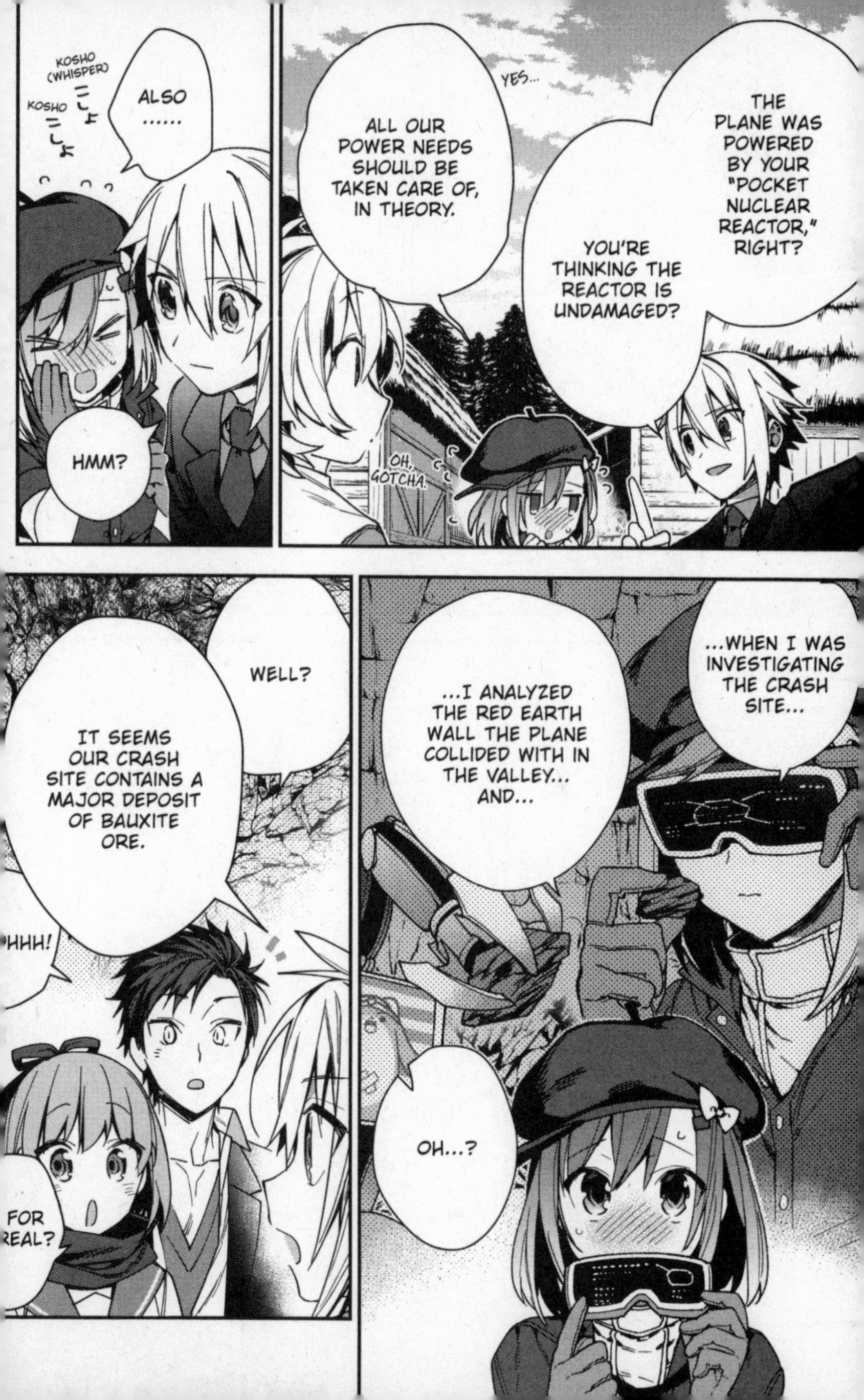
THE PLANE WAS POWERED BY YOUR "POCKET NUCLEAR REACTOR," RIGHT?
YOU'RE THINKING THE REACTOR IS UNDAMAGED?
YES...
ALL OUR POWER NEEDS SHOULD BE TAKEN CARE OF, IN THEORY.
OH, GOTCHA.
ALSO ......
KOSHO (WHISPER)
こしょ
KOSHO
こしょ
HMM?
...WHEN I WAS INVESTIGATING THE CRASH SITE...
...I ANALYZED THE RED EARTH WALL THE PLANE COLLIDED WITH IN THE VALLEY... AND...
OH...?
WELL?
IT SEEMS OUR CRASH SITE CONTAINS A MAJOR DEPOSIT OF BAUXITE ORE.
HHH!
FOR REAL?

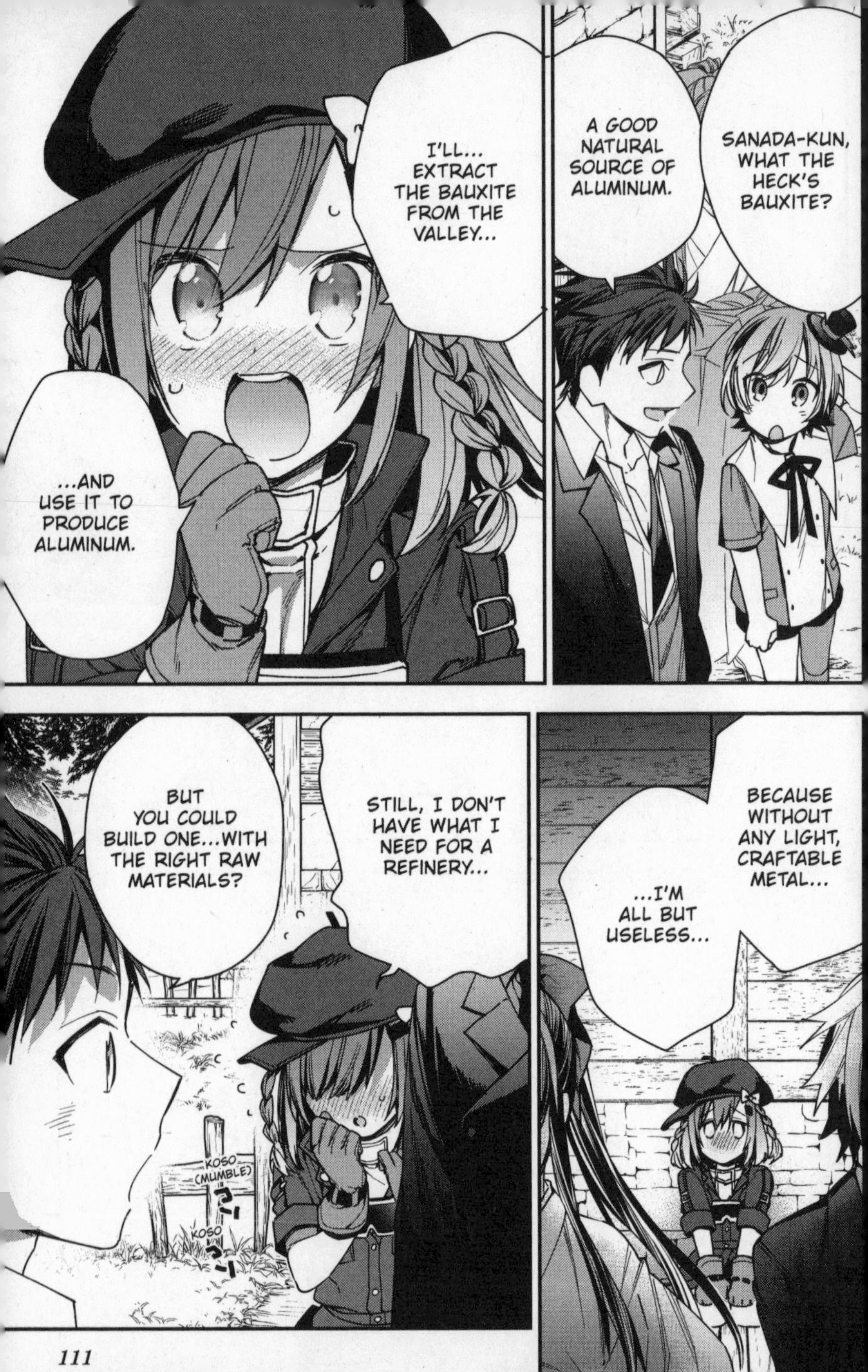
SANADA-KUN, WHAT THE HECK'S BAUXITE?
A GOOD NATURAL SOURCE OF ALUMINUM.
I'LL... EXTRACT THE BAUXITE FROM THE VALLEY...
...AND USE IT TO PRODUCE ALUMINUM.
BECAUSE WITHOUT ANY LIGHT, CRAFTABLE METAL...
...I'M ALL BUT USELESS...
STILL, I DON'T HAVE WHAT I NEED FOR A REFINERY...
BUT YOU COULD BUILD ONE...WITH THE RIGHT RAW MATERIALS?
KOSO (MUMBLE)
KOSO

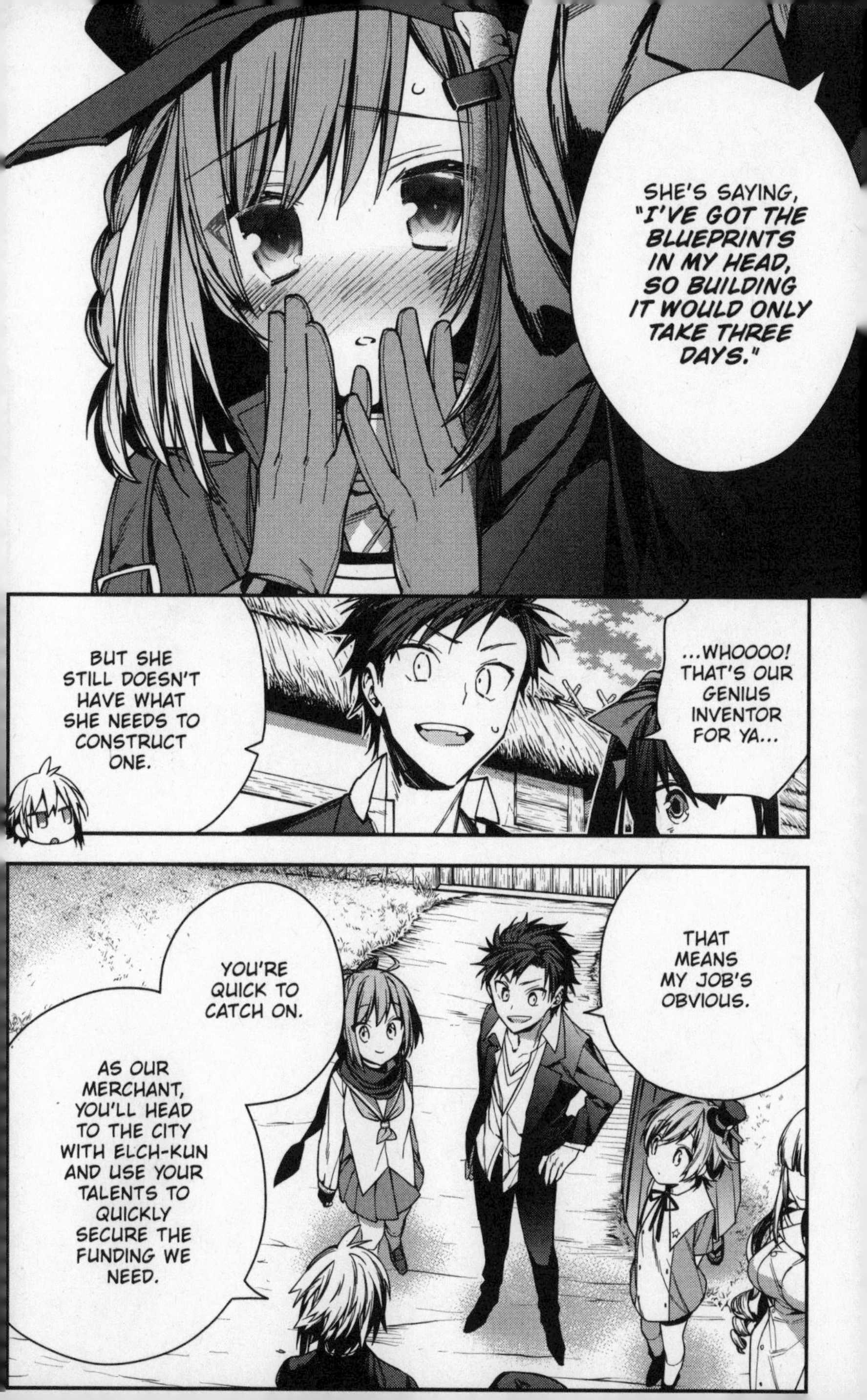
SHE'S SAYING, "I'VE GOT THE BLUEPRINTS IN MY HEAD, SO BUILDING IT WOULD ONLY TAKE THREE DAYS."
...WHOOOO! THAT'S OUR GENIUS INVENTOR FOR YA...
BUT SHE STILL DOESN'T HAVE WHAT SHE NEEDS TO CONSTRUCT ONE.
THAT MEANS MY JOB'S OBVIOUS.
YOU'RE QUICK TO CATCH ON.
AS OUR MERCHANT, YOU'LL HEAD TO THE CITY WITH ELCH-KUN AND USE YOUR TALENTS TO QUICKLY SECURE THE FUNDING WE NEED.

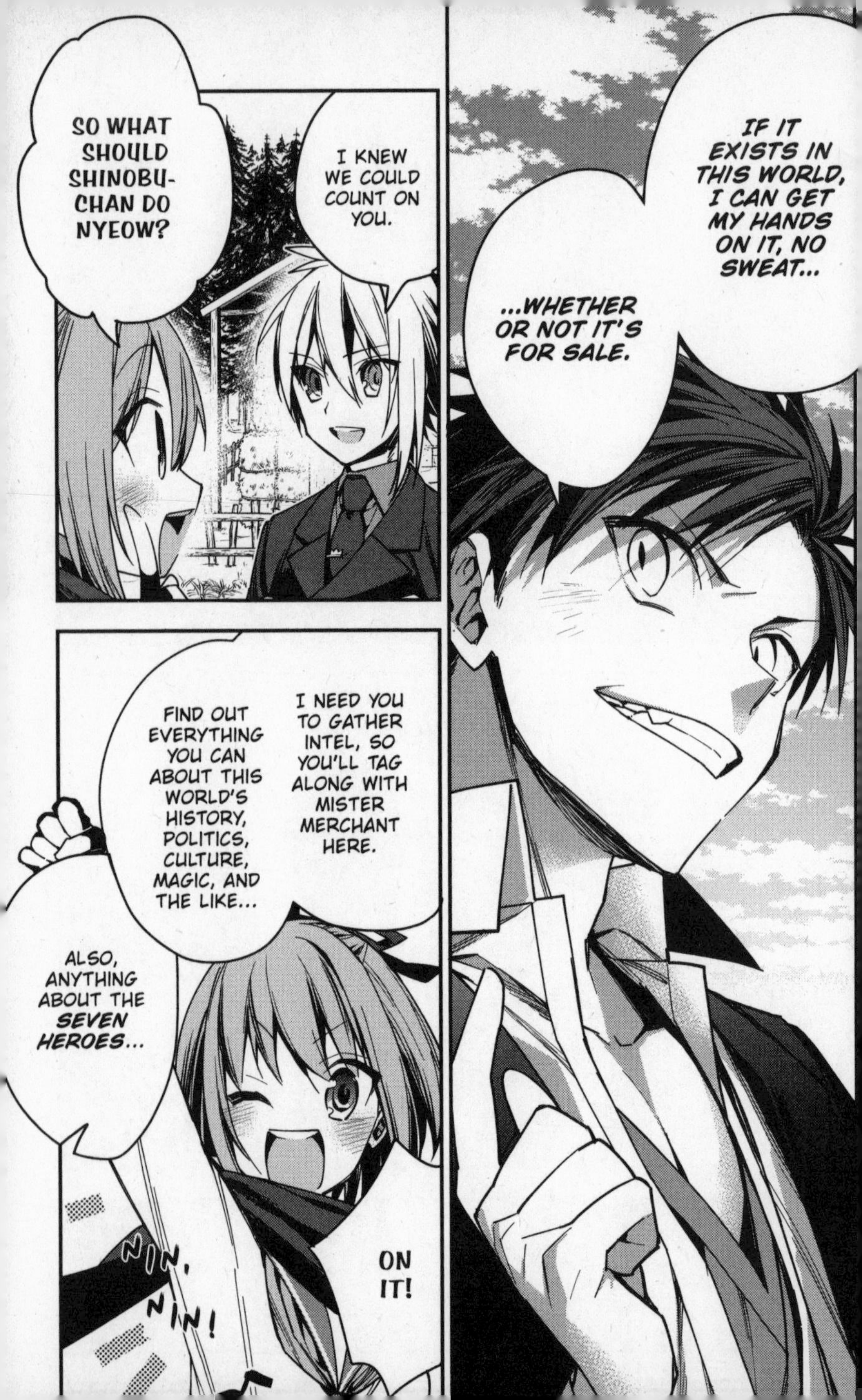
IF IT EXISTS IN THIS WORLD, I CAN GET MY HANDS ON IT, NO SWEAT...
...WHETHER OR NOT IT'S FOR SALE.
I KNEW WE COULD COUNT ON YOU.
SO WHAT SHOULD SHINOBU-CHAN DO NYEOW?
I NEED YOU TO GATHER INTEL, SO YOU'LL TAG ALONG WITH MISTER MERCHANT HERE.
FIND OUT EVERYTHING YOU CAN ABOUT THIS WORLD'S HISTORY, POLITICS, CULTURE, MAGIC, AND THE LIKE...
ALSO, ANYTHING ABOUT THE SEVEN HEROES...
ON IT!
NIN, NIN!

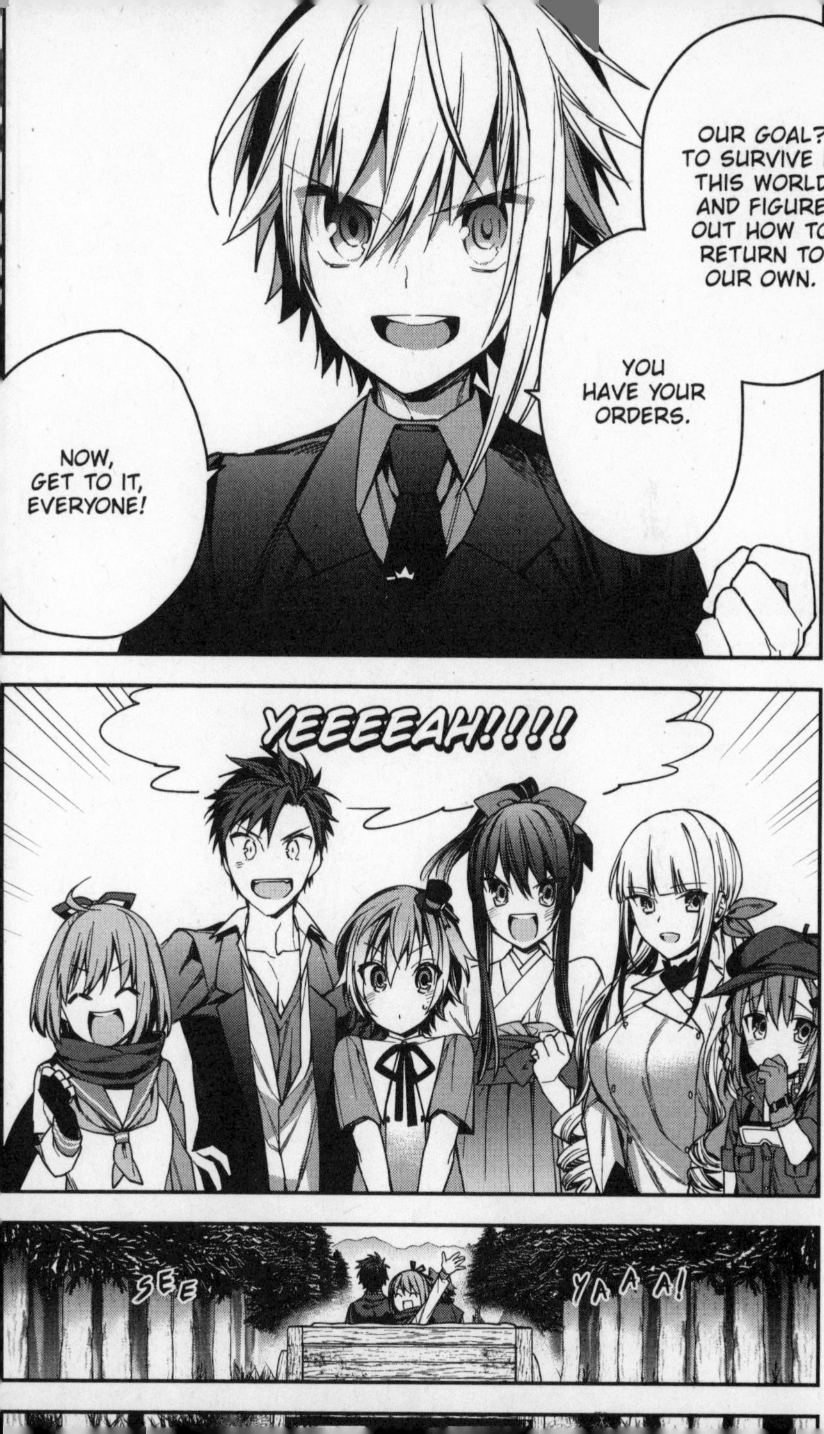
OUR GOAL? TO SURVIVE IN THIS WORLD AND FIGURE OUT HOW TO RETURN TO OUR OWN.
YOU HAVE YOUR ORDERS.
NOW, GET TO IT, EVERYONE!
YEEEEAH!!!!
YAAA!
SEE

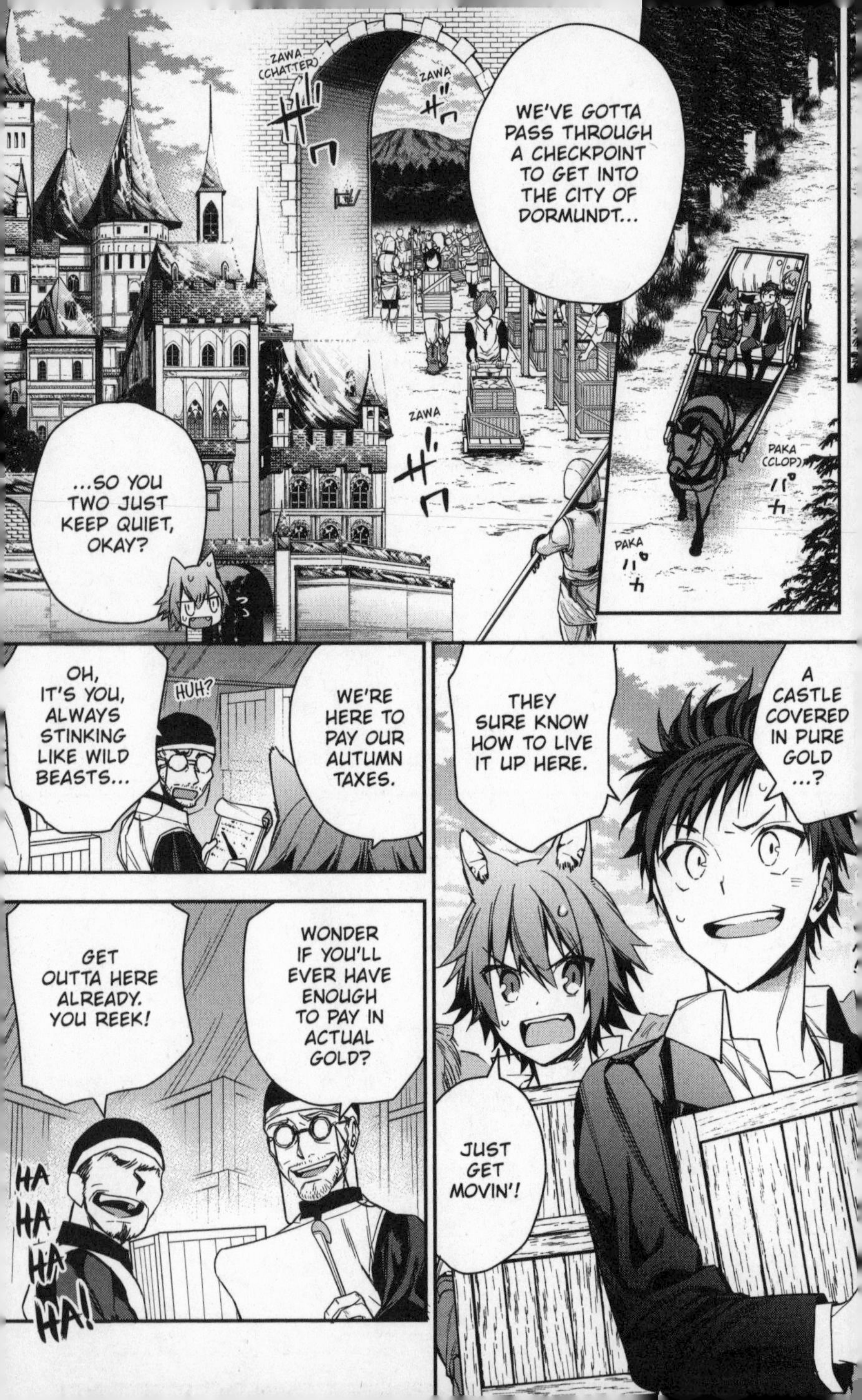
WE'VE GOTTA PASS THROUGH A CHECKPOINT TO GET INTO THE CITY OF DORMUNDT...
PAKA (CLOP)
PAKA
ZAWA (CHATTER)
ZAWA
ZAWA
...SO YOU TWO JUST KEEP QUIET, OKAY?
A CASTLE COVERED IN PURE GOLD ...?
THEY SURE KNOW HOW TO LIVE IT UP HERE.
JUST GET MOVIN'!
WE'RE HERE TO PAY OUR AUTUMN TAXES.
HUH?
OH, IT'S YOU, ALWAYS STINKING LIKE WILD BEASTS...
WONDER IF YOU'LL EVER HAVE ENOUGH TO PAY IN ACTUAL GOLD?
GET OUTTA HERE ALREADY. YOU REEK!
HA HA HA HA!

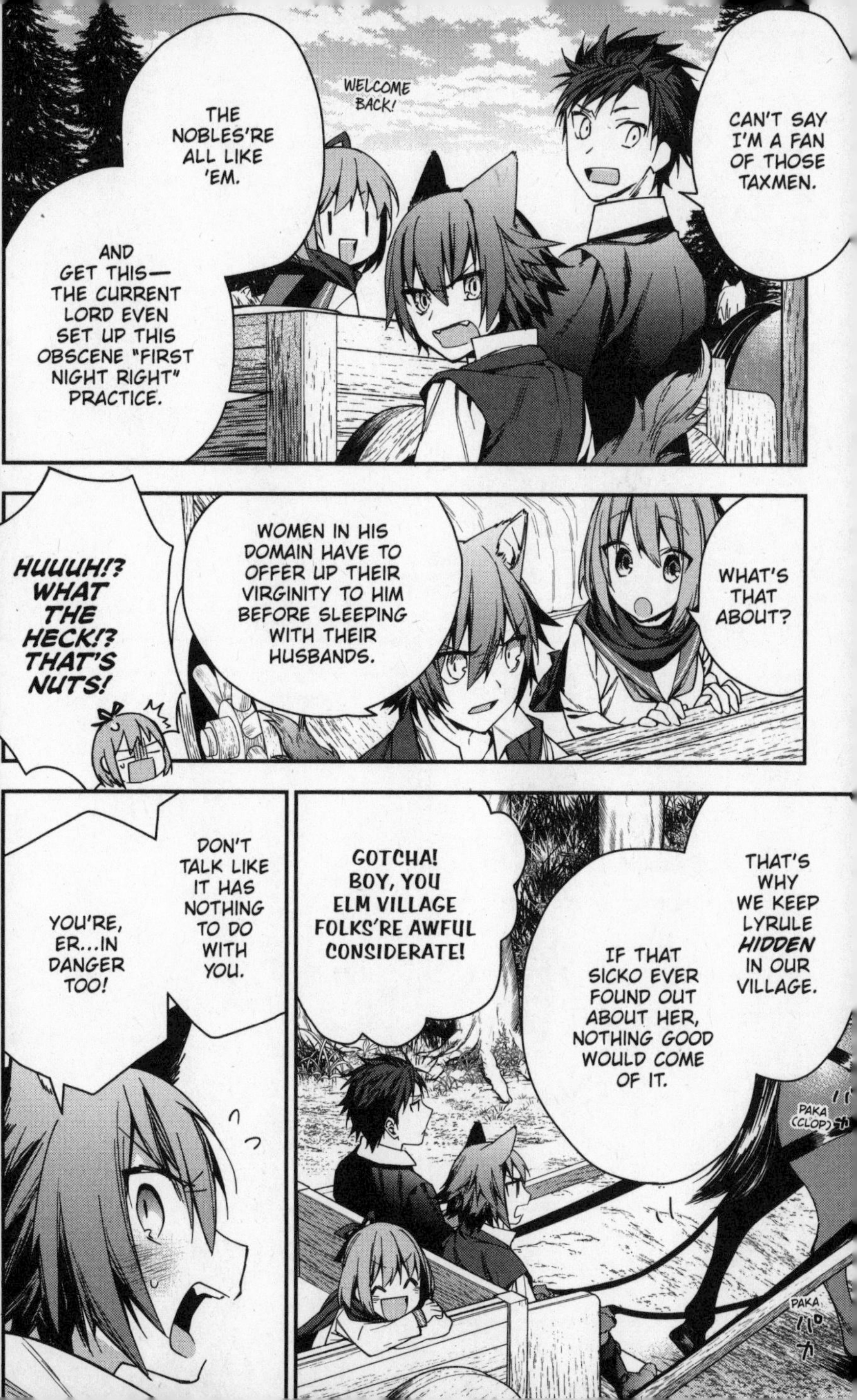
CAN'T SAY I'M A FAN OF THOSE TAXMEN.
WELCOME BACK!
THE NOBLES'RE ALL LIKE 'EM.
AND GET THIS—THE CURRENT LORD EVEN SET UP THIS OBSCENE "FIRST NIGHT RIGHT" PRACTICE.
WHAT'S THAT ABOUT?
WOMEN IN HIS DOMAIN HAVE TO OFFER UP THEIR VIRGINITY TO HIM BEFORE SLEEPING WITH THEIR HUSBANDS.
HUUUH!? WHAT THE HECK!? THAT'S NUTS!
THAT'S WHY WE KEEP LYRULE HIDDEN IN OUR VILLAGE.
IF THAT SICKO EVER FOUND OUT ABOUT HER, NOTHING GOOD WOULD COME OF IT.
PAKA (CLOP)
GOTCHA! BOY, YOU ELM VILLAGE FOLKS'RE AWFUL CONSIDERATE!
PAKA
DON'T TALK LIKE IT HAS NOTHING TO DO WITH YOU.
YOU'RE, ER...IN DANGER TOO!

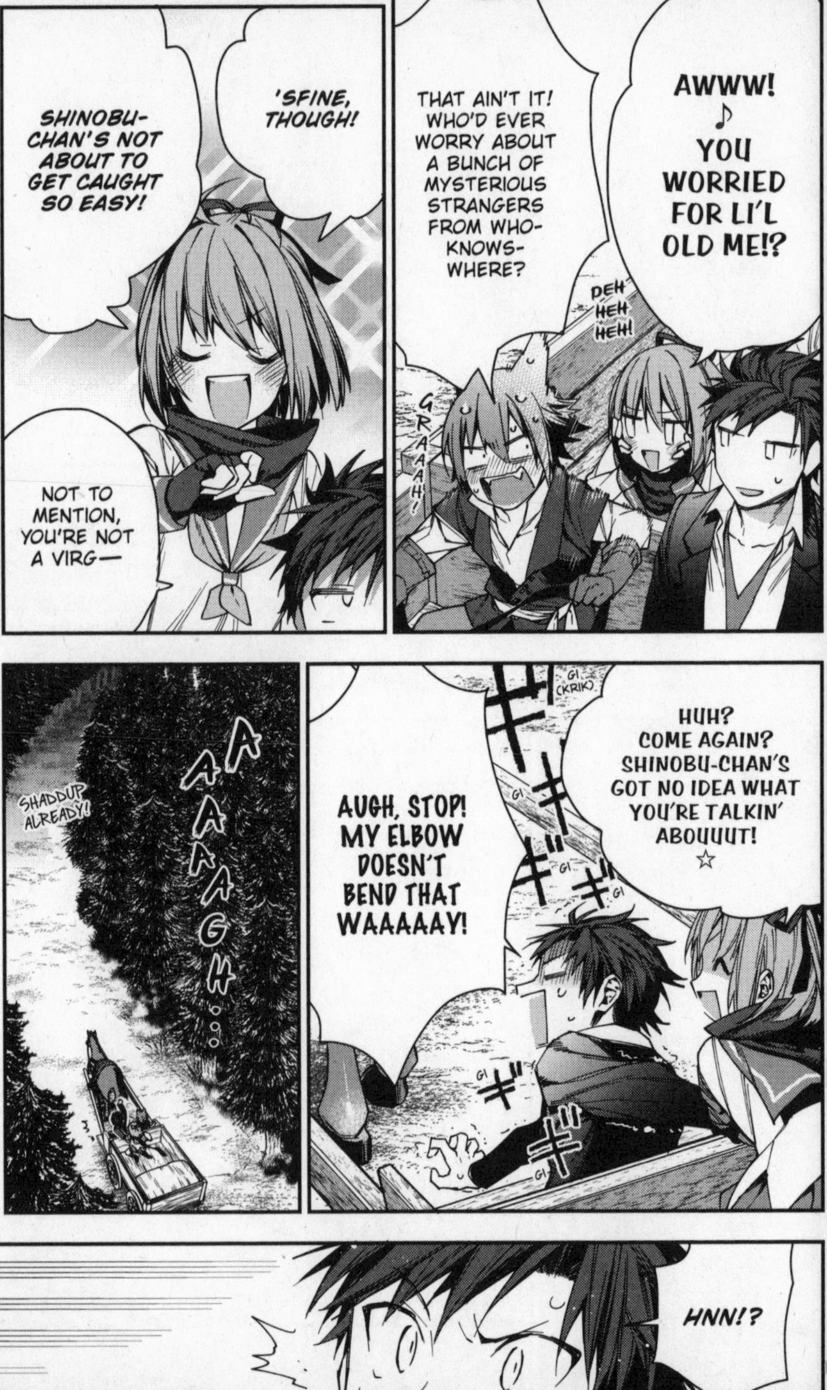
AWWW! ♪ YOU WORRIED FOR LI'L OLD ME!?
THAT AIN'T IT! WHO'D EVER WORRY ABOUT A BUNCH OF MYSTERIOUS STRANGERS FROM WHO-KNOWS-WHERE?
DEH HEH HEH!
GRAAAAH!
'SFINE, THOUGH!
SHINOBU-CHAN'S NOT ABOUT TO GET CAUGHT SO EASY!
NOT TO MENTION, YOU'RE NOT A VIRG—
HUH? COME AGAIN? SHINOBU-CHAN'S GOT NO IDEA WHAT YOU'RE TALKIN' ABOUUUT! ☆
GI (KRIK)
GI
GI
GI
AUGH, STOP! MY ELBOW DOESN'T BEND THAT WAAAAAY!
GI
GI
AAAAAGH...
SHADDUP ALREADY!
HNN!?

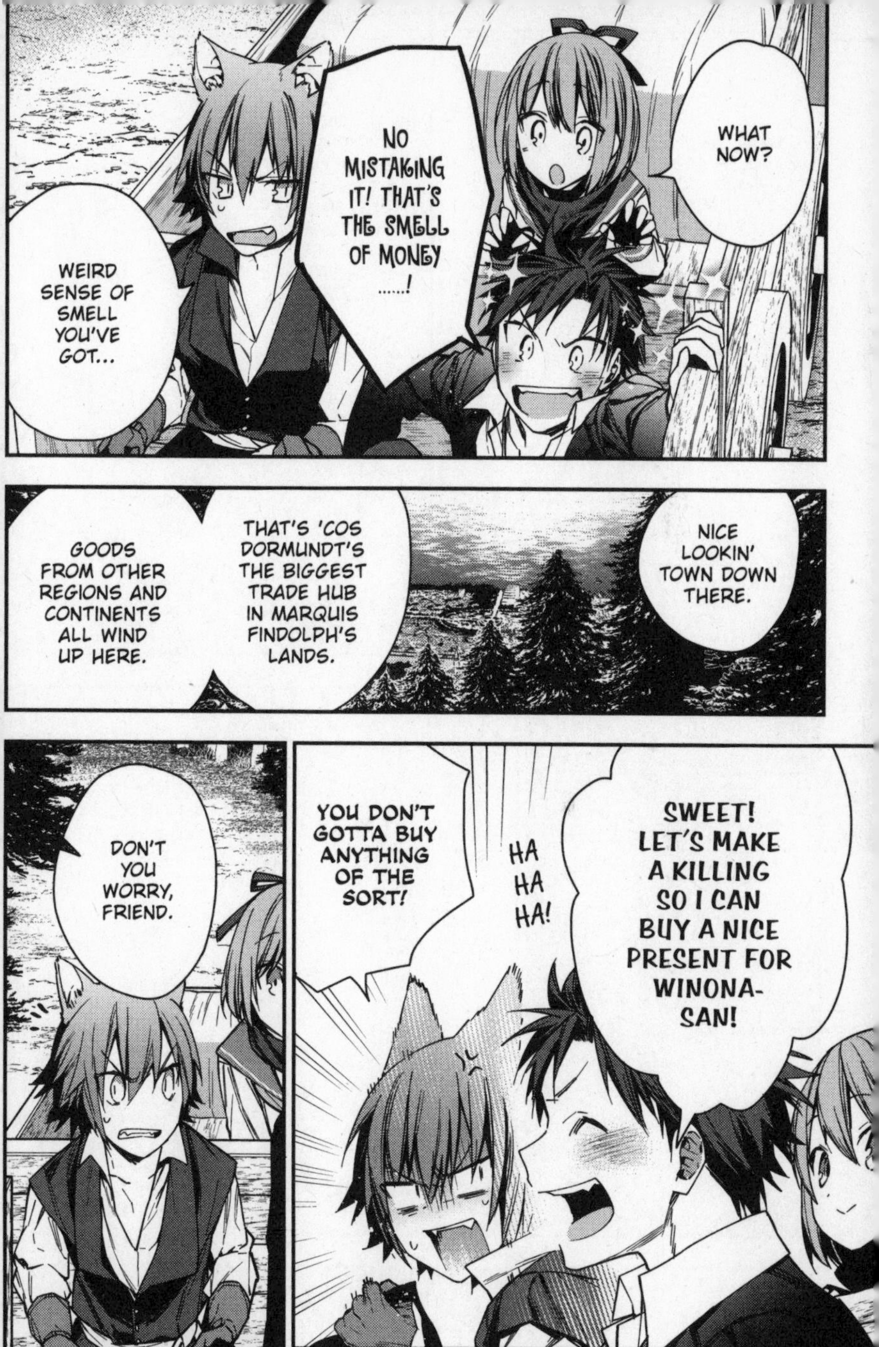
WHAT NOW?
NO MISTAKING IT! THAT'S THE SMELL OF MONEY ......!
WEIRD SENSE OF SMELL YOU'VE GOT...
NICE LOOKIN' TOWN DOWN THERE.
THAT'S 'COS DORMUNDT'S THE BIGGEST TRADE HUB IN MARQUIS FINDOLPH'S LANDS.
GOODS FROM OTHER REGIONS AND CONTINENTS ALL WIND UP HERE.
SWEET! LET'S MAKE A KILLING SO I CAN BUY A NICE PRESENT FOR WINONA-SAN!
HA HA HA!
YOU DON'T GOTTA BUY ANYTHING OF THE SORT!
DON'T YOU WORRY, FRIEND.

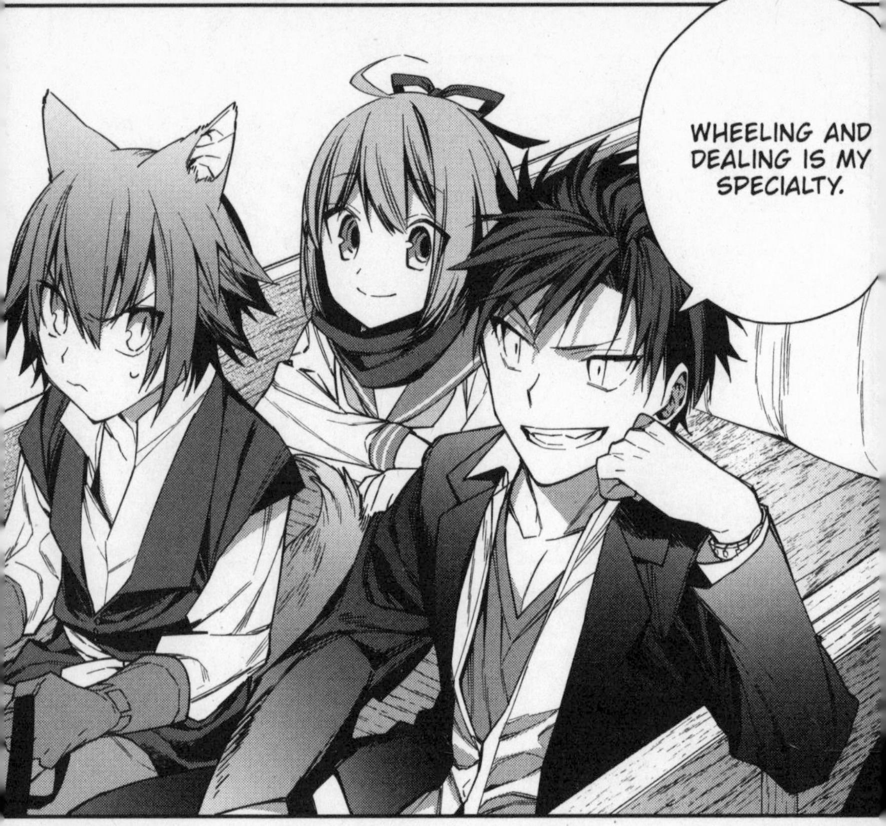
WHEELING AND DEALING IS MY SPECIALTY.
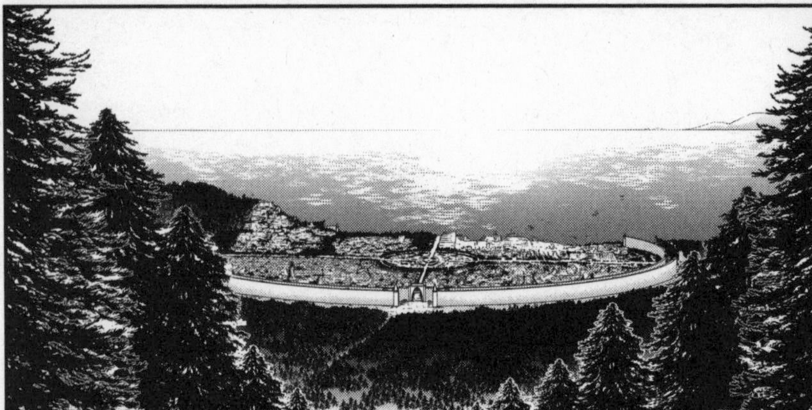

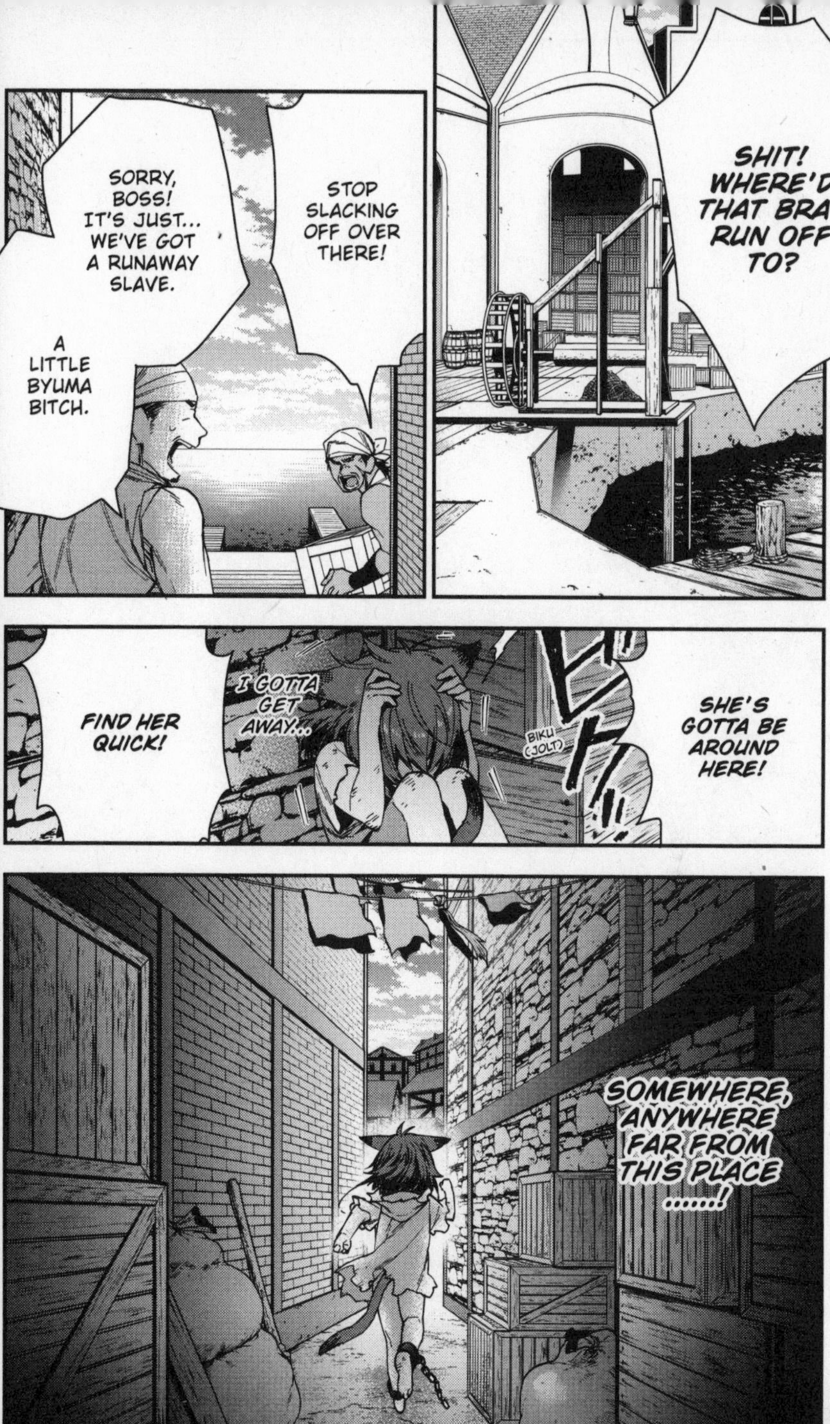
SHIT! WHERE'D THAT BRAT RUN OFF TO?
STOP SLACKING OFF OVER THERE!
SORRY, BOSS! IT'S JUST... WE'VE GOT A RUNAWAY SLAVE.
A LITTLE BYUMA BITCH.
SHE'S GOTTA BE AROUND HERE!
BIKU (JOLT)
I GOTTA GET AWAY...
FIND HER QUICK!
SOMEWHERE, ANYWHERE FAR FROM THIS PLACE ......!

HIGH SCHOOL
PRODIGIES HAVE
IT EASY EVEN IN
ANOTHER
WORLD!

CHARACTER FILE 05

Ringo Oohoshi

One of the high school prodigies. The brain behind the "pocket nuclear fission reactor," the "nuclear waste neutralizer," and other such inventions that are centuries ahead of their time. She had an unrequited crush on Tsukasa in middle school.

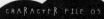

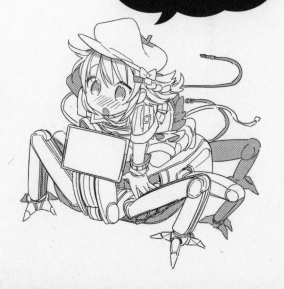

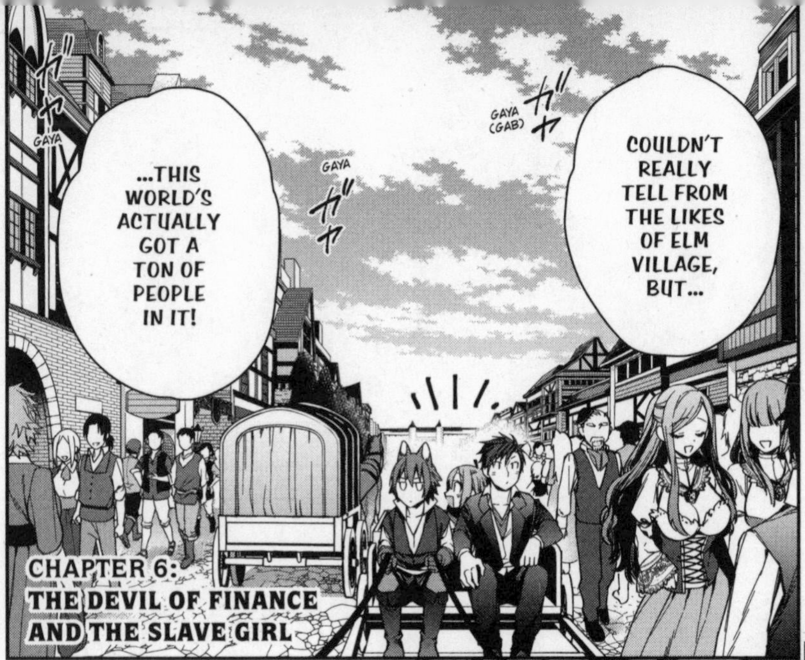
GAYA (GAB)
COULDN'T REALLY TELL FROM THE LIKES OF ELM VILLAGE, BUT...
GAYA
GAYA
...THIS WORLD'S ACTUALLY GOT A TON OF PEOPLE IN IT!

CHAPTER 6: THE DEVIL OF FINANCE AND THE SLAVE GIRL

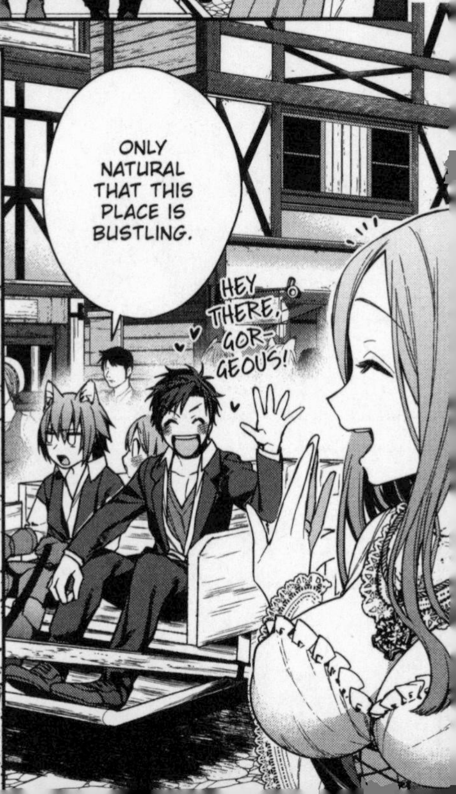
ONLY NATURAL THAT THIS PLACE IS BUSTLING.
HEY THERE, GORGEOUS!

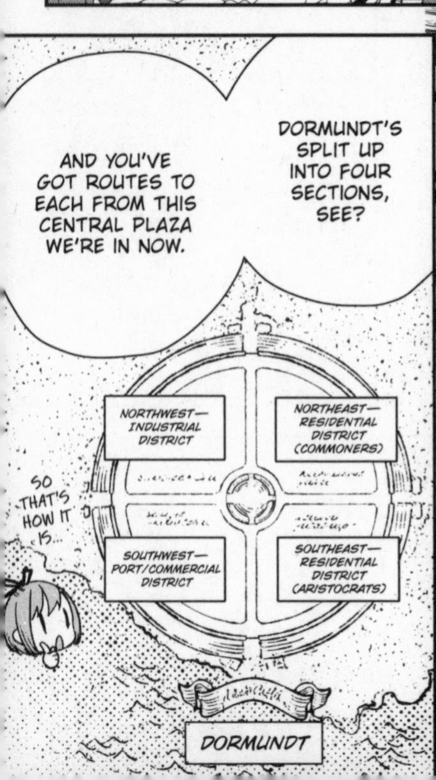
DORMUNDT'S SPLIT UP INTO FOUR SECTIONS, SEE?
AND YOU'VE GOT ROUTES TO EACH FROM THIS CENTRAL PLAZA WE'RE IN NOW.
NORTHWEST—INDUSTRIAL DISTRICT
NORTHEAST—RESIDENTIAL DISTRICT (COMMONERS)
SOUTHWEST—PORT/COMMERCIAL DISTRICT
SOUTHEAST—RESIDENTIAL DISTRICT (ARISTOCRATS)
DORMUNDT
SO THAT'S HOW IT IS...

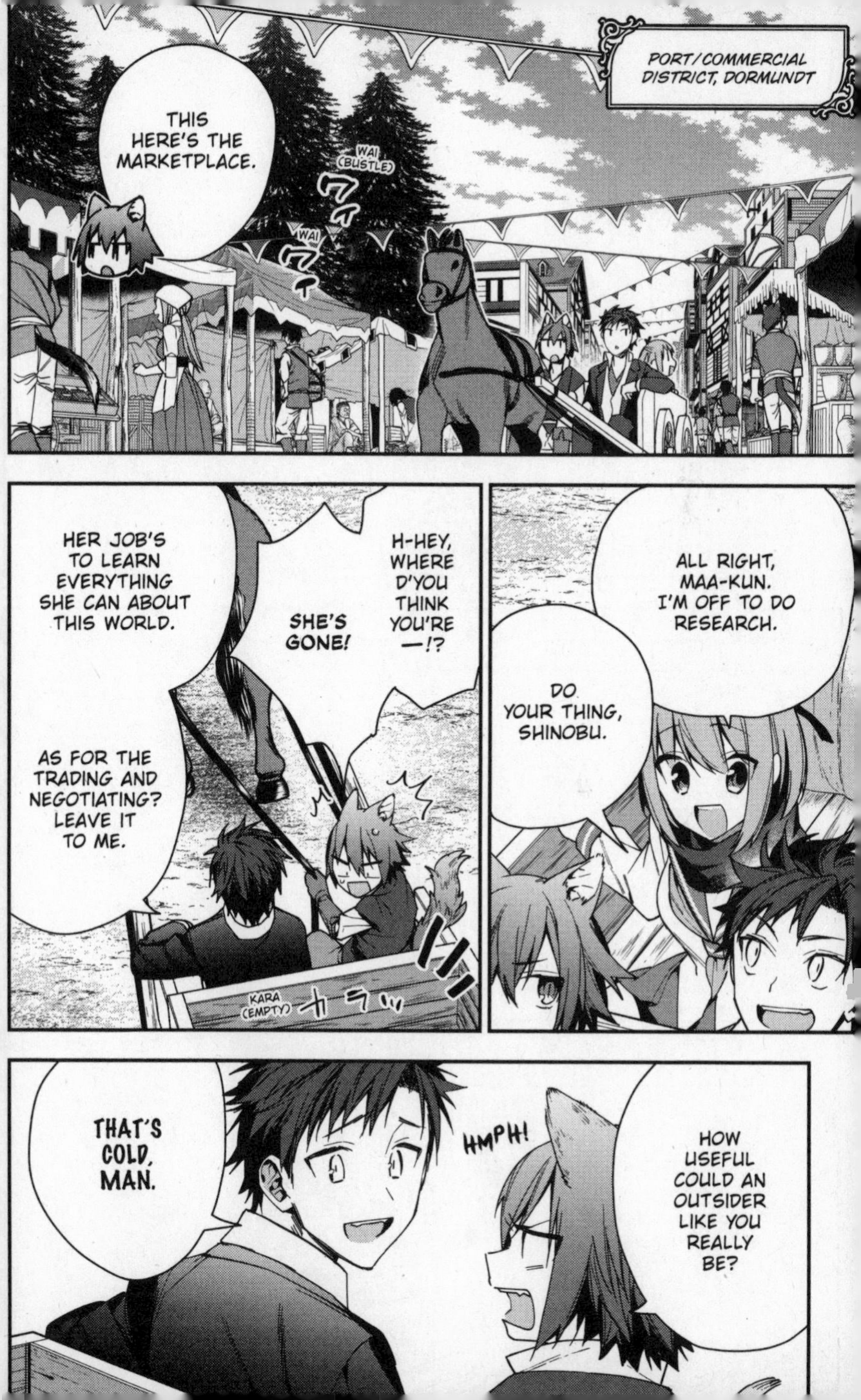
PORT/COMMERCIAL DISTRICT, DORMUNDT
WAI (BUSTLE)
WAI
THIS HERE'S THE MARKETPLACE.
ALL RIGHT, MAA-KUN. I'M OFF TO DO RESEARCH.
DO YOUR THING, SHINOBU.
H-HEY, WHERE D'YOU THINK YOU'RE —!?
SHE'S GONE!
HER JOB'S TO LEARN EVERYTHING SHE CAN ABOUT THIS WORLD.
AS FOR THE TRADING AND NEGOTIATING? LEAVE IT TO ME.
KARA (EMPTY)
HOW USEFUL COULD AN OUTSIDER LIKE YOU REALLY BE?
HMPH!
THAT'S COLD, MAN.

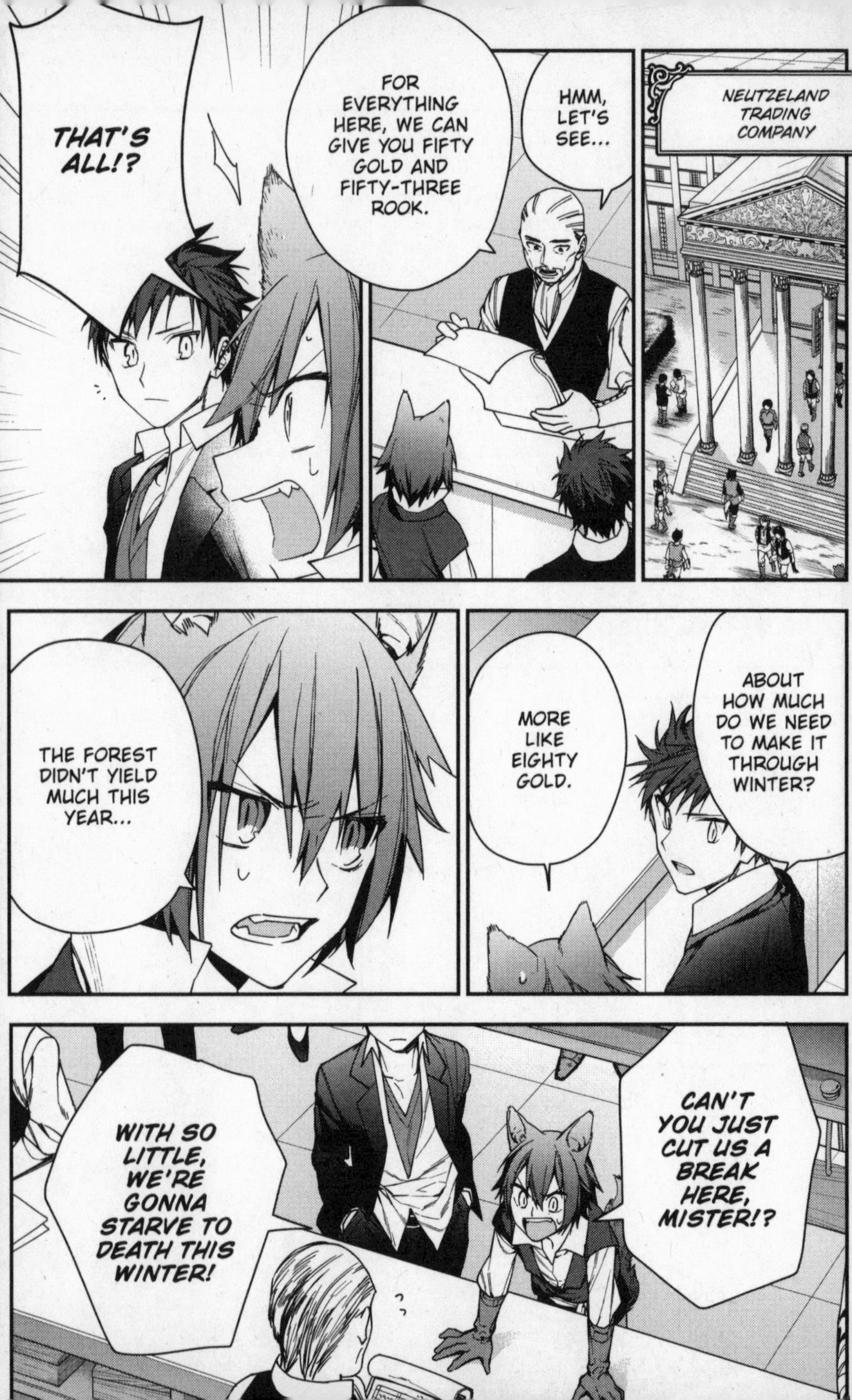
NEUTZELAND TRADING COMPANY
HMM, LET'S SEE...
FOR EVERYTHING HERE, WE CAN GIVE YOU FIFTY GOLD AND FIFTY-THREE ROOK.
THAT'S ALL!?
ABOUT HOW MUCH DO WE NEED TO MAKE IT THROUGH WINTER?
MORE LIKE EIGHTY GOLD.
THE FOREST DIDN'T YIELD MUCH THIS YEAR...
CAN'T YOU JUST CUT US A BREAK HERE, MISTER!?
WITH SO LITTLE, WE'RE GONNA STARVE TO DEATH THIS WINTER!

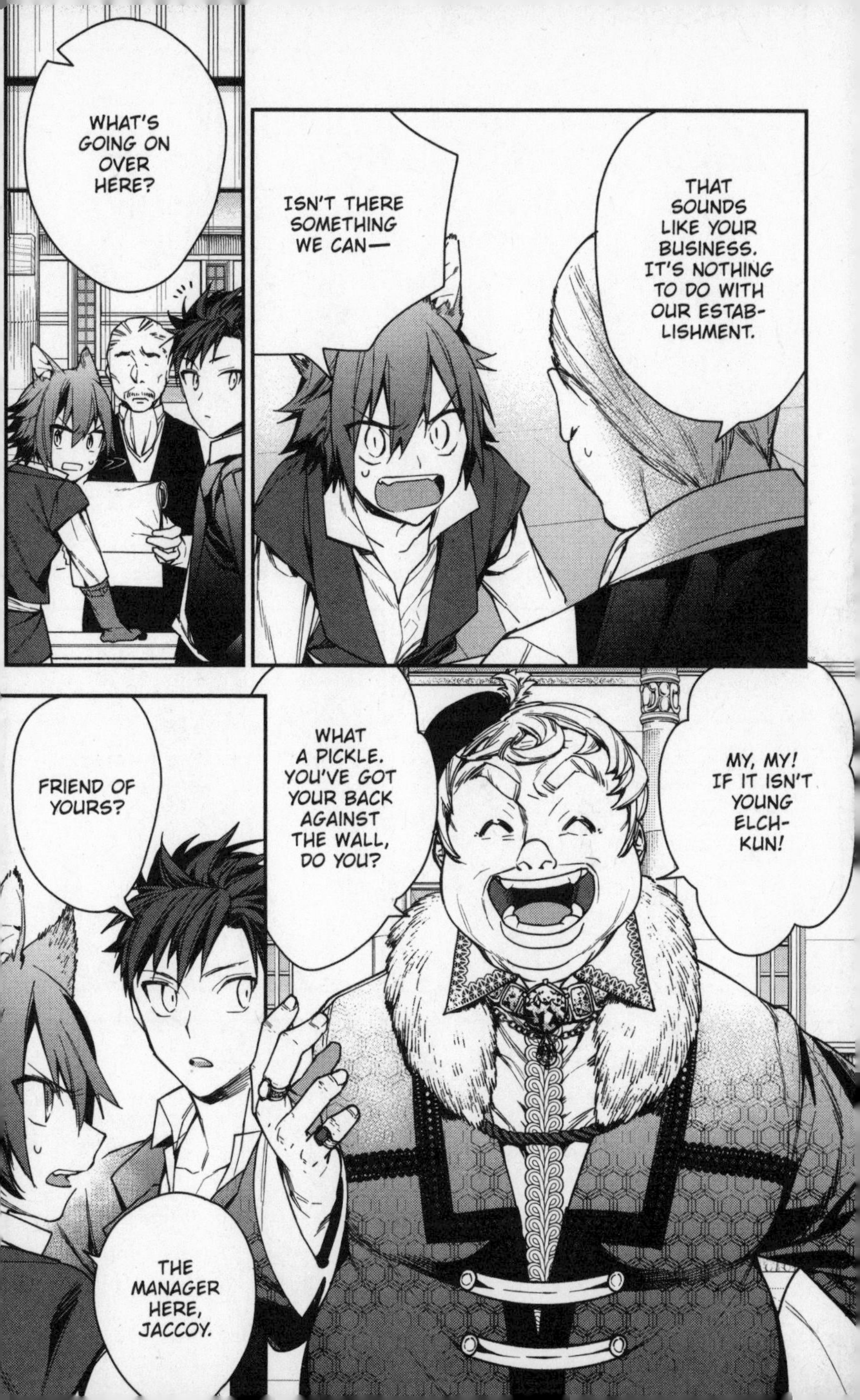
THAT SOUNDS LIKE YOUR BUSINESS. IT'S NOTHING TO DO WITH OUR ESTAB-LISHMENT.
ISN'T THERE SOMETHING WE CAN—
WHAT'S GOING ON OVER HERE?
MY, MY! IF IT ISN'T YOUNG ELCH-KUN!
WHAT A PICKLE. YOU'VE GOT YOUR BACK AGAINST THE WALL, DO YOU?
FRIEND OF YOURS?
THE MANAGER HERE, JACCOY.

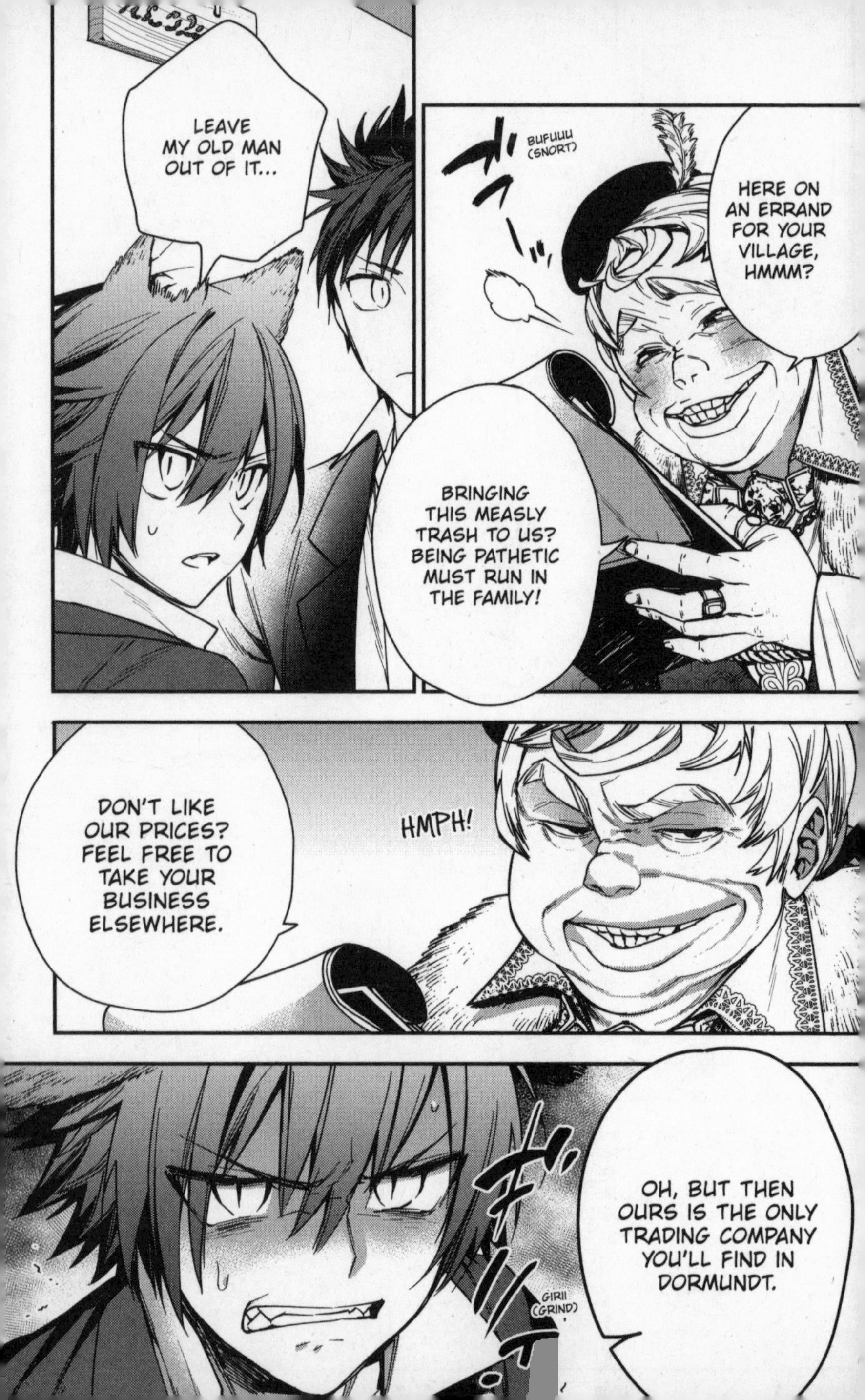
HERE ON AN ERRAND FOR YOUR VILLAGE, HMMM?
BUFUUU (SNORT)
BRINGING THIS MEASLY TRASH TO US? BEING PATHETIC MUST RUN IN THE FAMILY!
LEAVE MY OLD MAN OUT OF IT...
HMPH!
DON'T LIKE OUR PRICES? FEEL FREE TO TAKE YOUR BUSINESS ELSEWHERE.
OH, BUT THEN OURS IS THE ONLY TRADING COMPANY YOU'LL FIND IN DORMUNDT.
GIRII (GRIND)

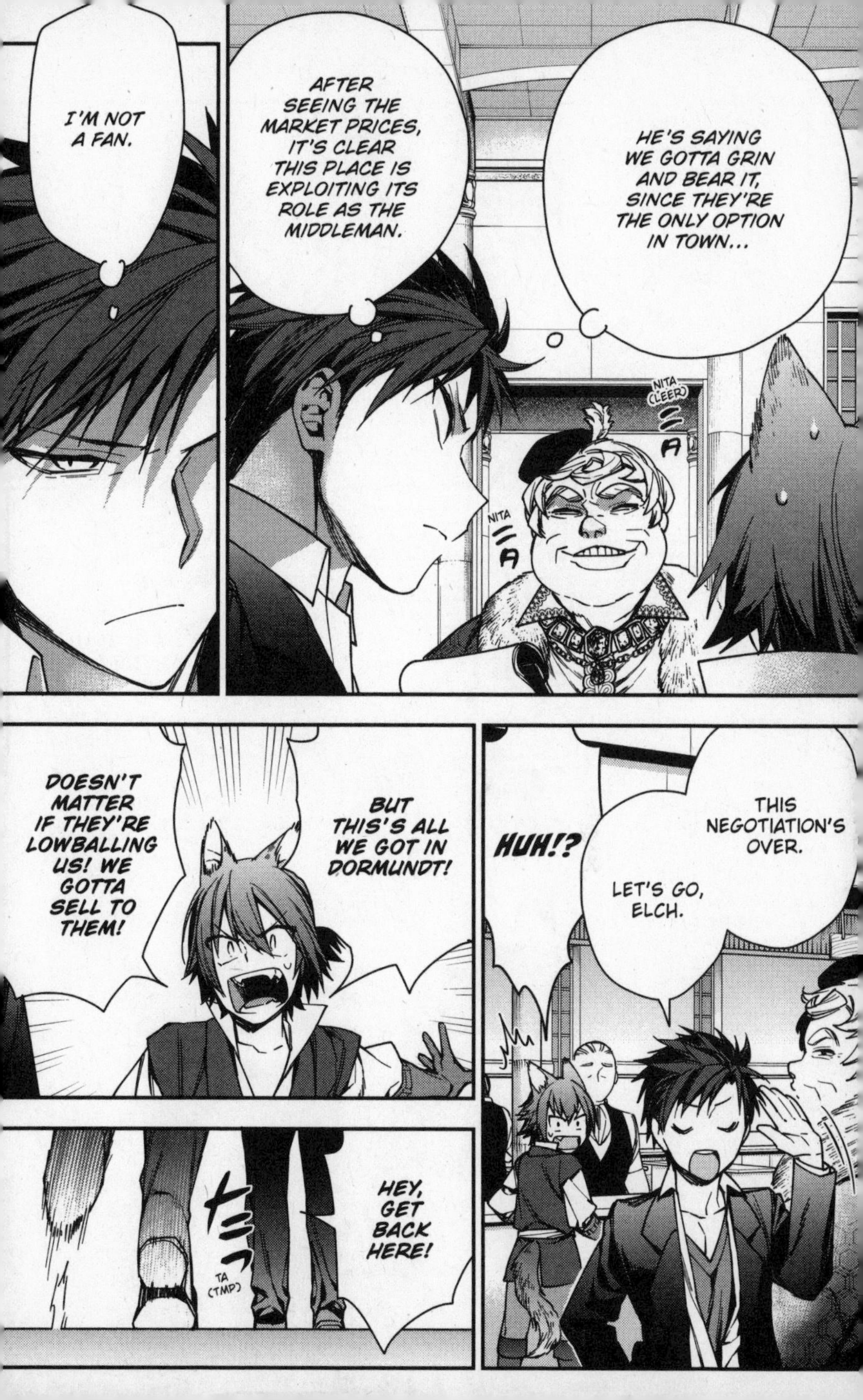

HE'S SAYING WE GOTTA GRIN AND BEAR IT, SINCE THEY'RE THE ONLY OPTION IN TOWN...
NITA (LEER)
NITA
AFTER SEEING THE MARKET PRICES, IT'S CLEAR THIS PLACE IS EXPLOITING ITS ROLE AS THE MIDDLEMAN.
I'M NOT A FAN.
THIS NEGOTIATION'S OVER.
LET'S GO, ELCH.
HUH!?
BUT THIS'S ALL WE GOT IN DORMUNDT!
DOESN'T MATTER IF THEY'RE LOWBALLING US! WE GOTTA SELL TO THEM!
HEY, GET BACK HERE!
TA (TMP)

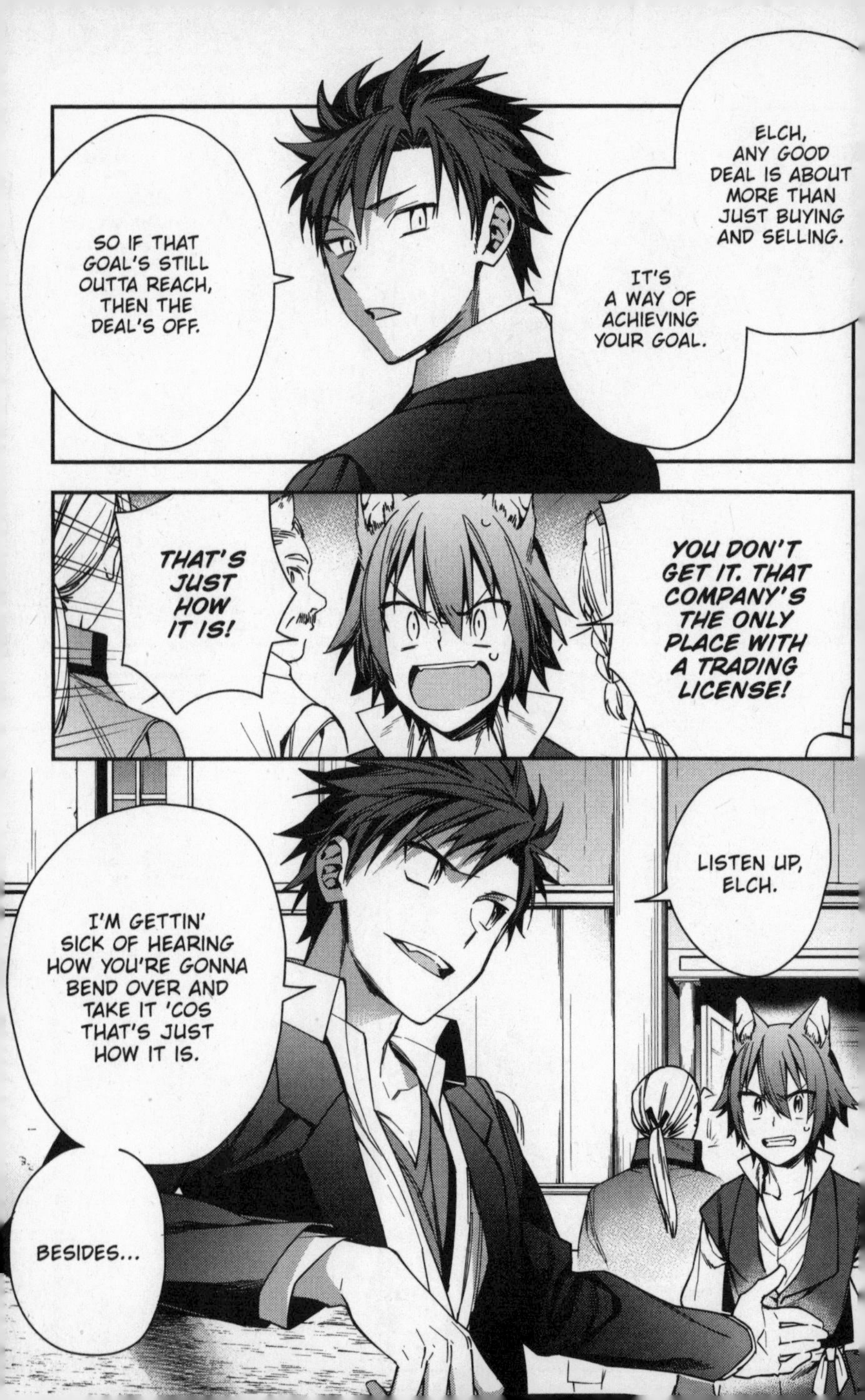
ELCH, ANY GOOD DEAL IS ABOUT MORE THAN JUST BUYING AND SELLING.
IT'S A WAY OF ACHIEVING YOUR GOAL.
SO IF THAT GOAL'S STILL OUTTA REACH, THEN THE DEAL'S OFF.
YOU DON'T GET IT. THAT COMPANY'S THE ONLY PLACE WITH A TRADING LICENSE!
THAT'S JUST HOW IT IS!
LISTEN UP, ELCH.
I'M GETTIN' SICK OF HEARING HOW YOU'RE GONNA BEND OVER AND TAKE IT 'COS THAT'S JUST HOW IT IS.
BESIDES...

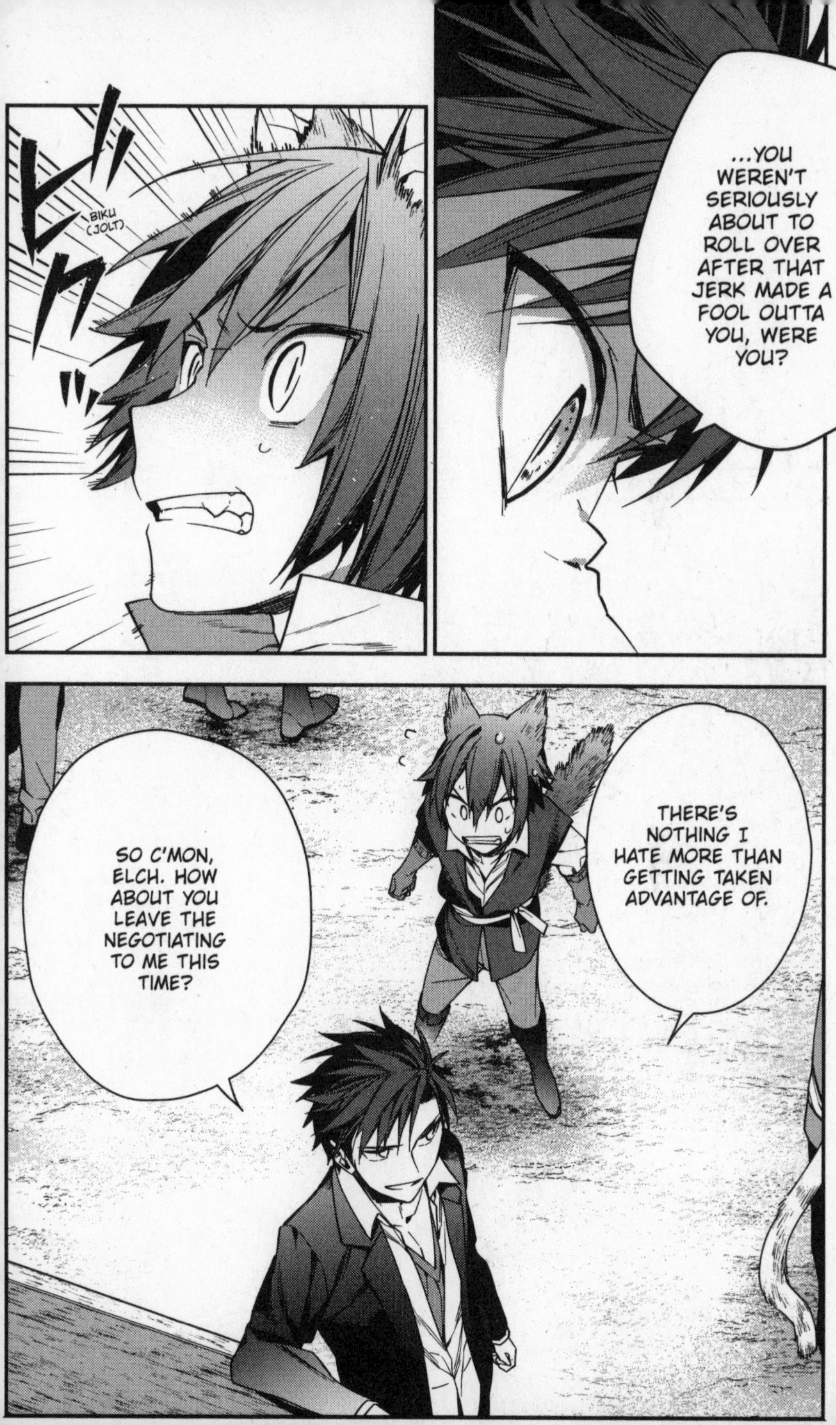
...YOU WEREN'T SERIOUSLY ABOUT TO ROLL OVER AFTER THAT JERK MADE A FOOL OUTTA YOU, WERE YOU?
BIKU (JOLT)
THERE'S NOTHING I HATE MORE THAN GETTING TAKEN ADVANTAGE OF.
SO C'MON, ELCH. HOW ABOUT YOU LEAVE THE NEGOTIATING TO ME THIS TIME?

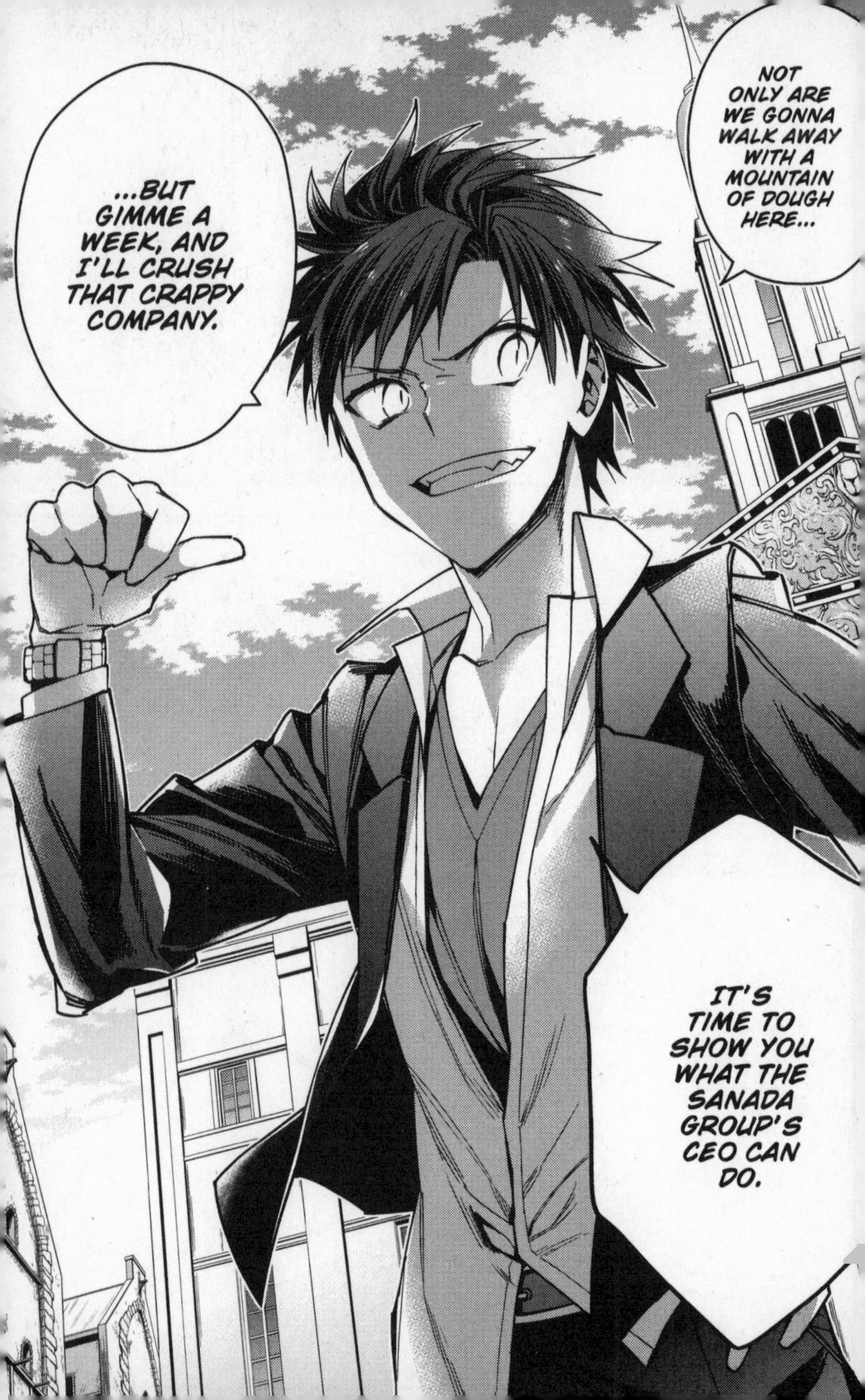
NOT ONLY ARE WE GONNA WALK AWAY WITH A MOUNTAIN OF DOUGH HERE...
...BUT GIMME A WEEK, AND I'LL CRUSH THAT CRAPPY COMPANY.
IT'S TIME TO SHOW YOU WHAT THE SANADA GROUP'S CEO CAN DO.

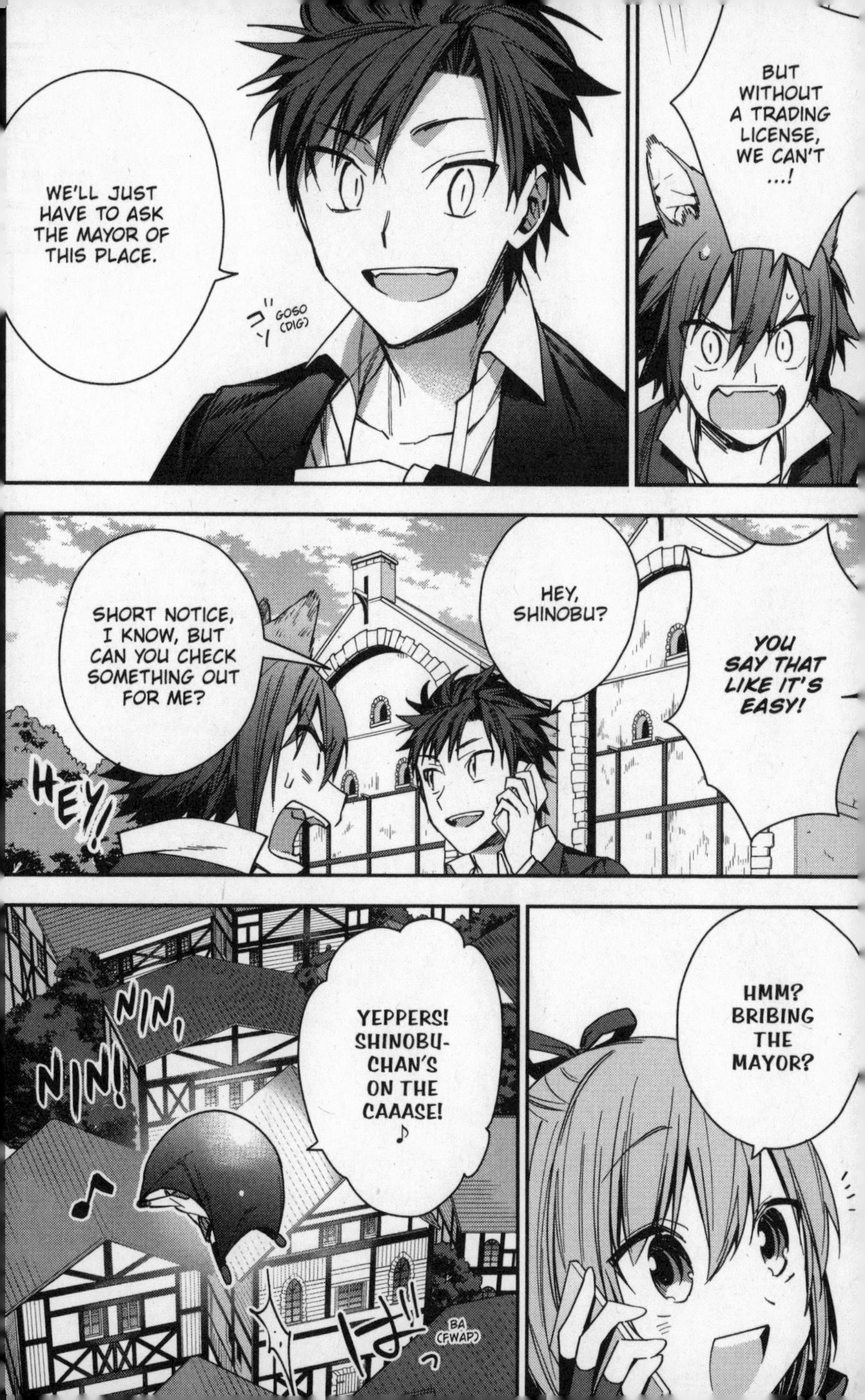
BUT WITHOUT A TRADING LICENSE, WE CAN'T ...!
WE'LL JUST HAVE TO ASK THE MAYOR OF THIS PLACE.
GOSO (DIG)
YOU SAY THAT LIKE IT'S EASY!
HEY, SHINOBU?
SHORT NOTICE, I KNOW, BUT CAN YOU CHECK SOMETHING OUT FOR ME?
HEY!
HMM? BRIBING THE MAYOR?
YEPPERS! SHINOBU-CHAN'S ON THE CAAASE! ♪
NIN, NIN!
BA (FWAP)

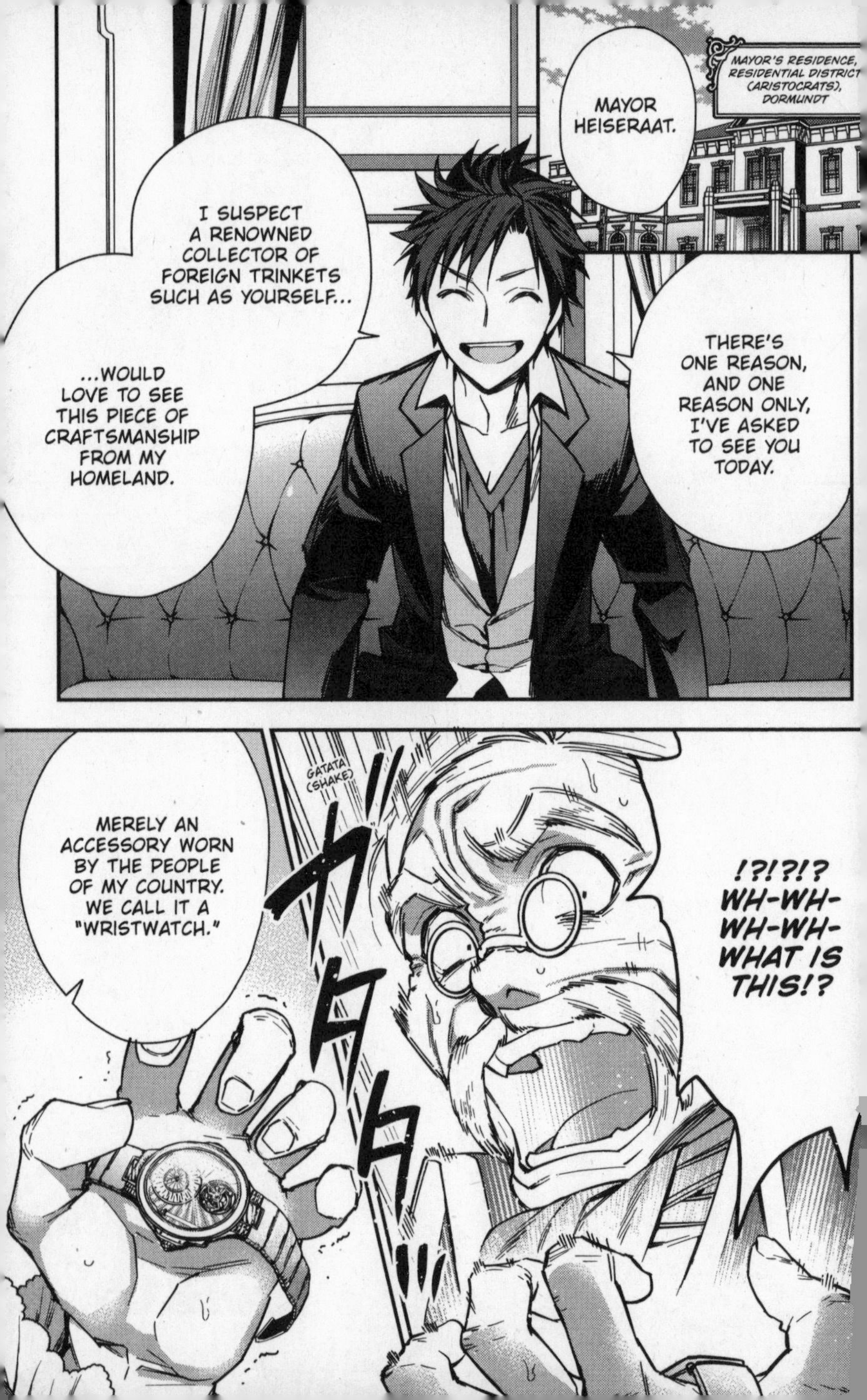
MAYOR'S RESIDENCE, RESIDENTIAL DISTRICT (ARISTOCRATS), DORMUNDT
MAYOR HEISERAAT.
THERE'S ONE REASON, AND ONE REASON ONLY, I'VE ASKED TO SEE YOU TODAY.
I SUSPECT A RENOWNED COLLECTOR OF FOREIGN TRINKETS SUCH AS YOURSELF...
...WOULD LOVE TO SEE THIS PIECE OF CRAFTSMANSHIP FROM MY HOMELAND.
!?!?!? WH-WH-WH-WH-WHAT IS THIS!?
GATATA (SHAKE)
MERELY AN ACCESSORY WORN BY THE PEOPLE OF MY COUNTRY. WE CALL IT A "WRISTWATCH."

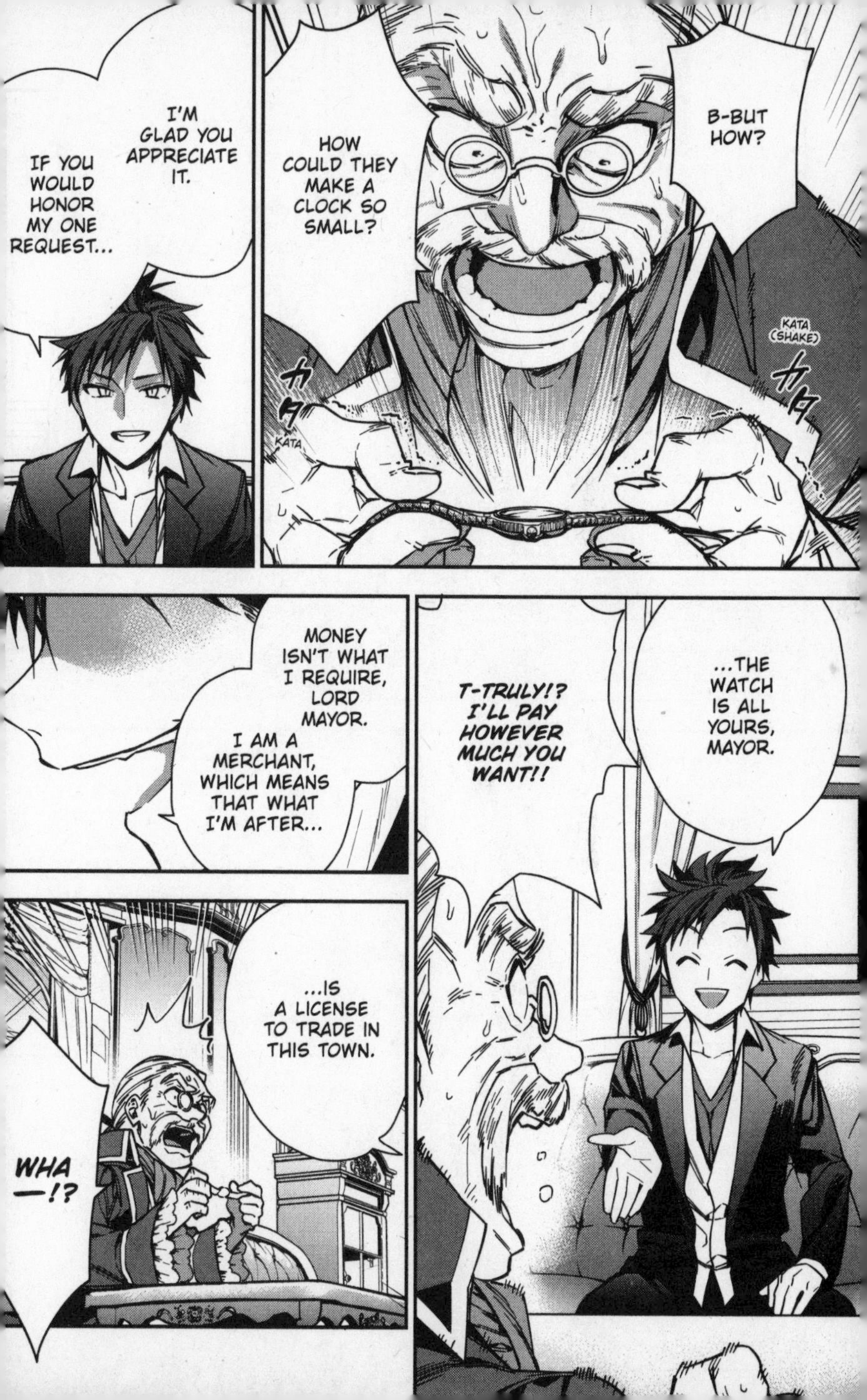
B-BUT HOW?
HOW COULD THEY MAKE A CLOCK SO SMALL?
KATA (SHAKE)
KATA
I'M GLAD YOU APPRECIATE IT.
IF YOU WOULD HONOR MY ONE REQUEST...
...THE WATCH IS ALL YOURS, MAYOR.
T-TRULY!? I'LL PAY HOWEVER MUCH YOU WANT!!
MONEY ISN'T WHAT I REQUIRE, LORD MAYOR.
I AM A MERCHANT, WHICH MEANS THAT WHAT I'M AFTER...
...IS A LICENSE TO TRADE IN THIS TOWN.
WHA—!?

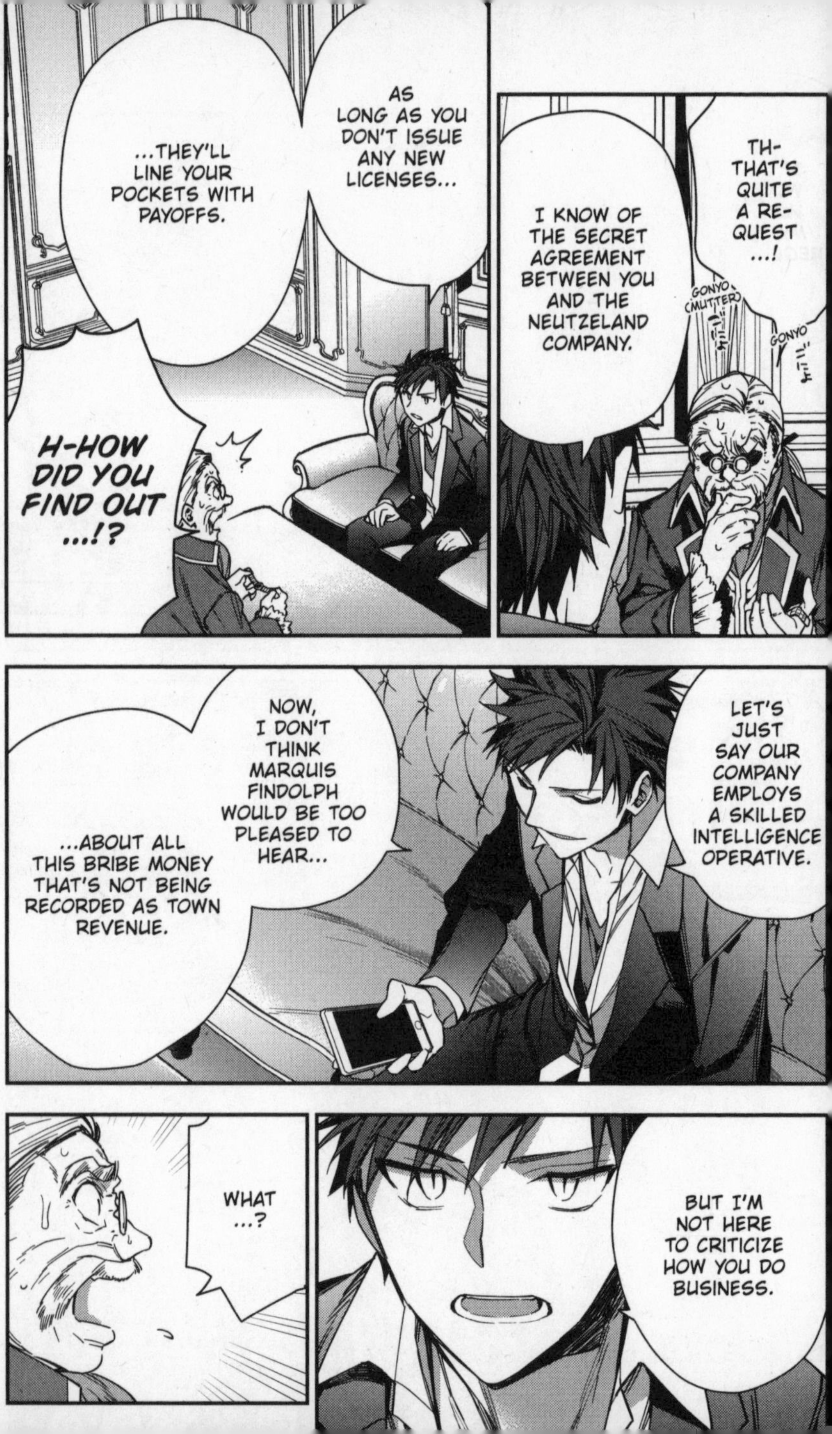
TH-THAT'S QUITE A RE-QUEST ...!
GONYO (MUTTER)
GONYO
I KNOW OF THE SECRET AGREEMENT BETWEEN YOU AND THE NEUTZELAND COMPANY.
AS LONG AS YOU DON'T ISSUE ANY NEW LICENSES...
...THEY'LL LINE YOUR POCKETS WITH PAYOFFS.
H-HOW DID YOU FIND OUT ...!?
LET'S JUST SAY OUR COMPANY EMPLOYS A SKILLED INTELLIGENCE OPERATIVE.
NOW, I DON'T THINK MARQUIS FINDOLPH WOULD BE TOO PLEASED TO HEAR...
...ABOUT ALL THIS BRIBE MONEY THAT'S NOT BEING RECORDED AS TOWN REVENUE.
BUT I'M NOT HERE TO CRITICIZE HOW YOU DO BUSINESS.
WHAT ...?

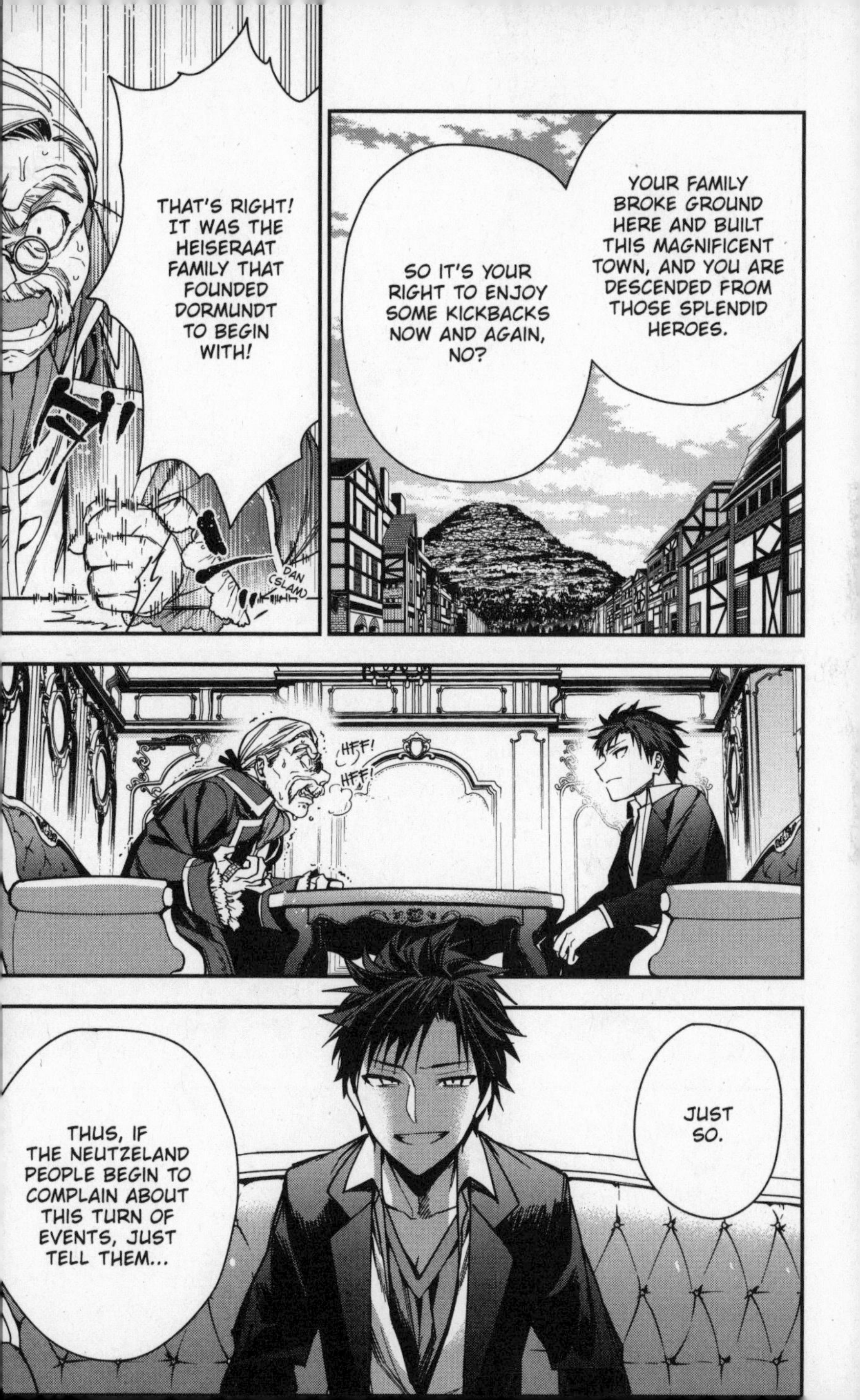

YOUR FAMILY BROKE GROUND HERE AND BUILT THIS MAGNIFICENT TOWN, AND YOU ARE DESCENDED FROM THOSE SPLENDID HEROES.
SO IT'S YOUR RIGHT TO ENJOY SOME KICKBACKS NOW AND AGAIN, NO?
THAT'S RIGHT! IT WAS THE HEISERAAT FAMILY THAT FOUNDED DORMUNDT TO BEGIN WITH!
DAN (SLAM)
HFF!
HFF!
JUST SO.
THUS, IF THE NEUTZELAND PEOPLE BEGIN TO COMPLAIN ABOUT THIS TURN OF EVENTS, JUST TELL THEM...

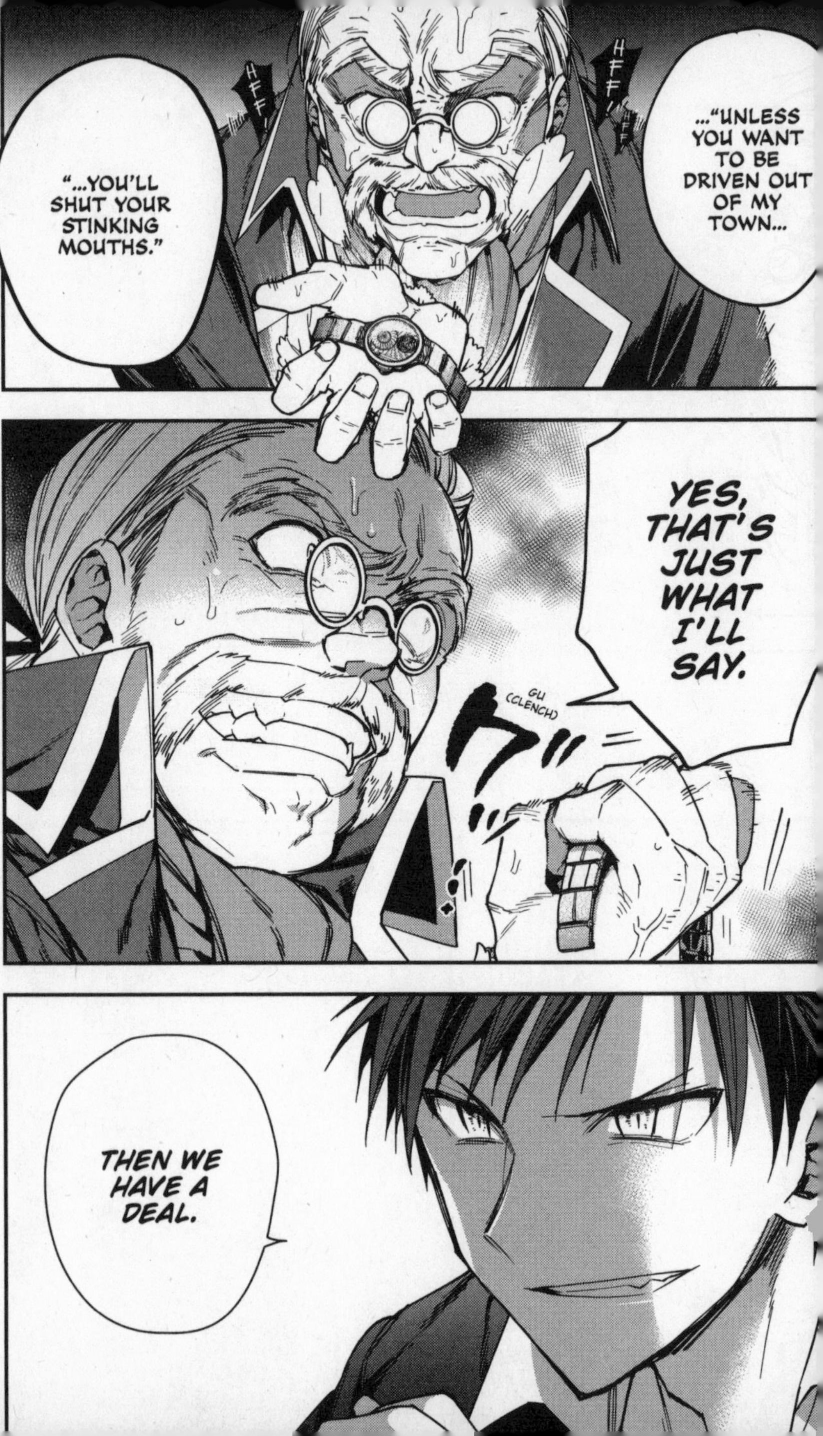
HFF!
HFF
..."UNLESS YOU WANT TO BE DRIVEN OUT OF MY TOWN...
HFF!
"...YOU'LL SHUT YOUR STINKING MOUTHS."
YES, THAT'S JUST WHAT I'LL SAY.
GU (CLENCH)
THEN WE HAVE A DEAL.

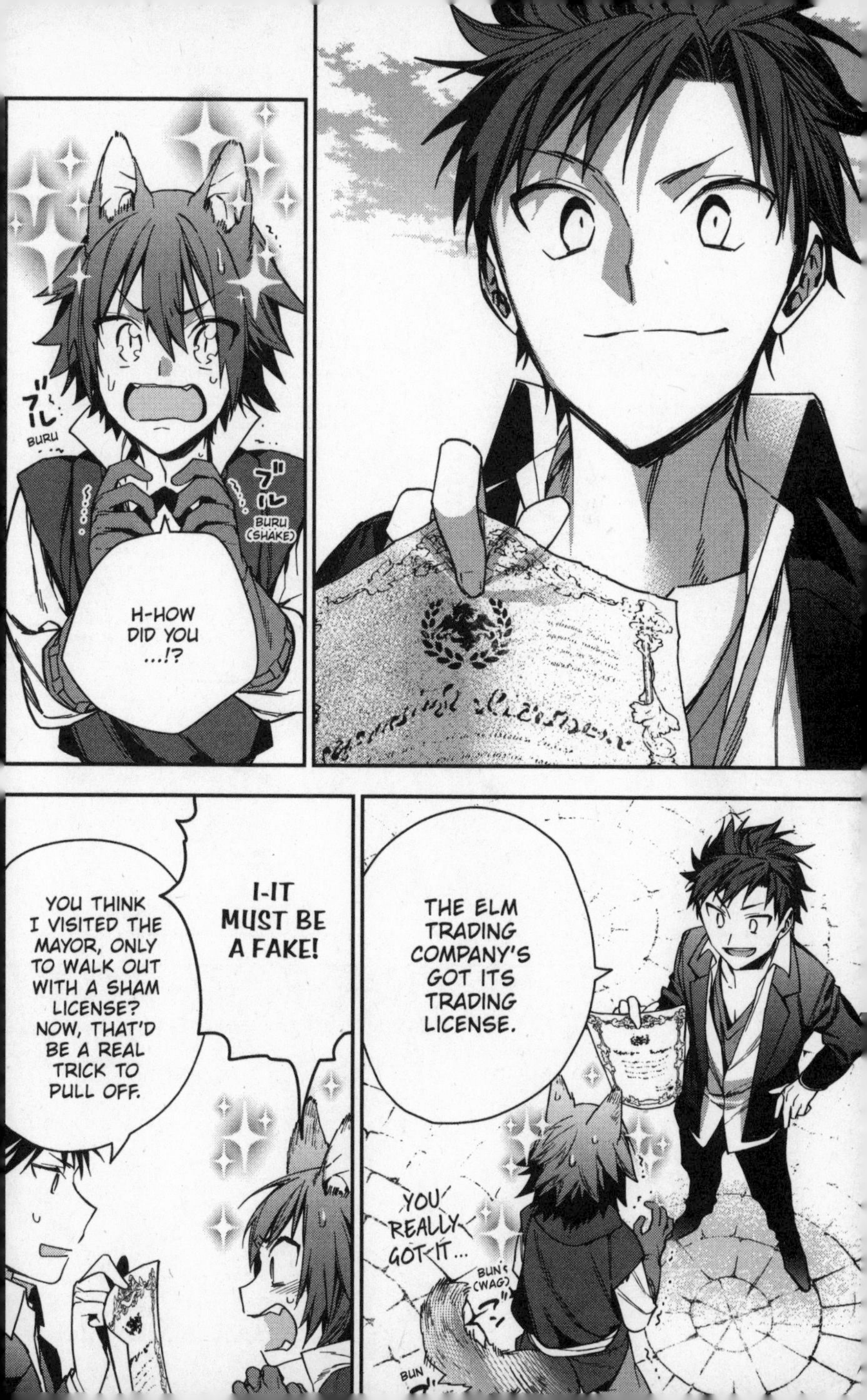
ブル
BURU (SHAKE)
H-HOW DID YOU ...!?
ブル
BURU
THE ELM TRADING COMPANY'S GOT ITS TRADING LICENSE.
YOU REALLY GOT IT...
BUN (WAG)
BUN
I-IT MUST BE A FAKE!
YOU THINK I VISITED THE MAYOR, ONLY TO WALK OUT WITH A SHAM LICENSE? NOW, THAT'D BE A REAL TRICK TO PULL OFF.

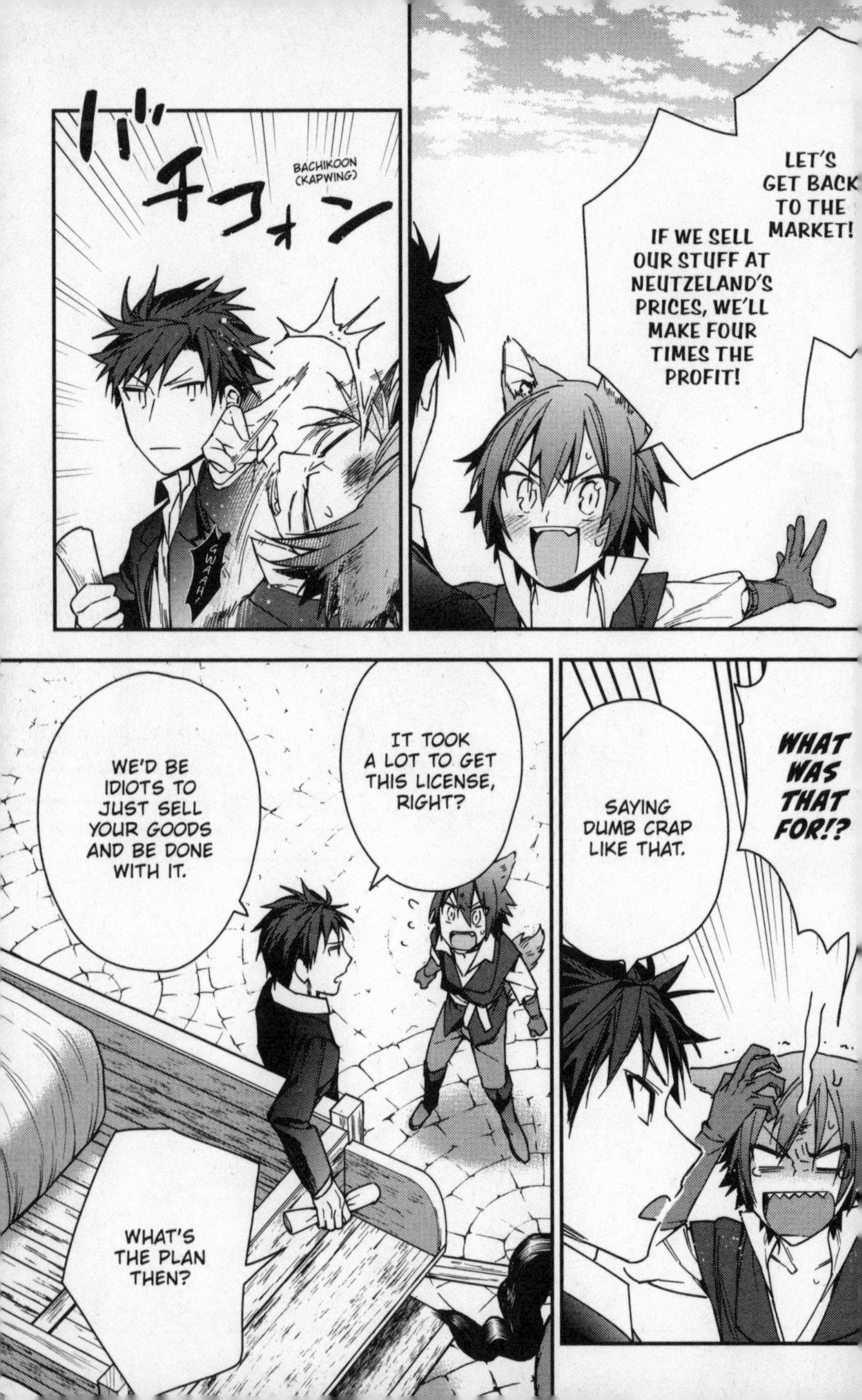
LET'S GET BACK TO THE MARKET!
IF WE SELL OUR STUFF AT NEUTZELAND'S PRICES, WE'LL MAKE FOUR TIMES THE PROFIT!
バチコォン
BACHIKOON (KAPWING)
GWAAH!
WHAT WAS THAT FOR!?
SAYING DUMB CRAP LIKE THAT.
IT TOOK A LOT TO GET THIS LICENSE, RIGHT?
WE'D BE IDIOTS TO JUST SELL YOUR GOODS AND BE DONE WITH IT.
WHAT'S THE PLAN THEN?

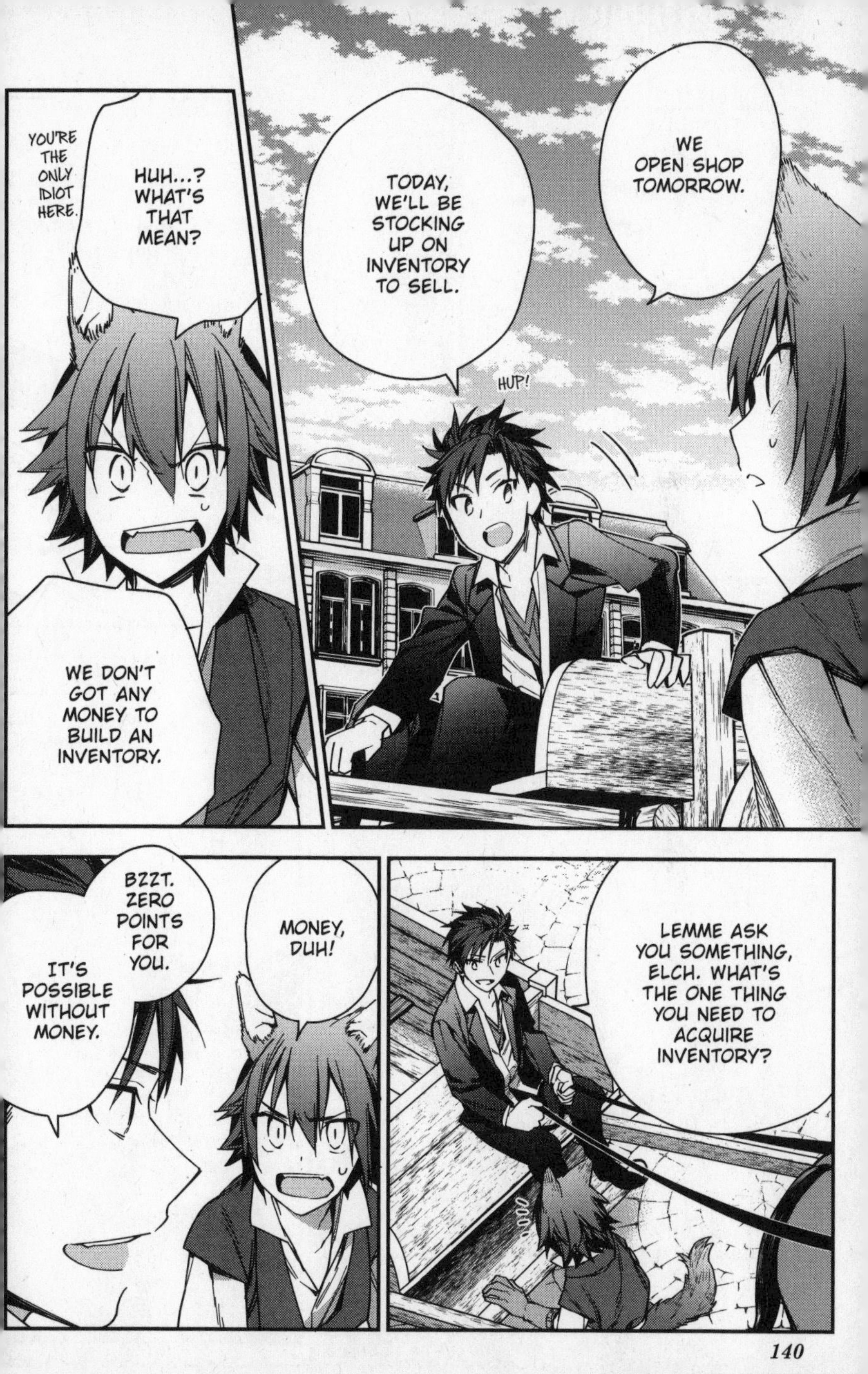
WE OPEN SHOP TOMORROW.
TODAY, WE'LL BE STOCKING UP ON INVENTORY TO SELL.
HUP!
HUH...? WHAT'S THAT MEAN?
YOU'RE THE ONLY IDIOT HERE.
WE DON'T GOT ANY MONEY TO BUILD AN INVENTORY.
LEMME ASK YOU SOMETHING, ELCH. WHAT'S THE ONE THING YOU NEED TO ACQUIRE INVENTORY?
MONEY, DUH!
BZZT. ZERO POINTS FOR YOU.
IT'S POSSIBLE WITHOUT MONEY.

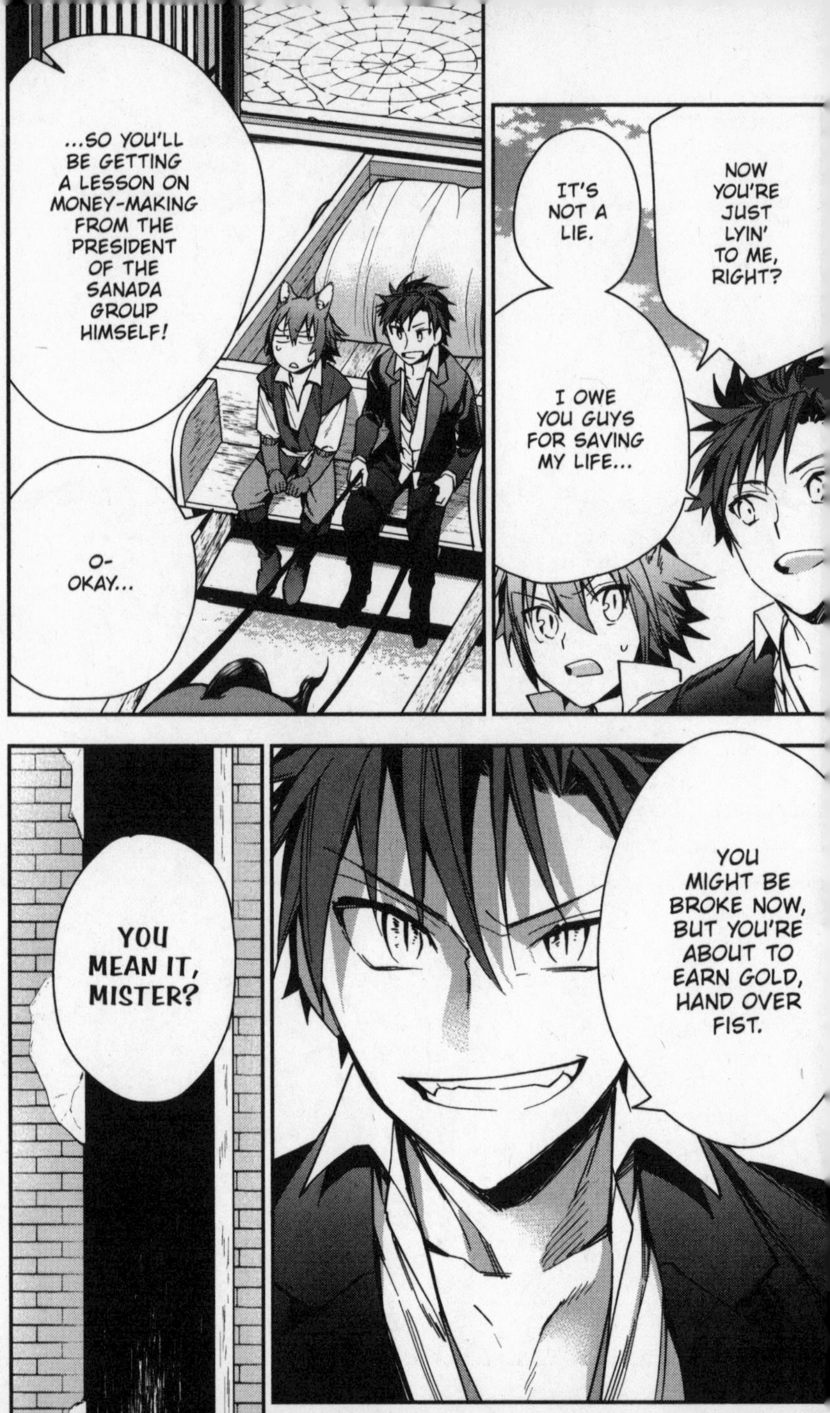
NOW YOU'RE JUST LYIN' TO ME, RIGHT?
IT'S NOT A LIE.
I OWE YOU GUYS FOR SAVING MY LIFE...
...SO YOU'LL BE GETTING A LESSON ON MONEY-MAKING FROM THE PRESIDENT OF THE SANADA GROUP HIMSELF!
O- OKAY...
YOU MIGHT BE BROKE NOW, BUT YOU'RE ABOUT TO EARN GOLD, HAND OVER FIST.
YOU MEAN IT, MISTER?

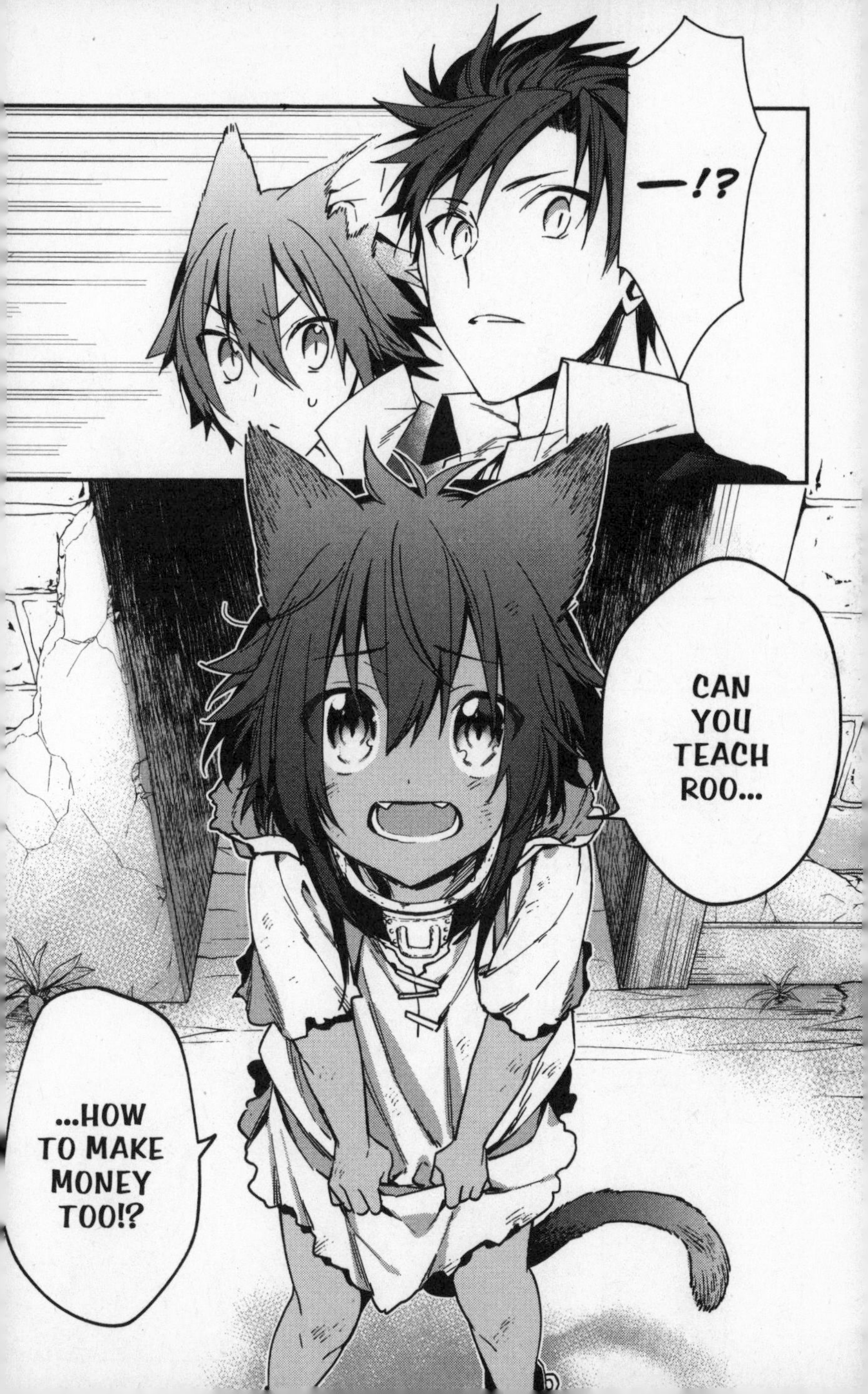
—!?
CAN YOU TEACH ROO...
...HOW TO MAKE MONEY TOO!?

HIGH SCHOOL
PRODIGIES HAVE
IT EASY EVEN IN
ANOTHER
WORLD!

CHARACTER FILE 06

Prince Akatsuki

One of the high school prodigies. Clairvoyance, telekinesis, teleportation—this illusionist can do it all. His classical features often get him mistaken for a girl, which is a sore spot for him.

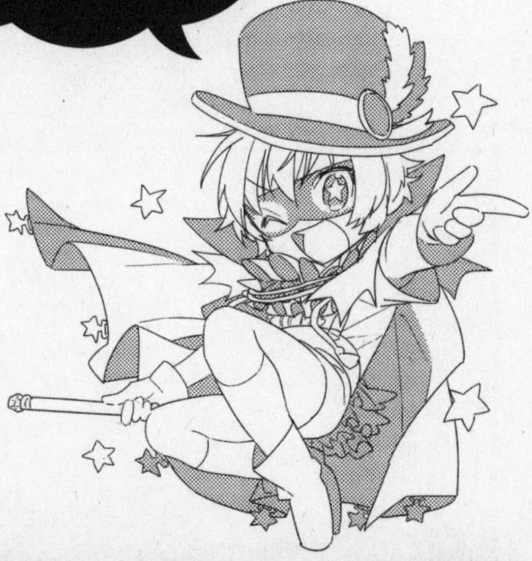

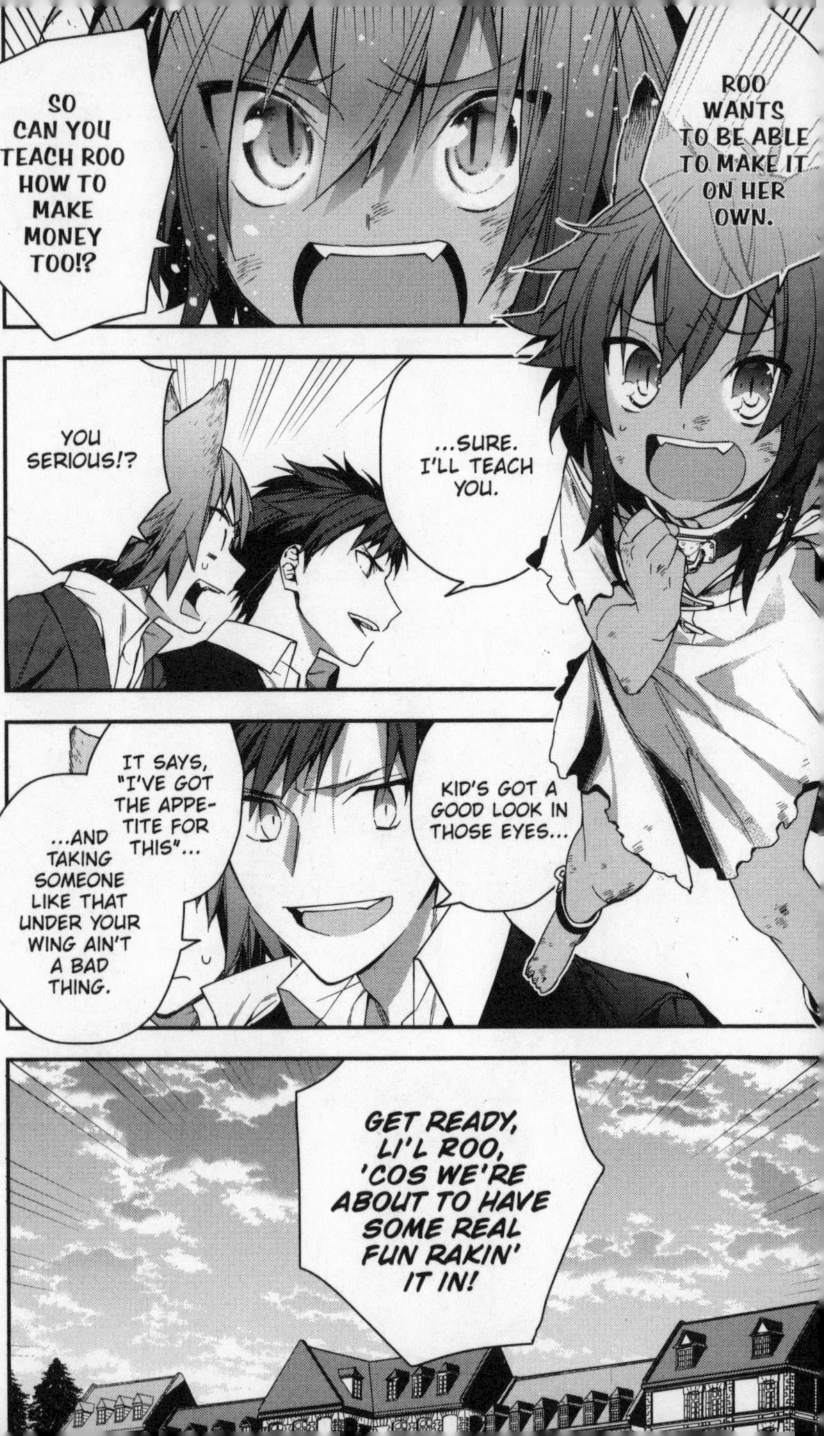
ROO WANTS TO BE ABLE TO MAKE IT ON HER OWN.
SO CAN YOU TEACH ROO HOW TO MAKE MONEY TOO!?
...SURE. I'LL TEACH YOU.
YOU SERIOUS!?
KID'S GOT A GOOD LOOK IN THOSE EYES...
IT SAYS, "I'VE GOT THE APPETITE FOR THIS"...
...AND TAKING SOMEONE LIKE THAT UNDER YOUR WING AIN'T A BAD THING.
GET READY, LI'L ROO, 'COS WE'RE ABOUT TO HAVE SOME REAL FUN RAKIN' IT IN!

CHAPTER 7: A NEW ALLY

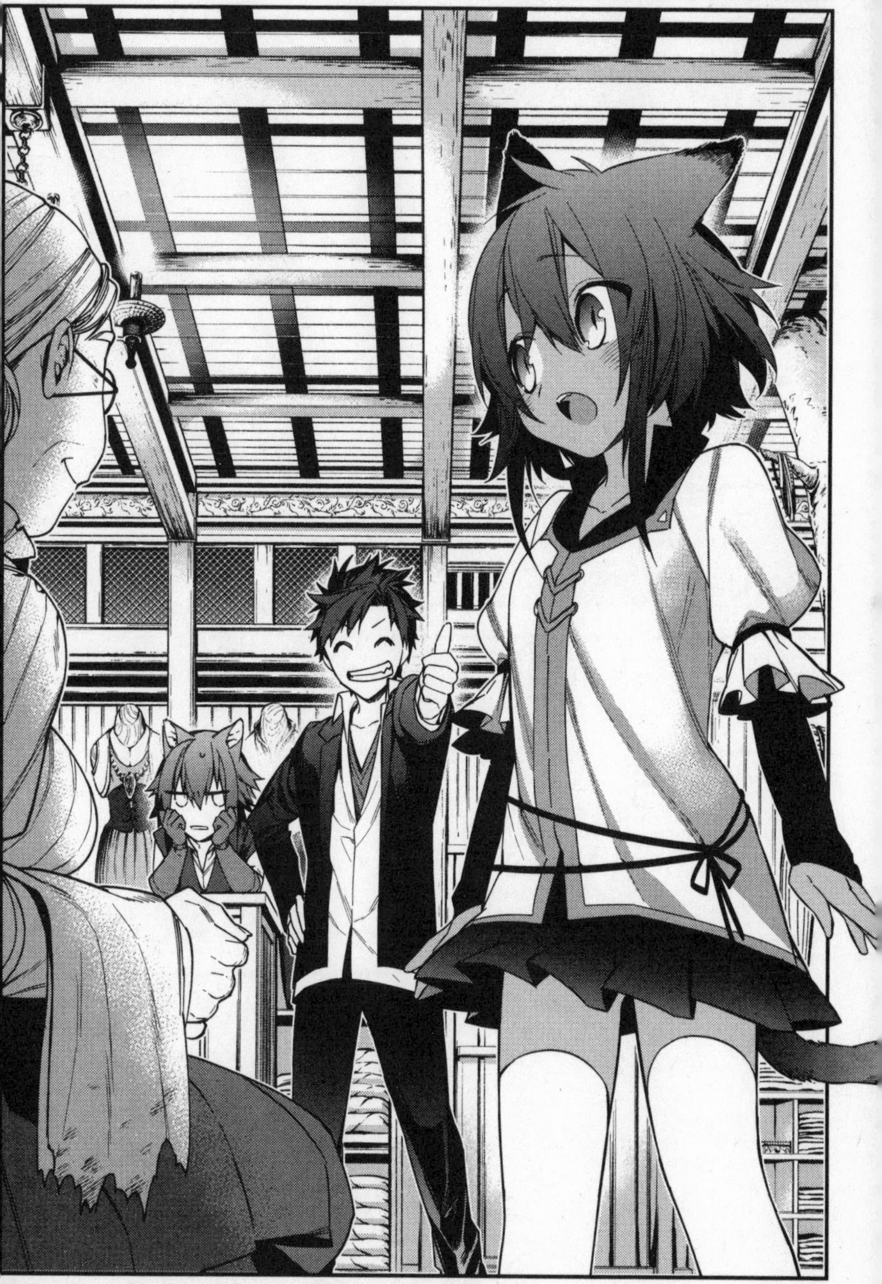

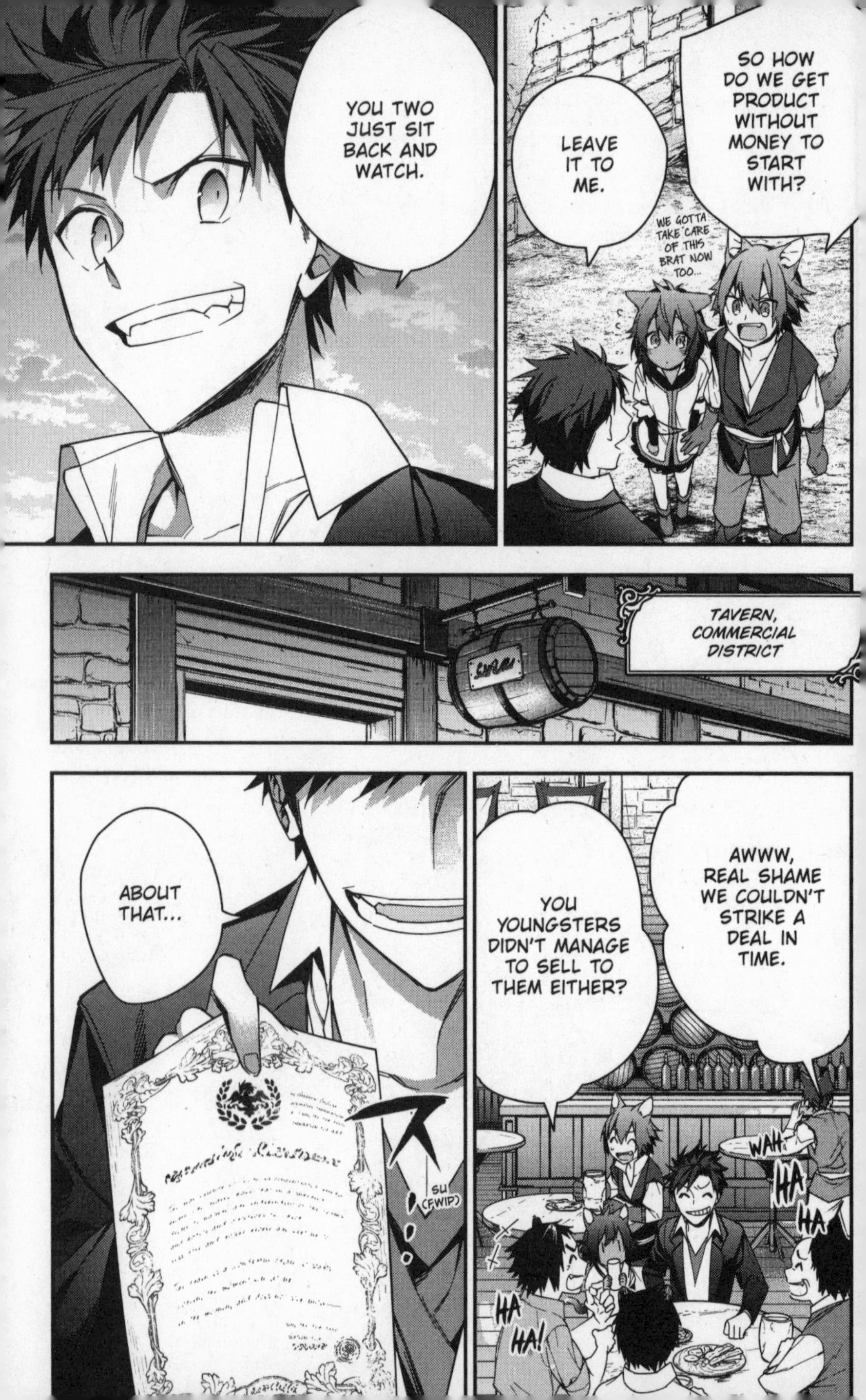
SO HOW DO WE GET PRODUCT WITHOUT MONEY TO START WITH?
LEAVE IT TO ME.
WE GOTTA TAKE CARE OF THIS BRAT NOW TOO...
YOU TWO JUST SIT BACK AND WATCH.
TAVERN, COMMERCIAL DISTRICT
AWWW, REAL SHAME WE COULDN'T STRIKE A DEAL IN TIME.
YOU YOUNGSTERS DIDN'T MANAGE TO SELL TO THEM EITHER?
WAH HA HA HA
HA HA!
ABOUT THAT...
SU (FWIP)

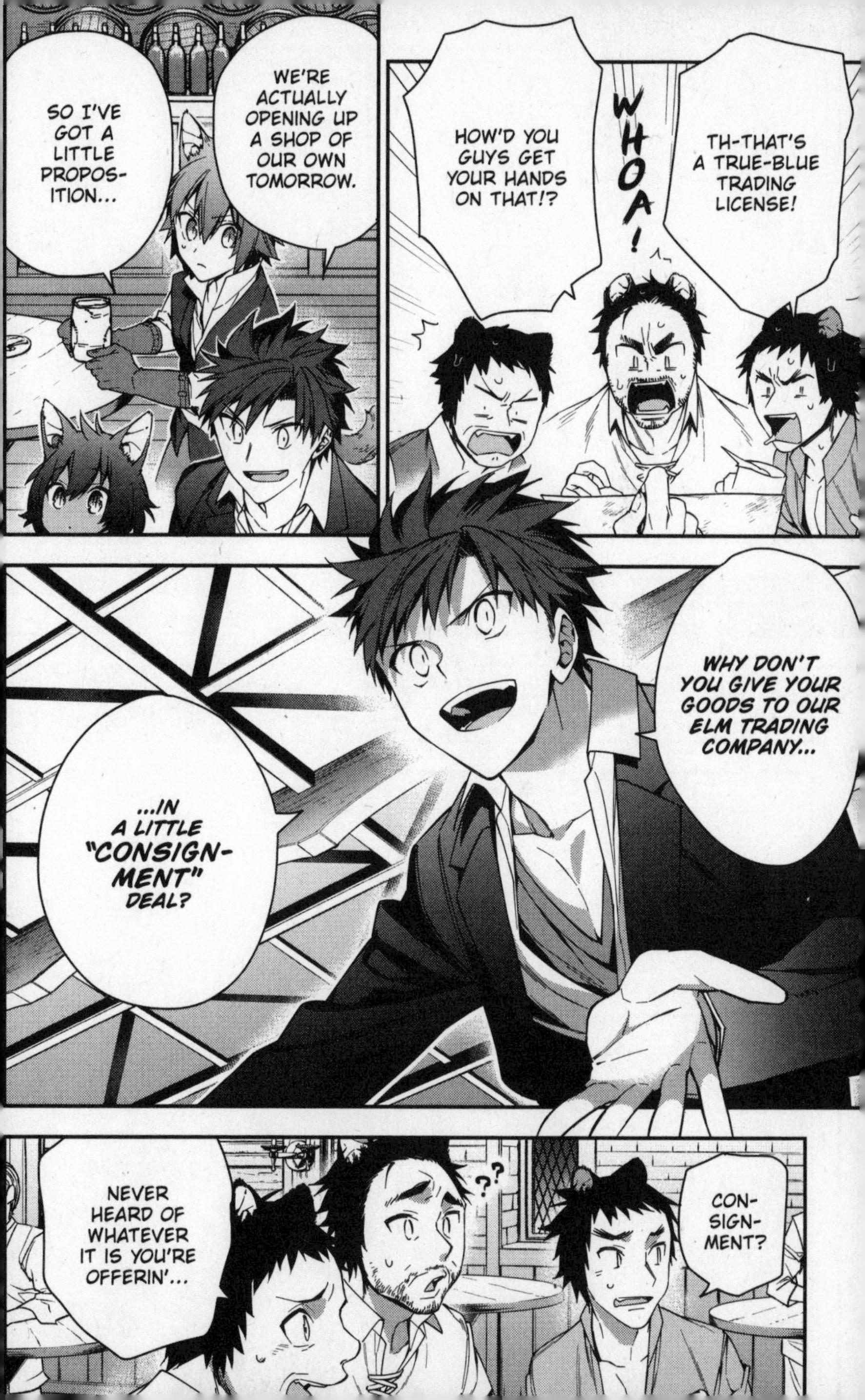

TH-THAT'S A TRUE-BLUE TRADING LICENSE!
WHOA!
HOW'D YOU GUYS GET YOUR HANDS ON THAT!?
WE'RE ACTUALLY OPENING UP A SHOP OF OUR OWN TOMORROW.
SO I'VE GOT A LITTLE PROPOSITION...
WHY DON'T YOU GIVE YOUR GOODS TO OUR ELM TRADING COMPANY...
...IN A LITTLE "CONSIGNMENT" DEAL?
CONSIGNMENT?
??
NEVER HEARD OF WHATEVER IT IS YOU'RE OFFERIN'...

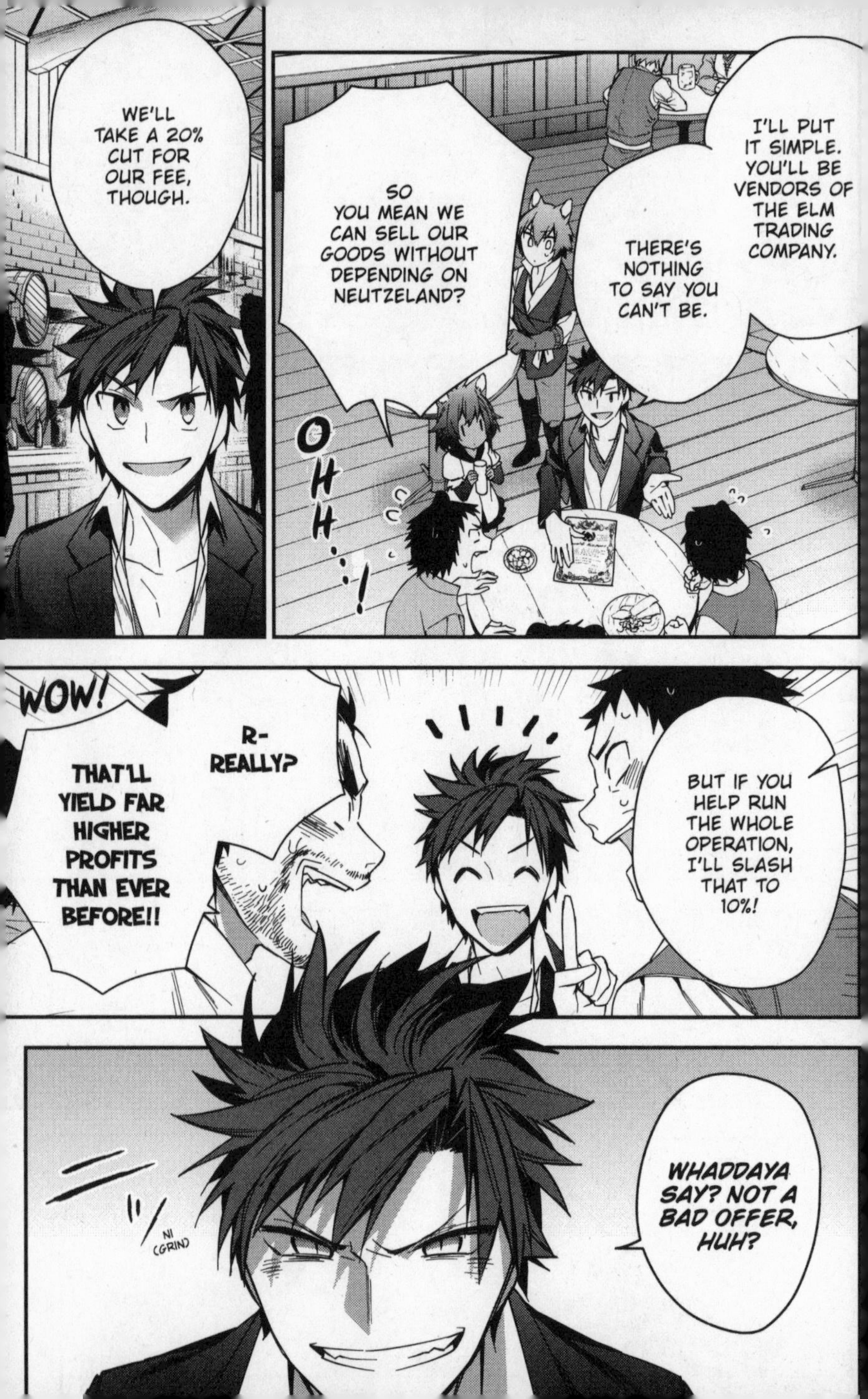
I'LL PUT IT SIMPLE. YOU'LL BE VENDORS OF THE ELM TRADING COMPANY.
THERE'S NOTHING TO SAY YOU CAN'T BE.
SO YOU MEAN WE CAN SELL OUR GOODS WITHOUT DEPENDING ON NEUTZELAND?
OHH...!
WE'LL TAKE A 20% CUT FOR OUR FEE, THOUGH.
BUT IF YOU HELP RUN THE WHOLE OPERATION, I'LL SLASH THAT TO 10%!
R-REALLY?
WOW!
THAT'LL YIELD FAR HIGHER PROFITS THAN EVER BEFORE!!
WHADDAYA SAY? NOT A BAD OFFER, HUH?
NI (GRIN)

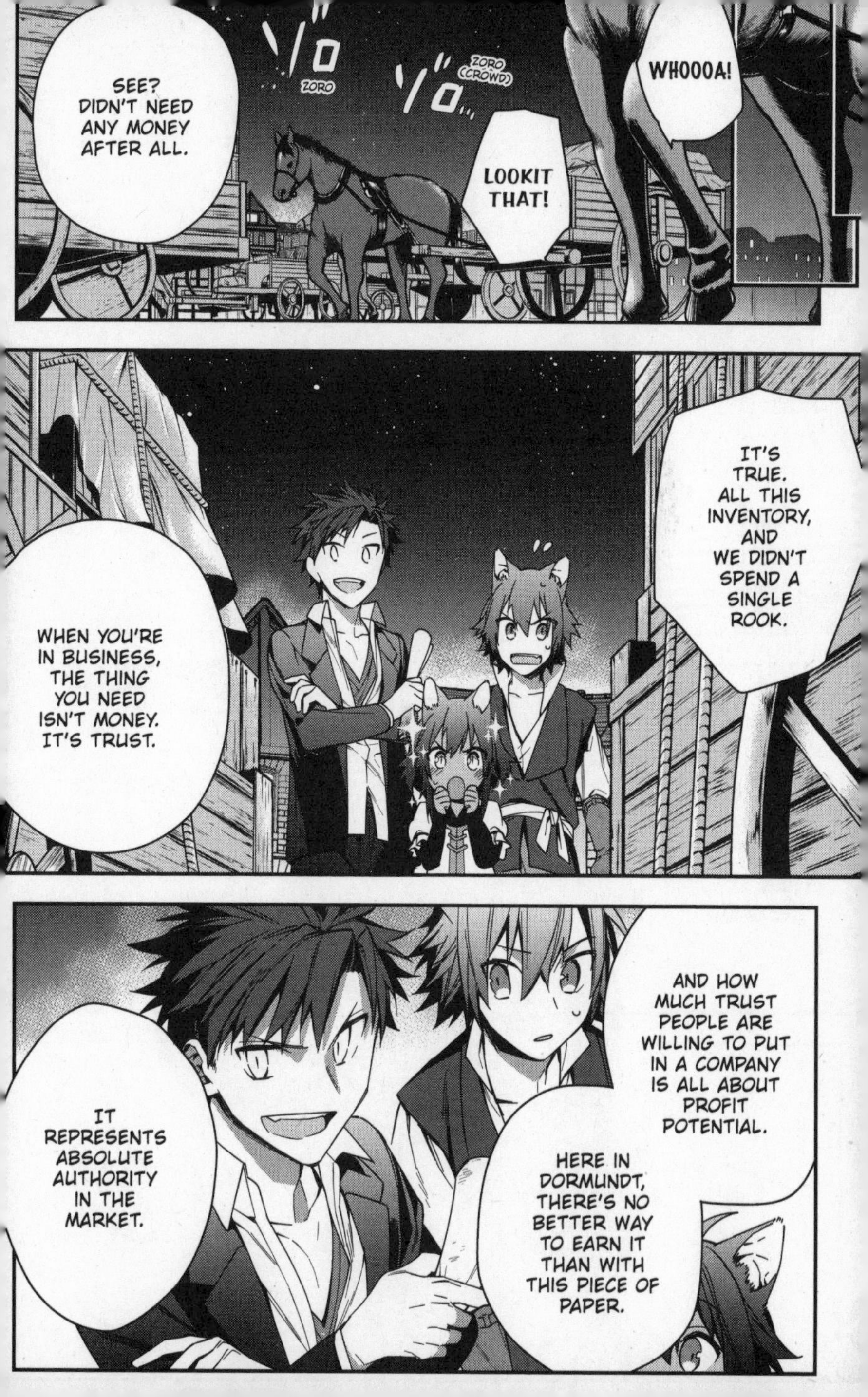
WHOOOA!
ZORO (CROWD)
LOOKIT THAT!
ZORO
SEE? DIDN'T NEED ANY MONEY AFTER ALL.
IT'S TRUE. ALL THIS INVENTORY, AND WE DIDN'T SPEND A SINGLE ROOK.
WHEN YOU'RE IN BUSINESS, THE THING YOU NEED ISN'T MONEY. IT'S TRUST.
AND HOW MUCH TRUST PEOPLE ARE WILLING TO PUT IN A COMPANY IS ALL ABOUT PROFIT POTENTIAL.
HERE IN DORMUNDT, THERE'S NO BETTER WAY TO EARN IT THAN WITH THIS PIECE OF PAPER.
IT REPRESENTS ABSOLUTE AUTHORITY IN THE MARKET.

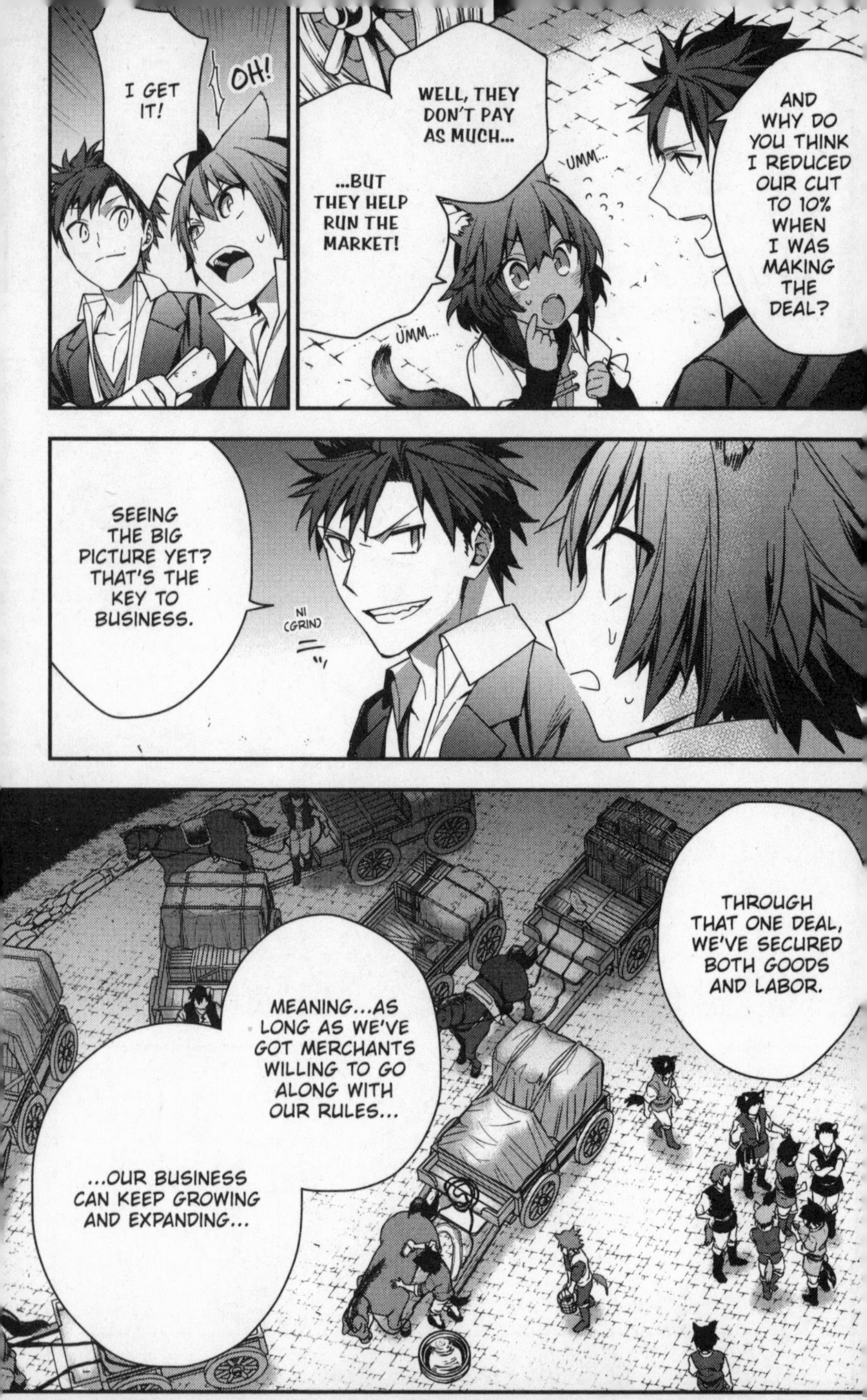
AND WHY DO YOU THINK I REDUCED OUR CUT TO 10% WHEN I WAS MAKING THE DEAL?
UMM...
WELL, THEY DON'T PAY AS MUCH...
...BUT THEY HELP RUN THE MARKET!
UMM...
OH!
I GET IT!
SEEING THE BIG PICTURE YET? THAT'S THE KEY TO BUSINESS.
NI (GRIN)
THROUGH THAT ONE DEAL, WE'VE SECURED BOTH GOODS AND LABOR.
MEANING...AS LONG AS WE'VE GOT MERCHANTS WILLING TO GO ALONG WITH OUR RULES...
...OUR BUSINESS CAN KEEP GROWING AND EXPANDING...

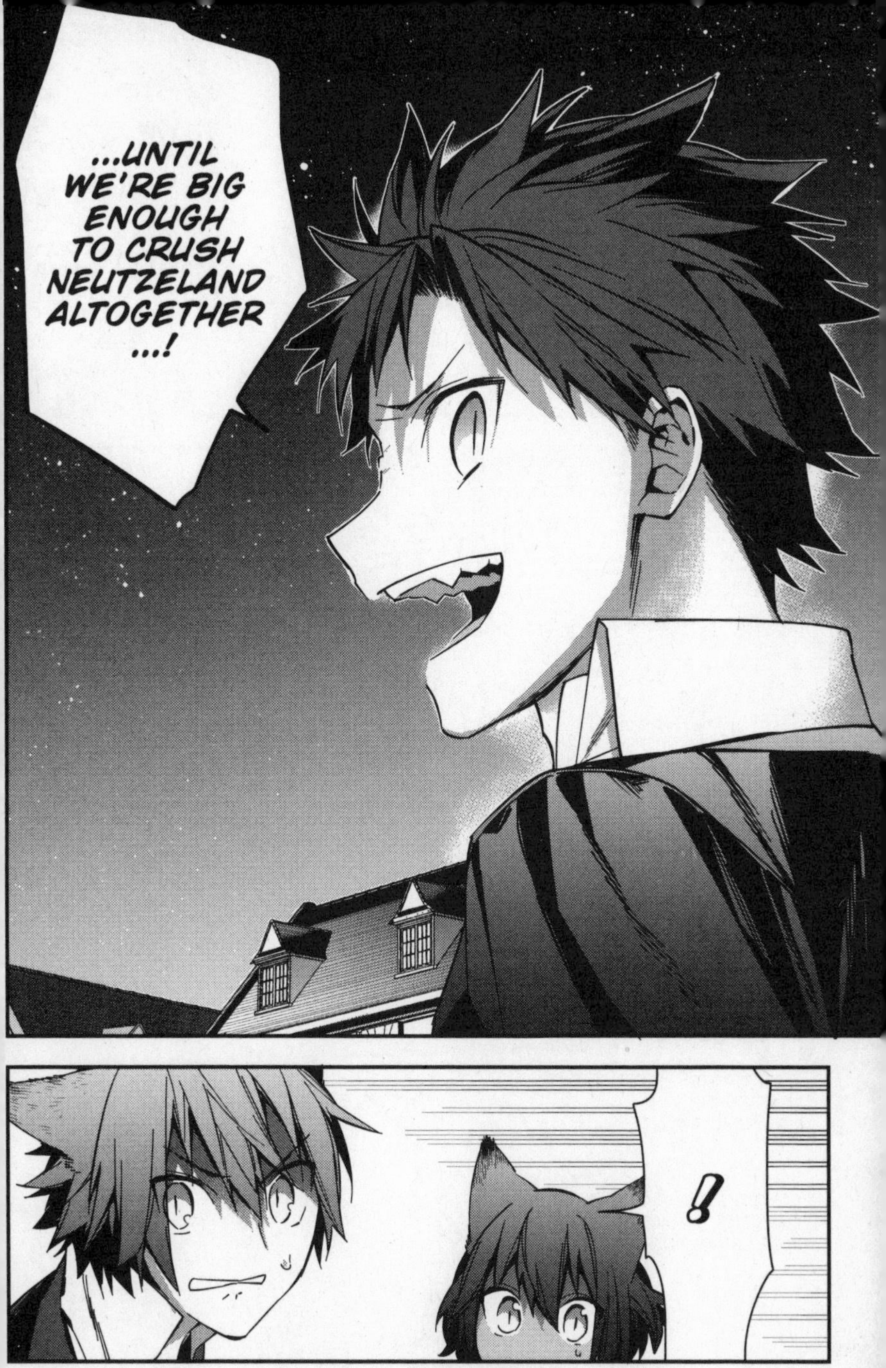
...UNTIL WE'RE BIG ENOUGH TO CRUSH NEUTZELAND ALTOGETHER ...!
!

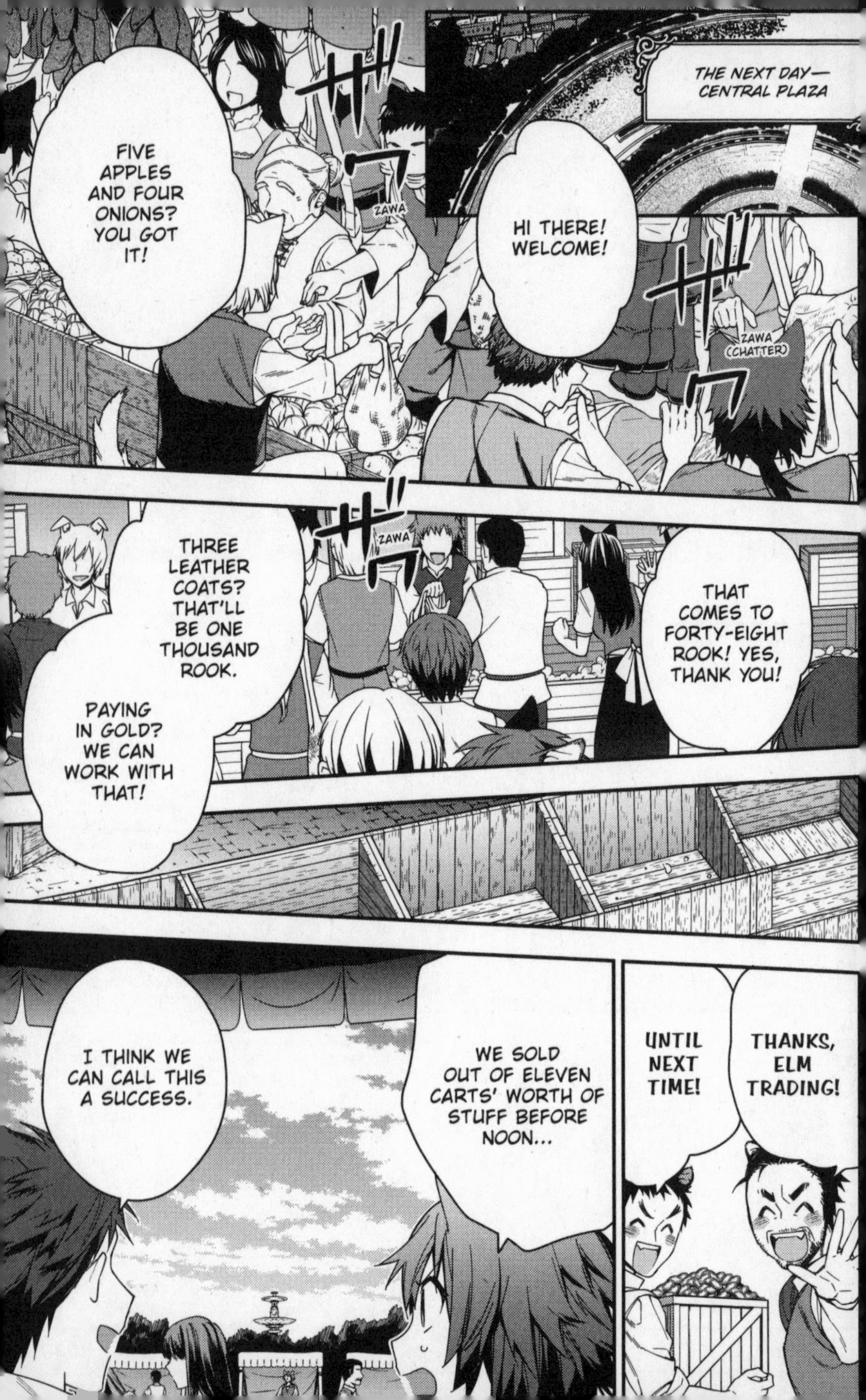
THE NEXT DAY—
CENTRAL PLAZA
HI THERE! WELCOME!
ZAWA
(CHATTER)
ZAWA
FIVE APPLES AND FOUR ONIONS? YOU GOT IT!
THAT COMES TO FORTY-EIGHT ROOK! YES, THANK YOU!
ZAWA
THREE LEATHER COATS? THAT'LL BE ONE THOUSAND ROOK.
PAYING IN GOLD? WE CAN WORK WITH THAT!
THANKS, ELM TRADING!
UNTIL NEXT TIME!
WE SOLD OUT OF ELEVEN CARTS' WORTH OF STUFF BEFORE NOON...
I THINK WE CAN CALL THIS A SUCCESS.

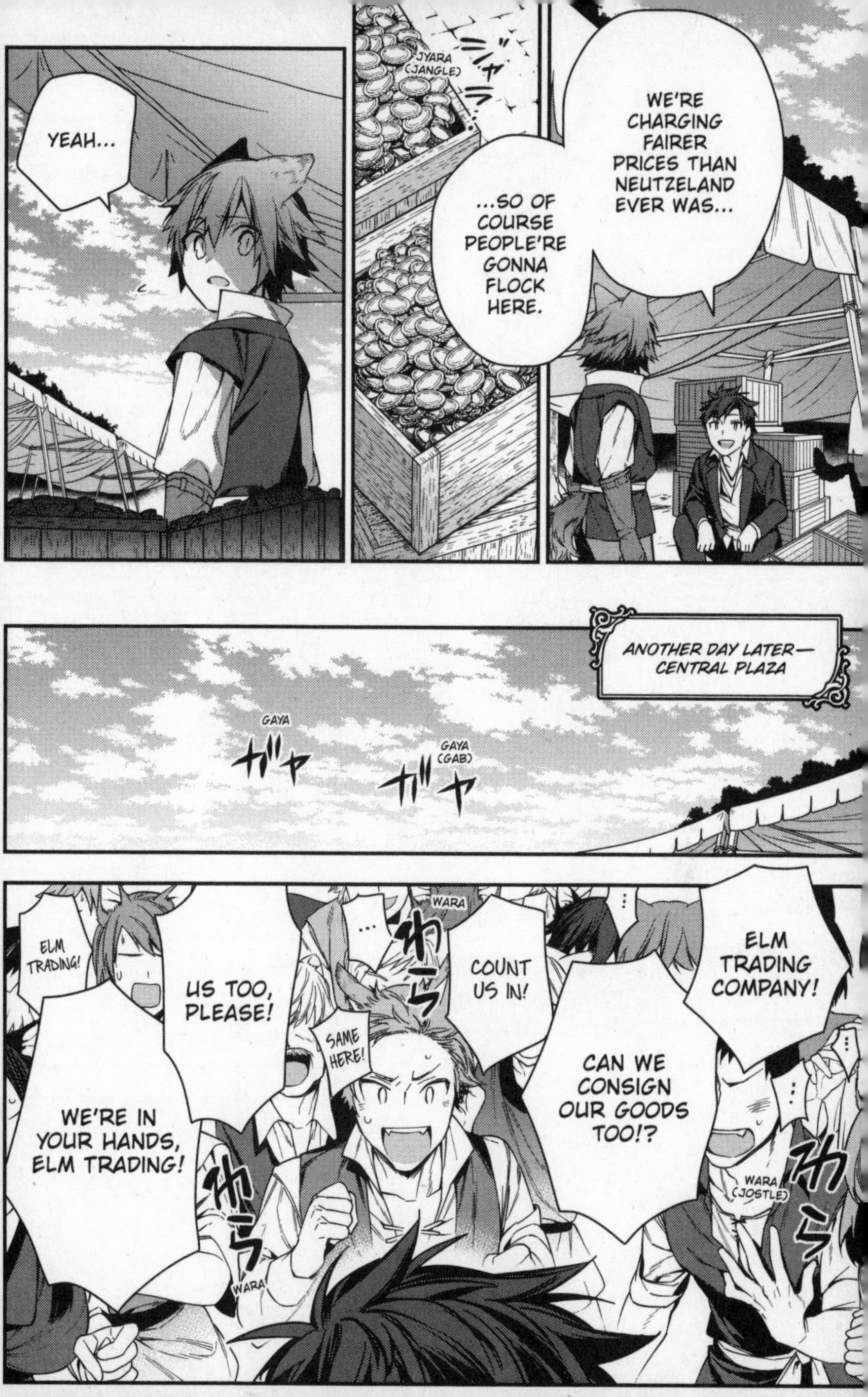
WE'RE CHARGING FAIRER PRICES THAN NEUTZELAND EVER WAS...
...SO OF COURSE PEOPLE'RE GONNA FLOCK HERE.
JYARA (JANGLE)
YEAH...
ANOTHER DAY LATER— CENTRAL PLAZA
GAYA (GAB)
GAYA
ELM TRADING COMPANY!
CAN WE CONSIGN OUR GOODS TOO!?
WARA (JOSTLE)
COUNT US IN!
WARA
SAME HERE!
US TOO, PLEASE!
ELM TRADING!
WE'RE IN YOUR HANDS, ELM TRADING!
WARA

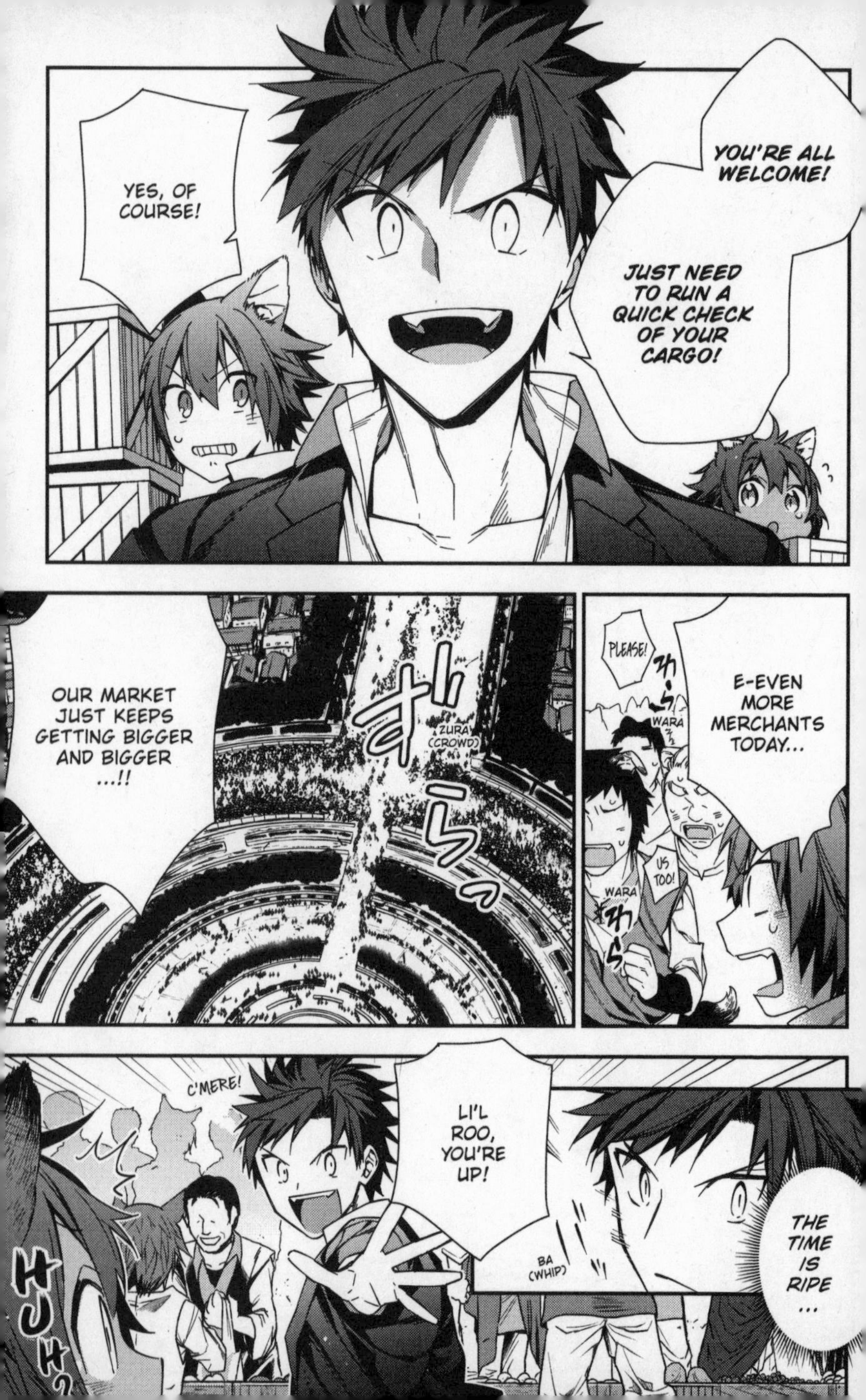
YOU'RE ALL WELCOME!
JUST NEED TO RUN A QUICK CHECK OF YOUR CARGO!
YES, OF COURSE!
E-EVEN MORE MERCHANTS TODAY...
PLEASE!
WARA
US TOO!
WARA
OUR MARKET JUST KEEPS GETTING BIGGER AND BIGGER ...!!
ZURA (CROWD)
THE TIME IS RIPE ...
LI'L ROO, YOU'RE UP!
BA (WHIP)
C'MERE!

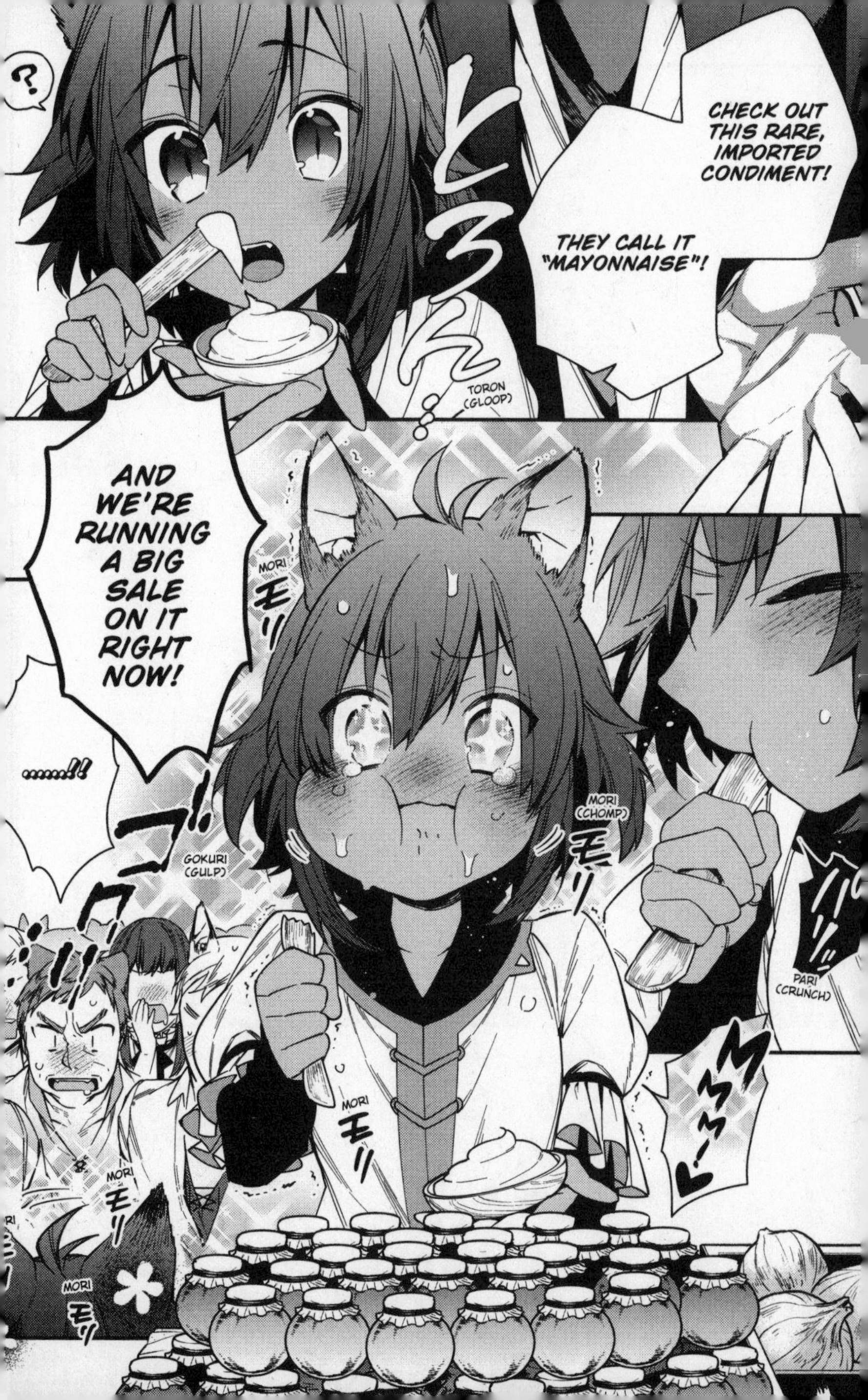
CHECK OUT THIS RARE, IMPORTED CONDIMENT!
THEY CALL IT "MAYONNAISE"!
TORON (GLOOP)
?
AND WE'RE RUNNING A BIG SALE ON IT RIGHT NOW!
PARI (CRUNCH)
MORI (CHOMP)
MORI
......!!
GOKURI (GULP)
MORI
MORI
MORI

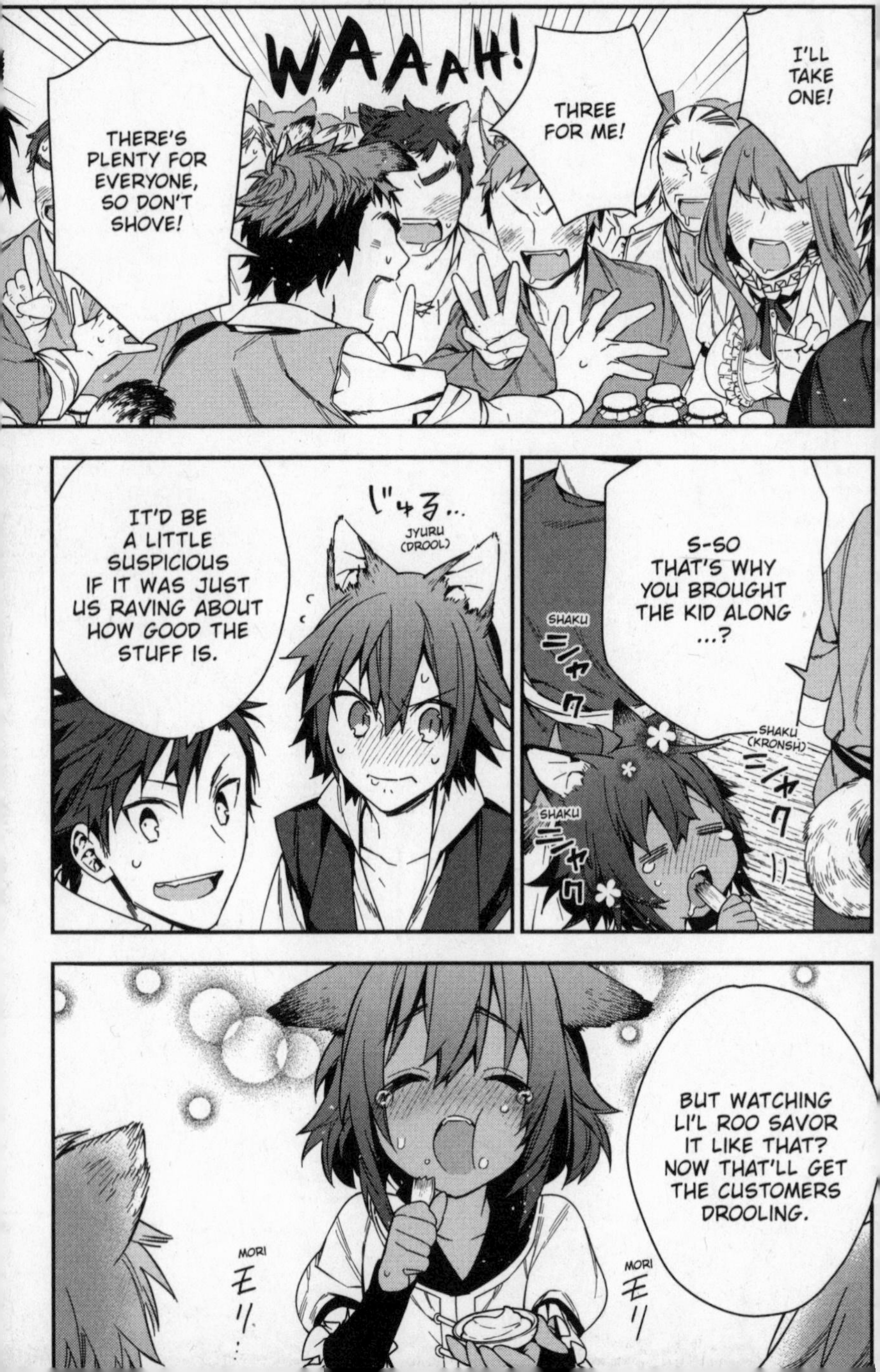
I'LL TAKE ONE!
THREE FOR ME!
WAAAH!
THERE'S PLENTY FOR EVERYONE, SO DON'T SHOVE!
S-SO THAT'S WHY YOU BROUGHT THE KID ALONG ...?
SHAKU
シャク
SHAKU (KRONSH)
シャク
SHAKU
シャク
じゅる…
JYURU (DROOL)
IT'D BE A LITTLE SUSPICIOUS IF IT WAS JUST US RAVING ABOUT HOW GOOD THE STUFF IS.
BUT WATCHING LI'L ROO SAVOR IT LIKE THAT? NOW THAT'LL GET THE CUSTOMERS DROOLING.
MORI
モリ
MORI
モリ

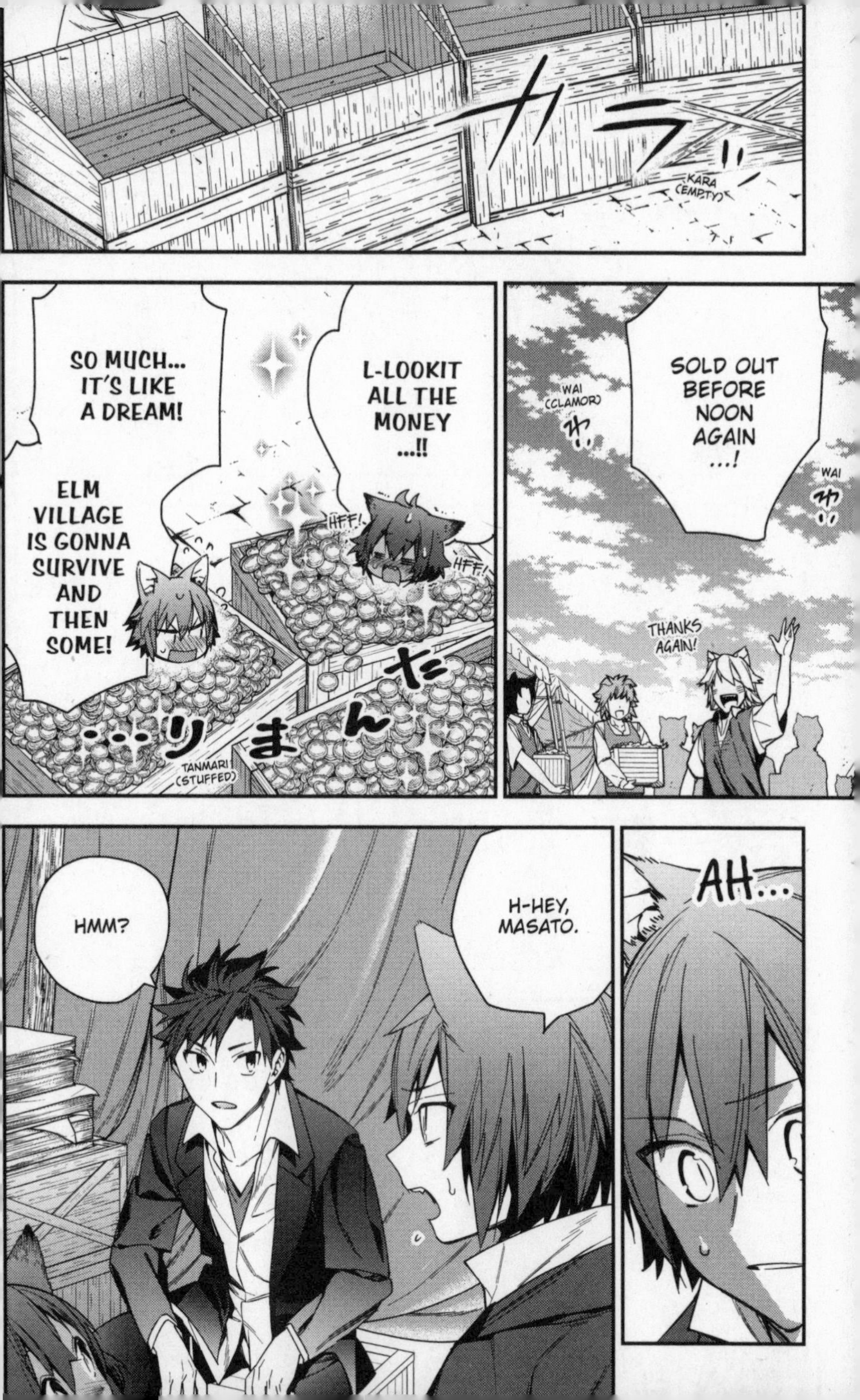
KARA (EMPTY)
SOLD OUT BEFORE NOON AGAIN ...!
WAI
WAI (CLAMOR)
THANKS AGAIN!
L-LOOKIT ALL THE MONEY ...!!
SO MUCH... IT'S LIKE A DREAM!
HFF!
HFF!
ELM VILLAGE IS GONNA SURVIVE AND THEN SOME!
TANMARI (STUFFED)
AH...
H-HEY, MASATO.
HMM?

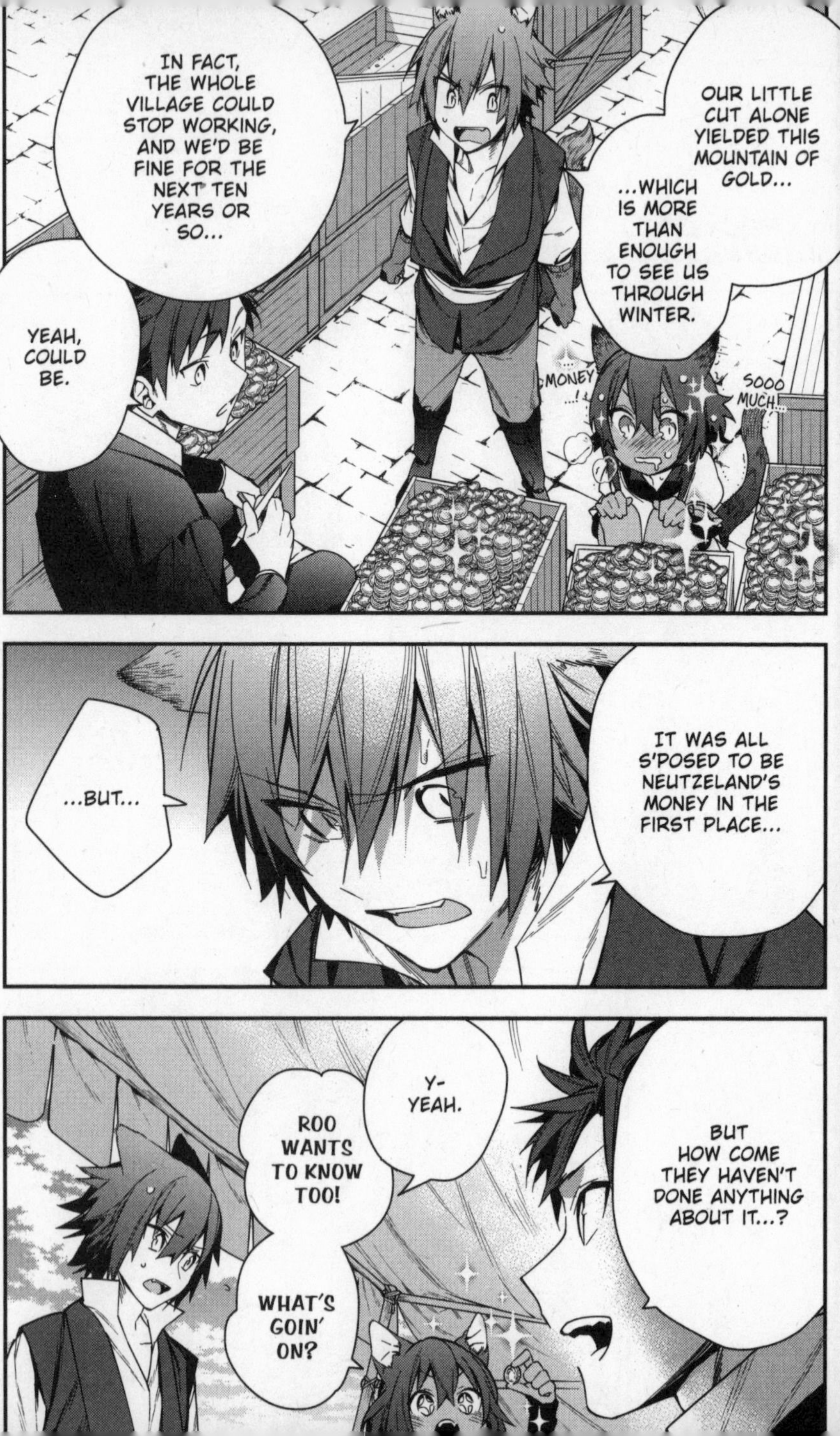
OUR LITTLE CUT ALONE YIELDED THIS MOUNTAIN OF GOLD...
...WHICH IS MORE THAN ENOUGH TO SEE US THROUGH WINTER.
IN FACT, THE WHOLE VILLAGE COULD STOP WORKING, AND WE'D BE FINE FOR THE NEXT TEN YEARS OR SO...
SOOO MUCH...
...MONEY...!
YEAH, COULD BE.
IT WAS ALL S'POSED TO BE NEUTZELAND'S MONEY IN THE FIRST PLACE...
...BUT...
BUT HOW COME THEY HAVEN'T DONE ANYTHING ABOUT IT...?
Y-YEAH.
ROO WANTS TO KNOW TOO!
WHAT'S GOIN' ON?

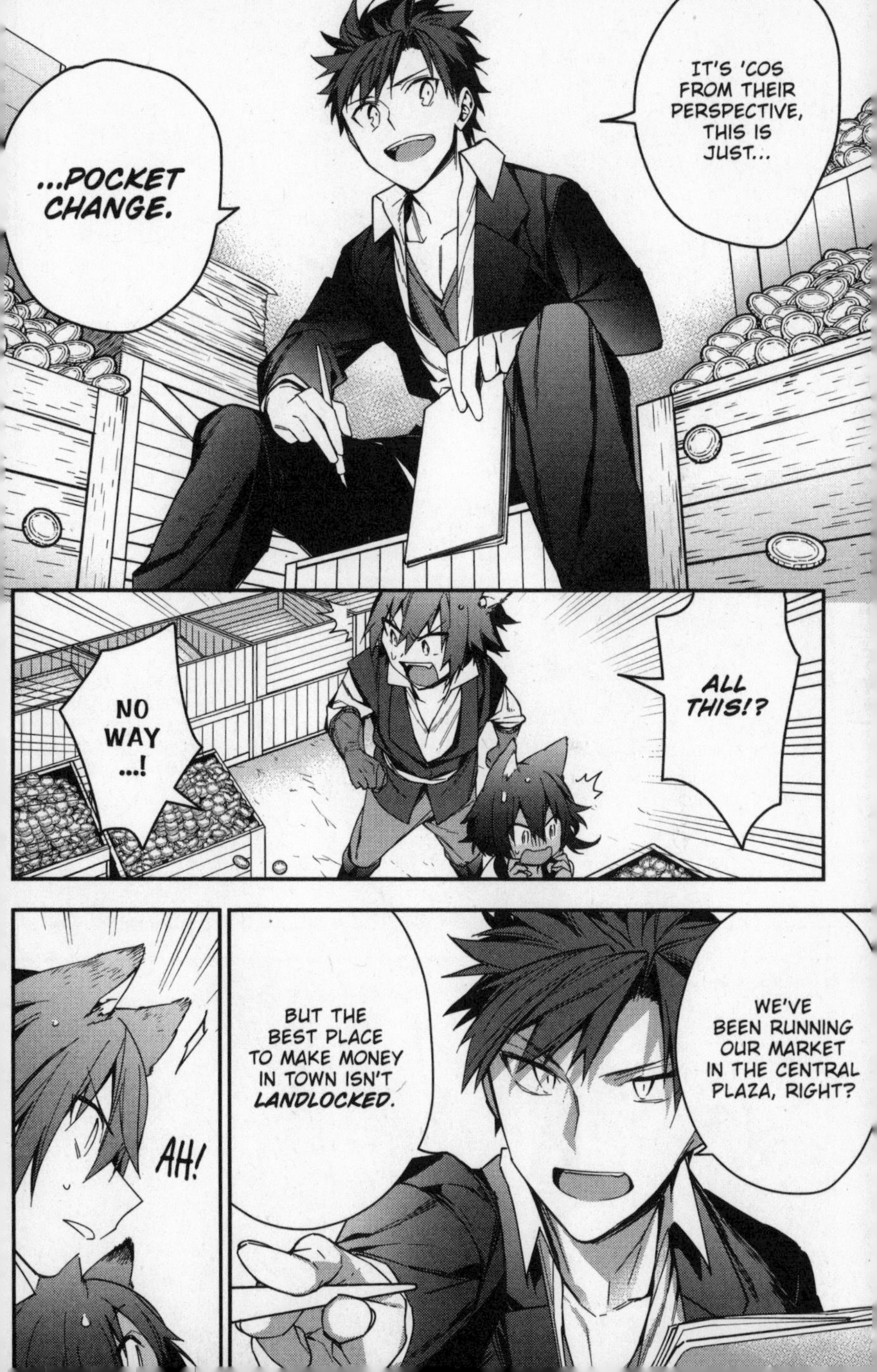
IT'S 'COS FROM THEIR PERSPECTIVE, THIS IS JUST...
...POCKET CHANGE.
ALL THIS!?
NO WAY ...!
WE'VE BEEN RUNNING OUR MARKET IN THE CENTRAL PLAZA, RIGHT?
BUT THE BEST PLACE TO MAKE MONEY IN TOWN ISN'T *LANDLOCKED*.
AH!

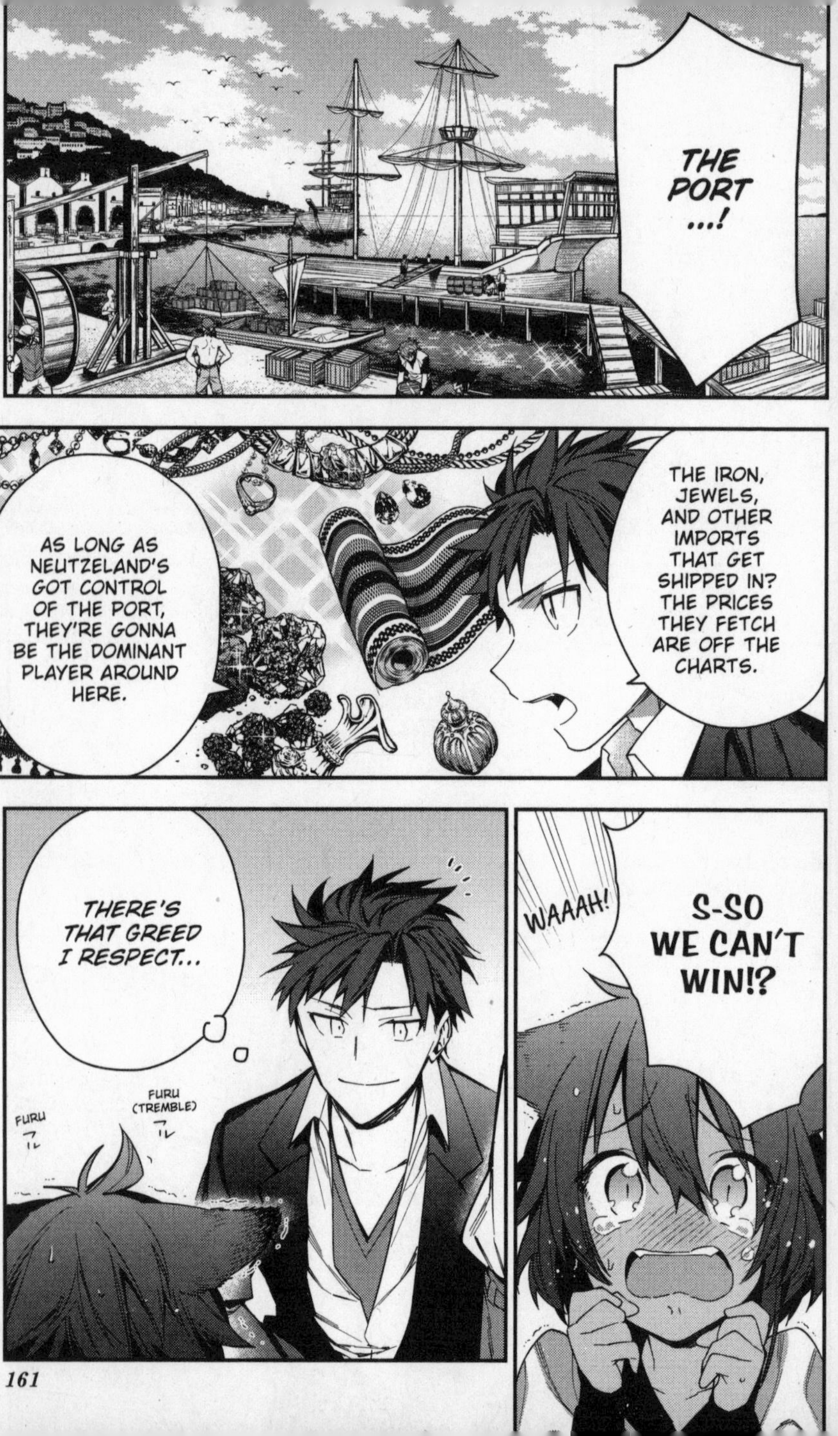
THE PORT ...!
THE IRON, JEWELS, AND OTHER IMPORTS THAT GET SHIPPED IN? THE PRICES THEY FETCH ARE OFF THE CHARTS.
AS LONG AS NEUTZELAND'S GOT CONTROL OF THE PORT, THEY'RE GONNA BE THE DOMINANT PLAYER AROUND HERE.
S-SO WE CAN'T WIN!?
WAAAH!
THERE'S THAT GREED I RESPECT...
FURU (TREMBLE)
FURU

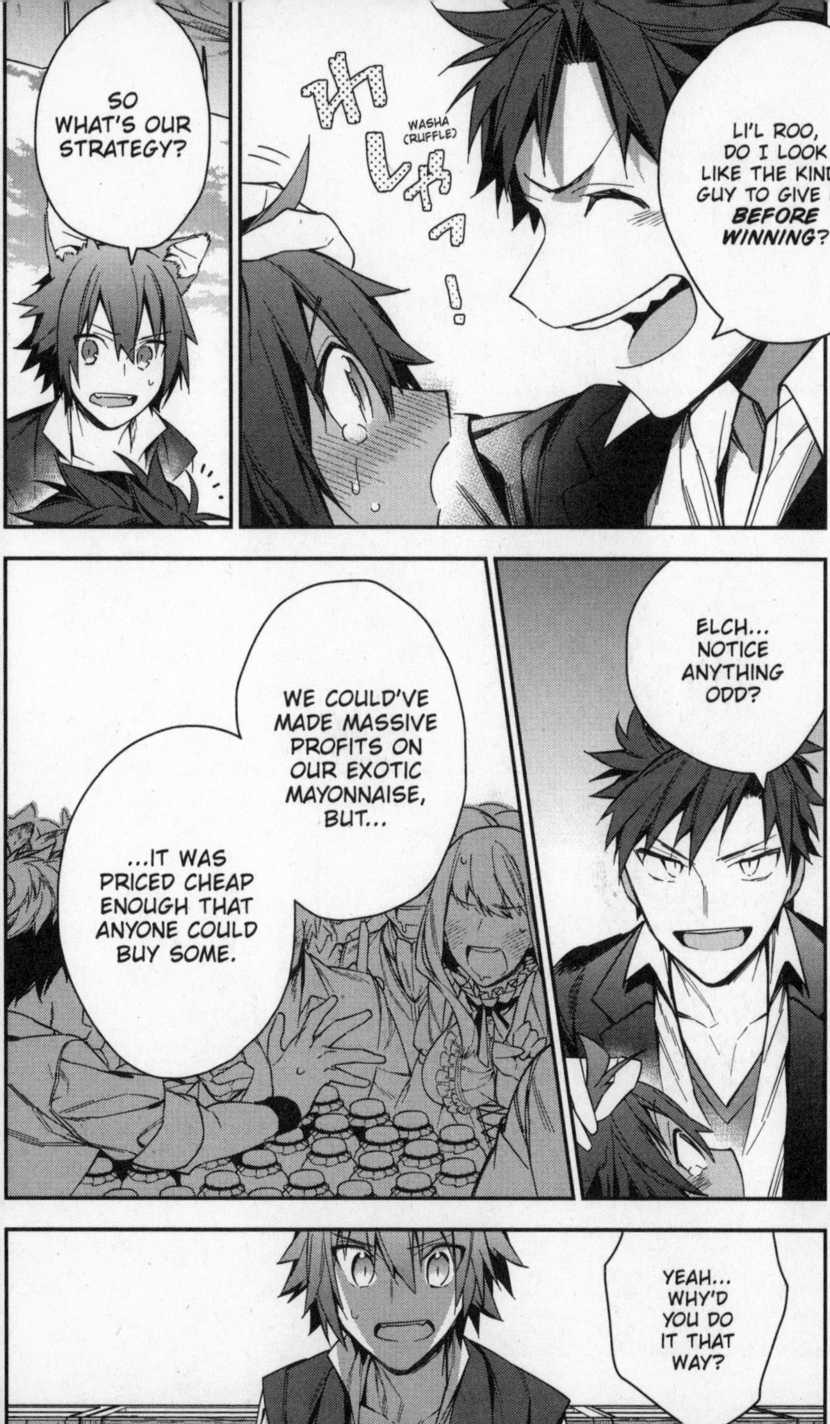
WASHA (RUFFLE)
LI'L ROO, DO I LOOK LIKE THE KINDA GUY TO GIVE UP ***BEFORE WINNING***?
SO WHAT'S OUR STRATEGY?
ELCH... NOTICE ANYTHING ODD?
WE COULD'VE MADE MASSIVE PROFITS ON OUR EXOTIC MAYONNAISE, BUT...
...IT WAS PRICED CHEAP ENOUGH THAT ANYONE COULD BUY SOME.
YEAH... WHY'D YOU DO IT THAT WAY?

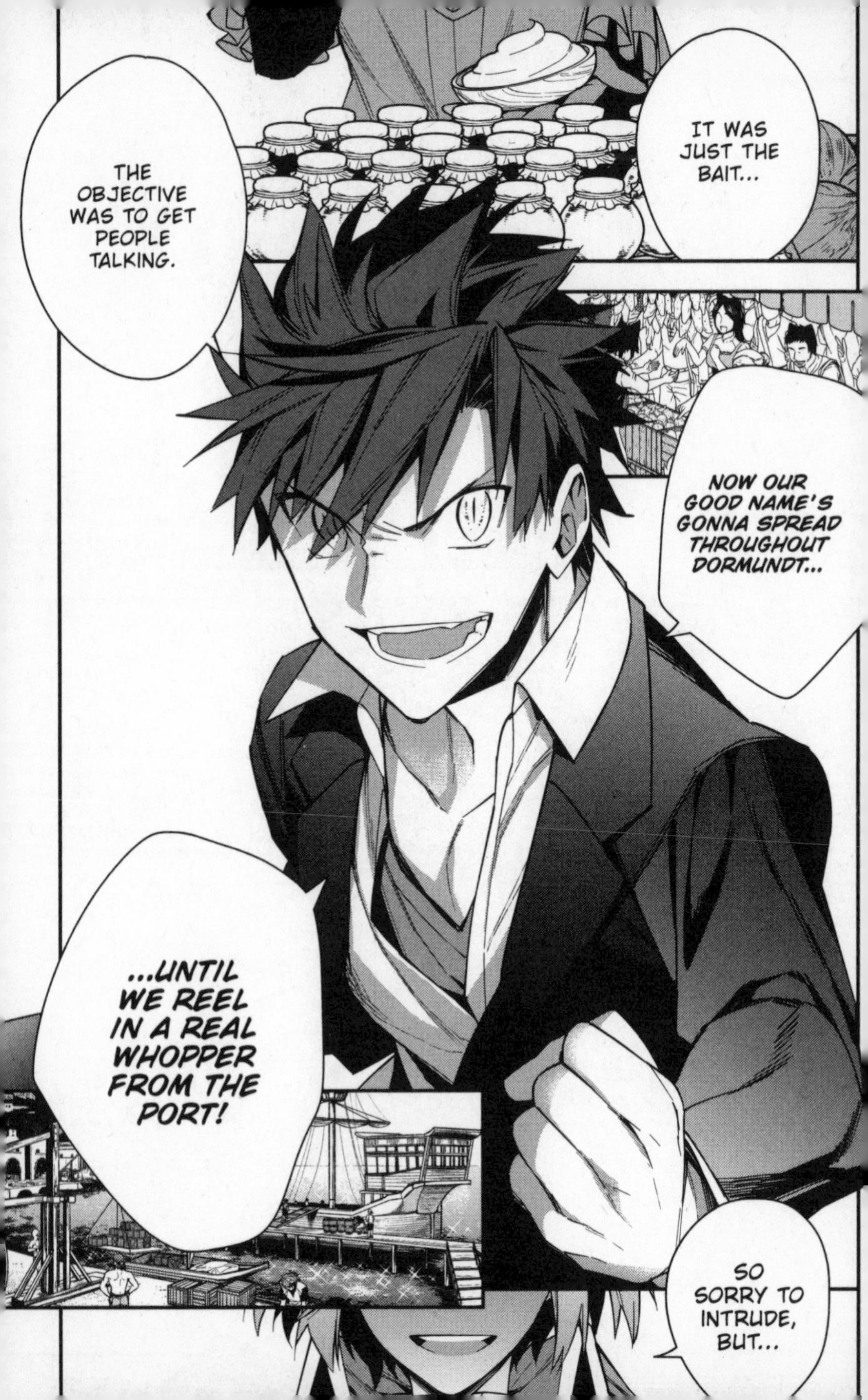
IT WAS JUST THE BAIT...
THE OBJECTIVE WAS TO GET PEOPLE TALKING.
NOW OUR GOOD NAME'S GONNA SPREAD THROUGHOUT DORMUNDT...
...UNTIL WE REEL IN A REAL WHOPPER FROM THE PORT!
SO SORRY TO INTRUDE, BUT...

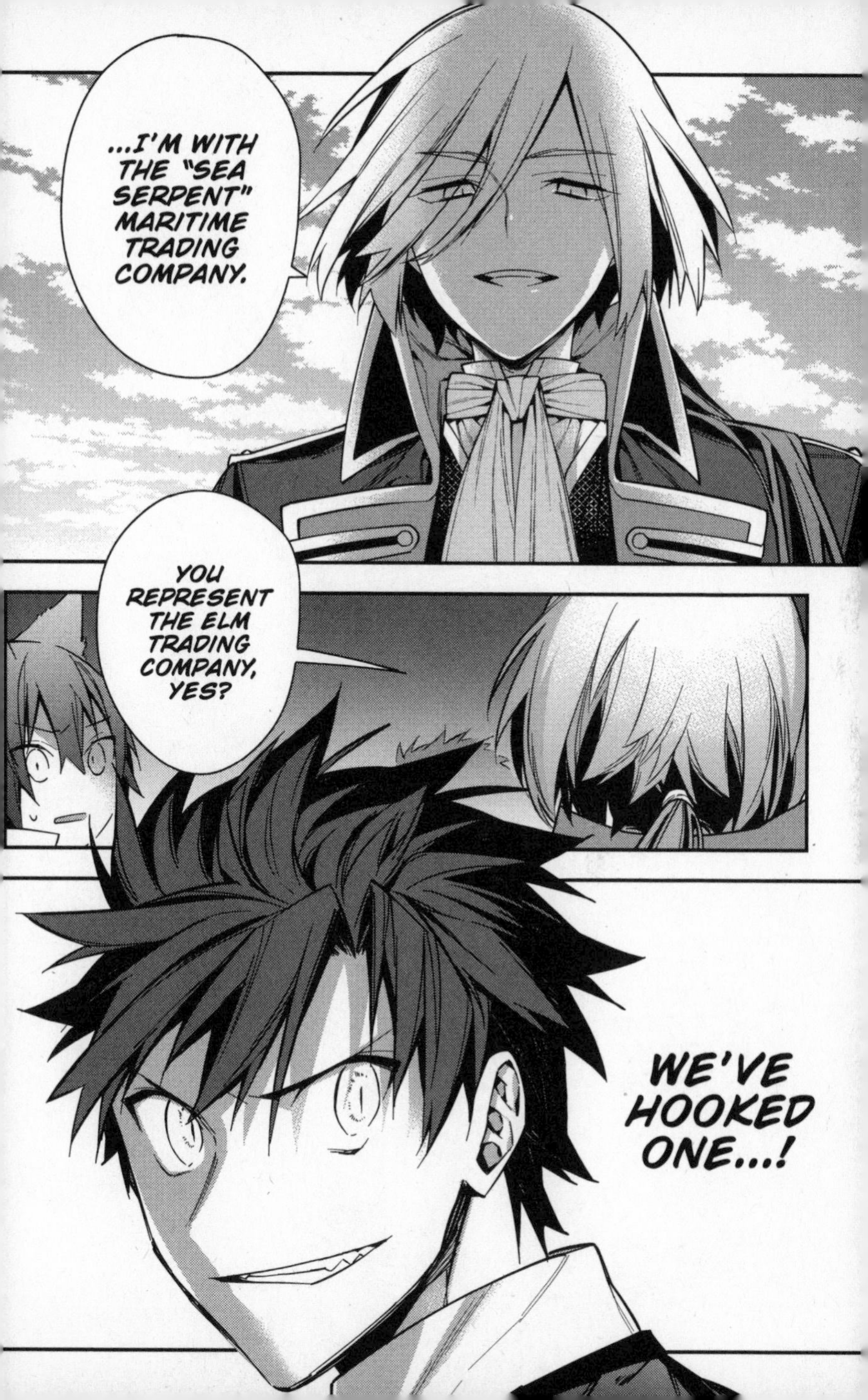
...I'M WITH THE "SEA SERPENT" MARITIME TRADING COMPANY.
YOU REPRESENT THE ELM TRADING COMPANY, YES?
WE'VE HOOKED ONE...!

HIGH SCHOOL
PRODIGIES HAVE
IT EASY EVEN IN
ANOTHER
WORLD!

CHARACTER FILE 07

Keine
Kanzaki

One of the high school prodigies.
There's no malady she can't heal,
and not a single person has died on
her operating table to date. She went
to the same middle school as Aoi.

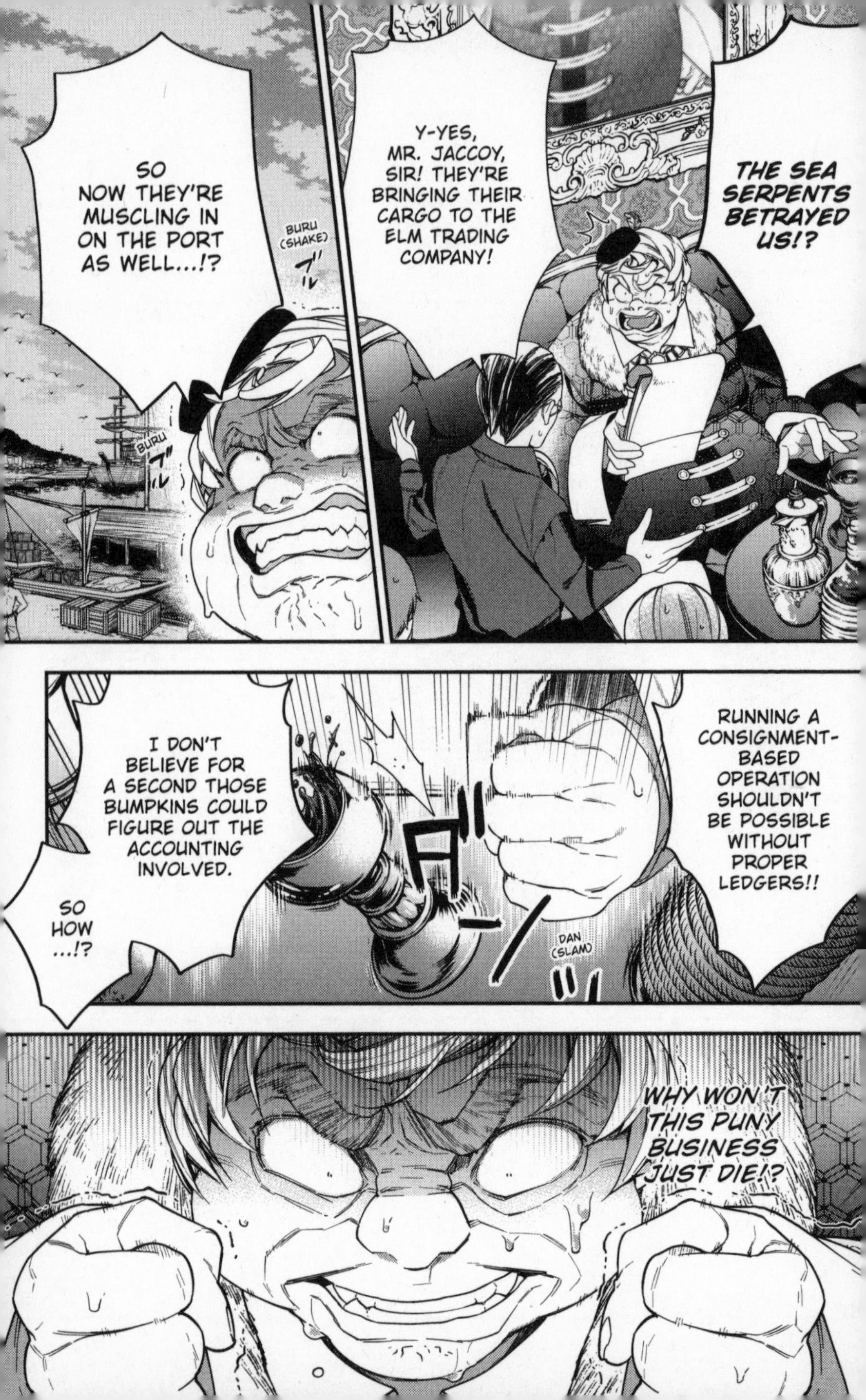
THE SEA SERPENTS BETRAYED US!?
Y-YES, MR. JACCOY, SIR! THEY'RE BRINGING THEIR CARGO TO THE ELM TRADING COMPANY!
BURU (SHAKE)
BURU
SO NOW THEY'RE MUSCLING IN ON THE PORT AS WELL...!?
RUNNING A CONSIGNMENT-BASED OPERATION SHOULDN'T BE POSSIBLE WITHOUT PROPER LEDGERS!!
DAN (SLAM)
I DON'T BELIEVE FOR A SECOND THOSE BUMPKINS COULD FIGURE OUT THE ACCOUNTING INVOLVED.
SO HOW ...!?
WHY WON'T THIS PUNY BUSINESS JUST DIE!?

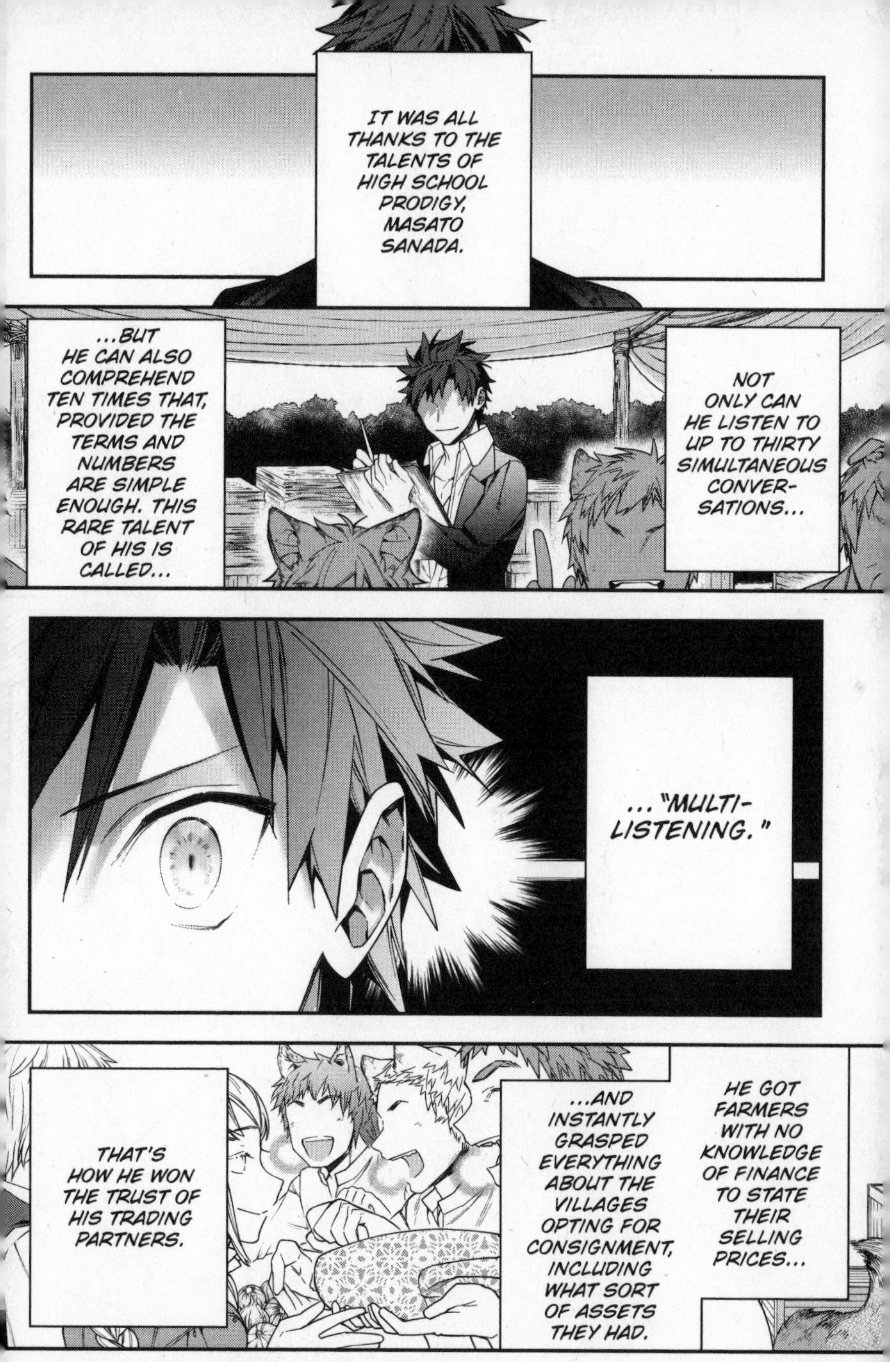
IT WAS ALL THANKS TO THE TALENTS OF HIGH SCHOOL PRODIGY, MASATO SANADA.
NOT ONLY CAN HE LISTEN TO UP TO THIRTY SIMULTANEOUS CONVER-SATIONS...
...BUT HE CAN ALSO COMPREHEND TEN TIMES THAT, PROVIDED THE TERMS AND NUMBERS ARE SIMPLE ENOUGH. THIS RARE TALENT OF HIS IS CALLED...
..."MULTI-LISTENING."
HE GOT FARMERS WITH NO KNOWLEDGE OF FINANCE TO STATE THEIR SELLING PRICES...
...AND INSTANTLY GRASPED EVERYTHING ABOUT THE VILLAGES OPTING FOR CONSIGNMENT, INCLUDING WHAT SORT OF ASSETS THEY HAD.
THAT'S HOW HE WON THE TRUST OF HIS TRADING PARTNERS.

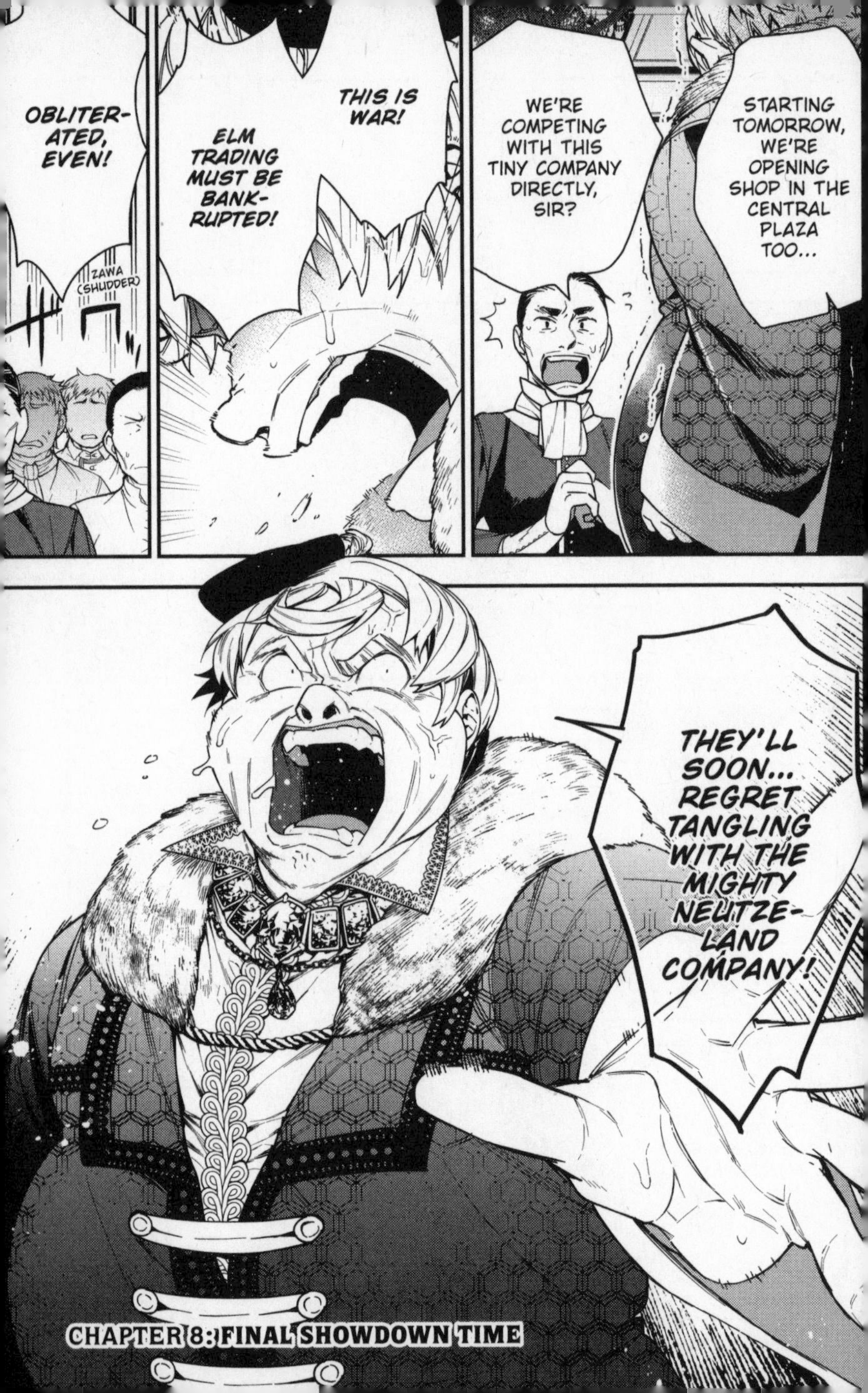
STARTING TOMORROW, WE'RE OPENING SHOP IN THE CENTRAL PLAZA TOO...
WE'RE COMPETING WITH THIS TINY COMPANY DIRECTLY, SIR?
THIS IS WAR!
ELM TRADING MUST BE BANK-RUPTED!
OBLITER-ATED, EVEN!
ZAWA (SHUDDER)
THEY'LL SOON... REGRET TANGLING WITH THE MIGHTY NEUTZE-LAND COMPANY!

CHAPTER 8: FINAL SHOWDOWN TIME

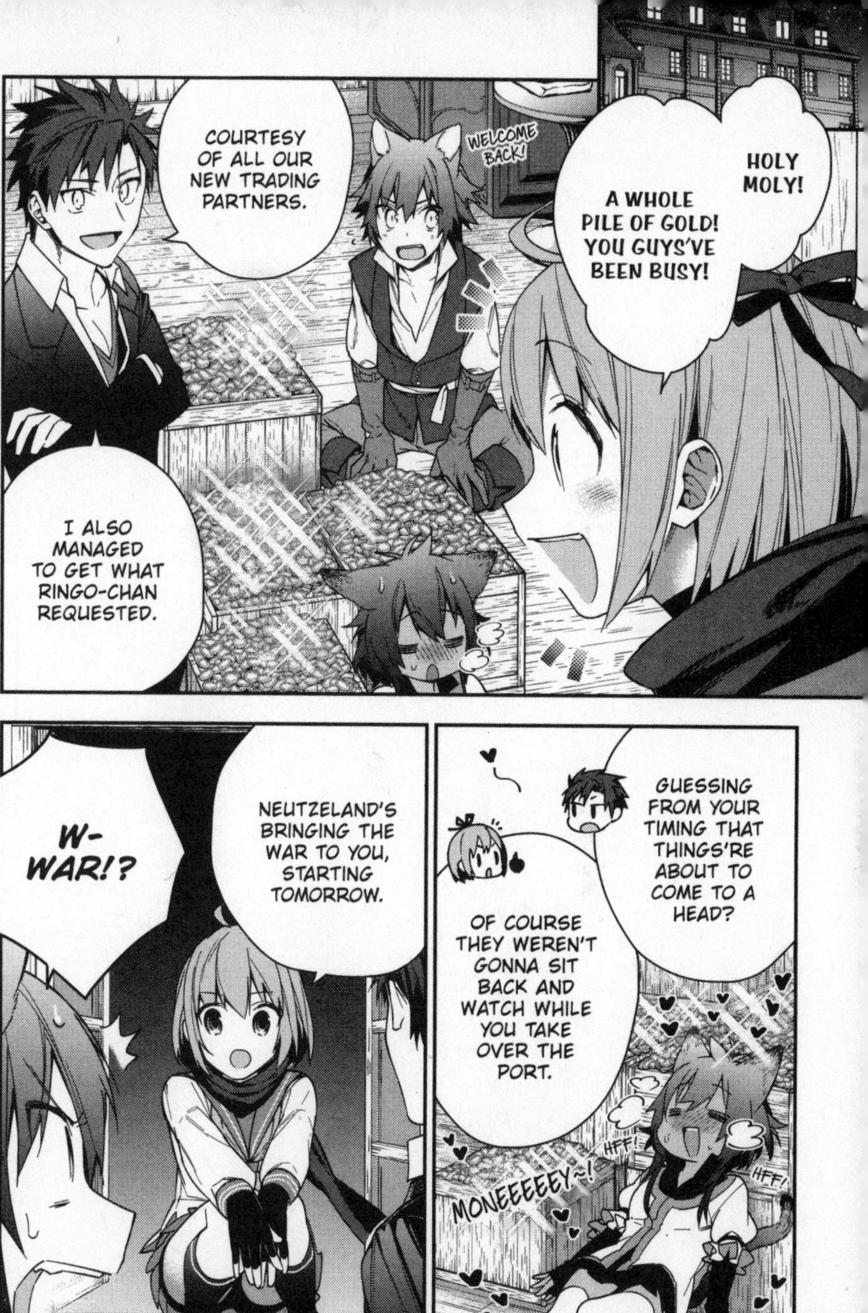
HOLY MOLY!
A WHOLE PILE OF GOLD! YOU GUYS'VE BEEN BUSY!
WELCOME BACK!
COURTESY OF ALL OUR NEW TRADING PARTNERS.
I ALSO MANAGED TO GET WHAT RINGO-CHAN REQUESTED.
GUESSING FROM YOUR TIMING THAT THINGS'RE ABOUT TO COME TO A HEAD?
OF COURSE THEY WEREN'T GONNA SIT BACK AND WATCH WHILE YOU TAKE OVER THE PORT.
HFF!
HFF!
MONEEEEEY~!
NEUTZELAND'S BRINGING THE WAR TO YOU, STARTING TOMORROW.
W-WAR!?

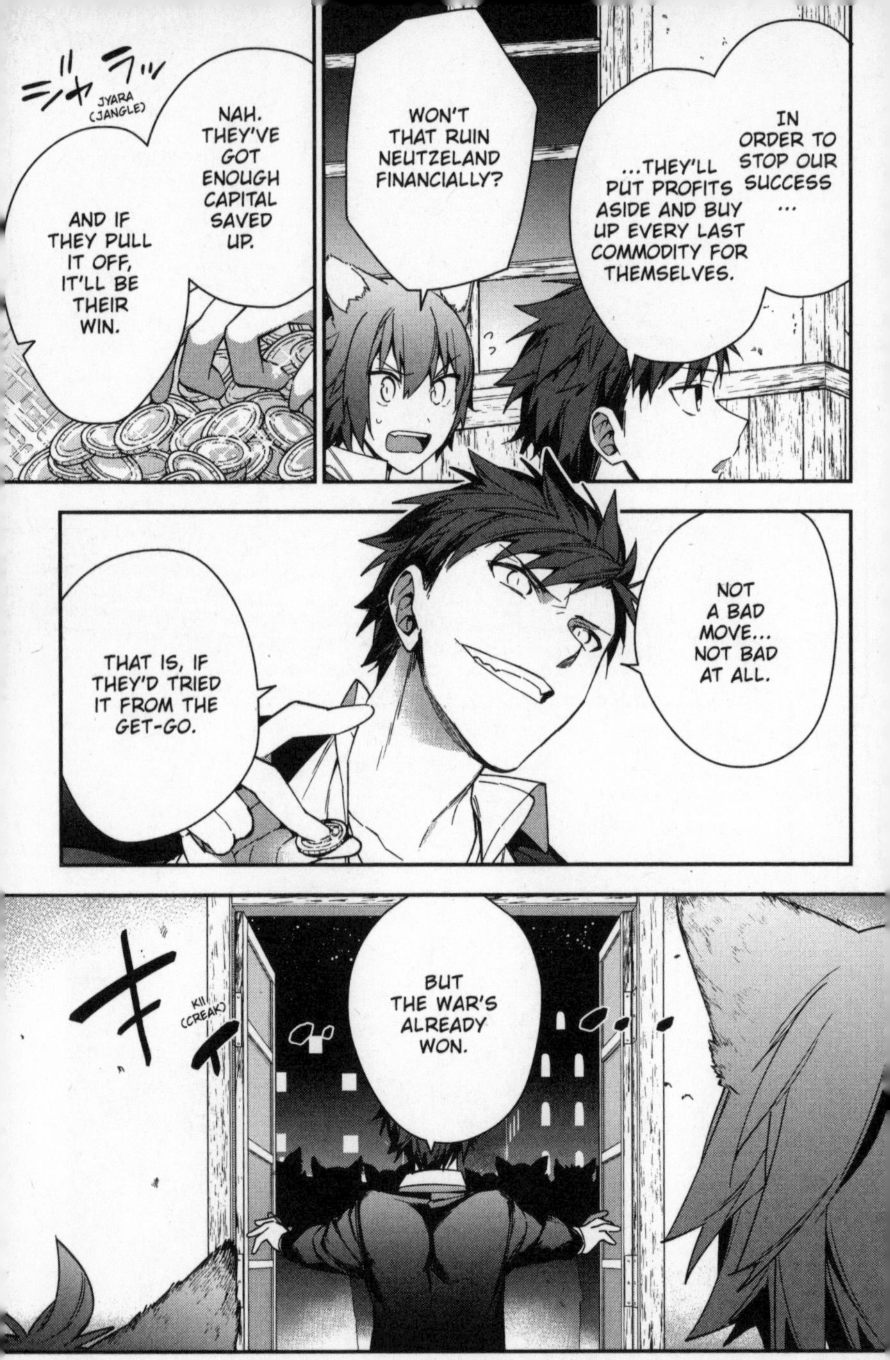
IN ORDER TO STOP OUR SUCCESS...
...THEY'LL PUT PROFITS ASIDE AND BUY UP EVERY LAST COMMODITY FOR THEMSELVES.
WON'T THAT RUIN NEUTZELAND FINANCIALLY?
JYARA (JANGLE)
NAH. THEY'VE GOT ENOUGH CAPITAL SAVED UP.
AND IF THEY PULL IT OFF, IT'LL BE THEIR WIN.
NOT A BAD MOVE... NOT BAD AT ALL.
THAT IS, IF THEY'D TRIED IT FROM THE GET-GO.
BUT THE WAR'S ALREADY WON.
KII (CREAK)

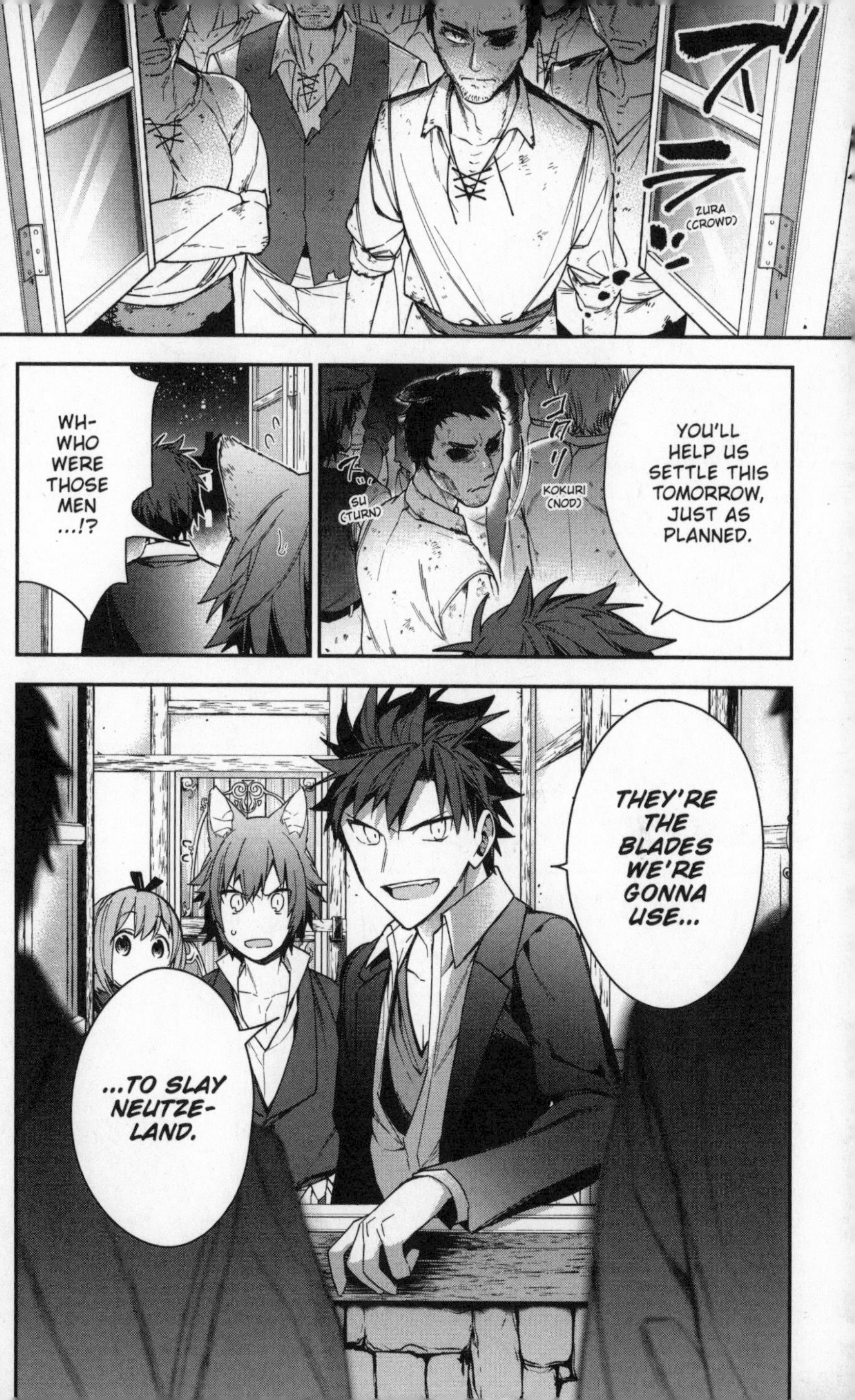
ZURA (CROWD)
YOU'LL HELP US SETTLE THIS TOMORROW, JUST AS PLANNED.
KOKURI (NOD)
SU (TURN)
WH-WHO WERE THOSE MEN ...!?
THEY'RE THE BLADES WE'RE GONNA USE...
...TO SLAY NEUTZE-LAND.

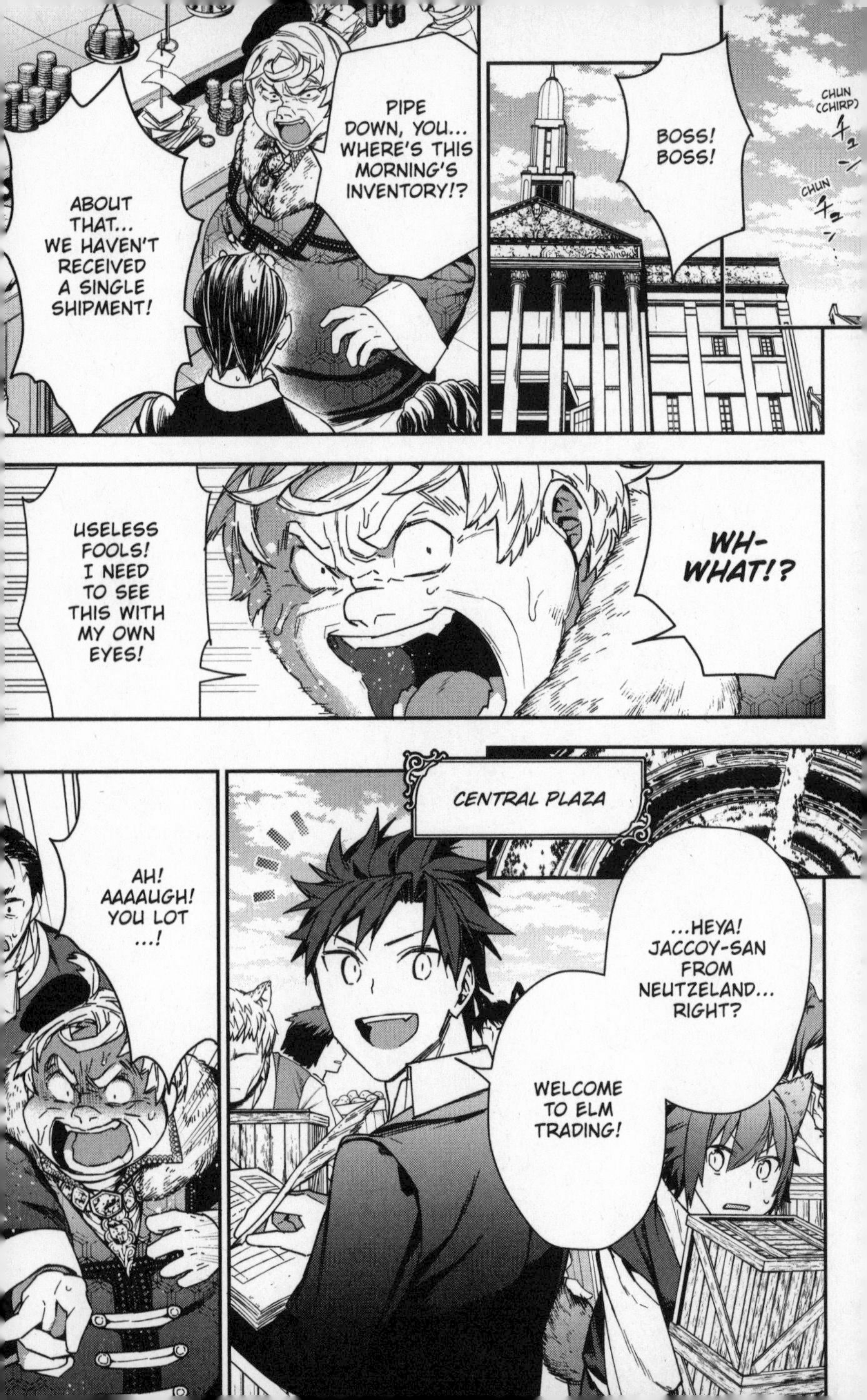
CHUN (CHIRP)
CHUN
BOSS! BOSS!
PIPE DOWN, YOU... WHERE'S THIS MORNING'S INVENTORY!?
ABOUT THAT... WE HAVEN'T RECEIVED A SINGLE SHIPMENT!
WH-WHAT!?
USELESS FOOLS! I NEED TO SEE THIS WITH MY OWN EYES!
CENTRAL PLAZA
...HEYA! JACCOY-SAN FROM NEUTZELAND... RIGHT?
WELCOME TO ELM TRADING!
AH! AAAAUGH! YOU LOT ...!

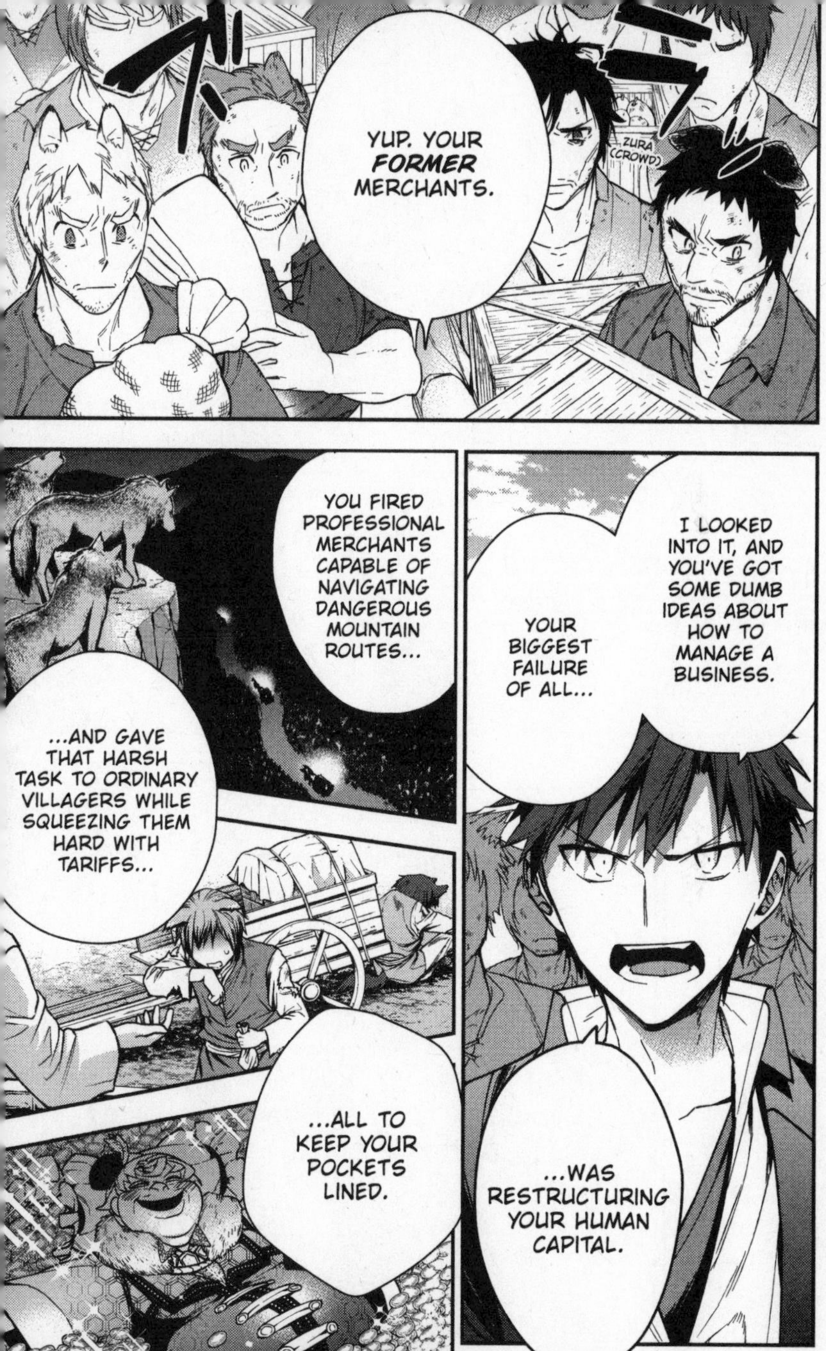
ZURA (CROWD)
YUP. YOUR *FORMER* MERCHANTS.
I LOOKED INTO IT, AND YOU'VE GOT SOME DUMB IDEAS ABOUT HOW TO MANAGE A BUSINESS.
YOUR BIGGEST FAILURE OF ALL...
...WAS RESTRUCTURING YOUR HUMAN CAPITAL.
YOU FIRED PROFESSIONAL MERCHANTS CAPABLE OF NAVIGATING DANGEROUS MOUNTAIN ROUTES...
...AND GAVE THAT HARSH TASK TO ORDINARY VILLAGERS WHILE SQUEEZING THEM HARD WITH TARIFFS...
...ALL TO KEEP YOUR POCKETS LINED.

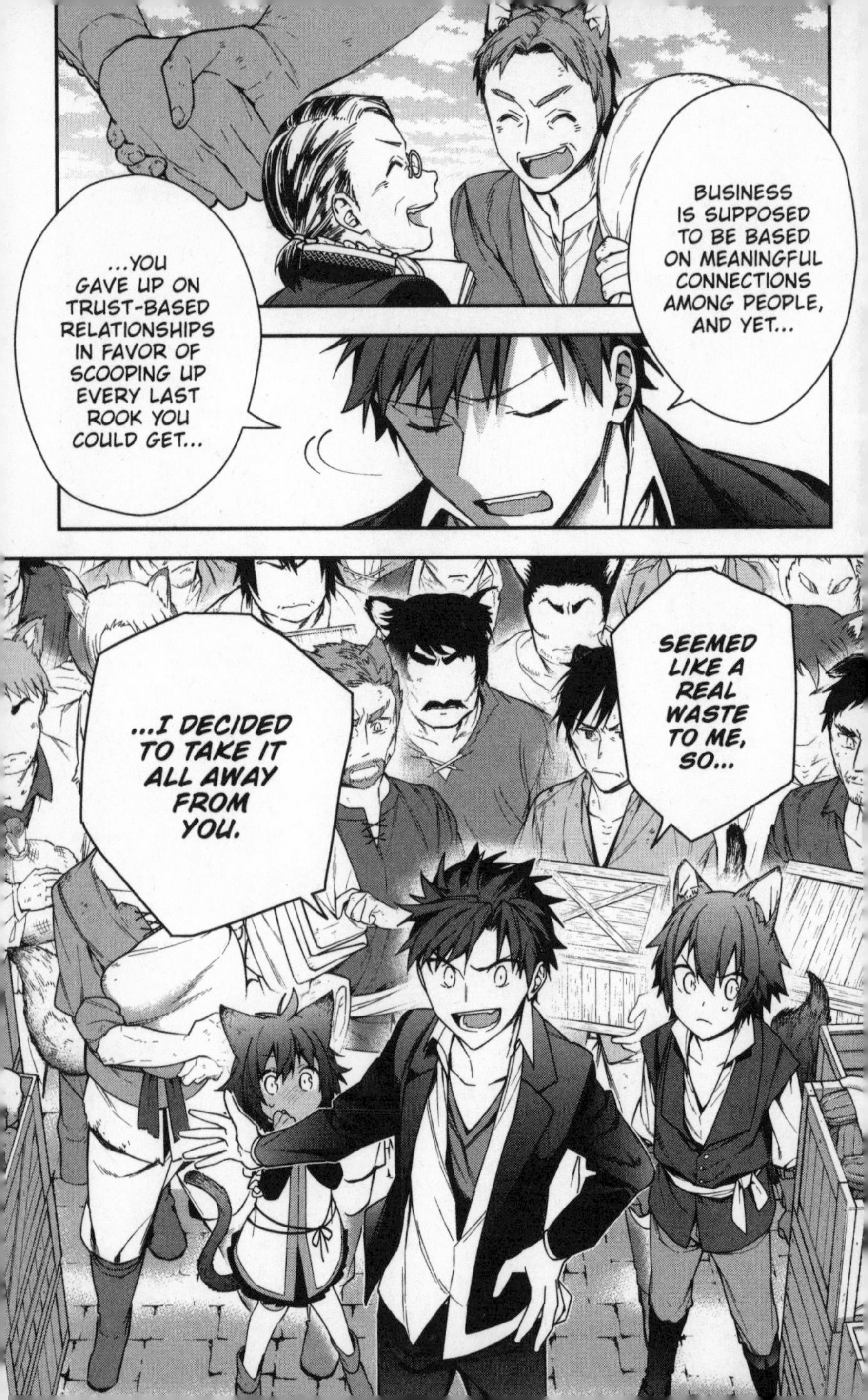
BUSINESS IS SUPPOSED TO BE BASED ON MEANINGFUL CONNECTIONS AMONG PEOPLE, AND YET...
...YOU GAVE UP ON TRUST-BASED RELATIONSHIPS IN FAVOR OF SCOOPING UP EVERY LAST ROOK YOU COULD GET...
SEEMED LIKE A REAL WASTE TO ME, SO...
...I DECIDED TO TAKE IT ALL AWAY FROM YOU.

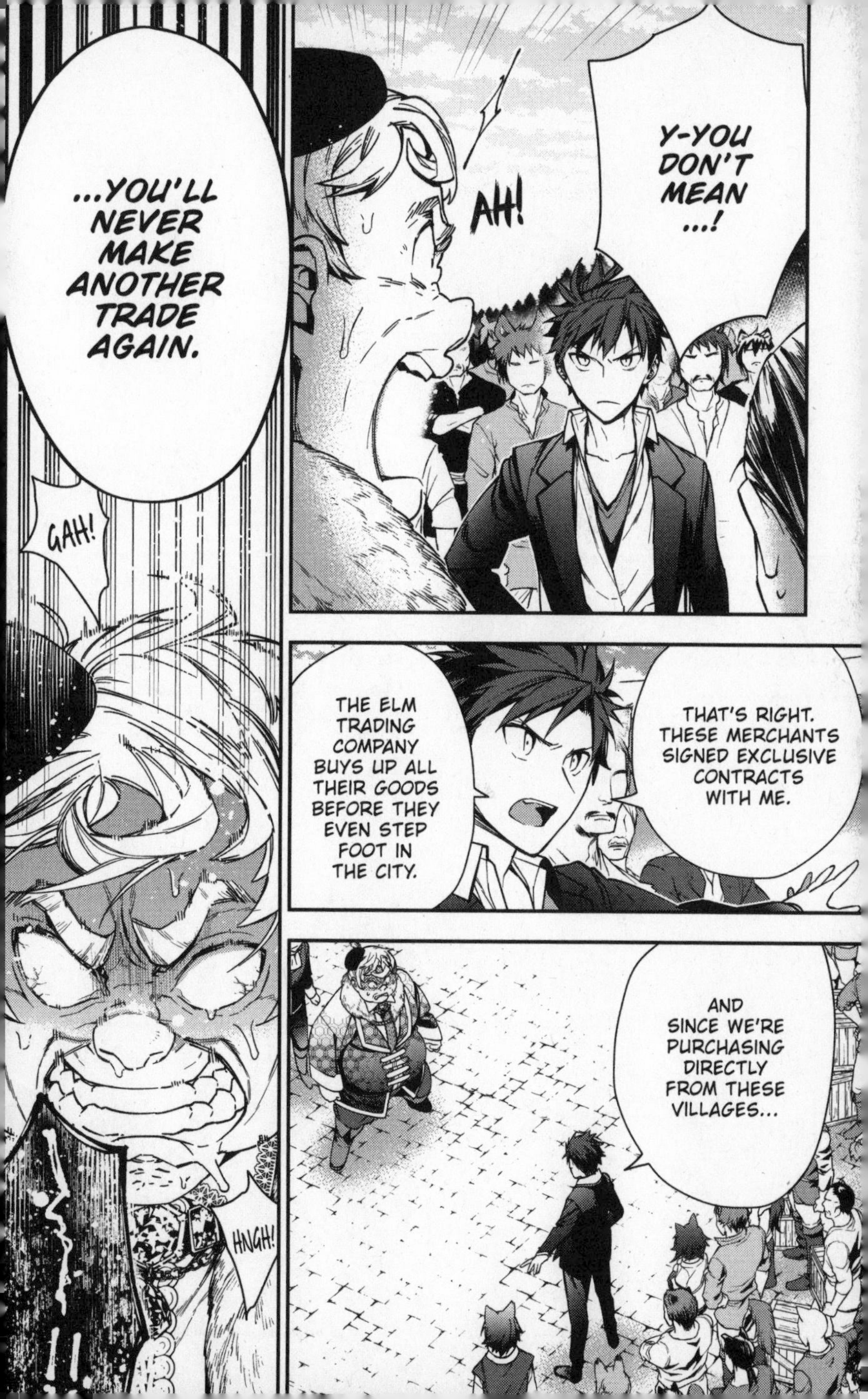
Y-YOU DON'T MEAN ...!
AH!
THAT'S RIGHT. THESE MERCHANTS SIGNED EXCLUSIVE CONTRACTS WITH ME.
THE ELM TRADING COMPANY BUYS UP ALL THEIR GOODS BEFORE THEY EVEN STEP FOOT IN THE CITY.
AND SINCE WE'RE PURCHASING DIRECTLY FROM THESE VILLAGES...
...YOU'LL NEVER MAKE ANOTHER TRADE AGAIN.
GAH!
HNGH!

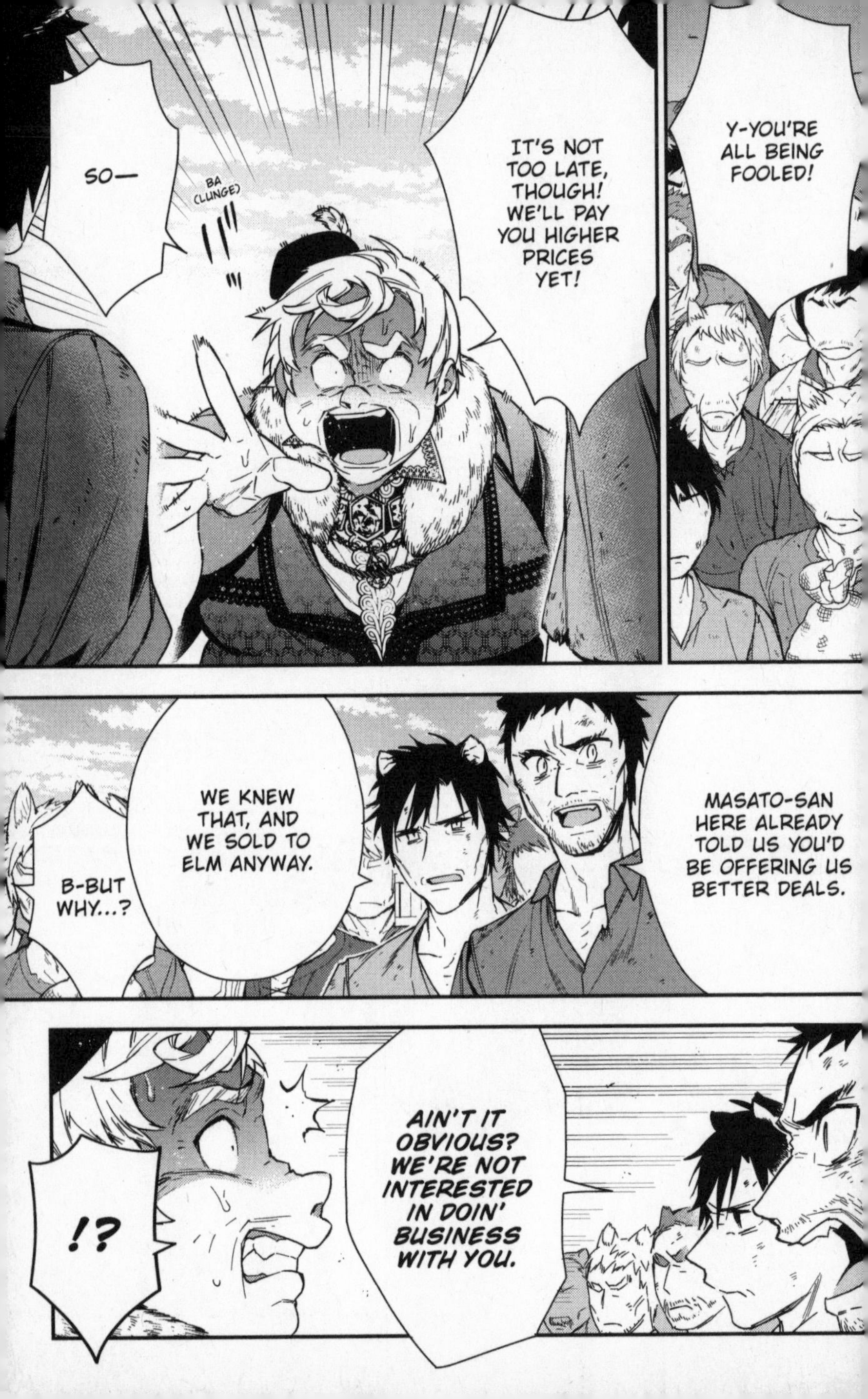
Y-YOU'RE ALL BEING FOOLED!
IT'S NOT TOO LATE, THOUGH! WE'LL PAY YOU HIGHER PRICES YET!
BA (LUNGE)
SO—
MASATO-SAN HERE ALREADY TOLD US YOU'D BE OFFERING US BETTER DEALS.
WE KNEW THAT, AND WE SOLD TO ELM ANYWAY.
B-BUT WHY...?
AIN'T IT OBVIOUS? WE'RE NOT INTERESTED IN DOIN' BUSINESS WITH YOU.
!?

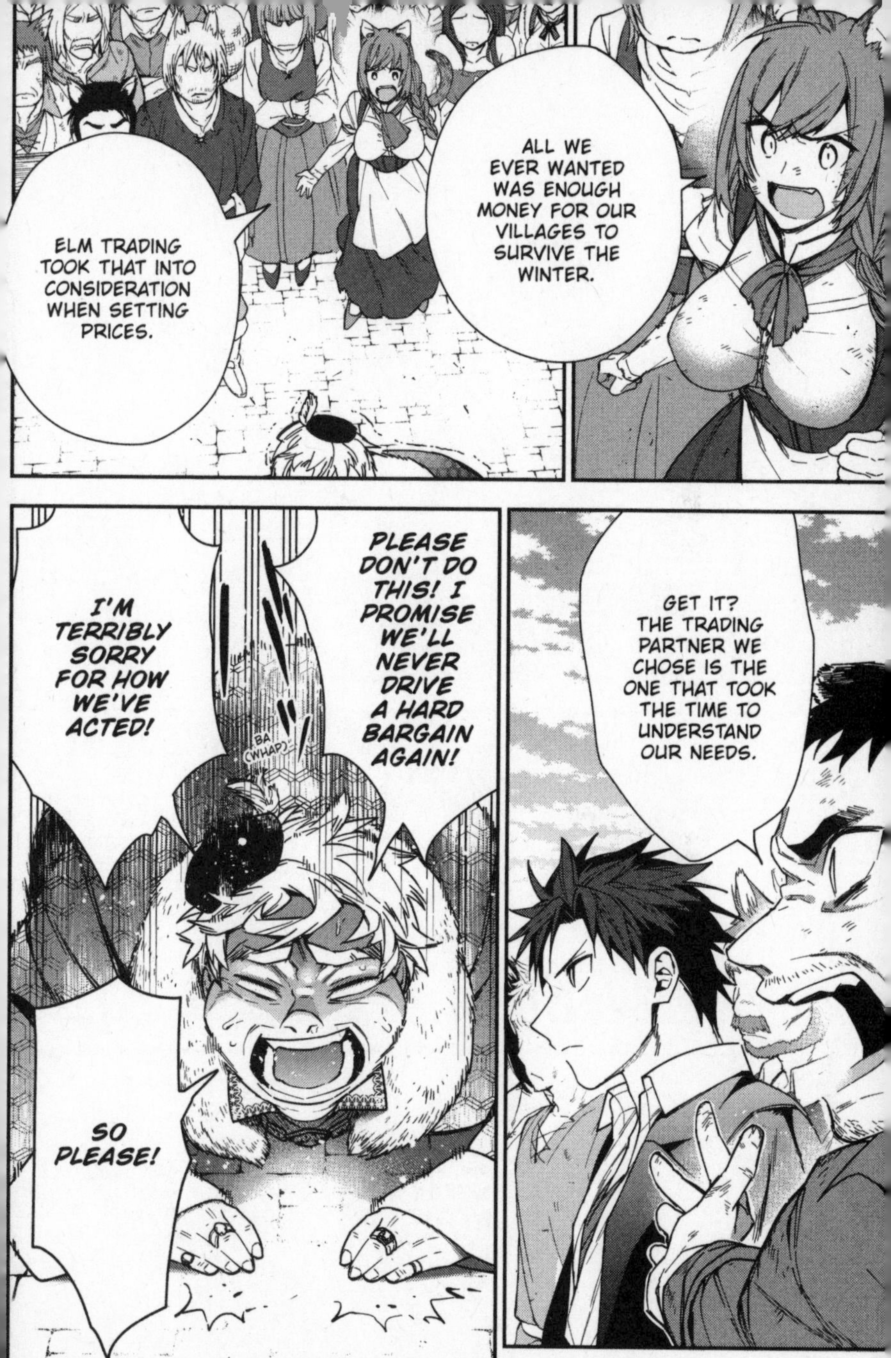
ALL WE EVER WANTED WAS ENOUGH MONEY FOR OUR VILLAGES TO SURVIVE THE WINTER.
ELM TRADING TOOK THAT INTO CONSIDERATION WHEN SETTING PRICES.
GET IT? THE TRADING PARTNER WE CHOSE IS THE ONE THAT TOOK THE TIME TO UNDERSTAND OUR NEEDS.
PLEASE DON'T DO THIS! I PROMISE WE'LL NEVER DRIVE A HARD BARGAIN AGAIN!
I'M TERRIBLY SORRY FOR HOW WE'VE ACTED!
BA (WHAP)
SO PLEASE!

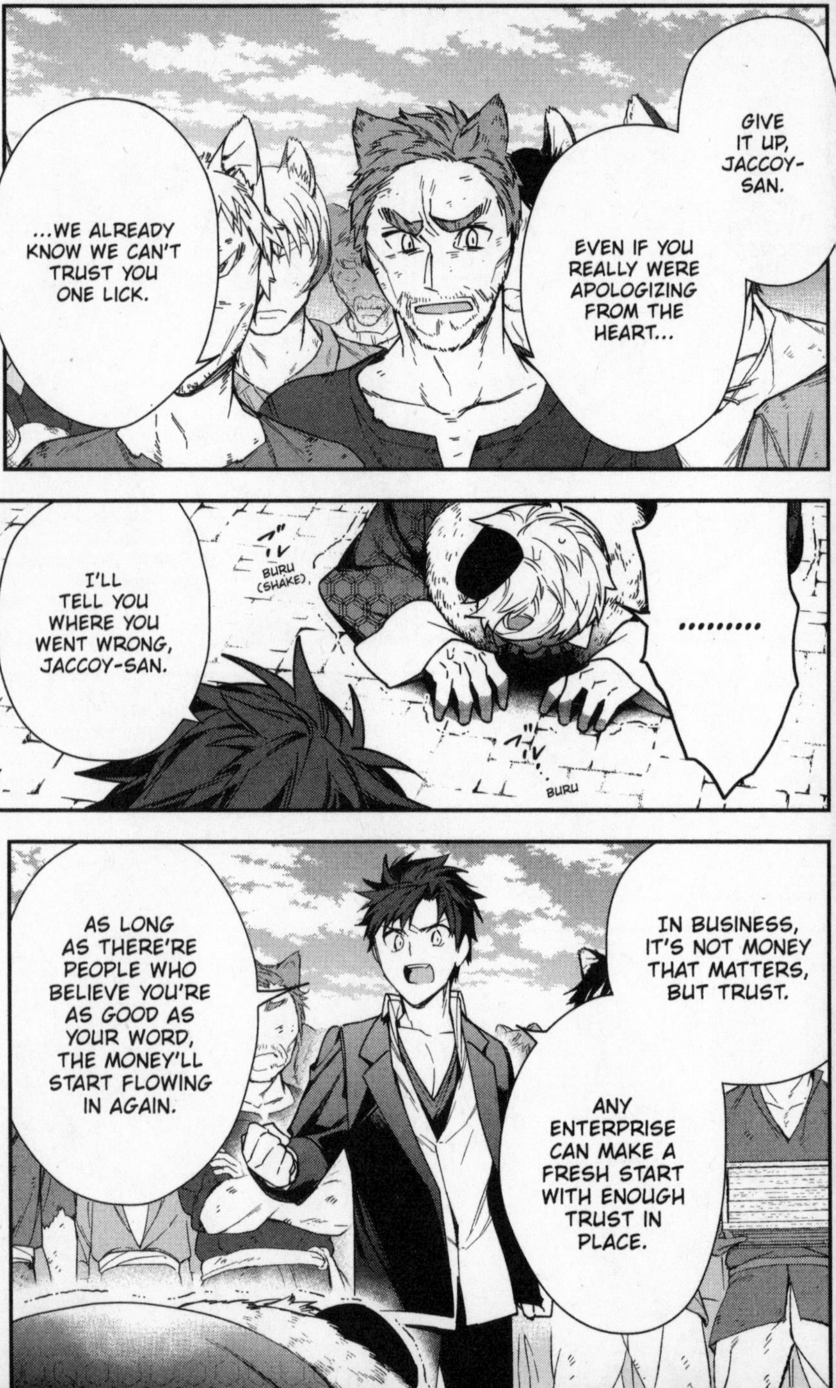
GIVE IT UP, JACCOY-SAN.
EVEN IF YOU REALLY WERE APOLOGIZING FROM THE HEART...
...WE ALREADY KNOW WE CAN'T TRUST YOU ONE LICK.
....
ブル BURU (SHAKE)
ブル BURU
I'LL TELL YOU WHERE YOU WENT WRONG, JACCOY-SAN.
IN BUSINESS, IT'S NOT MONEY THAT MATTERS, BUT TRUST.
ANY ENTERPRISE CAN MAKE A FRESH START WITH ENOUGH TRUST IN PLACE.
AS LONG AS THERE'RE PEOPLE WHO BELIEVE YOU'RE AS GOOD AS YOUR WORD, THE MONEY'LL START FLOWING IN AGAIN.

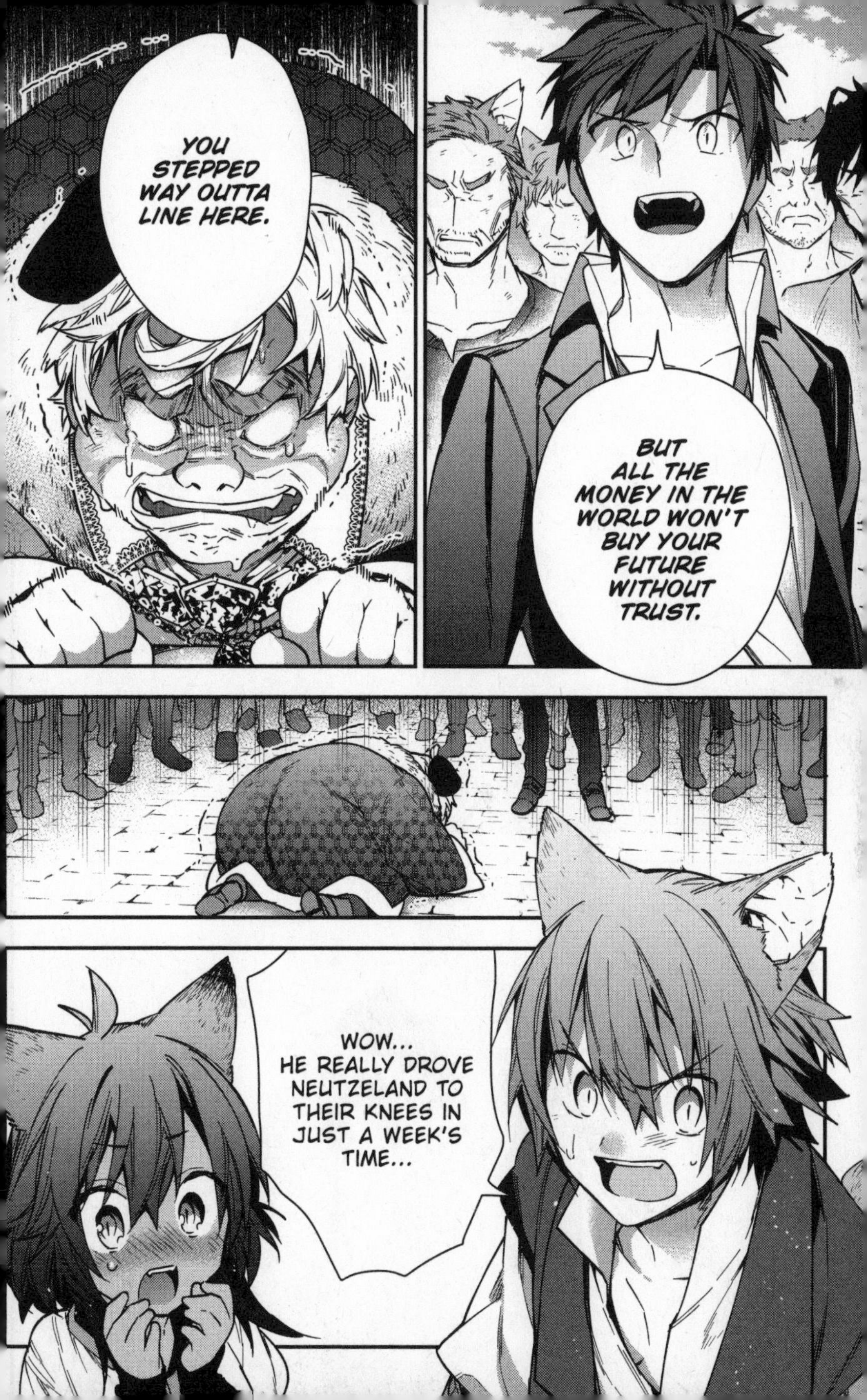
BUT ALL THE MONEY IN THE WORLD WON'T BUY YOUR FUTURE WITHOUT TRUST.
YOU STEPPED WAY OUTTA LINE HERE.
WOW... HE REALLY DROVE NEUTZELAND TO THEIR KNEES IN JUST A WEEK'S TIME...

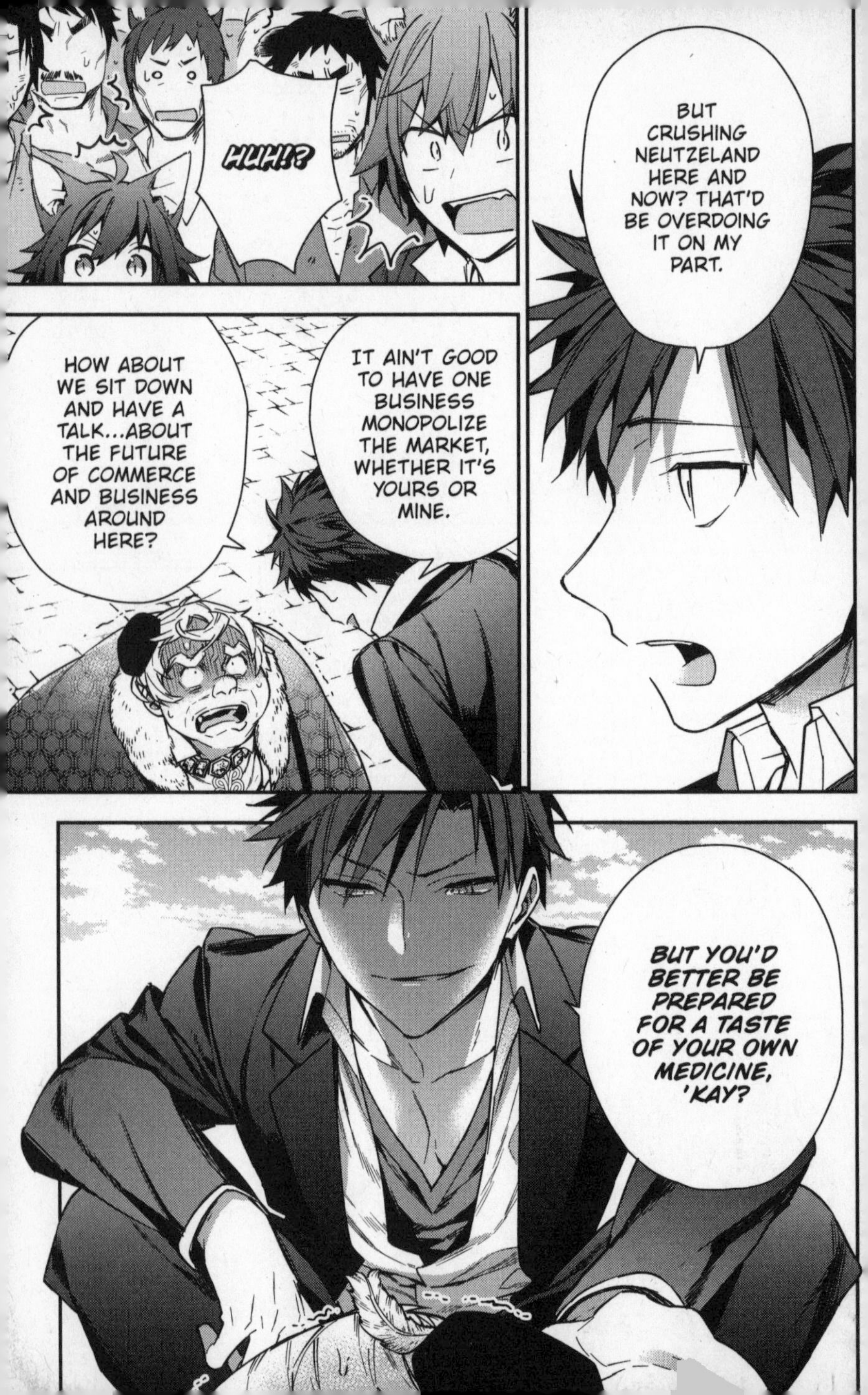
BUT CRUSHING NEUTZELAND HERE AND NOW? THAT'D BE OVERDOING IT ON MY PART.
HUH!?
IT AIN'T GOOD TO HAVE ONE BUSINESS MONOPOLIZE THE MARKET, WHETHER IT'S YOURS OR MINE.
HOW ABOUT WE SIT DOWN AND HAVE A TALK...ABOUT THE FUTURE OF COMMERCE AND BUSINESS AROUND HERE?
BUT YOU'D BETTER BE PREPARED FOR A TASTE OF YOUR OWN MEDICINE, 'KAY?

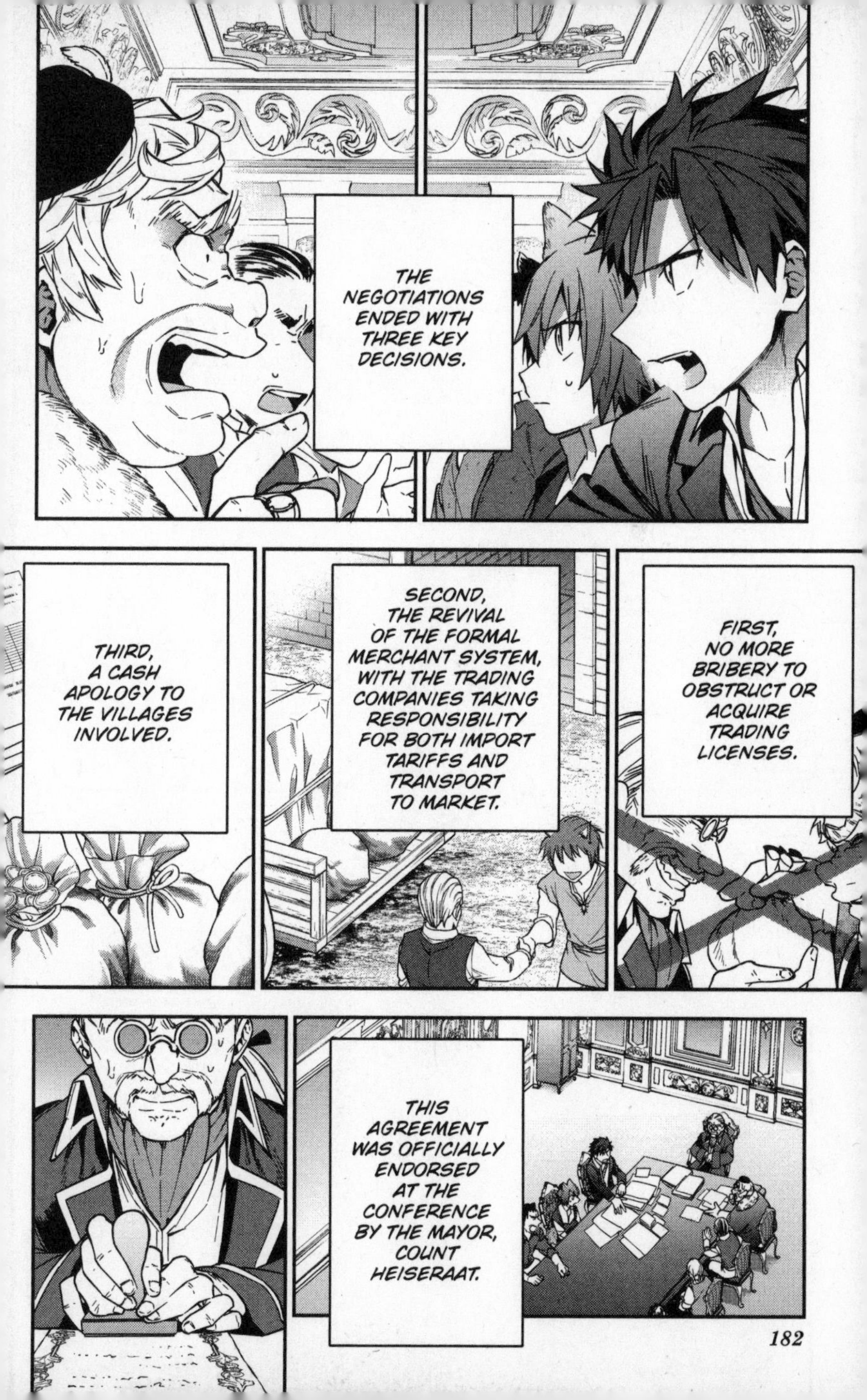
THE NEGOTIATIONS ENDED WITH THREE KEY DECISIONS.
FIRST, NO MORE BRIBERY TO OBSTRUCT OR ACQUIRE TRADING LICENSES.
SECOND, THE REVIVAL OF THE FORMAL MERCHANT SYSTEM, WITH THE TRADING COMPANIES TAKING RESPONSIBILITY FOR BOTH IMPORT TARIFFS AND TRANSPORT TO MARKET.
THIRD, A CASH APOLOGY TO THE VILLAGES INVOLVED.
THIS AGREEMENT WAS OFFICIALLY ENDORSED AT THE CONFERENCE BY THE MAYOR, COUNT HEISERAAT.

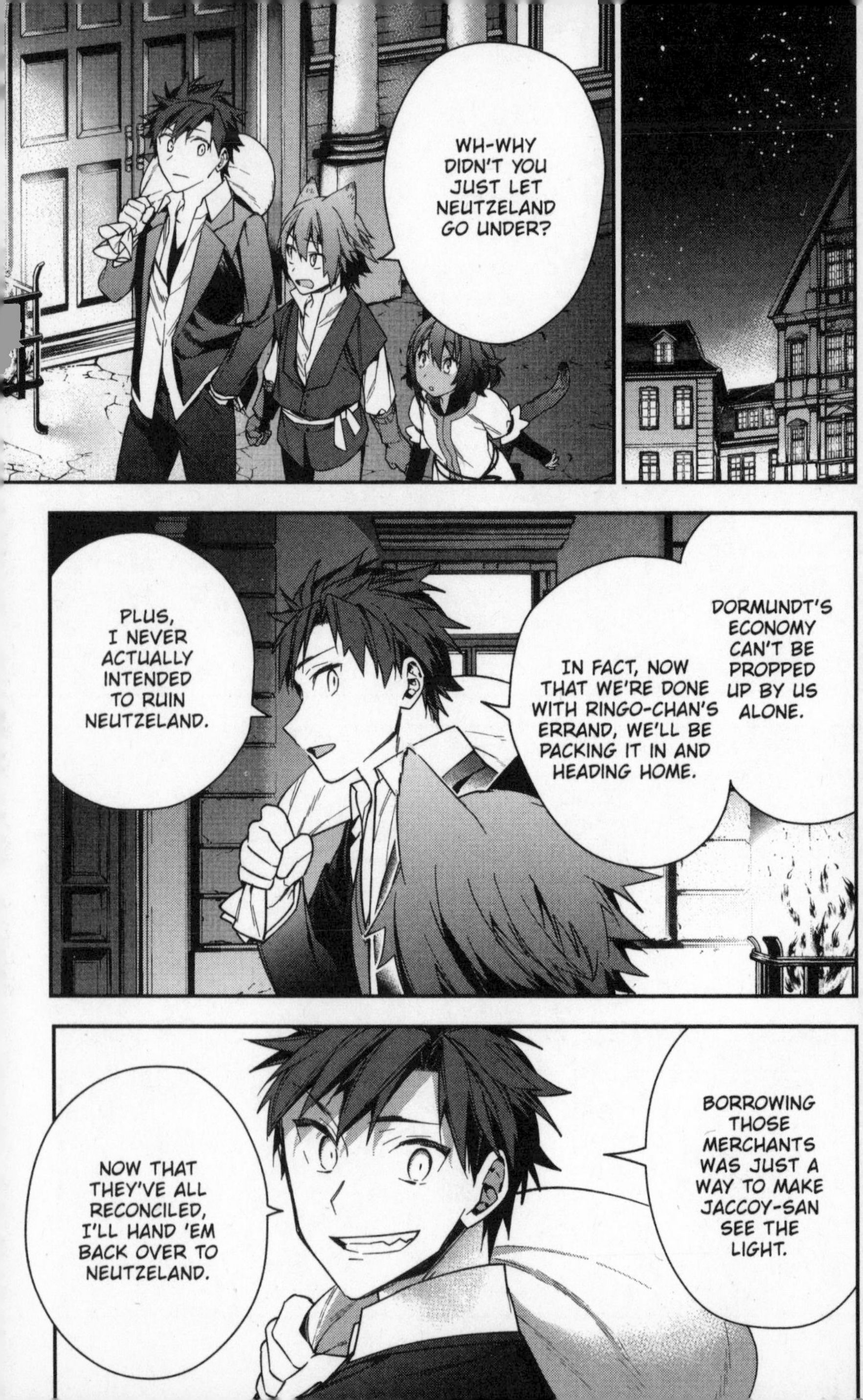
WH-WHY DIDN'T YOU JUST LET NEUTZELAND GO UNDER?
DORMUNDT'S ECONOMY CAN'T BE PROPPED UP BY US ALONE.
IN FACT, NOW THAT WE'RE DONE WITH RINGO-CHAN'S ERRAND, WE'LL BE PACKING IT IN AND HEADING HOME.
PLUS, I NEVER ACTUALLY INTENDED TO RUIN NEUTZELAND.
BORROWING THOSE MERCHANTS WAS JUST A WAY TO MAKE JACCOY-SAN SEE THE LIGHT.
NOW THAT THEY'VE ALL RECONCILED, I'LL HAND 'EM BACK OVER TO NEUTZELAND.

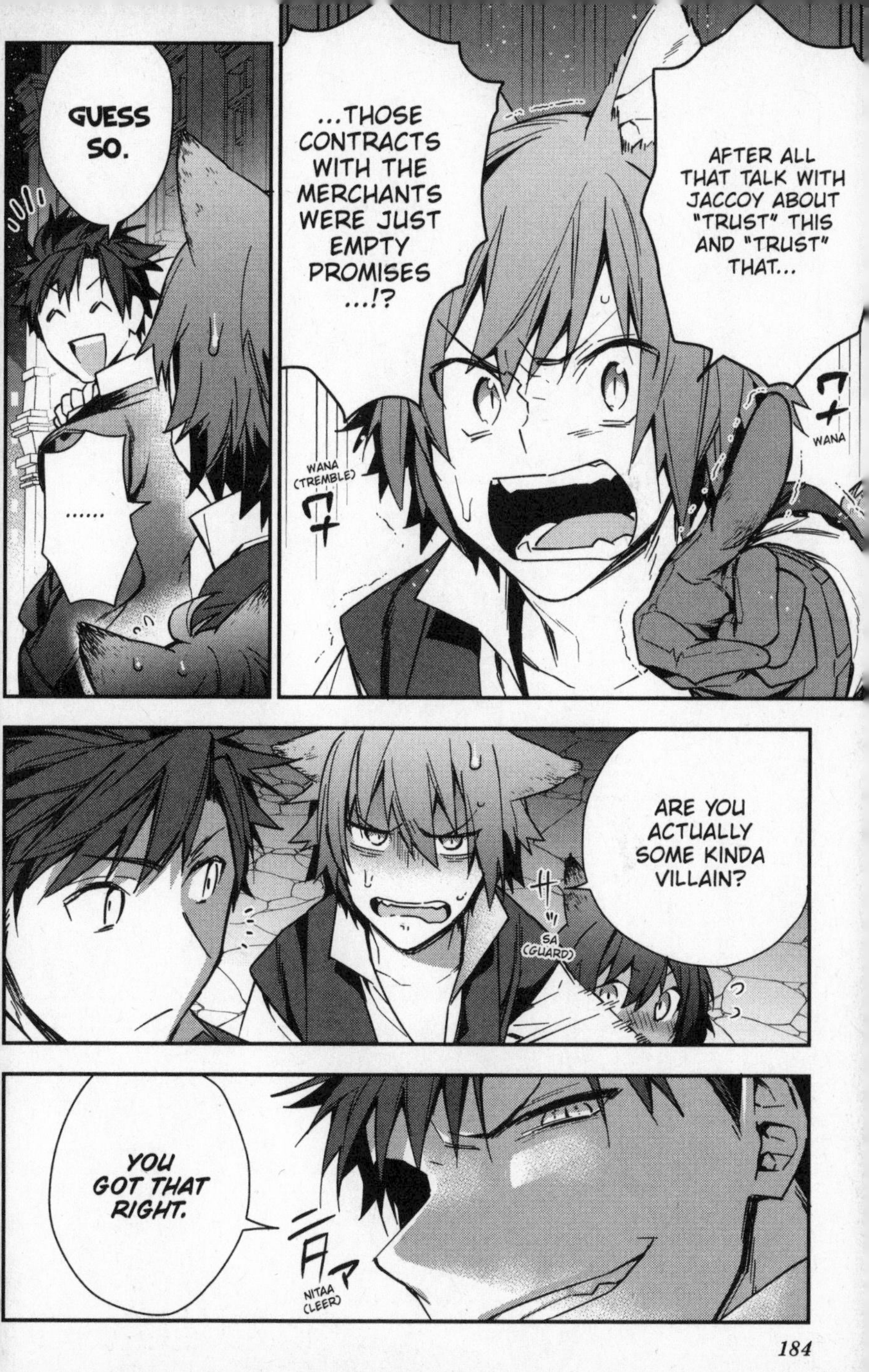
AFTER ALL THAT TALK WITH JACCOY ABOUT "TRUST" THIS AND "TRUST" THAT...
...THOSE CONTRACTS WITH THE MERCHANTS WERE JUST EMPTY PROMISES ...!?
WANA
WANA (TREMBLE)
GUESS SO.
......
ARE YOU ACTUALLY SOME KINDA VILLAIN?
SA (GUARD)
NITAA (LEER)
YOU GOT THAT RIGHT.

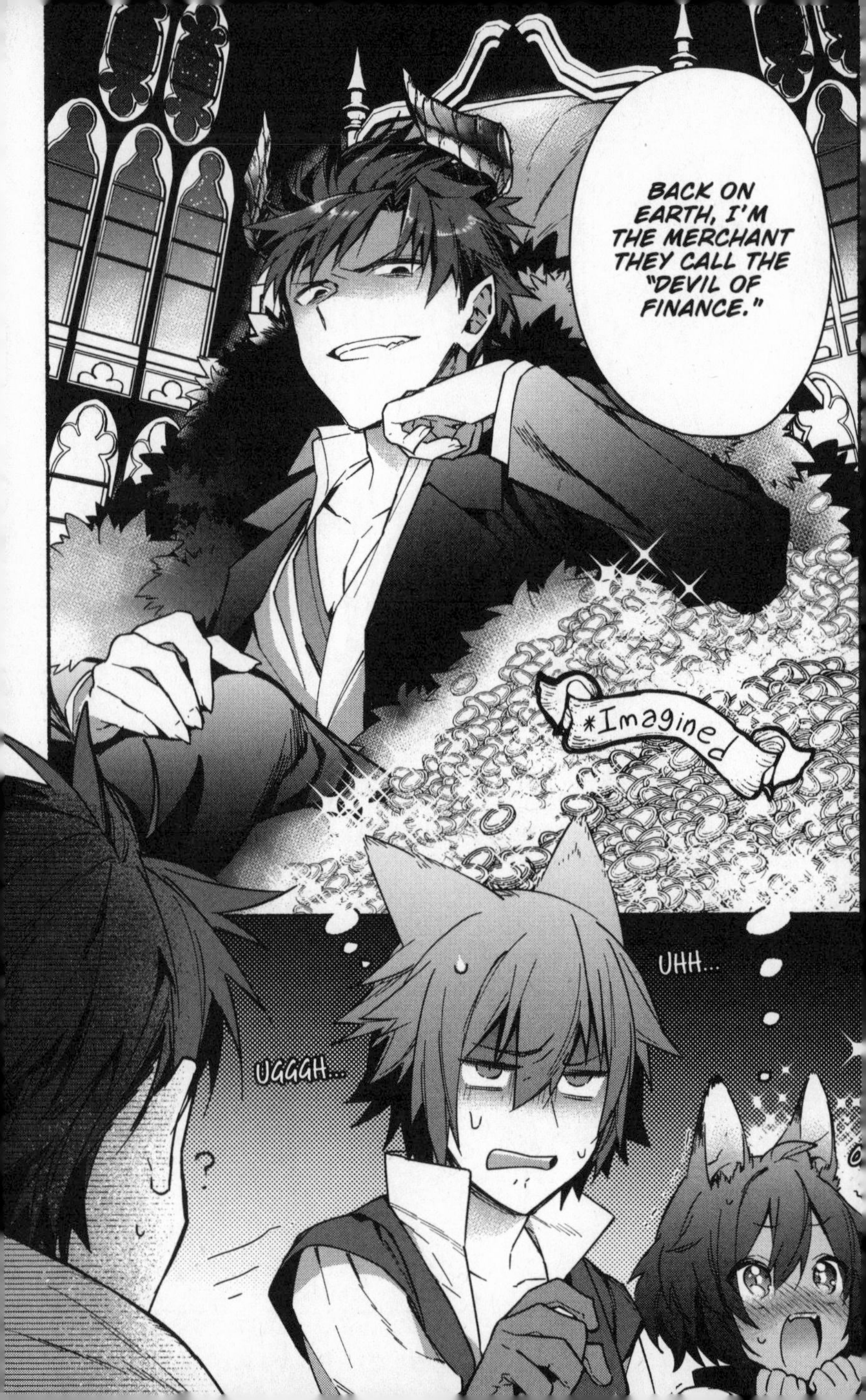
BACK ON EARTH, I'M THE MERCHANT THEY CALL THE "DEVIL OF FINANCE."
*Imagined
UHH...
UGGGH...
?

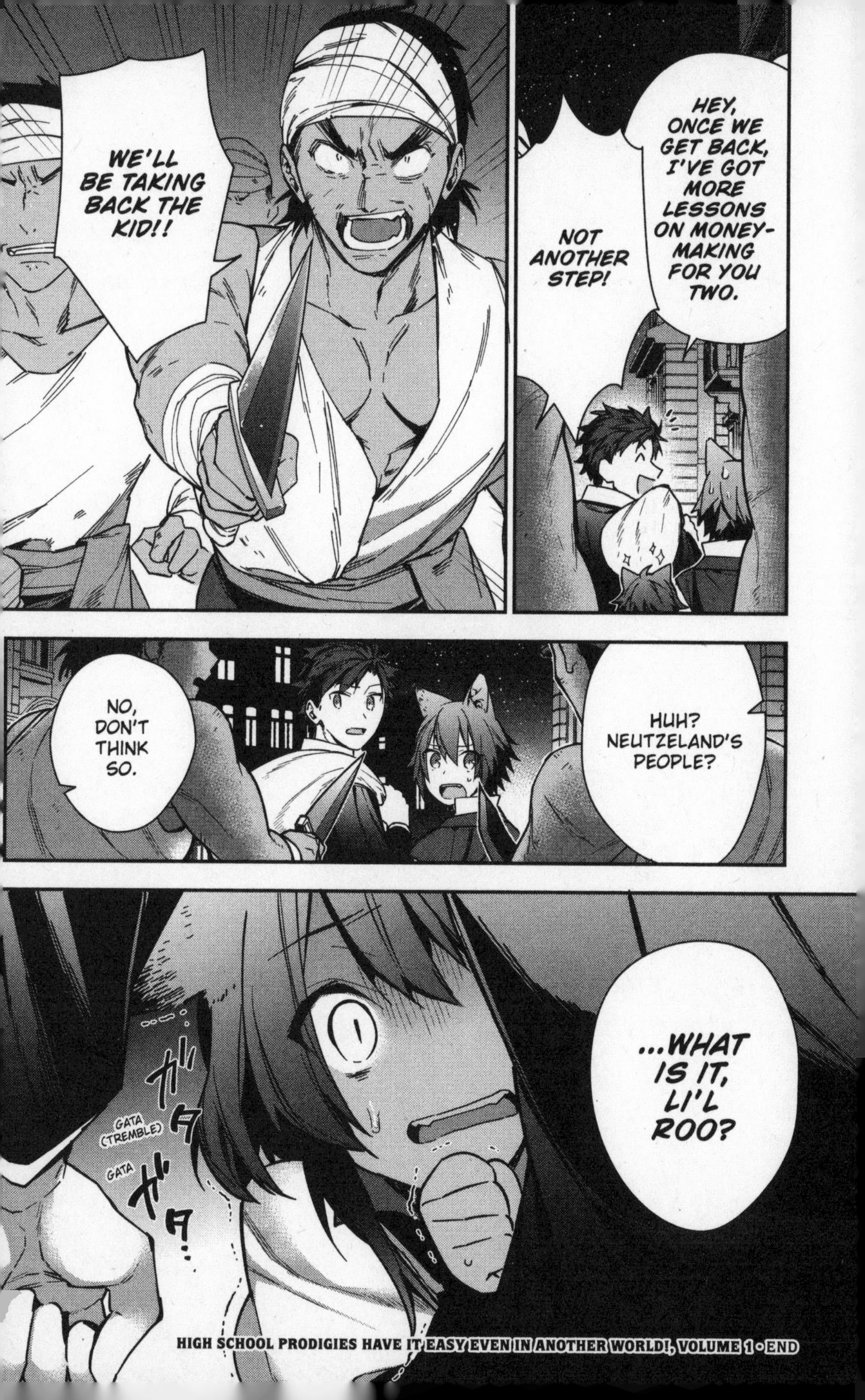
HEY, ONCE WE GET BACK, I'VE GOT MORE LESSONS ON MONEY-MAKING FOR YOU TWO.
NOT ANOTHER STEP!
WE'LL BE TAKING BACK THE KID!!
HUH? NEUTZELAND'S PEOPLE?
NO, DON'T THINK SO.
...WHAT IS IT, LI'L ROO?
GATA (TREMBLE)
GATA
HIGH SCHOOL PRODIGIES HAVE IT EASY EVEN IN ANOTHER WORLD!, VOLUME 1 • END

TRANSLATION NOTES

COMMON HONORIFICS

no honorific: Indicates familiarity or closeness; if used without permission or reason, addressing someone in this manner would constitute an insult.

-san: The Japanese equivalent of Mr./Mrs./Miss. If a situation calls for politeness, this is the fail-safe honorific.

-sama: Conveys great respect; may also indicate that the social status of the speaker is lower than that of the addressee.

-kun: Used most often when referring to boys, this indicates affection or familiarity. Occasionally used by older men among their peers, but it may also be used by anyone referring to a person of lower standing.

-chan: An affectionate honorific indicating familiarity used mostly in reference to girls; also used in reference to cute persons or animals. Variants include **-chin**.

-senpai: A suffix used to address upperclassmen or more experienced coworkers.

-sensei: A respectful term for teachers, artists, or high-level professionals.

Page 13
Ringo's A.I. companion's name, **Kumausa**, is a combination of "bear" (*kuma*) and "rabbit" (*usagi*). However, Kumausa definitely favors its bear side when it comes to peppering its dialogue with puns.

Page 20
Prime Minister **Tsukasa** Mikogami's first name is written with the kanji that means "to govern."

Page 23
Shinobu's cry of "**Nin, nin!**" points to her ninja heritage, as does her first name, the kanji of which is the *nin* in ninja. *Shinobu* can also mean "to conceal oneself."

Page 43
Altan, the name of the native tongue in the other world, is *Aruto-go* in Japanese, making it a possible play on the word "alternate."

Page 58
Onee-chan ("big sister") and **onii-chan** ("big brother") and are often used to address siblings but can also be used when addressing unrelated young people who are older than the speaker. These words can also be used as honorifics; for example, Tsukasa-*niichan* on page 82.

Page 70
Aoi Ichijou uses the old-fashioned *gozaru* sentence ending in Japanese, making her sound like a samurai from ages past.

CHARACTER FILE 08

Aoi Ichijou

One of the high school prodigies. A swordmaster whose blade cuts across war zones resonant with gunfire. She employs the Ichijou Rishin style and firmly believes her sword ought to protect the defenseless.

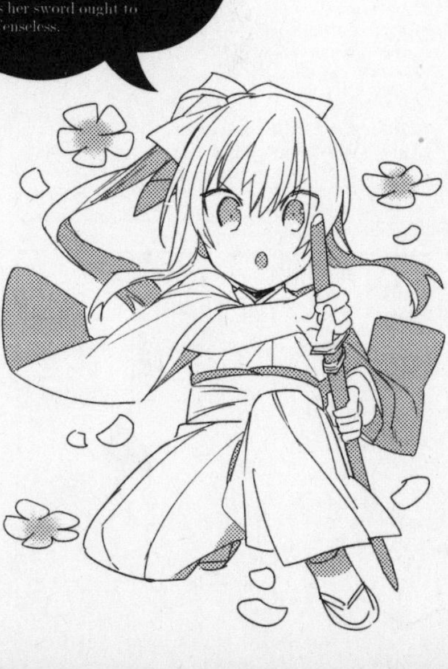

THE DAILY LIVES OF THE HIGH SCHOOL PRODIGIES

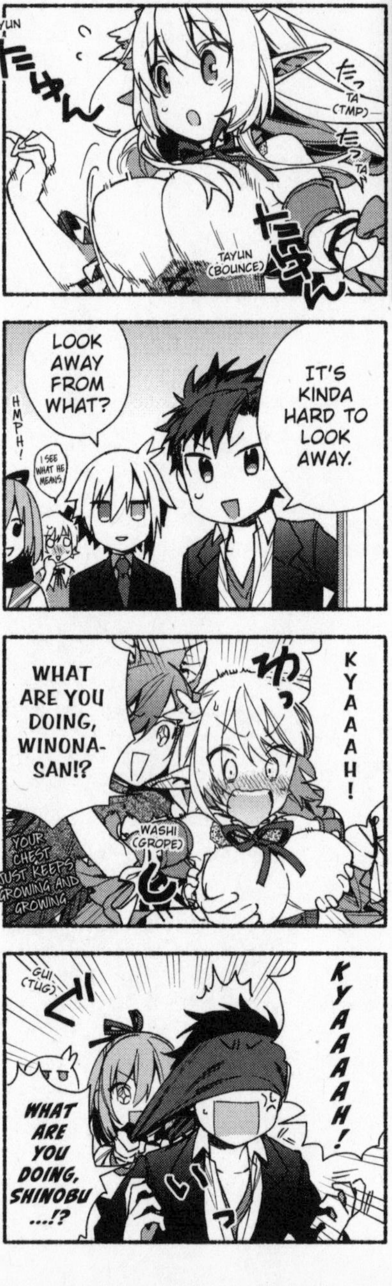
TAYUN
TA (TMP)
TA
TAYUN (BOUNCE)
IT'S KINDA HARD TO LOOK AWAY.
LOOK AWAY FROM WHAT?
HMPH!
I SEE WHAT HE MEANS.
KYAAAAH!
WHAT ARE YOU DOING, WINONA-SAN!?
WASHI (GROPE)
YOUR CHEST JUST KEEPS GROWING AND GROWING
KYAAAAAH!
GUI (TUG)
WHAT ARE YOU DOING, SHINOBU...!?

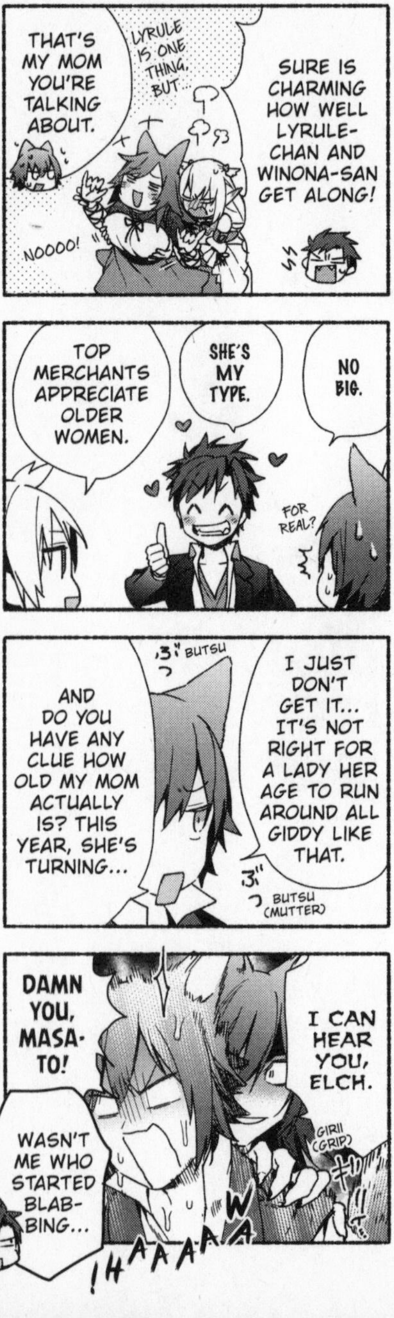
SURE IS CHARMING HOW WELL LYRULE-CHAN AND WINONA-SAN GET ALONG!
LYRULE IS ONE THING, BUT
THAT'S MY MOM YOU'RE TALKING ABOUT.
NOOOO!
NO BIG.
SHE'S MY TYPE.
TOP MERCHANTS APPRECIATE OLDER WOMEN.
FOR REAL?
BUTSU
I JUST DON'T GET IT... IT'S NOT RIGHT FOR A LADY HER AGE TO RUN AROUND ALL GIDDY LIKE THAT.
AND DO YOU HAVE ANY CLUE HOW OLD MY MOM ACTUALLY IS? THIS YEAR, SHE'S TURNING...
BUTSU (MUTTER)
I CAN HEAR YOU, ELCH.
DAMN YOU, MASATO!
GIRII (GRIP)
WASN'T ME WHO STARTED BLABBING...
WAAAAAH!

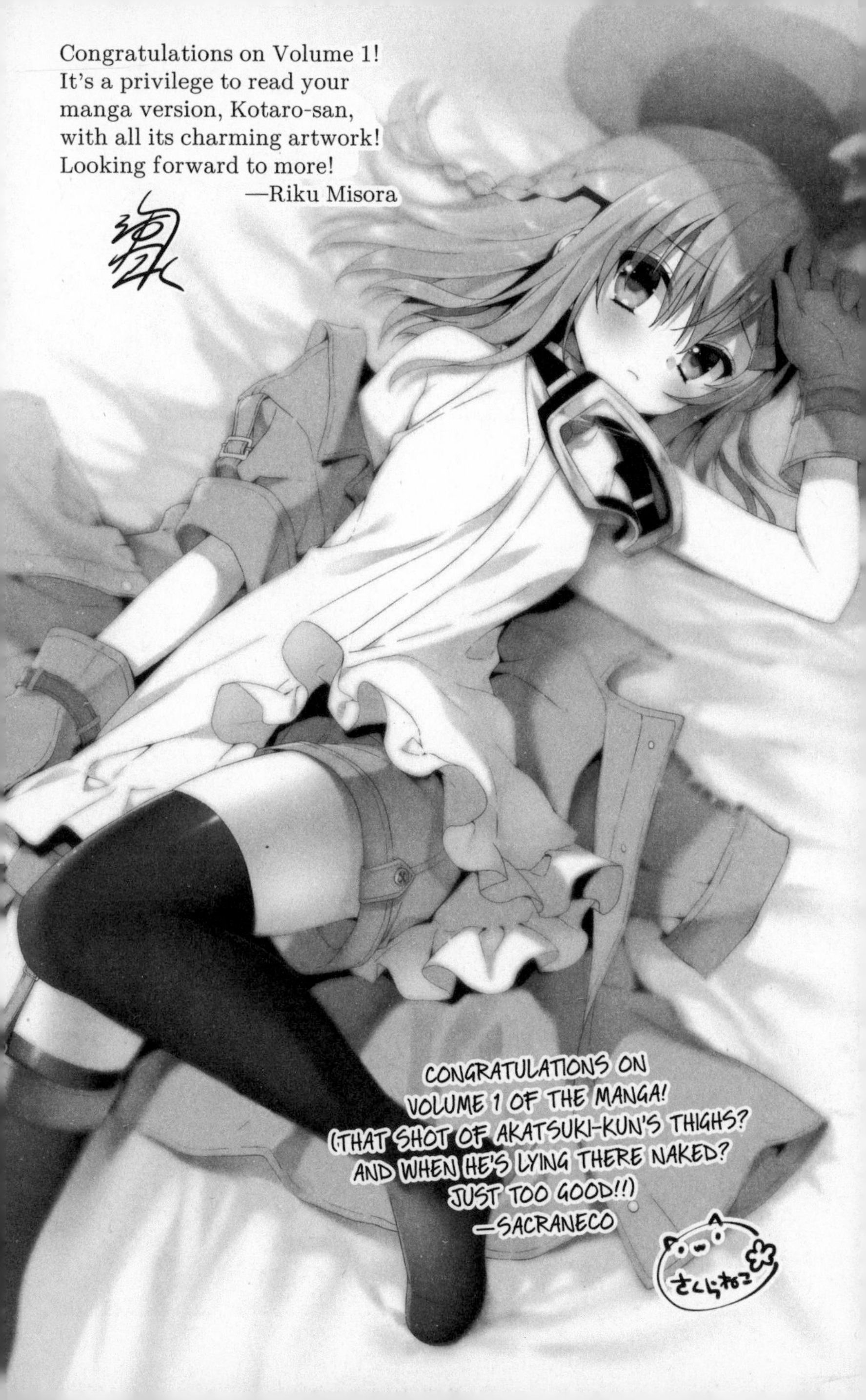
Congratulations on Volume 1!
It's a privilege to read your manga version, Kotaro-san, with all its charming artwork!
Looking forward to more!
—Riku Misora
CONGRATULATIONS ON VOLUME 1 OF THE MANGA!
(THAT SHOT OF AKATSUKI-KUN'S THIGHS? AND WHEN HE'S LYING THERE NAKED? JUST TOO GOOD!!)
—SACRANECO

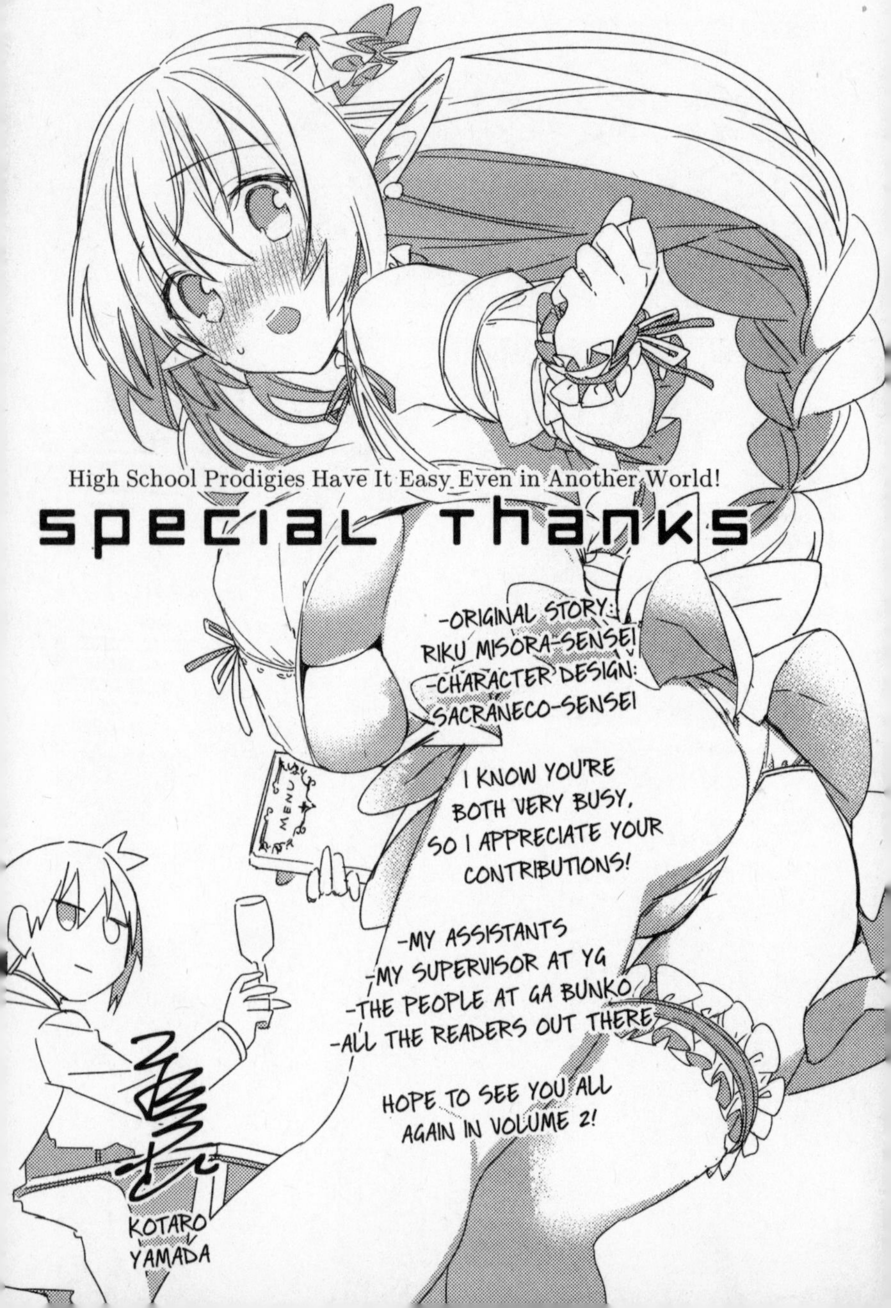
High School Prodigies Have It Easy Even in Another World!
special thanks
-ORIGINAL STORY:
RIKU MISORA-SENSEI
-CHARACTER DESIGN:
SACRANECO-SENSEI
MENU
I KNOW YOU'RE
BOTH VERY BUSY,
SO I APPRECIATE YOUR
CONTRIBUTIONS!
-MY ASSISTANTS
-MY SUPERVISOR AT YG
-THE PEOPLE AT GA BUNKO
-ALL THE READERS OUT THERE
HOPE TO SEE YOU ALL
AGAIN IN VOLUME 2!
KOTARO
YAMADA

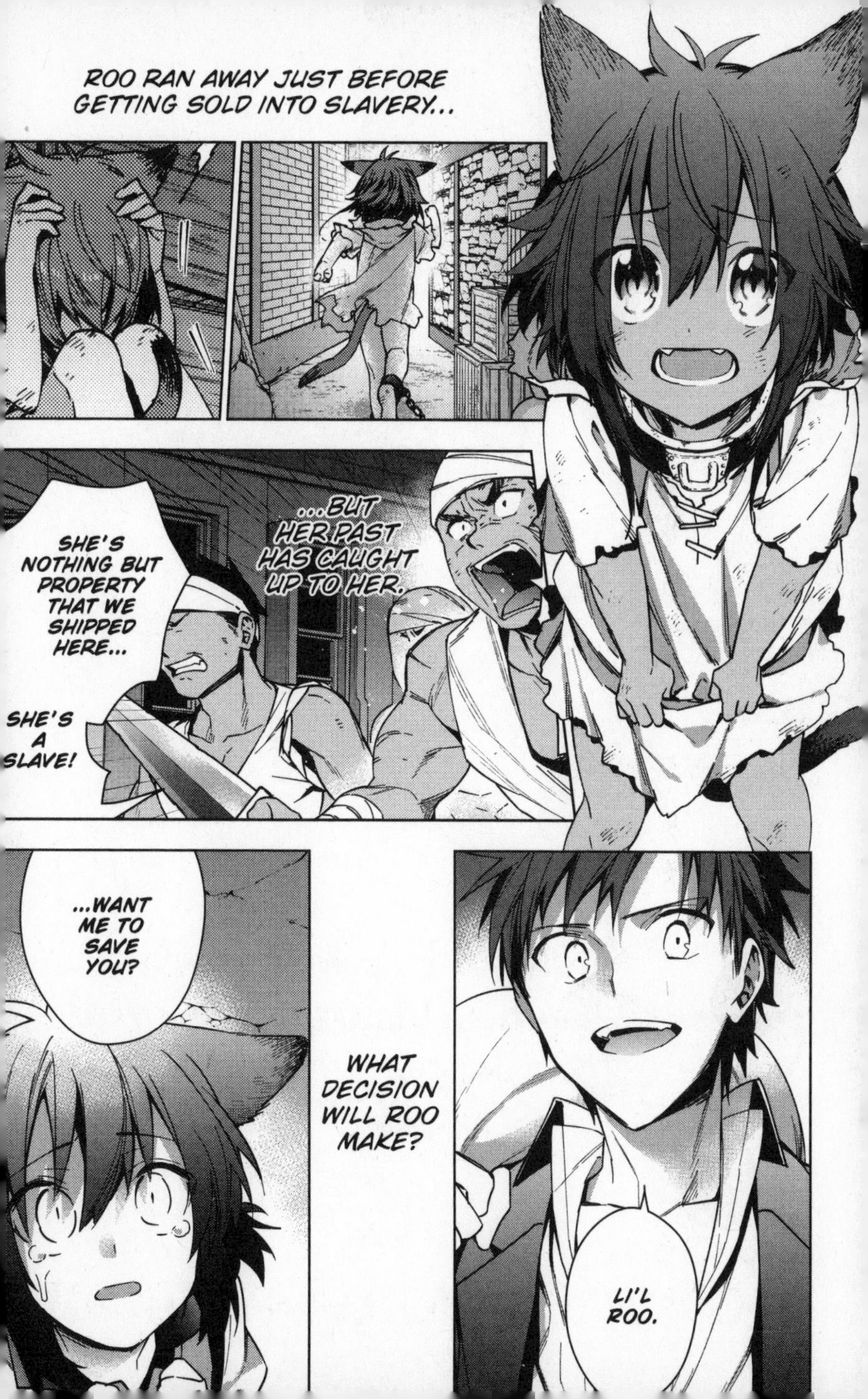
ROO RAN AWAY JUST BEFORE GETTING SOLD INTO SLAVERY...
...BUT HER PAST HAS CAUGHT UP TO HER.
SHE'S NOTHING BUT PROPERTY THAT WE SHIPPED HERE...
SHE'S A SLAVE!
WHAT DECISION WILL ROO MAKE?
LI'L ROO.
...WANT ME TO SAVE YOU?

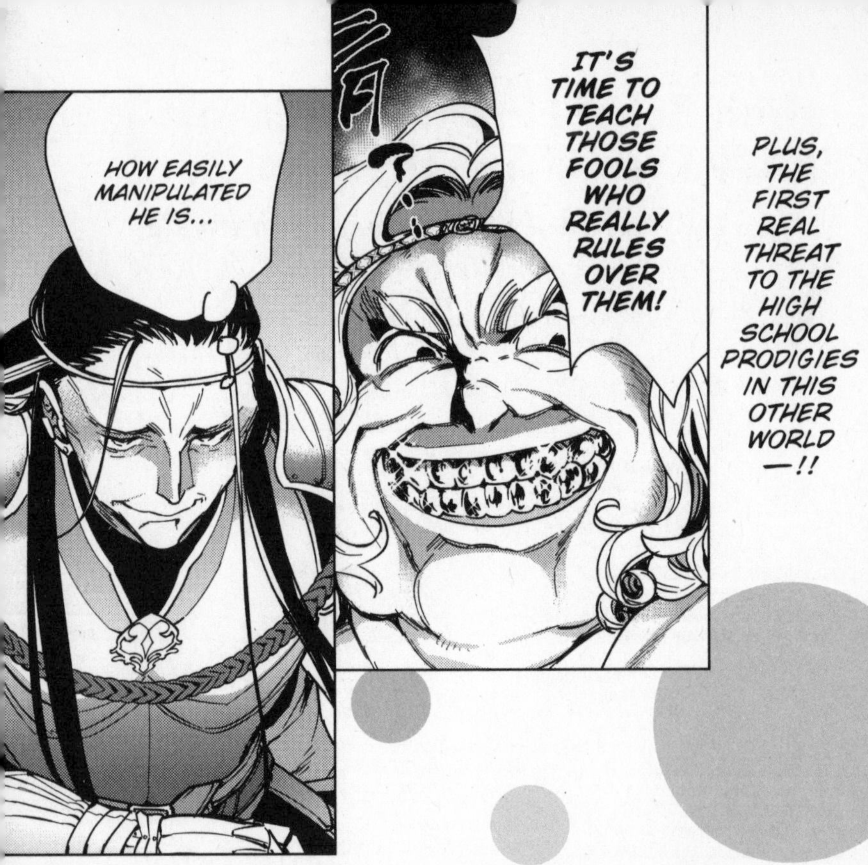
PLUS, THE FIRST REAL THREAT TO THE HIGH SCHOOL PRODIGIES IN THIS OTHER WORLD—!!
IT'S TIME TO TEACH THOSE FOOLS WHO REALLY RULES OVER THEM!
HOW EASILY MANIPULATED HE IS...

High School Prodigies Have It Easy Even in Another World! 1

STORY BY Riku Misora   ART BY Kotaro Yamada

CHARACTER DESIGN BY Sacraneco

Translation: Caleb D. Cook
Lettering: Brandon Bovia

CHOUJIN KOUKOUSEI TACHI WA ISEKAI DEMO YOYU DE IKINUKU YOUDESU! vol. 1
© Riku Misora / SB Creative Corp. Character Design: Sacraneco
© 2016 Kotaro Yamada / SQUARE ENIX CO., LTD.
First published in Japan in 2016 by SQUARE ENIX CO., LTD.
English translation rights arranged with SQUARE ENIX CO., LTD.
and Yen Press, LLC through Tuttle Mori Agency, Inc.

English translation © 2018 by SQUARE ENIX CO., LTD.

Yen Press
1290 Avenue of the Americas
New York, NY 10104

Visit us at yenpress.com

facebook.com/yenpress
twitter.com/yenpress

yenpress.tumblr.com
instagram.com/yenpress

First Yen Press Edition: October 2018

Yen Press is an imprint of Yen Press, LLC.
The Yen Press name and logo are trademarks of Yen Press, LLC.

Library of Congress Control Number: 2018948324

ISBNs: 978-1-9753-0134-7 (paperback)
978-1-9753-0135-4 (ebook)

10 9 8 7 6 5 4 3 2 1

WOR

Printed in the United States of America